MGF and TF
Restoration Manual

MGF and TF
Restoration Manual

Roger Parker

THE CROWOOD PRESS

First published in 2012 by
The Crowood Press Ltd
Ramsbury, Marlborough
Wiltshire SN8 2HR

www.crowood.com

This impression 2018

British Library Cataloguing-in-Publication Data
A catalogue record for this book is available from the British Library.

ISBN 978 1 84797 400 6

Acknowledgements
This list is perhaps unusually short since most of this book is information I have gained from
personal involvement with the cars and people who designed and built them over what is now
eighteen years. There will, however, always be some whose help is invaluable and the person
who comes head and shoulders above others is my son Matt, a very skilled motor engineer in
his own right, whose help has been immeasurable. His hands may be seen here in some of the
images taken when we have been working on the many MGF and TFs that we deal with, as well
as on our own 'fleet', which at the time of writing consists of three MGFs, both MPi and VVC, a
TF 160 and four other K series engined MGs and Rovers.

Great credit must also go to my wife Carol, who has consistently kept tea and coffee on
tap during the many lonely evenings and weekends she has silently put up with as this book
progressed and absorbed more and more time.

I must also thank Richard Monk, Jonathan Kimber and Richard Ladds, my colleagues at the
MG Owners Club, who have been very supportive during the writing of this book in a variety of
ways, especially during the winter of 2011/12 when my focus was almost entirely on this book.

Typeset by Jean Cussons Typesetting, Diss, Norfolk

Printed and bound in Malaysia by Times Offset (M) Sdn Bhd

contents

Fig. 1.1   Early Mk 1 MGF 1.8i (MPi) suffering from a holed piston.

introduction

What is it that attracts people to the MGF and MG TF and drives many to buy them, when over the years there has been so much 'Rover and MG bashing' by the press? Some of this has been related to self-inflicted injuries to the cars' reputations that mainly revolve around engine reliability, or the lack of it, associated with head gasket failures.

I suggest that this is because the cars project an image of simple fun and enjoyment from driving that you just can't get from a modern tin-top car. It starts with easy recognition of the car's shape and even in silhouette it stands out from the crowd. It doesn't pretend to be anything other than what it is – a two-seat open-top sporting car – and this format has always been associated with fun with a capital F. Other modern saloon/hatch cars may deliver stunning performance with four-wheel drive and aggressive appendages to differentiate them from their mundane siblings, but they still lack individual character.

The MG character includes both positive and negative attributes. Some of the low points are occasionally deep, but without these how would you appreciate the highs? I believe this is why the MGF and MG TF was the UK's top selling two-seat sports car for each of the years it was in full production, up to and including 2004. Some will hate the prospect of lows causing inconvenience and expense, but equally the phrase 'boringly reliable' tells its own story on how owners often become dissatisfied with this type of car. Indeed I have had conversations with owners who have migrated from Japanese and German makes because of that lack of character. From the MG perspective what would be ideal is something that takes away some of the negative aspects while retaining the positives, or even improving them. Within this book I intend to illustrate how this can be achieved.

It may seem strange to be looking at a book that covers restoration of the MGF and MG TF, the latter especially as it was in production until 2011. The earliest TFs are now ten years old, while the oldest MGFs are nearly out of their teens, well past the time when many saloon cars are being recycled. One aspect that usually leads to a car being recycled is when repair costs are weighed against the car's value. The low prices these cars currently command, something that the MG Rover collapse has much to do with, doesn't mean that the cars are intrinsically bad, just that some owners are not prepared to pay and prefer to change. In many cases the faults may not be that deep and so 'repair and restoration' can end up costing somewhat less than the costs of buying a competitor that doesn't currently need any work: it just needs a little forward vision.

The MGF was in production between 1995 and the end of 2001, and as such is of an age when many examples will have a mechanical condition commensurate with their age and six-figure mileages. To the immense credit of the designers, many cars have survived in a structurally and mechanically sound state. This offers the prospect of MG sports car ownership without the huge costs and complications of needing a complete body restoration, as is so

Fig. 1.2 *The body cosmetics, though, are good, as seen from the reflection in this wing.*

Fig. 1.3 *The interior is very clean and the telltale driver's seat is in good order.*

often the expected situation with the pre-1980 MGs.

There are still quite a number of early cars with one or two owners from new, with very low mileages. When these come on the market, for whatever reason, owners can expect to receive relatively little from even well above average cars, so the purchaser will get even more car for their money. Interestingly, one factor driving many of these cars onto the market is a sudden, more serious mechanical issue, usually a head gasket failure, where professional rectification costs are so high they often exceed the value of the car.

This allows the mechanically adept buyer to buy cheaply: between £500 and £600 is common. (I bought a very clean 1998 VVC MOT failure in 2011 for £350, for example; doing the necessary repairs with my son Matt will cost about the same again.) This is the sort of route I would see many benefiting from by spending relatively little but putting in plenty of time and energy in repairs, and ending up with a car that sits well with others costing four times as much.

One problem with a book covering 'restoration' is that the focus may well be perceived as returning the car to a near-showroom condition. Such an exercise will always be costly in both money and effort. There will be some aspects that lean that way, but I am very aware that a car bought for less than one or two thousand pounds may not be meant as one to own for the next ten or twenty years. Economical repairs, however, can offer you enjoyment for

several years in the knowledge that in the end you will have gained good value for money.

A long-standing problem that affects most cars, irrespective of make, is that while their values plummet as they age, the costs of spares and repair labour doesn't drop, and often increases. Parts and repairs start to take on a much higher proportion of the car's value and this becomes a big disincentive for owners to keep on with original parts and dealers. For these reasons I will divert from the 'return to showroom condition' approach and suggest cheaper alternative routes to solving a problem.

From having seen how cheaply MGFs can be bought, with the TF not far behind, it has to be said that these

are cars with great potential. As a bonus you get something out of the ordinary and end up with an economic, effective, reliable – yes, reliable – modern MG sports car that will give a great deal of enjoyment. Do you now feel more inclined to put a toe in the MG water?

Finding a suitable donor car is really quite simple as a steady stream of cheap cars is always to be seen on eBay, in *Autotrader* and adverts in local papers, MG magazines and MG Clubs within the UK. Finding one of those low-mileage, one-owner cars in need of the type of work I described previously is just a case of sitting back and monitoring the sales as they do come along reasonably regularly. Many others, however, may have already spotted these opportunities to make

Fig. 1.4 *A 1998 MGF bought in 2011 for £350 that needed very little work for its MOT.*

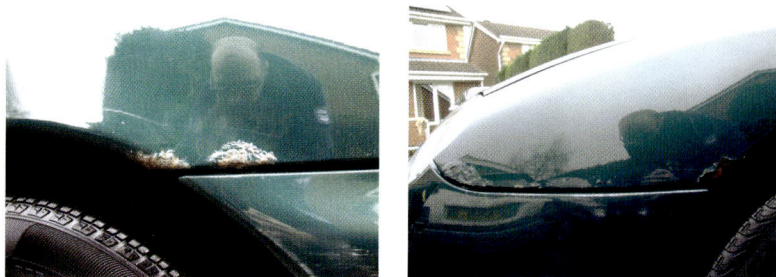

Figs. 1.5 and 1.6   Both front and rear wings show edge rusting caused by living near the sea.

a little money, so prompt action is required to snap up any cars appearing.

This also illustrates a need to be able to assess a car accurately. Research using buying guides, the MG Clubs and the Internet is valuable, but most important of all is to gain actual hands-on familiarization by seeing as many cars as you can while keeping your wallet locked away. Once you have seen five or six cars you will have gained a much better appreciation of the model and what the market is currently offering, and by reading this book you will have some knowledge about many of the areas in which you will probably have to do some work. Note in particular that there is no specific buyer's guide section; the whole book is a buyer's guide as it covers all and more than any 'buying guide' will give you.

I have to balance the rose-tinted spectacles approach, though, by saying that there are some real 'dogs' on the market. This reinforces the need for preparation and gaining knowledge *before* the wallet is released. If the first car you see is a really good one, and it has sold by the time you have seen enough to know that it was a good one, never fear – others equally good

will come along in the not too distant future.

Those not comfortable with their abilities to select a car may not perhaps be best placed to consider taking on a car needing much work. Where a potential purchaser wishes to have some support, try to take an informed friend along to the viewing to act as a first-level 'filter'. If the car passes this filter then consider having the car professionally examined by one of the usual suppliers of these services, or seek the advice of an MG specialist to provide that assessment. If you are worried about the car being sold before the examination, offer a holding deposit and enter into an agreement with the seller that the sale is subject to the result of a professional examination. Sellers confident in their cars will usually agree to this.

Finding an MG specialist within reach of the car's location can be made easier by using the 'Pre-purchase inspection system' offered by the MG Owners Club (www.mgownersclub.co.uk). The Club Members' Recommended Suppliers list, which is updated annually via feedback from a questionnaire, names MG specialists who offer pre-purchase

inspections at variable cost, set by the individual specialist. MGF and TF specialists are not yet as common as classic MG specialists, but it is encouraging to report that many classic MG specialists are starting to offer services to the MGF and TF owner too.

PARTS SUPPLY

One of the pressures on residual values created by the collapse of MG Rover has been a widely held belief that spares support for the cars has collapsed as well. This is far from the truth, however, since the MG parts company responsible for the supply of spares, XPart, was sold well over a year before the collapse to Caterpillar Logistics, part of Caterpillar Inc., a multinational company associated with earth-moving equipment and very much more.

With a huge and solid parent, the XPart operation has flourished and was able to step in and fill the void by creating an alternative dealer network under the XPart Autoservice Centre network. This includes many former MG Rover dealers and has subsequently grown to roughly the size of the former MG Rover network and continues to provide support to MG and Rover owners.

In addition to XPart's supply of genuine MG parts there is a growing alternative parts supply industry, just as was seen with the classic MG spares market. Clearly having a car that was designed to draw heavily upon the 'parts bins' of other Rover models is a considerable help, as a range of common parts used on a number of different cars means that there is a bigger market

Fig. 1.7   XPart's main warehouse has 637,000 sq ft of parts storage.

Fig. 1.8   Racking for MG and Rover parts extends over twenty-two miles.

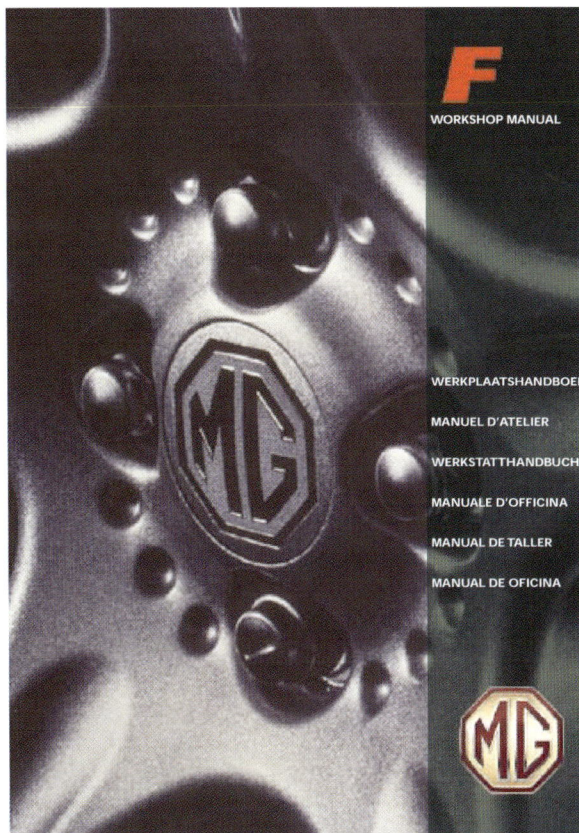

LEFT: *Fig. 1.9   Front cover of the MGF workshop manual. (MG Rover)*

ABOVE: *Fig. 1.10   MG TF 'RAVE' dealer workshop manual. (XPart)*

for suppliers to aim at and encourages them to invest in supplying that need. The fact that spares are available from a widening range of suppliers also shows them responding to the increasing number of new owners spending more money on their purchases.

Just as the classic MG spares market has expanded to offer better ranges and service than applied at any time when the MG Midget and MGB were in production, the active MG enthusiast scene surrounding the MGF and TF bodes well that the future spares supply for these models will develop in a similar way.

WORKSHOP MANUAL

I will be referring regularly to the workshop manual throughout this book. It is worth noting, however, that there has never been a non-MG factory workshop manual, so you are restricted to those produced by Rover and MG Rover. Most of these were supplied specifically for dealers in CD format under the title of RAVE, although for several years MG Rover did produce in-house versions designed for the individual owner. These were expensive, costing almost £50, but even so sold well and

stocks soon vanished once MG Rover collapsed. Since that time Brooklands Books have published paper versions with the information taken from the original CD data. The MGF paper manual is a comprehensive document with more than 800 pages, but doesn't contain the electrical or electrical wiring diagram sub-manuals, which are available separately and should be regarded as a matching pair.

The Brooklands Books TF manual contains both normal manual and electrical manuals in one book, but the downside is that the print size is smaller to fit everything in a single publication. For 2010, XPart reintroduced the complete set of TF manuals on CD at a price then of £33, significantly under the last MG Rover price. These are available from many MG specialists and XPart dealers; the MG Owners Club also holds stocks for members to buy.

MGF MODELS

Unlike many cars that need badges and other information emblazoned on their sides and rump telling the world the make and model, because without that confirmation it looks like every other car around it, the MGF has just a clear

MG badge on the bonnet and boot. (That translates to hood and trunk for transatlantic readers, so when I start talking about hoods and hardtops remember I am talking about weather protection for the occupants.)

MGFs originally reached customers at the end of summer 1995 with just a single model with a multi-point injection (MPi) 1796cc K series 16-valve twin cam engine. This was the first appearance of the largest production version of the 4-cylinder K series, although it was to be installed in a number of other Rover and MG vehicles (and even a hovercraft). It produced 120Ps (118bhp) that was directed to the rear wheels through a five-speed Rover PG1 series gearbox and gave the car a competitive 120mph top speed and acceleration from standstill to the benchmark 60mph in around 8½ seconds.

Good fuel economy has been an unsung attribute of these cars, and the MGF should deliver more than 30mpg (imperial) in full urban conditions. Give it any sort of longer run and 40mpg should be very easy to crack with just normal driving styles. (I have achieved just over 50mpg with one of my MGFs, carefully set up with minor

Fig. 1.11   MGF Trophy 160 SE. (MG Rover)

economy modifications that I will return to in Chapter 6.)

Six months after the launch of the MGF 1.8i came the performance version of the MGF, initially referred to as the MGF 1.8i VVC, but later simply known as the MGF VVC model. VVC stands for Variable Valve Control, which applies to the clever technology that controls the opening and closing of the inlet valves so that the time they are open can be varied depending on the specific rpm and load on the engine.

VVC is a complex system, dubbed by some wag as Very Very Complicated, but in compensation it delivers a much wider power band with the power peak rpm rising from 5,500rpm to 7,000rpm,

Fig. 1.12   (Left) standard displacer and (right) Trophy 160 displacer; note the differences in the alloy pistons.

together with an extra peak of 25bhp. Torque was increased too but it peaked at higher rpms, so the PG1 gearbox featured a 10 per cent lower final drive to make the most of this free revving engine. The VVC adds a useful 10mph to the MGF top speed and acceleration is noticeably sharper, with more than a second shaved off the benchmark 0–60mph sprint. Unlike many tuned engines, the VVC does not drink vast extra quantities of fuel and manages within a whisker of the excellent returns of a 1.8i.

After the launch of the VVC there followed a period of relative inactivity dictated by BMW, which saw the MGF as a competitor to its Z3. Only the arrival of special edition models, such as the Abingdon, higher profile concepts at motor shows and speed record attempts kept interest simmering. What was actually desired by owners, and indeed many elements within Rover, however, were developments to provide greater performance options that would take full advantage of the MGF's handling qualities.

Not until mid-1999 was there any significant change to the model line-up. The arrival of the 2000 model year facelift, commonly referred to as 2000MY, significantly freshened up

the range with mainly new cosmetic exterior and interior features, including an adjustable height steering column, smoked front and side indicators, and one new model, the Steptronic.

In simple terms Steptronic was an MGF with a constantly variable auto (CVT) gearbox that filled a hole in the model range for an automatic transmission. The marketing approach cleverly tried to connect the CVT (previously very much associated with the Dutch DAF small car ranges) with Formula 1, since with some clever mapping within the gearbox controller it was able to deliver six 'fixed' ratios that were controlled by steering wheel control button switches, or the floor selector. This was quite novel, but it never sold in volume.

Unfortunately, the dynamics delivered by this option were somewhat distant from F1 as the relatively low power of the 120Ps engine, hindered by the CVT gearbox absorbing more power than the manual gearbox, meant that the steering wheel gear change buttons had more correlation to being an engine noise volume control.

Many have questioned why the VVC engine was not fitted as the gearbox has a suitably high power and torque capability, but the actual issue preventing this was that the gearbox was restricted to a maximum input rotational speed of 6,000rpm, so using the VVC engine, which didn't deliver peak power until 7,000rpm, was pointless. Interestingly I later had a much more positive experience with a Steptronic model tuned by PTP Ltd. This delivered 140bhp within that 6,000rpm limit and the difference was quite marked, turning the steering wheel switches into performance switches.

Not long after the introduction of the Steptronic and the 2000 model year changes, BMW departed and took the name Steptronic with them. The newly independent MG Rover neatly solved the issue of the now nameless model by renaming it Stepspeed, although no other changes were made.

BMW's departure allowed MG Rover to expand the MGF range with a new 1.6-litre model at the entry level, using the 1589cc K series engine more commonly seen in many of Rover's small saloon models. Surprisingly this engine was less than 10bhp adrift of the 1796cc version and not much further apart in the torque stakes either. This meant that the MGF 1.6i, as it was titled, was still a respectable performer and provided the best average fuel consumption, which was just a smidgen under 40mpg for the combined cycle.

As befits an entry level model, the price was less than the existing models. While the equipment list was shorter in standard form, it could be easily expanded and many buyers added options. Externally the only visual clues to these models being the entry level were the black plastic finish for the door handle assembly, mirrors and the side air vents. Perhaps the most obvious item missing from the specification list was remote central locking, which meant that unlocking and locking had to be done with the key in the driver's door lock, not an issue if you are not used to having it, but much missed if you are.

At the other end of the model range was the new Trophy 160 SE, which featured a 160Ps (158bhp) spec engine. This was the most powerful 4-cylinder K series engine to date and offered a useful extra 15bhp over the previous 145Ps (143bhp) VVC. The power increase came from some very mild tuning by changing to a much more efficient dual cold air inlet air filter, 52mm bore throttle body (from 48mm) and some minor tweaks inside the exhaust system.

The engine was actually just a small part of the new model, which featured two very new and bright exterior colours, Trophy Yellow and Trophy Blue, which noticeably set these models apart. There was also a red and black option for those less keen on standing out like a daffodil on a traffic island.

By far the most significant change to the Trophy spec was the use of a significantly firmer version of the Hydragas suspension, which was also lowered by 20mm. The drop actually came from a shortened pushrod tube, not a lowering knuckle as is sometimes reported. This was matched by the adoption of new 16in alloy wheels, which were needed to clear new MG branded AP Racing four-piston front brake calipers that gripped 64mm larger diameter discs, at 304mm diameter.

Surprisingly, these new brakes were not available with ABS, although this deficiency was not immediately apparent when you first experienced them, since previous experience of normal MGF brakes did not prepare you for the power of the new four-pot brakes trying to reshape your nose against the windscreen!

This specification was not only intended as a top of the range model for general use, but was specifically honed for the track day enthusiast. The suspension was not just firm but hard. Once on a track, however, the model was transformed into a really well sorted and quick car. It was not as responsive as a Lotus Elise, since a direct comparison between the heavy steel-bodied MG and the glass fibre Elise, which is about 25 per cent lighter, is not realistic, but it was a well-received improvement that helped the MGF finish its production period on a high note.

MG TF MODELS

MGF production finished at the end of 2001 after 77,269 cars had been built. The new TF was then released into the media gaze on 5 January 2002. Here was a car that had much sharper lines and lost much of the 'friendly face' aspect of the MGF. At the time this was seen as a positive development and also moved the car from the perspective of many from a feminine look to masculine. A downside of this more extreme look is that it has dated more quickly. The use of a nametag previously featured on the 1953–1955 TF Midget, a car with a continuing high profile within MG circles, also caused a stir.

In detail the new TF was much more than an MGF with new bumpers, headlights and boot lid. There were some very significant changes under the skin, not least the suspension, which featured new steel springs with no sign of Hydragas; this was not initially intended as a universal fit, but was imposed by the Hydragas supplier and cost implications. The new steel spring suspension was not simply a change from Hydragas to a steel spring, but was far more comprehensive (*see* Chapter 4).

The downside to this otherwise positive development was that the ride was very firm indeed: not as hard as the MGF Trophy 160 SE model, but definitely hard enough to put off many potential buyers. I certainly noted this when driving cars at the Press launch of the TF. As I was considering changing my three-year-old MGF, I decided then that, since there was no ride advantage with the standard suspension, I would have the lowered 'Sport Pack 1' suspension option on my new TF 160, which offered a small handling improvement and slightly better aesthetics.

TF subframes were modified to take the new steel spring and damper units. Additional significant changes were seen at the rear with new cast trailing arms and lower arms, the rear of which were pivoting much closer to the cars centreline rather than on each outer subframe member. There was much less change at the front as it was already quite effective, but additional front subframe stiffening, plus other body stiffening by approximately 20 per cent, meant handling took a step forward.

The change of headlamp saw the previously separate front indicator move within the new headlamp. This was possible since both headlamp dip and main beam were now of the smaller 'Projector' type, which use small diameter lenses, resembling 'bottle bottom' type spectacle lenses, so that all of the lamps' reflector functions were focused by these lenses. The side

Fig. 1.13   MG TF with optional hard top. (MG Rover)

Fig. 1.14   MG TF headlamp.

sill also allowed the side air intakes to benefit from improved airflow.

At the rear the bumper panel mirrored the angular changes seen at the front. A consequence that was not generally appreciated was the need for the exhaust to have slightly longer tailpipes. The boot lid also saw a change with the central section gaining a defined kick up; this was not just cosmetic, but helped promote better extracting airflow through the boot vents.

The TF range was split into four models designated by numbers that equated to their engine power outputs: the entry level 1.6-litre 115; the 1.8-litre 120 Stepspeed; the new spec 1.8-litre 135; and finally the 160 model, which used a further modified version of the MGF Trophy 160 SE engine. Since the Stepspeed models had previously seen slow sales, MG Rover elevated the equipment levels in the 120 and deliberately placed it between the 135 and 160 models in order to raise its profile. It didn't seem to make much difference, as sales were never that strong and it is a model that remains at a disadvantage compared to the manual models.

One reason may have been the introduction in the UK on 1 March 2001, the last year of MGF production, of a modified annual tax system based on the car's CO_2 output, rather than the

lamp also remained within the headlamp assembly, but now in a small pencil holder that made it pretty useless other than as a parking lamp.

The basic shape of the headlamps remained as on the MGF, but the inner end was now longer and the lamp took on more of a teardrop shape, which ate very slightly into the bumper space. With the bumper losing the indicators, however, a new moulding was needed

anyway and this has a more angular shape than the MGF bumper.

Moving down the sides towards the rear, there was some obvious 'muscling out' of the previous MGF curved under round sill shape. This was not just cosmetic as the reshaping provided added strength to the body structure. This was amplified by the forming of the rear wing and side sill as a single panel rather than two. The new shape of the previous simple two engine capacity system: up to 1549cc or 1549cc and higher. (The CO_2 ratings for cars available at this date are listed in Appendix A, along with performance and fuel economy information.)

The TF as a range continued until the collapse of MG Rover in April 2005. Ironically this was just after the TF's notoriously hard suspension had been relieved and a more robust glass rear window replaced the plastic one in the hood. By then some 39,295 had been built, according to figures obtained directly from MG Rover's production data three days after the company went into Administration; this total included the car production scheduled for the week when the lines stopped, so incorporating the cars later finished by the Administrators.

A lesser-known fact about the TF relates to its four-star Euro NCAP safety rating for passenger protection; if the passenger airbag had been fitted as standard this could have been even higher. Its impressive three-star rating for pedestrian safety, which achieved a level many mainstream manufacturers are still trying to attain ten years later, was mainly due to the low front and relatively 'soft' bonnet, as there is no 'hard' engine just underneath.

MG Rover may have been financially weak, but its team was highly skilled. After the company's collapse its skill base was scattered, but much of that engineering talent was gathered together by SAIC Motor, the Chinese company that was close to becoming more than just a partner with MG Rover. The resulting team that did great things with little money for MG Rover now found themselves part of the new SMTC (SAIC Motor Technical Centre UK Ltd) with a far better financed parent. This initially operated from Leamington Spa, but moved back into comprehensively refurbished facilities at Longbridge to provide them with the means to justifiably become SAIC's lead design and engineering centre.

MG MOTOR TF

MG has a curious history of reviving its production models in modified forms. Even though the MGB went out of production in 1980, for example, a heavily modified MGB based limited edition model, the MG RV8, appeared in 1992 (a model, incidentally, that I was personally involved in getting off the ground). Then in August 2008 production of the TF resumed in a slightly modified format at Longbridge in the form of the MG Motor (the Chinese company's UK production operation) TF LE500.

Aside from updating the engine to conform to EU4 level compliance – something that MG Rover almost achieved – the EU4 spec retained virtually the same power despite the need to use a 'pre-cat' in the exhaust manifold, which is known to cost some power. Cosmetically the car received a slightly modified front bumper that is visually something halfway between the original TF and MGF styles.

The first of the new models was the LE500 (500 being built), which featured a very high standard specification for significantly less than the same car would have cost in MG Rover days. This was followed in mid-2009 by the 'basic' TF 135 specification and shortly after by the TF 85th Anniversary, intended to mark the MG brand's anniversary.

The 85th Anniversary car, of which fifty-two were made, may have appeared to be another cosmetic variation, but a number of individual suspension developments gave it the best ride and handling of any TF. The benefits of holding the former engineering team together showed in the way their total familiarity with the TF enabled them to hone the 85th's suspension to great effect, using special Bilstein dampers and Eibach anti-roll bars with uprated links.

For the first time different sized wheels were used at front and rear, although it had been standard on all MGF and TF models, except for some early 16in equipped MGFs, to have tyres of a different size at the front and the rear. This 16in diameter wheel design, in a very individual 'flowing' style known as 'Twist of Pepper', differed from anything that went before and was both designed and made in the UK.

The TF swansong was the 2010, 135 model, which saw new and bigger door mirrors as a response to changing UK legislation. Some examples featured the 85th Anniversary wheels as a bonus, although this was more a case of using up old stock.

The end of production was finally announced in April 2011, although the last batch of cars was actually finished in May 2010. A total of 906 MG Motor TFs were built in the UK, together with a very small number of TFs built in China.

DRIVING THE MGF AND TF

To enjoy the pleasures of top-down

Fig. 1.15   Toyo Proxes S953 Snowprox 215/40 ×16 tyres on an MGF.

LEFT: *Fig. 1.16   When winter tyres are not enough snow chains will fit cars with 15in wheels and tyres. (Roger Martin)*

ABOVE: *Fig. 1.17   As there is limited wheel arch clearance, these 'snow socks' are more practical, easily carried in the boot and relatively easy to fit.*

motoring to the full means keeping speeds below 60mph (100km/h) and keeping off main routes to properly appreciate the surrounding sights, smells and sounds. Higher speed introduces wind noise and buffeting, although raising the side windows and the use of a 'windstop' are very effective at reducing buffeting. Main roads away from towns see much higher traffic speeds, which means a significant increase in traffic noise that is often unpleasant.

Both the MGF and TF are designed to deliver the best top-down driving pleasure in temperate climates. As they are soft-top cars this means dry and ideally warmer days. From forty continuous years of owning soft-top MGs, however, I can add that dry and very cold bright days provide an uplifting driving experience as long as you wrap up well. Climates where there is continuous strong sunshine are not ideal for the use of open-top cars with the hood lowered, because it easy for the occupants to become sunburnt.

At the opposite extreme winter driving in snow is not a good experience in cars still riding on their summer tyres. Such tyres are far too focused on grip in wet or dry conditions above around 7° Celsius and they perform very badly in snow. Those living in areas where winter tyres are mandated will know how much better these tyres perform

on snow and ice, as my limited experience confirms.

It is less easy to quantify references made by tyre manufacturers to the general performance of winter tyres being better when ambient temps fall below 7°C in wet and dry conditions. Having been caught out in snow conditions with the original summer Goodyear Eagle F1 GSD2 tyres, I now have a spare set of wheels with Toyo winter tyres in the standard sizes.

Snow chains can only be used on cars with 15in diameter wheels and standard-sized tyres because of clearance issues. Those using them in snow conditions report how effective they are even when attached to the original summer tyres.

SAFETY CONSIDERATIONS

A few words here on safety will not go amiss. Since everyone has to start somewhere, and some reading this may well be undertaking their first car project, before commencing any work on your car consider the following points:

◆ Always select a level piece of ground that has a solid material base, such as concrete or block. Tarmac can be hard enough where you use motorway grade materials and a deep enough base, but home

driveway tarmac will often not be able to support spot loads from a jack or axle stand feet and will sink. In these cases you will need to use load-spreading 'pads', such as 12mm or 19mm thick plywood, which is widely available and relatively cheap, and can be easily cut to convenient sizes.

◆ These pads can be sized to be a little bigger than the axle stand and cut individually for each stand, ramp or jack, or you can keep the plywood at its original sheet size and drive the car onto it in order to have a firm base under a large area of the car. (The assumption here is the sheets of plywood come in 8 × 4ft sheets.) Good quality plywood, and specifically marine types, last very well; I had a 4 × 4ft sheet of non-Marine ply for over a decade, mostly kept outside, stood on its end against the back of the garage wall.

◆ The positioning of tyres on ramps is pretty obvious, but I will labour the point anyway: always ensure that the tyre is centralized, fully at the top of the ramp, and in contact against the raised stop bar.

◆ The positioning of axle stands is more varied. My advice is that axle stands should be fitted under any 'hard point' of the car. Hard points are any substantial sections of the car's understructure, which generally include jacking points, chassis sections and points where suspension bolts to the car's structure. In the case of the MGF and TF you will usually find that jacking up on the subframe, and then locating the stands under another part of the subframe, more than adequate. When looking to work on the subframe the stands can be moved to the body jacking points (*see below*).

◆ Ensure that the stand's saddle (the top of the stand on which the car rests) is in a position where it can't slip. When placing the stand under the car do it with an outstretched arm and don't be tempted to crawl under the car, taking both stands with you to save time. Place one stand under the one side and then walk around to the other. Place that one under the car and lower the jack slowly, watching how the car and stand saddles engage with each other. Stop and adjust the stand position if necessary to ensure a solid contact and safe support.

◆ When lifting a car remember that it is better to lift and then adjust the height of each stand in small increments rather than going for a full lift in one go. This is especially valid when using four stands to lift a car fully off the ground, since once one end is raised and on stands, and you start to jack up the other end, it is normal to find that as you raise the car the jack pulls on it and the stands that are already place can see one of their three feet start to lift. This is one reason why small incremental stages of jacking up (and also lowering) are safer than the whole lift done in one go as it allows the car to be supported. If needed you can go back and lift the car in order to reseat it where any stand is being pulled.

◆ When you need unrestricted access to the subframes you should place stands under alternative 'hard points' instead of the subframes. Choose to place the stands under jacking points or, if appropriate for the planned work, under the subframe to body mounting points.

Although not directly related to safety considerations – although it could be if the driveway owner is easily upset – it should be remembered that if you have an expensively laid drive, not only does the use of plywood spread the load and make a safer lift, but it also insulates the driveway from direct physical damage and from any leaking fluids.

You may also want to take this driveway preservation a stage further by obtaining a large section of builders' plastic sheeting and place this on the drive under the plywood before you start, as this will catch all the debris and make for a simple and easy clean up when you have finished. If you plan to do rustproofing and apply anti-rust treatment to the subframes and the rest of the car's underside, buy a sheet big enough to have at least a two-foot overlap all round.

Once the car is raised sufficiently to give you good access underneath, it is time to look at your personal protection. Depending on what work you are doing this will mean goggles, usually some gloves and sometimes earplugs. (The latter is something only those who have had a bit of debris drop in their eyes or ears when crawling under a car will truly appreciate.) There is of course a limit to where you will be able to access, but for practical maintenance purposes this will be good enough.

Catering for the possibility of fire is an important precaution to take. Here the main cause will be from fuel leaks and having exposed types of heater in the garage where sources of ignition can be found. I have seen many petrol fires, so I always have at least two fire extinguishers to hand in the garage that are currently in date. When working on a car's fuel system, or if any part of the fuel system is exposed, then ideally the work should be done outside where the best ventilation is found, or supply as much ventilation in the garage as possible and don't rely on any heating that can generate an ignition source.

It is also logical not to smoke anywhere near the car or garage. Yet the number of 'dipstick drivers' who are to be seen puffing away when they pull in at petrol stations, and then feel hard done by when the station's staff shout at them, means this warning has to be made here.

Electrical safety is also an aspect demanding careful consideration. It is the common logical step to disconnect the battery of the car before any electrical work is commenced. With the MGF and TF there is the additional consideration, especially with all MGFs and early TFs with the Lucas 5AS alarm system, that to disengage the immobilizer after the battery has been disconnected means re-synchronizing the remote fob to the car's alarm ECU. This is a simple process done by using the key in the driver's door and the fob in a set sequence (*see* Chapter 5). The important point is that if the key doesn't operate the central locking, then it is indicative that there is no communication between the driver's door lock and the ECU, so you will not be able to disable the immobilizer after reconnecting the battery. This needs to be dealt with first.

The same consideration needs to be applied to radio codes: is your radio coded, do you have the code, and do you have the procedure to input that code? If not, find the missing information before committing to disconnecting the battery.

Connected to the electrical system is the SRS (Supplementary Restraint System), more commonly known as the Air Bag system. These explosive devices can seriously injure or even kill if you are too close when they go off. This can happen when someone working on the car is too close, usually disconnecting or reconnecting part of the system without having gone through the very necessary battery disconnection and the waiting period of fifteen minutes to allow residual power to drain away. The safety process is reproduced later (*see* Chapter 3) and a reminder is set at appropriate points where disturbance of the SRS may be needed.

Fig. 2.1   MGF and TF body shells were manufactured in a collaborative deal with Stadco.

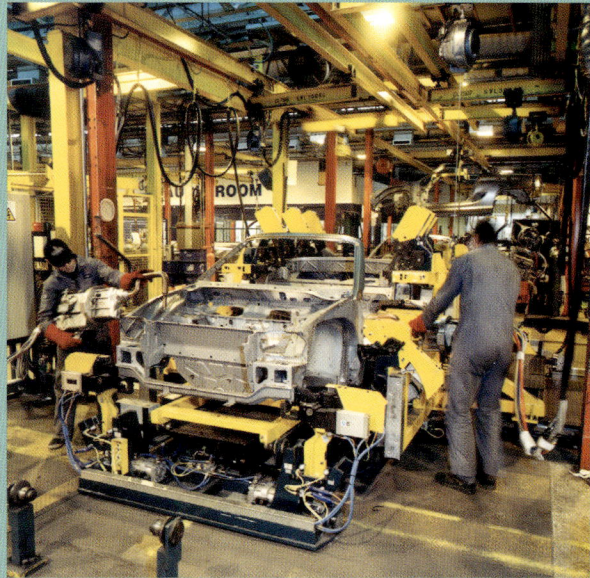

Fig. 2.2   Stadco's assembly plant in Coventry.

2

body structure and external panels

OVERVIEW

When introduced in 1995, the MGF was a paragon of ingenuity on the part of the team led by the late Chief Engineer Brian Griffin. They created a great car from limited resources and components already on the company's parts shelves, and proved how skilled they were. The appreciation of how good the car was can be seen in contemporary road tests.

It was the Rover Metro at the very bottom of the Rover car range that provided much of the new MGF's content. The logic in this can be seen through the fact that the Metro used steel subframes to support the engine, transmission, steering, suspension and brakes, and these subframes were then bolted into the Metro body.

Look closer at the MGF and TF front bulkhead, and the Metro roots are obvious, although the external shape of the MGF and the TF is quite unlike the Metro. The use of the Metro subframe and suspension, however, did provide some restrictions on the overall body dimensions, especially the width.

The MGF body itself is a steel monocoque construction with huge inbuilt strength and rigidity for a body without a roof structure. This was because it was designed as such. It may not be as good as many modern saloon cars, but is certainly more than competitive against comparable two-seat sports cars and usually better than saloon cars with a roof chop. Indeed, the TF is actually 20 per cent stiffer than an MGF and some of the updates that give the

Fig. 2.3   The unpainted bodies, known as 'body in white' (assembled bodies), were shipped direct to Longbridge. (MG Rover)

TF that bonus can be incorporated into the MGF (*see* Section 3 below).

A big advantage over classic MGs is that the body steel has a zinc phosphate surface treatment that provides significant anti-corrosion protection. This has been proven with most cars suffering little corrosion, except where the surface layer has been penetrated, for example, after body repairs. The front wing lower edges, around the side repeaters and the wheel arches are the most common problem areas.

The design of the MGF as a soft-top car from the outset incorporated some specific bonus features, such as a reinforced windscreen frame to add considerable rigidity and protection in the event of the car overturning. It is not that instability is an issue, but having this safety feature in the background is comforting. Behind the facia there is also a massive cross brace tube that makes scaffolding look puny. This helps reduce scuttle shake, although early cars could suffer from insufficient welding of this to the body and creaking behind the dashboard would occur. The TF is better and the MGF can benefit from TF additions. The TF also achieved very creditable Euro NCAP four-star occupant safety and three-star pedestrian safety ratings, the latter being something many current cars have difficulty reaching.

BODY REPAIRS

Before I start going into detail on how to do this or that, I want to make it clear that I am not going to repeat workshop manual processes. I am making the reasonable assumption that readers will have a good level of mechanical knowledge and already have the 'Body Manual' sub-manual of the original Rover workshop manual. Indeed it is essential to have a workshop manual on hand and there is only the MG factory workshop manual or published copies of same, as Haynes and other publishers have not produced MGF or TF manuals.

The MGF and TF have traditional welded steel bodies to form a rigid structure. The bonnet, boot, doors and front wings are all bolt-on steel panels, while the front and rear bumpers are bolt-on moulded plastic panels. Obviously significant repairs to these bolt-

Fig. 2.4   *The heavy tube cross brace adds considerable structure. Some early cars, however, had insufficient welding, which could break and allow movement within the end sockets. Here an attempt was made to rectify this with big exhaust type clamps rather than do a proper weld repair.*

on panels is best done by replacement with a new or good used panel, but the traditional methods of repairing the steel panels, and filling minor damage with body filler, can still be used very successfully.

Bumpers

Plastic front and rear bumper repairs present more difficulty than steel. They are easily cracked with minor parking errors, so are usually easier to replace than repair. Repairing cracked bumpers and even refitting broken pieces can be done using a plastic welding tool that feeds molten plastic just like a hot glue gun to 'weld' the crack or broken pieces back into a single solid bumper. Experience shows that the quality of results is variable, however, and so as long as new and second-hand spares availability remains good this route is preferable.

The other bonus with plastic, of course, is that it doesn't corrode, but this must be weighed against the not uncommon sight of paint colour fading at a different rate on plastic parts compared to the rest of the body, and so taking on a different hue. Painting also requires different initial preparation to the plastic surface to ensure good paint adhesion.

Minor body damage is something that home restorers can tackle themselves. If damage is more serious but confined to the bolt-on panels, it is a relatively simple matter of unbolting one and bolting on the replacement.

A common mistake is that what may appear to be local damage will often have affected the adjoining section(s) due to the designed-in safety body crushability, which is only seen when trying to fit a replacement panel. Even so this will often still be within the scope of the home mechanic. If buying a damaged salvage car, however, do take someone very familiar with these cars' structures to stop you buying one needing more extensive and expensive repairs.

Probably the most common panels that need to be repaired or replaced, aside from bumpers, are frontal panels following the most common nose-to-tail bumps. If you were that car in front, though, the next most common damage is to the rear.

Front Bumpers

'Fender bender' (minor) impacts involving a damaged plastic bumper are usually well within the scope of home correction. Behind the front bumper is a structural support, called an armature, to which the bumper is bolted and which provides most of the support to turn what, off the car, is a very floppy moulding into the firm and rigid panel that gives the car the frontal shape we are all familiar with.

TOP LEFT: *Fig. 2.5   At the front of the MGF and TF is a bolt-on box support beam called an armature. This supports the bumper and provides some impact absorption …*

TOP RIGHT: *Fig. 2.6   … by way of two collapsible sections at each end (one shown here).*

LEFT: *Fig. 2.7   The TF armature differs very slightly, with additional bumper mounting brackets.*

This armature is an alloy box bar that is bolted to the front of the car's body via two sacrificial mounting plinths at either end. These are an integral part of the armature and have a collapsible construction that is intended to absorb smaller impact energy and prevent damage from being transmitted into the car's structure. The MG TF's armature has additions riveted to it, as shown here.

After a 'fender bender' incident owners often criticize the armature's weakness when it has to be replaced, but they fail to appreciate that the impact energy absorbed has stopped the damage extending into the front panels and headlamps, which would make the repair much more difficult and expensive.

Dealing with a front bumper replacement on an MGF or TF is a simple operation and well covered in the workshop manual, but I have a few extra hints that I hope will make life easier.

The MGF front bumper has two main bolts securing it to the armature, hidden behind the indicator units. Many of these lamps are damaged by careless or incorrect removal in what is actually a simple process. The correct removal involves inserting a small flat screwdriver into a slot on the grille side

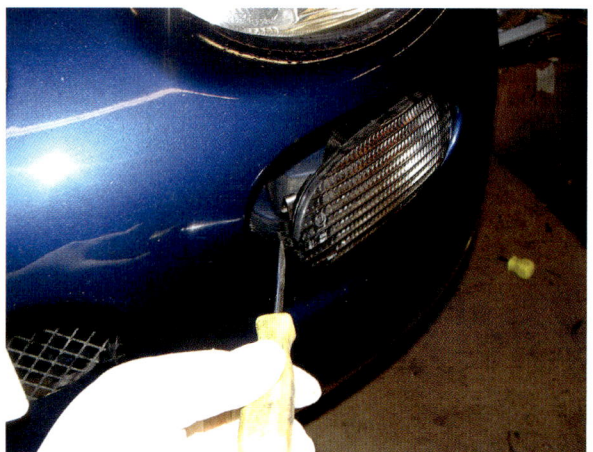

LEFT: *Fig. 2.8   At the rear are two smaller square support box structures commonly called 'crush cans' seen here indicated by arrows.*

ABOVE: *Fig. 2.9   MGF bumper removal needs the indicator units removed. Carefully insert a screwdriver and gently lever it against the lamp's plastic spring clip, before pulling out the unit.*

of the indicator, applying gentle pressure against the plastic clip that is a moulded part of the lamp and easing the lamp out, as shown in the accompanying images.

If you are not familiar with this method, I find that wrapping a bit of masking tape or similar around the bottom inch or so of the screwdriver provides some added insurance against damaging the paint. The leverage force is such that it shouldn't place any stress on the paint on the indicator aperture edge of the bumper. Once this end of the indicator is free, the whole unit simply lifts out. There is then just the simple quick-release electrical plug to disconnect and the indicator can be placed aside. Repeat for the other indicator.

Returning to the issue of bumper removal, start by removing the five self-tapper screws holding the top edge of the bumper where it meets the bonnet. Remove the two screws per side holding each end of the bumper in the wheel arches to the lower edge of the front wings, and then just loosen (no need to remove) the two additional screws between the end screws and the headlamps.

Bumper removal is then a matter of removing the two bolts at the rear of the indicator apertures. Always have an assistant ready to hold the bumper, since once it is removed the bumper becomes like floppy tissue paper and wants to fall face down onto a hard surface. Carefully lift the bumper off and place it face down on soft material somewhere out of harm's way.

Only those cars fitted with headlamp washers, non-MG additional lamps or front parking sensors will need any additional items being disconnected

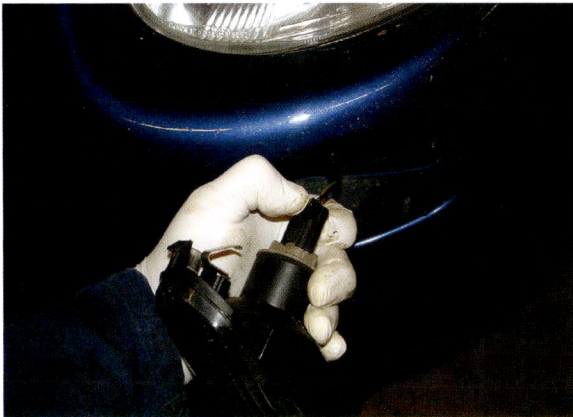
Fig. 2.10   Unclip the electrical plug and remove the lamp.

Fig. 2.11   With the lamp removed the main bumper securing bolts are visible.

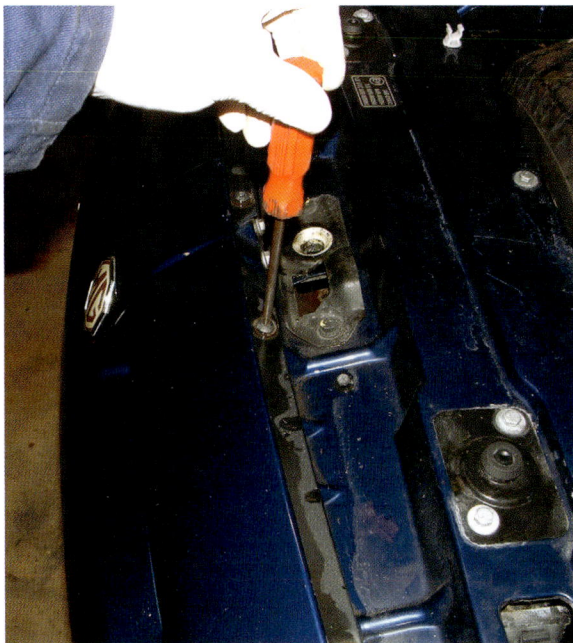

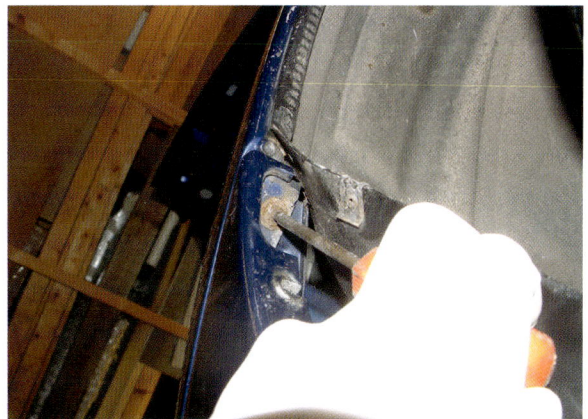

MIDDLE LEFT: Fig. 2.12   Bumper removal starts with removing the top five screws at the bonnet edge.

MIDDLE RIGHT: Fig. 2.13   Remove the screws at the edge of the bumper in the wheel arches.

BOTTOM RIGHT: Fig. 2.14   Pull the arch liner out of the way to access the two screws a little towards the headlamp, on the same level as the previous screws, but loosen them only a couple of turns.

LEFT: *Fig. 2.15   Carefully remove the bumper and lay it face down on a soft material to prevent damaging the paint.*

ABOVE: *Fig. 2.17   Whereas MGF fog lamps are fitted to the body, TF fog lamps are attached to the back of the bumper, as indicated, and have to be unplugged before the bumper is removed.*

Fig. 2.16   TF bumper removal follows a similar pattern to the MGF, but the main bumper bolts are always accessible.

Rear Bumpers

Removing and refitting the rear bumper really needs no additional guidance than the workshop manual provides as it is simple, although it is necessary for an assistant to support the bumper as it is still floppy, if not as much as the front. It is worth pointing out that the rear 'crush cans' are the same for both the MGF and TF, even though there is no listing in the XPart Electronic Parts Catalogue (EPC) for a TF.

A common problem is that the two single main bolts screw into captive nuts and these cans corrode, and it doesn't have to be that severe to find the 'can' metal ripped apart when trying to undo the bolts. When this happens you should weld in a new captive nut or replace the cans.

TF Bumpers on the MGF

When it comes to fitting the MG TF front bumper to the MGF, the TF

before the bumper can be removed. Surprisingly, the factory-fitted official MG fog lamp kit doesn't have any connection to the bumper, as this is bolted to the body immediately behind the bumper and so doesn't impinge on bumper removal.

The TF front bumper is fitted in a very similar way, but some important differences make the removal simpler, since moving the TF indicators into the extended headlamp has left the main bolts accessible. On the downside, though, the fog lamps are secured to the back of the bumper, so the wiring plug needs to be disconnected before removal. Other than these differences, and the possible addition of items such as headlamp washers, the same MGF removal process applies.

Refitting is more of a fiddle than removal, and it is certainly important to have an assistant again to hold the bumper while you negotiate the edges into place. Note specifically how the bumper fits around the headlamps, which is always where the most unsightly gaps can occur.

Fig. 2.18   TF rear 'crush cans' are the same as the MGF's and the bolts fixing the 'can' to the bumper may corrode.

headlamps have to be regarded as an integral part of this conversion. The reasons are obvious in that the separate MGF indicators are integrated into the TF headlamps and the different shape requires bigger headlamp cut-outs, although the bonnet and front wings are unchanged.

The bumper to body mountings are different. Although changing the front armature, as the mounting bracket is called (see Fig. 2.5 and Fig. 2.6), to the TF one will allow the TF bumper to be a bolt-on fit to an MGF, the TF headlamps will not fit until modifications are made to the headlamp panel or TF panels are fitted. Finally, the headlamp wiring plugs are completely different to cater for the indicators. This complicates things as those electrical plugs are an integral part of the car's wiring loom and not sold separately, so you either have to buy a complete loom (expensive) or look for a smashed-up car to cut the plugs from and then do some neat cutting, joining, soldering and insulating.

At the rear the bumper is mounted in the same way as the MGF, and because the new panel has a more vertical line to the moulding rather than the 'folding in' style of the MGF, the TF exhaust tailpipes are longer to project sufficiently beyond the bumper and look correct. If you stick with an MGF exhaust, don't be too surprised if on the first long journey you find heat deformity on the bumper around the tailpipes.

Interchangeability of Panels

While there are many differences between the MGF and TF, the front wings, doors and bonnets are identical. Internal panels are generally going to be those that are already welded onto the main body structure, so sourcing these as spare panels may seem a little far-fetched, but when you consider that some MGF panels have not always been available since MG Rover's collapse, cutting out a straight panel from a breaker's car starts to make sense. TF panels have not been quite so adversely affected – so far.

The MGF and TF share many parts, but when the TF was launched MG Rover saw a need to separate the two models and deliberately made life difficult for the MGF owner who wanted to fit TF external parts. This was to protect the individuality of the TF and MG Rover customers who bought a new TF, although in time a small number of MGFs with TF panels still appeared.

The main MGF to TF body differences were the bumpers, headlamps, boot lid, rear wings and sills. In my opinion the marriage of the TF front and rear bumpers and headlights with the rounded MGF side sill panels is not a happy one, which may explain the relative unpopularity of this conversion. Very few cars were converted even after second-hand parts became readily available, although changing MGF panels for TF ones is not that complex.

TF rear wings were not changed just for styling purposes. There were also aerodynamic benefits from reshaping the engine air intake vent from a round format into a triangular one, and structural from being integrated into the sill panel.

Hidden from view there was also a small addition in the form of expanded foam in the A pillars. When expanded it fully filled the internal void and added a small degree of additional rigidity. The A pillar changes are out of reach of MGF owners, although I expect some might visit their local DIY store for a can of builders' foam. Certainly the option of welding the sill to the rear wing is something that can be applied to an MGF to aid the structure.

The significant change in the shape of the TF's sill matched a similarly reshaped lower rear wing section. The TF changes added strength, improved airflow and many thought they looked better. Finally, the boot lid gained a pronounced kick-up trailing edge, again in the name of improved aerodynamics. It helps draw more air out of the engine

TOP LEFT: *Fig. 2.19 The sill of an MGF is a separate panel.*

TOP FAR RIGHT: *Fig. 2.20 The TF's sill is part of the rear wing panel and has a different shape.*

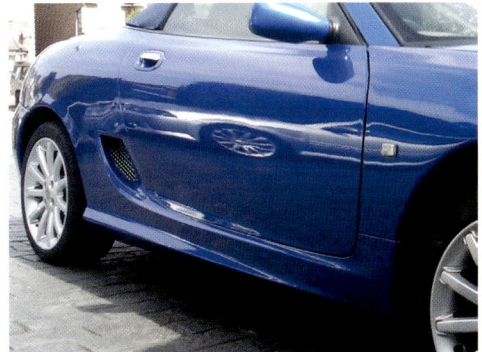

BOTTOM RIGHT: *Fig. 2.21 The boot of the MGF has a flat profile and less integrated high-level brake lamp.*

BOTTOM FAR RIGHT: *Fig. 2.22 The TF has a raised rear edge to the boot lid and a well-integrated high-level brake lamp.*

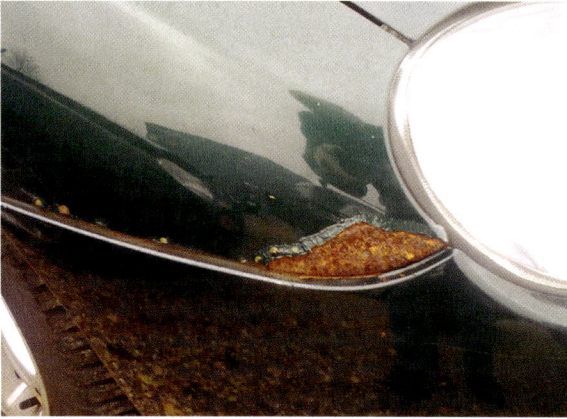

Fig. 2.23   While structural corrosion is not a common problem, cars can suffer more near the sea. A new or second-hand wing is a better option with this sort of corrosion.

Fig. 2.24   Even if you manage to find a replacement wing in the 'same' colour, shade and tint differences often make it a different colour and repainting is unavoidable.

LEFT: Fig. 2.25   Two hinges hold the door to the body and the wing must be removed to access the bolts joining the hinge to the body.

RIGHT: Fig. 2.26   The door check strap roll pin can be drifted out when removing the door.

bay, and for some years I have used a TF boot lid on my MGF.

These panels are easily interchangeable, involving simply unbolting the MGF boot lid and bolting on the TF one (or the other way around, if anyone wishes). The only difficulty involves threading the wiring through the inside of the boot panel. On the other hand the rear wing and sills are welded to the body and I have yet to see an MGF owner go to the trouble of having both rear wings and sills cut off to be replaced by the TF panels. Bumpers and headlamps are a different story and some MGF owners have fitted these TF parts to give their MGFs an updated look.

Replacement Front Wings

MGF and TF front wings are simple pressings and bolt on using six bolts with three screws. Removing a front wing is quite straightforward. The wing's plastic undershield is first removed to give access to the bolts

located behind the wing near the door. This also allows better access to the screws between bumper and wing edge and the screw between wing and headlamp, which is often badly rusted and leads to the plastic headlamp 'foot' breaking. Refitting is just as simple as the removal; as it is a bolt-on panel there is the opportunity to fine tune the fit against the surrounding panels.

This makes finding better condition second-hand wings a viable option, even in the correct colour, but colour tint differences with the same body colour may make repainting unavoidable.

Fitting Replacement Doors

Doors are bulky and heavy items, especially when fully assembled with glass. This may seem to be obvious, but it needs to be mentioned to ensure you have enough support when one or both hinges are disconnected. It is much easier to strip or generally work on a door that is securely bolted to the

car and held at a convenient working height, than one that has been removed.

The door has two hinges bolted to it with a two-bolt fixing per hinge to the door and a three-bolt fixing to the A pillar. The bolts holding the hinge to door are easy to access, so when changing a door it is easiest to consider door removal by way of unbolting these rather than the bolts holding the hinge to the A pillar (*see below*). Unfortunately that removal is not only related to the hinges, but is somewhat more complex.

The first issue is that the electrical wiring that enters the door to cater for central locking, electric windows and speakers doesn't have a simple and convenient quick release multi-plug. Instead the wiring is an extension of the main harness, which means you have to disconnect each wiring plug individually from inside the door, unclip the wiring from the various internal retaining clips and feed it out of the front edge of the door, so at least a partial door strip is required.

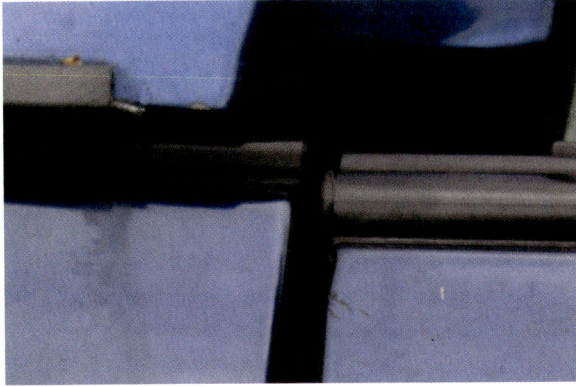

Fig. 2.27 Door hinge wear shows with the back edge of the door dropping, as can be seen in this image.

Fig. 2.28 The door is securely supported while the hinges are being attended to.

Once the wiring is dealt with you can then move to the door check strap, which needs to be disconnected. This can be achieved by drifting out the roll pin seen at the end of the strap nearest the A pillar. Alternatively the two bolts holding the main strap to the door may both be accessed from inside the door through the speaker aperture, after this has been removed.

What now remains is the relatively simple removal of the door. Its weight, however, must be considered, so that dictates a good strong additional pair of hands to hold the door while the four bolts that hold the hinges to the door are removed and it is then lifted away. Replacement is a true reversal of this process, although it is advisable to feed most of the wiring into the door first, and then bolt the door onto the hinges, followed by the check strap. Take care when checking the door fit to the aperture, just in case the door hits the sill. There is nothing more galling than knowing you could so easily have avoided that paint damage.

Repairing Door Hinges

A perennial problem for the MGF and TF is that wear in the door hinges will see the doors start to sag. This will, of course, be directly proportional to the amount of use a car gets and the lubrication that the hinges are afforded during their life. The driver's door is usually the one that shows problems first, simply because the car will not be carrying a passenger all the time.

This issue is first seen with the door catching the striker plate more heavily on the body B pillar, and more effort is needed to shut the door. Adjusting the striker will provide some relief for a while, but this is a case of treating the symptom not the cause. Over time the problem worsens, leading to the rear lower part of the door catching on the sill, damaging the paint, and on bumpy roads this can generate annoying rattles.

A very rough estimate of the rate of wear applicable to the driver's door hinges would suggest that few or no problems are seen on cars up to 40,000 miles, but by 60,000 miles wear in the bushes will be evident. By 80,000 miles this wear is likely to have gone through the bushes and started to ovalize the hinge holes.

The cause is always that the movement between the hinge halves using the hinge pin as a pivot is carrying the significant weight of the door, exacerbated by the door being long for easy access, and that increases the overall door weight. In this instance that also increases the leverage forces, so effectively putting more stress on the hinges' pivot points.

In some respects we are fortunate that the original hinge design incorporates separate bushes on the door half of the hinge. The material used in these bushes appears to have been designed to make them sacrificial items and so helping to reduce the wear seen on the hinge pin. It is therefore disappointing that, while this design was present, there was never any facility to buy just replacement bushes and pins as official MG parts.

In fact the only factory replacement part you can buy is a complete hinge, subject to availability (and there have been times when none were available). At a 2011 list price of just under £26.50 each, plus VAT, a new hinge is not too expensive when compared with some other parts. Fitting a complete hinge is somewhat time-consuming at an official allocated time of nearly 1¾ hours per door because access to the fixings holding the hinge to the body are hidden. That time doesn't account for painting the new bare cast hinge body colour, so if fitted professionally there would be an even higher cost.

At the time of writing there were good stock levels of new hinges, but if these drop out of availability again the obvious suggestion would be to search for second-hand. Indeed the rate of cars being broken for spares is still high, so there is currently plenty of second-hand stock. The problem of course is that, aside from the very few low mileage cars, most drivers' door hinges will have excessive wear affecting the bushes and pins, and unfortunately many will have ovalized holes.

At this point it is worth noting that when the hinge holes do wear, it is only found in the part that bolts to the door; that is why only these holes have the bushes. The hinge pin has a splined end that is a tight interference fit into the body-mounted part of the hinge, just like a wheel stud that bites into the hub flange. Therefore this part of the hinge and pin are static, leaving only the door-mounted part of the hinge turning against the pin.

Fortunately, the MG specialist trade has noted this and created replacement parts to fill the void. The MGF Centre (www.mgfcentre.com) has door repair kits that include bushes, new pins and the important 'E' clip (circlip), while Mike Satur (www.mikesatur. com) has replacement hinge bushes. As

Fig. 2.29   Carefully lever off the retaining 'E' clip to a point where it can be removed with long-nosed pliers so not to see it ping off into the distance.

Fig. 2.30   The hinge pin can now be drifted out.

Fig. 2.31 Once loose the pin can be withdrawn. Note the position it comes out, as refitting it 180 degrees around overcomes minor pin wear.

Fig. 2.32 The bolts holding the hinge half to the door can now be undone and that half removed. Note that the door edges have been covered in masking tape as a precaution against paint damage.

spares supply for MGs is a big market, it is likely that other suppliers will be able to offer this type of spare to cover what the original MG factory parts sources can't.

The fitting of replacement hinges, though it can be done relatively easily without specialist tools, is not covered in the workshop manual. The process shown here also applies to the passenger door and is the same for both MGF and TF.

The door is opened and supported around the mid- to end position to take the tension that would otherwise be present if the hinges were holding the door's weight. In this instance a small wheeled seat happened to provide the perfect height to give this support and the seat obviously is kind to the door's paint.

Next take the tension from the two bolts holding the top hinge to the door, but do not remove at this stage. Now move to the top of the hinge pin where you will see a three-eared circlip ('E' clip), which needs to be removed. Do not approach this roughly, but ease it off enough until you can pull it away with pliers, otherwise it may ping off into the distance, never to be found again. As it is not a standard replacement MG part, it will be a big inconvenience if you lose it.

Once the circlip is off and safely stored, turn your attention to the hinge pin. This is fitted from the underside. With the help of a pin punch and hammer, tap the top of the pin to move it downwards. Initially you may find it won't move because the lower part of the pin has a tight interference fit, so add a little more energy to the taps and it will slowly start to move, until you are able to remove it by hand.

Fig. 2.33   The wear on the bush in the hinge is quite obvious.

TOP LEFT: *Fig. 2.34   Worn bushes are easy to tap out.*
TOP RIGHT: *Fig. 2.35   The depth of wear on an old bush is clearly evident when compared to a new one (left).*
LEFT: *Fig. 2.36   New bushes are tapped into the hinge.*
BELOW: *Fig. 2.37   The removed blue pin shows wear not visible on the orange pin. The wear was overcome, however, by turning the blue pin 180 degrees before refitting it.*

At this point you may want to make a mark on the top of the pin as a reference against the hinge. As the pin wears on one side only, it is possible to reuse the pin by turning it by 180 degrees, so moving the unworn side of the pin to the thrust side and slightly reducing door drop.

Now remove the two hinge bolts to the door and remove that half of the hinge, noting that the door will stand safely if supported correctly, and of course it still has the bottom hinge and check strap securing it to the car.

Take the removed half hinge to the bench in order to give some attention to the two bushes in the hinge holes, making sure they have a 'top hat' shape. Tap out the bushes from the top of the 'top hat'; if it is heavily worn they are likely to drop out fairly easily. Then fit the replacement bushes in the opposite way and tap into place.

The repaired hinge half is refitted and the bolts loosely fitted. The reason for lightly refitting the bolts is that this gives this part of the hinge some freedom of movement, making alignment and refitting of the pin simple. Remember the hint about turning the pin 180 degrees, then either squeeze it in place and finally tap in the last bit, or carefully tap it in all the way until you can see the circlip groove. The circlip is refitted with care to avoid the clip

Fig. 2.38   As there is limited space for hammers and tapping, use large grips so that the pins can be refitted gently but powerfully.

Fig. 2.39   Finally tap the pin fully home and once the circlip groove is visible then refit the 'E' clip.

LEFT: Fig. 2.40   The lower hinge is dealt with in the same way as the top hinge.
CENTRE: Fig. 2.41   Both hinges had suffered the same degree of bush wear.
RIGHT: Fig. 2.42   Once both hinges were repaired the door now sat level.

springing off, and then the hinge-to-door bolts are fully tightened.

The same process is applied to the bottom hinge. The space is a little more limited, but the job is still straightforward.

Unfortunately, the passenger door hinges are not the same as the driver's side: they are handed and marked R and L for obvious identification.

Replacing the Boot Lid

The boot lid is one of the simpler panels on the car to change as it is secured very simply by four bolts to the two hinges. The only difficulty comes from the wiring, which is part of the main wiring loom. This is threaded from the left side of the car against the left hinge, into the boot between the inner and outer skins and fed up the left inside of the boot before running across to the boot rear centre area, where all the electrical items are located.

Fortunately there are a couple of tricks to make threading the wiring less difficult. First, it is best to tape up the removed plug ends of the wiring to make a single 'stem' rather than have a 'tree' with many 'branches' of loose wiring. This will be easier to feed through the narrow internal voids in the boot lid. If the boot lid is to be refitted, tie some very stout string to the end of the wiring. This will become a 'pull string' when you come to refit the boot lid.

If you fit a replacement boot lid you will need to use a guide rod or similar to feed the wiring through. The traditional guide rod is often a welding rod, but anything similar will do. An excellent choice is a flexible gripper rod, fitted

at one end with a press button; when pressed, four spring fingers come out and grab what you want to hold.

The trouble with any metal rod or probe, however, is that it will scratch the paint. While you may not consider a scratch inside an inaccessible panel is problematic, you certainly do not want to encourage corrosion in that scratch. This wouldn't be a problem for the short term, but the whole point of taking on this project is that you plan to own the car for a longer term and this might be a problem in the future.

In order to overcome the risk of scratching it you simply need to wrap some adhesive tape around the rod/gripper tool. The first stage in drawing the wiring through requires the

removal of the rubber bungs. Insert the tool from the upper hole (labelled 1 in the accompanying picture) as far as the wire entry point (3). Tape the wiring to the end of the tool and then pull/jiggle the tool upwards to feed the wiring to the upper hole 1. If this does not work, first pull the wiring through from hole 3 to hole 2, and then move it up to hole 1.

Then remove the wiring from the tool and insert it into the hole where the interior light fits and feed it from there to hole 1. Tape the wiring to the tool again and repeat the draw/jiggle to move the wiring to the interior light position. From there it is quite simple to move the different wires into their final positions.

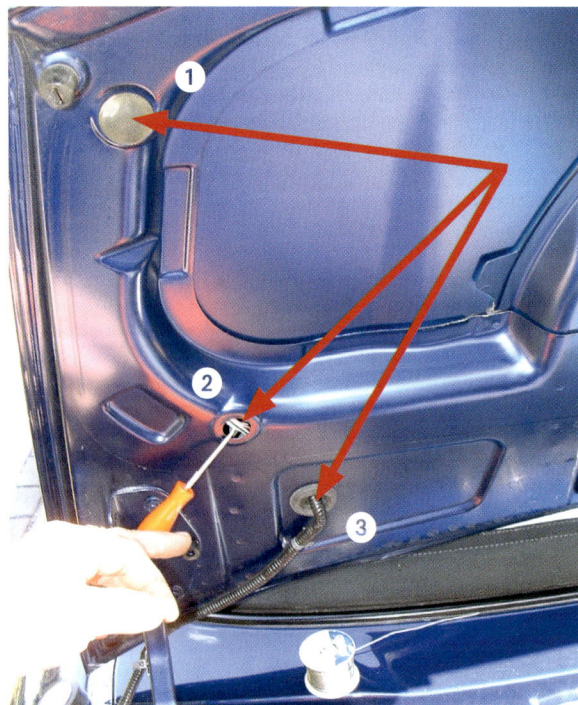

Fig. 2.43   Feeding wiring through a boot lid is fiddly. It can be made easier with a probe and by feeding the wiring between the numbers access holes and the central part of the lid.

GLASS AND ASSOCIATED COMPONENTS

Windscreen and Body Glass

The windscreen of the MGF and TF is bonded to the windscreen frame and adds to the body structure. The nature of this type of fitting means that removal and replacement of the windscreen is best left to the professionals, ideally one who has experience with the MGF and TF. Note that any water leaking after a windscreen change will result from the failure to apply an even bead of glass bonding sealant during fitting and will inevitably demand another screen replacement.

Most screen and body glass changes will be carried out following damage or breakage during driving. Replacement is often covered in insurance policies, at least it is in the UK, where only the 'windscreen excess' is paid by the policyholder. Replacement under insurance is also known when the glass suffers other forms of irreparable

Fig. 2.44   Before replacing a windscreen the old screen has to be removed. Because it is bonded it has to be cut out. Here a knife cuts through the bonding sealant to allow a thin wire to be inserted.

Fig. 2.45   The wire is attached to a winding wheel and mechanism, which is mounted to the inside of the glass using suckers.

Fig. 2.46   The wire is wound in, cutting through the sealant like a cheese wire.

Fig. 2.47   The glass is now completely severed from the car.

LEFT: Fig. 2.48   Most of the old sealant still in the windscreen frame is trimmed down to prevent the replacement glass sitting too high.

RIGHT: Fig. 2.49 Fresh sealant is then applied.

Fig. 2.50   Carefully pressing the new glass into the screen aperture spreads the sealant and ensures a good bond and weather protection.

Fig. 2.51   After fitting the windscreen allow the sealant a time to cure before the car is ready for use. Here the wipers and screen panel trim were removed to aid access, although this is not necessary.

damage, especially when visibility is inhibited by many years of grit pitting, which often only becomes apparent when driving into a rising or setting sun. The same applies to damage that inhibits the efficiency of the wipers, for example resulting in a big scratch arching across the screen.

Where no insurance cover exists, however, owners will have to pay the full costs of replacement, which at the time of writing was approximately £150 for the new screen and £20 for the trim seal, together with the removal of the existing screen and fitting the new.

Before the fitter leaves always check to make certain that the glass is seated no higher than the surrounding windscreen frame. When this occurs it usually indicates that the sealant/adhesive has been laid on too thickly and needs to be adjusted before it sets. Dealing with an incorrectly fitted screen once it is set in place is a major headache

and succeeding without breaking the screen is an achievement. Also check that the wipers are correctly adjusted and operate normally.

Door Glass

It is not often that door glass needs replacing as it is rarely broken in normal use other than through vandalism or related to theft, or if you're unlucky with a stone thrown up from next door's rotary mower! Aside from this, glass can become scratched from abrasive dirt being trapped between the weather seal and the glass.

Door glass is generally seen as body glass and usually has the same insurance cover as windscreens, something many UK owners seem to forget. Vandalism and theft-related damage will generally not raise any issues, but then neither should excess scratching that reduces visibility, especially in certain sunlight conditions.

Removal and replacement of the door glass is actually quite simple. The glass sits in a lower holder fixed to the lift mechanism by a couple of bolts that offer a quick release of the window. You should also remove the window stop that prevents the door glass rising too high. This is fitted through a hole in the lower front part of the window. (Window stops have their own problems; for more details *see* Chapter 3.) If the glass is tight when lifting it, the two fixings on the rear guide can be loosened to give much more freedom of movement.

Mirror Glass

Door mirrors on the pre-2000 model year MGF were always set manually, but had electric heating elements. The 2000 model year changes (VIN RD511059) introduced electric control. Not all MGF and TF models have been fitted with the electric control, however, depending on the model or export market, but all retained the heating.

There are many cosmetic aspects relating to why owners wish to change their mirrors (*see* Chapter 6), but in this section I will restrict the discussion to replacing the mirror glass. Many have to do this after damage, but it often has to be changed because the heating element has failed, something you certainly notice on frosty mornings.

Replacing the early manual mirror glass is a very simple operation: gently lever the outer trim, which carries the glass as an integral part, away from the body of the mirror, ease off the two

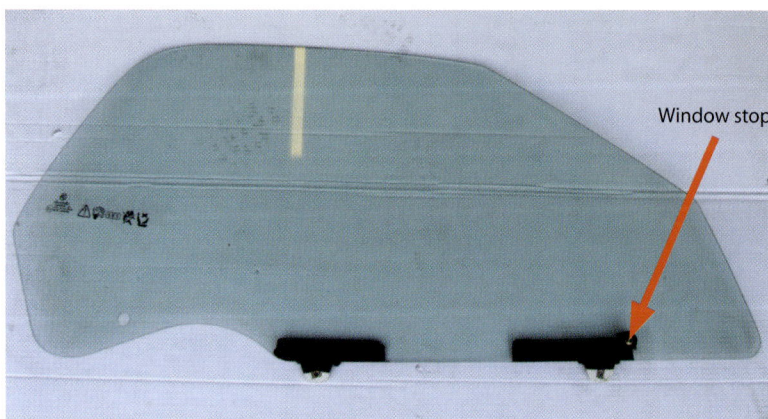

Window stop

Fig. 2.52   MGF and TF door glass, showing the position of the window stop.

Fig. 2.53 Sometimes the heated glass on manual door mirrors can fail. Replacement starts by splitting the mirror front from the body using a screwdriver.

Fig. 2.54 Once they are separated, there is access to the two electrical connectors.

RIGHT: Fig. 2.55 The connectors are usually very tight and pliers are often needed to separate them.

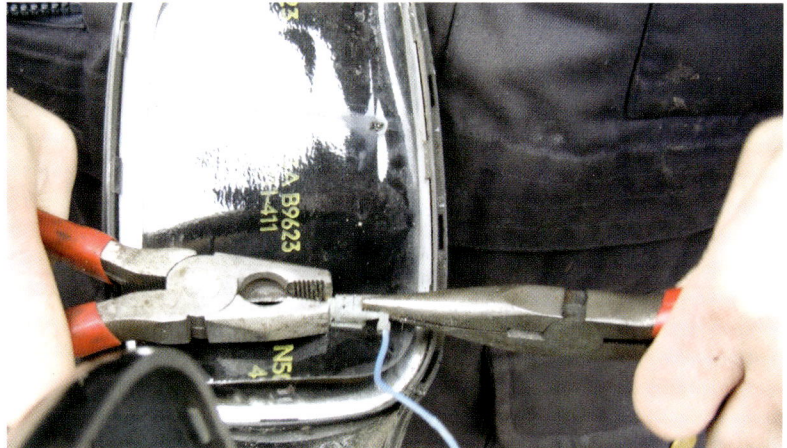

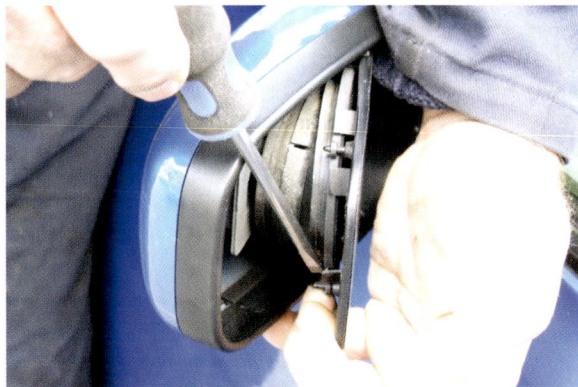
Fig. 2.56 In order to replace the glass in these electrically adjustable mirrors, it has to be eased out far enough until you can unclip the eight plastic hooks that hold the glass to the motor. The screwdriver tip indicates one of the hooks.

Fig. 2.57 Once disengaged from the motor, the glass electrical connections can be just as tight as on a manual mirror, so you may well need pliers to separate them.

Fig. 2.58 Retro-fitting the larger 2010 model year MG Motor TF door mirrors to earlier MGFs and TFs is almost straightforward.

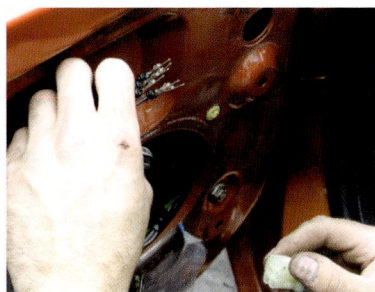
Fig. 2.59 As the plugs are wired differently, however, all the wires have to be picked out to fit in the matching connectors.

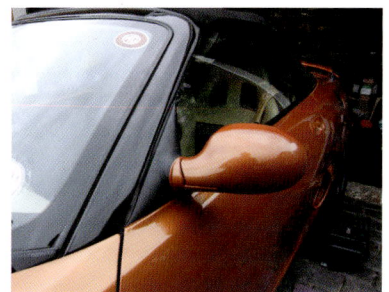
Fig. 2.60 The bigger reflective area on the new mirrors is an advantage.

ABOVE: Fig. 2.61   The glass hood window, introduced in 2005, is smaller but offers improved visibility and heated elements.

RIGHT: Fig. 2.62   The high positioning of the glass allows it to sit completely flat when the hood is lowered.

heated element spade connections and it is free, allowing the new glass to be connected and clipped back on.

The electrically adjustable mirror is a little different as the glass is clipped to a motorized mounting that provides the electrical adjustment. It needs a little courage to lever the outer edge of the mirror glass out to expose the inner workings and give room for a small flat blade screwdriver to detach the plastic hooks that are holding the glass to the mounting. It is then a matter of removing the heater element spade connections and the glass is free. Replacing with a new glass is a true reversal of the removal process.

It is possible to get replacement mirror glass that simply sticks onto the existing mirror, even if that is cracked. Although this works, you lose the heating function and if often looks like a stuck-on addition.

The door mirrors were a development of those fitted to other Rover Metro cars. Manual ones were used from 1995 to 2005, and electric options were used from 1999 to 2009 (with the break in production between 2005 and 2008). A change in legislation meant that for the last year of TF 135 production a larger design of mirror developed by MG Motor was fitted. These late mirrors can also be retrofitted to earlier cars, if they can be obtained.

Hood Glass Rear Window

The design of the MGF and TF hood allows for the rear section holding the rear window to be replaced as a separate section. For nearly the first ten years of MGF and TF production the rear window section in the hood was plastic and vulnerable, but for the 2005 model year, and beyond to the 2011 end of production, the rear window material was changed to glass. The clear advantages of this factory change to glass were received with a pretty universal response of 'about time too'.

An interesting element of the MG Rover production hood was that the base of the glass screen had a very pronounced curvature. Since there appeared to be a rather large depth of hood material below the glass, some people thought that the glass should have been deeper to give even better visibility. While the glass window was much smaller than the plastic one, from the driver's seat this was not an issue as the smaller surface area was more than offset by the glass's greater clarity, and heating elements now made a difference on days when it misted up.

The shape of the glass actually shows a greater depth of thought and design than appreciated. Here the curvature of the lower edge of the glass mirrors the curvature of the rear deck where the hood is attached to the body. The apparently excessively deep section of hood material under the glass screen

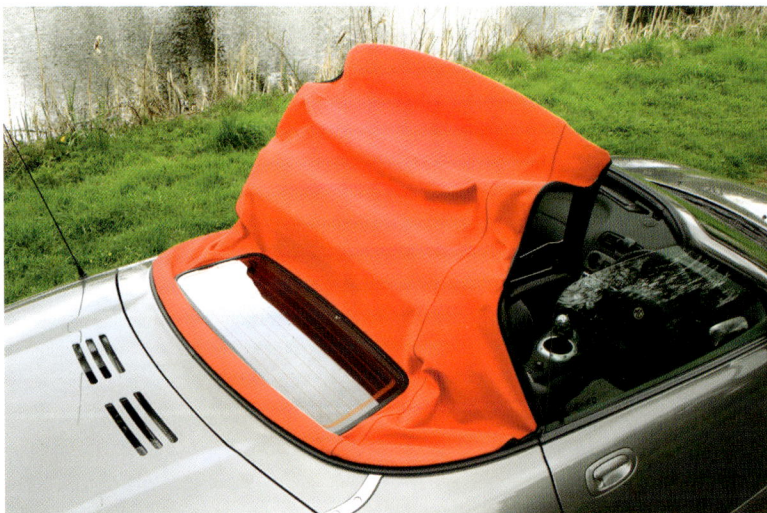

Fig. 2.63   The XPower hood with a glass window was made by BAS International.

Fig. 2.64   The XPower hood came in a range of 'loud' colours.

allows the glass to sit comfortably flat onto the rear engine cover carpet, so there are no spot loads on the glass. Larger and squared rear screen glass would not sit as comfortably and there would have been a greater risk of damage.

The production glass rear window was actually preceded on the market by an alternative glass rear window hood sold by MG Rover's 'MG Sport and Racing' offshoot, which was available with the hood material in a range of colours, some of them startlingly bright.

Retrofitting a glass window is possible, ideally using the 1998 model year on frame. Many specialists now supply rear hood sections with glass windows. Fitting is quite straightforward, if a little fiddly in places, but follow the instructions that come with the screen as there are some slight variations. Glass rear screens come with the very useful heated elements and these need the relay and switch normally associated with hard top fitting (*see* Chapter 5).

Fig. 2.65   Changing from a plastic rear window to glass can be simple.

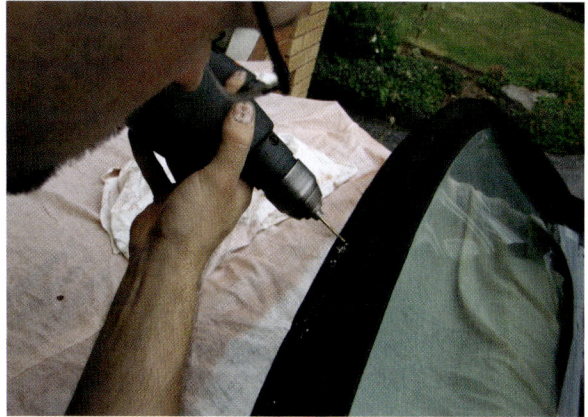

Fig. 2.66   Lift the hood from the rear deck and drill out the line of rivets under the window section.

Fig. 2.67   Drill out a couple of rivets either side holding the main hood material in order to give access to the window section end rivets.

Fig. 2.68   Gently lever off the retaining steel strip and keep it for re-use.

Fig. 2.69   Remove the end staple from the hood window zip. The zip can then be undone and separated into two.

Fig. 2.70   This allows the rear window section to be removed.

Fig. 2.71   The remains of the rivets are knocked out with a pin punch.

Fig. 2.72   The frame is cleaned up and painted, if necessary.

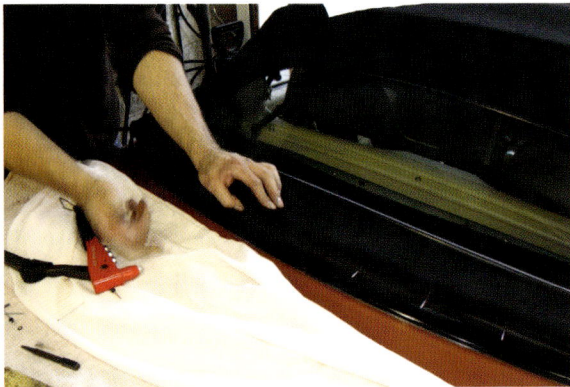

Fig. 2.73   The glass rear window section is laid in position and new rivets pushed through the steel strip, hood and frame.

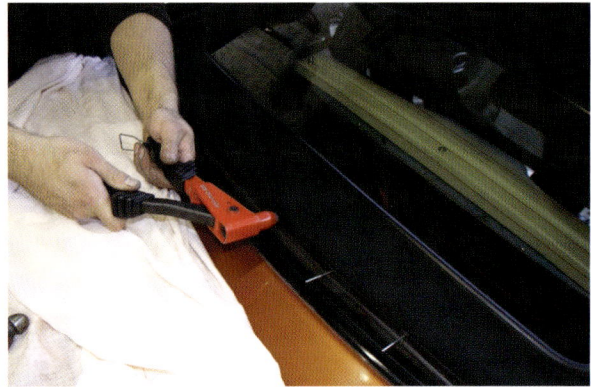

Fig. 2.74   The new rivets are secured with a rivet gun.

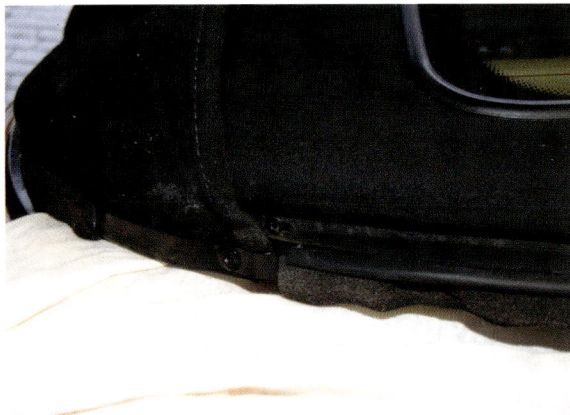

Fig. 2.75   Note that a bigger rivet is used for the end main hood sections. If rivets do not come in black, use a black felt tip pen to colour them.

Fig. 2.76   The zip is reconnected and the two parts are stapled together at one end. If the original main hood section zip is not in good condition, the other part of the new zip that comes with these window assemblies should also be fitted. This doubles the fitting time.

Hoods and Hardtops

All MGF and TFs share common body fixings for hoods and hardtops, so it is simple to swap hoods or hardtops from car to car. Pre-1998 model year MGFs had a less effective hood design that is easily identified by the longitudinal seams in the hood material, while the later models and TF all shared a cleaner and more weatherproof design.

Hoods are clipped to the body by the two obvious front clips to the windscreen and five spring clips holding it into the rear body channel. The frames are equally simple with two bolts per side holding it to the car's body. Accessing these bolts is a matter of removing the Tee bar plastic trim. Note the two additional 'J' shaped brackets attached to the same point. These are the hardtop rear anchor brackets and all cars were equipped with these as standard.

Hood maintenance is an important aspect of being able to achieve a long life from the hood. Coloured hoods degrade faster than the standard black hoods and are also less easy to re-colour. A task that is often forgotten is to properly clean and occasionally reproof a hood against water penetration and to make the material less attractive for mould growth on cars outside during the winter. There is a good range of specific cabriolet maintenance products on general sale; two common brands are Autoglym and Renovo.

The best advice would generally be to stick to one company's range of products and carefully follow the instructions. Before applying the product over the hood, it is essential to test a small inconspicuous area to make sure there is no unwanted reaction.

The task of renewing the hood is not that difficult when replacing the whole hood and frame as an assembly, but if just the material is being changed there are clear benefits having the hood fitted professionally. This also covers you for any error in the hood construction and anything in the fit that is not right. Fit a hood yourself and any material

Fig. 2.77 The original hood used on the MGF until the 1998 model year cars is easily identified by the two longitudinal seams in the material, running from front to back just above each door window.

Fig. 2.78 The seams are seen more clearly seen in this image, which also shows how the front corner of the hood material doesn't cover the edge of the hood frame.

Fig. 2.79 The later hood loses the longitudinal seams and there is much better material coverage on the frame corners.

Fig. 2.80 Two clips are used to attach the hood and hardtop to the windscreen header rail.

Fig. 2.81 Hoods are anchored into a recess around the rear of the cockpit area by five strong spring clips, which are covered by a moulded carpet.

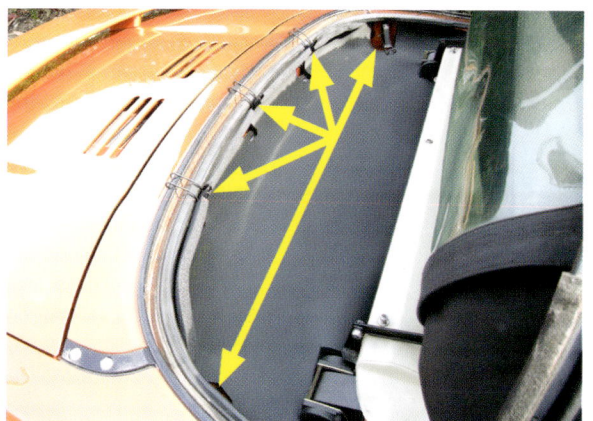

Fig. 2.82 Lifting the carpet allows a better view of the clips.

33

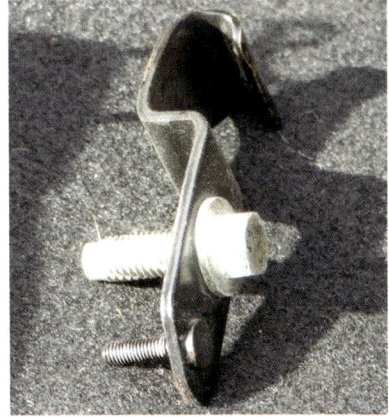

LEFT: *Fig. 2.83   The hood frame is anchored either side at the top of the B pillar area. Here the trim has been removed and the two anchor bolts and the 'J' shaped hardtop anchor bracket are indicated.*

Fig. 2.84   The anchor bolts and hardtop anchor bracket have been removed for clarity.

Fig. 2.85   Hardtops come in various styles. The original factory top, shown here, has a smooth rounded roof. When getting in the car after rain, you are likely to get a lapful of standing rainwater.

Fig. 2.86   The 'Heritage' top has a flatter profile and two small longitudinal creases in the top to discourage some of the rainwater from ending up in your lap.

Fig. 2.87   The heavy styled channels on the Stephen Palmer (SP) hardtop deal quite effectively with rainwater.

Fig. 2.88   When the frost had cleared it became obvious that this wasn't a frosted rear screen! The cause remained unknown.

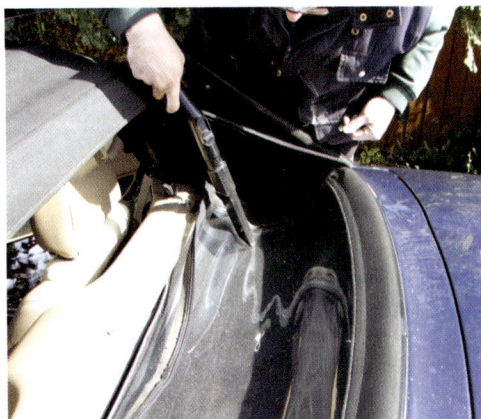

Fig. 2.89   Broken glass can get into inaccessible places that even a vacuum struggles to remove them from.

RIGHT: *Fig. 2.90 New rear screen and rubber.*

Fig. 2.91   The rubber is first fitted to the screen.

Fig. 2.92   The assembly is offered up and fitted to the hardtop with a little assistance from some liquid soap.

ridges and other small errors stand out like a sore thumb, and it's all down to you.

It is often asked whether a hard top from an MGF can be fitted to a TF, and vice versa. The simple answer is yes. New tops are still available, but are relatively expensive. As a result most purchases will be second-hand, but second-hand parts vary in quality and cannot be guaranteed, often resulting in the seals around door glass being a poor fit.

For this reason I always suggest that anyone looking to buy a hardtop adopt the 'try before you buy' approach, the only way you can assess if the top is a good fit or not. Remember that the cheapest transport of a hardtop is to go to the seller and fit it on the car, which answers any questions about the quality of fit and solves transport.

Most hardtops, irrespective of the maker, generally use the standard MG rear glass screen, so if you are unfortunate enough to suffer breakage then a replacement should not be too difficult to find. Fitting involves setting the traditional glass into a rubber seal, and then both are presented and pushed onto the lip of the aperture in the hardtop.

Heated Rear Window (HRW)

This was originally just an option fitted to hardtops, but the introduction of the optional MG Sport and Racing glass rear window hood changed this, and HRW became standard after the 2005 model year production cars adopted a glass window.

Every car was built with the wiring already in place for connecting the HRW by simply inserting a relay into the passenger compartment fuse box, an appropriate switch in the centre console and plugging in the window wiring. There are two main differences in detail, one when the switch design changed on the arrival of the 2000 model year cars, and then in mid-2003 when the SCU and a new fuse box introduced what are called micro blade fuses.

Two physically different types of relay were fitted: the older pre-mid 2003 standard relays and the later micro-sized relays. In both cases it is just a matter of inserting the relay into the unoccupied relay block. Earlier cars have a separate relay block, which may be tucked out of sight and around the right side of the passenger compartment fuse box, while the post-mid

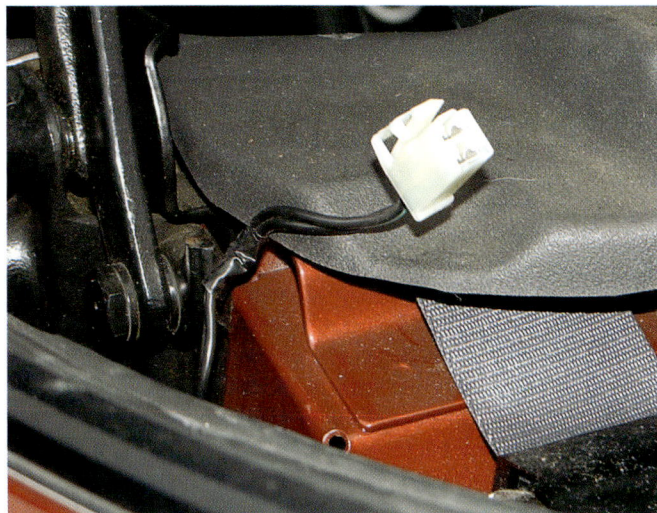

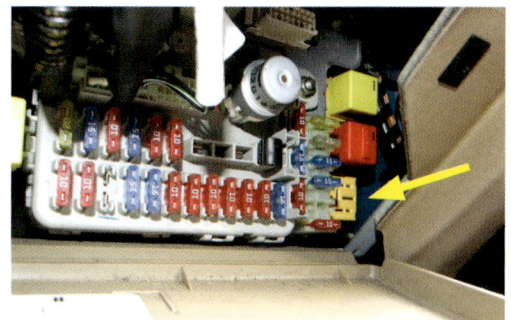

ABOVE: Fig. 2.93   All cars have wiring in place for a heated rear window, hidden under the carpet on the left side of the rear deck.

ABOVE RIGHT: Fig. 2.94   The wiring is plugged into the back of the switch blank in the centre console.

RIGHT: Fig. 2.95   More wires go to a vacant relay socket in the passenger compartment fuse box.

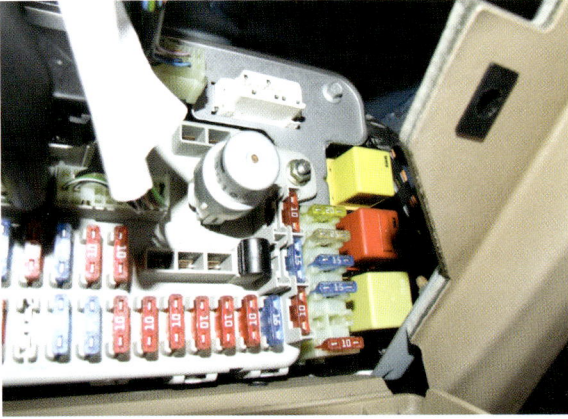

TOP LEFT: *Fig. 2.96   The heated rear window yellow relay is simply pushed into place.*

TOP RIGHT: *Fig. 2.97   Similarly the centre console switches are pushed into the existing electrical plugs and then clicked back into their slots in the centre console. This view shows the 2000 model year on.*

LEFT: *Fig. 2.98   The correct right-hand position on a square-shaped Mk 1 MGF switch.*

2003 models have the relay fitted to the main board.

As the switches are not interchangeable, you have to get the right one to fit the console. In every case, though, the HRW wiring plug is inserted into the back of the switch blank where the HRW switch locates, and it is nothing more complex than pushing out the blank, releasing the wiring and plug, clipping the wiring plug into the switch and inserting the switch back into the console.

Hood Plastic Rear Window Replacement

Replacing the rear window section with a replacement plastic window can be achieved in the same way that applies to replacing the section with a glass window. The original design of the hood foresaw that there would be a need for replacement rear windows and so it was made as a separate section, with a new window section as a standard spare part.

It is also possible to secure the services of a hood trimmer to replace just the plastic window section. This is very useful for cars that have a coloured hood for which there are no longer any replacement rear sections in the appropriate colour. Faded black hoods

Fig. 2.99   It was always expected that the plastic windows in hoods would need replacing before the hood, so they were designed as separate panels.

Fig. 2.100   Cracked and clouded window sections can be replaced by professional hood trimmers using the appropriate plastic screen materials in the same way the original was fitted.

Fig. 2.101   Windstops, intended to reduce buffeting from behind when driving with the hood lowered, have become common. There are two MG designs: a taller one for hoods with plastic windows and a shorter one for glass windows.

Fig. 2.102   When fitted the difference is obvious. The shorter one is intended to reduce scratching on the HRW elements, but also helps protect the plastic windows.

Fig. 2.103   MGF uses two modified Rover Metro front subframes. A rear subframe is here being refurbished, and has been blasted and rubbed down ready for painting.

Fig. 2.104   A coat of primer is then applied.

Fig. 2.105   The subframe is finished with Hammerite black.

Fig. 2.106   Home refurbishment of the subframe is very time consuming. A preferable course of action was to have this front subframe chemically dipped to clean back to the bare metal, rust blasted and then powder coated. The inside of the subframe box was Waxoyled for longevity.

can benefit in the same way, but for these there is the simpler option of re-colouring a black hood.

Windstops

These are the screens, usually folding, that fit on the Tee bar behind the seats. When in the vertical position they help reduce air buffeting for the occupants. There are two different sizes of the original Rover and MG Rover design using black mesh on a tubular frame: the taller was intended for use with the plastic rear window hoods and

the shorter one for glass rear window hoods. The difference was needed to allow for folding the windstop up and down without scraping against the rear window and damaging it.

A windstop can be quite effective at reducing the buffeting and as a result there are many different aftermarket designs using different materials, all doing the same job to a greater or lesser extent. Note that most windstops can't be used with aftermarket accessory roll hoops, and so the suppliers of the hoops often offer an integrated windstop that works with their hoops.

SUBFRAMES

What the engineers did for the MGF was simple and wholly logical. Using two modified Metro front subframes does not mean that you could have two engines, although I am slightly surprised that someone with the time and skill has not created a twin-engined MGF for fun (apart, that is, from the MG TF HPD200, which was based on a standard TF 160 rear drive but with a 40hp electric drive for the front wheels). No; the clever adaption comes from using two front subframes

Fig. 2.107   To overcome the need for one-off hubs on the front frame of the MGF and TF, engineers used the normal outer constant velocity joints without the joint normally used to connect to a driveshaft. This is seen here in the centre looking like a scooped-out half grapefruit.

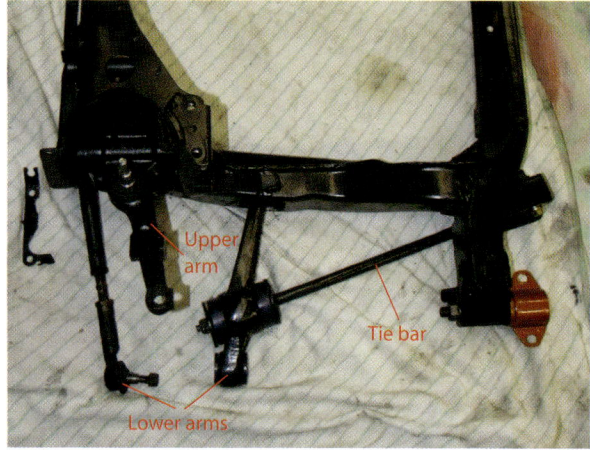

Fig. 2.108   Rear suspension control arm layout.

Fig. 2.109   MGF and TF subframes also gained additional end brackets to widen the mounting 'track' of the subframes to the body, indicated here on a rear subframe.

Fig. 2.110   View of the MGF and TF right-hand robust alloy engine mounting arm.

Fig. 2.111   The gearbox mounting arm is made of steel, as on the Metro, and is subject to corrosion. Here is one being refurbished.

and splitting the functions to provide what was needed.

At the front we see the suspension, brakes and steering are left in place, but no engine and transmission, while at the rear you find the engine, transmission, suspension and brakes, but the steering is omitted. It was not quite as simple as that, though: the suspension at the front, for example, suddenly had around 150kg less to support, so the Hydragas suspension needed some recalibration.

Then there was the fact that the front hubs were built up around a driveshaft: removing this would leave the wheel connected to the suspension by air alone. The clever solution was to leave the outer half of the constant velocity joint (CV joint) at the hub end of the drive shaft. This provided the required connection without the heavy cost of a one-off component. Look at the machined inner face of an MGF or MG TF front hub and you will see how it resembles the scooped out inside of half a grapefruit. This is where the ball bearings and other working parts of the former CV joint would normally fit.

The rear hubs need to be held in a fixed position, as there is no steering requirement, so a pair of fixed lower arms was fitted on a modified hub, using the same connection points on the subframe. Additionally the rear subframe needed a tie bar to help retain the suspension in the correct position when it was subjected to both braking

and drive torque, as well as a new lower engine mounting that was anchored from the sump to react against engine torque. The use of the PG1 series gearbox also needed a different mounting.

The way the subframes are mounted into the car's body saw new brackets

Fig. 2.112   As there is no engine and gearbox for the front to support, there is no need for supporting members. Box members add a little extra rigidity to the subframe.

TOP LEFT: Fig. 2.113   There is just a single front fixing bolt (here being removed) holding the box member to an MGF- and TF-specific additional bracket welded to the subframe. Here the subframe has been lowered in order to gain access.

TOP RIGHT: Fig. 2.114   MGF subframe-to-body bushes come in two densities, identified as black for early and green for later.

Fig. 2.115   MGF Trophy 160 SE models introduced solid subframe mountings, here painted orange, but they originally came painted blue or black. Note the absence of rubber infill, which seems to promote faster rusting on some cars.

Fig. 2.116   The mounting here is badly corroded. (Austin Garages)

Fig. 2.117   Further examples of corrosion removed from other cars. (Austin Garages)

welded onto the ends of MGF and TF subframes. This widens the distance between the left and right side mounting positions by approximately 30mm and also improves flexibility in the mounted height of the subframe relative to the body.

The Metro subframe also has two separate steel upper members for engine and gearbox support, whereas the MGF and TF right (engine) member is cast aluminium, which has the advantage of not corroding at anywhere near the rate of painted steel. These members have different shapes side to side: the right one has the engine mountings bolted to it and the left one has the gearbox mountings. While the engine mounting for an identically sized K series engine could simply adopt the simple Metro mounting, the MGF/TF mounting is far more robust.

The front subframe has no need for substantial separate members as there is no engine or gearbox to support. Instead there are simple light steel box members, which when fitted provide some extra rigidity to the front subframe. These box members can

suffer from corrosion, so they need protection.

The actual subframe is further modified with two raised plinths on the front to meet the upper box member base where it is secured with a single rather than the two bolts seen on the rear subframe. The rear of this upper member still uses two bolts in the same pattern as on the rear subframe. I have seen corrosion on cars as young as six years old, so it is reasonable to expect some will require replacements.

The subframe mountings to the body of the car are separate to the sub-frame. All MGFs, apart from the Trophy 160 SE models, have a rubber bushing insulating the single bolt to the subframe from the metal body of the mounting. This rubber was found in two slightly different densities for the front mountings on the front and rear subframes, one painted black and the other painted green.

The differences are small and if replacing just one it may as well be like for like. If you are replacing them all, however, go for the solid MGF Trophy or TF mountings, which provide a solid fixing of subframe to body. While slightly more noise and vibration is passed into the body, it provides a much more rigid fixing of subframe to the body and so reduces suspension geometry change.

These solid mountings were carried over into all TFs and are a justified modification on MGFs, but the drawback is that apparently they are more prone to corrosion than the rubber filled ones. The examples shown here of some that have had to be replaced should justify regular anti-corrosion checks and treatments.

TF Subframe Differences

One of the major developments that arrived with the TF was the change from the Hydragas system to a traditional style of steel coil spring suspension. The steel springs sit in a new strut-type suspension unit and require a different top method of fitting to the subframe that involves a closed cap design.

The rear suspension was also completely redesigned. While the rear suspension's front lower arm was still pivoting off the same point as the MGF's equivalent, the rear arm was nearly trebled in length so that it now pivoted on a newly created pivot point much closer to the vehicle's longitudinal centre line. Finally, there were substantial cast steel trailing arms, quite architec-

tural in design, with a new front pivot bracket on the front of the subframe.

One small change seen on the TF front subframe is also a good retrofit for MGF front subframes. This is a tubular steel cross brace, fitted between all four corners of the subframe, that was specifically designed to add structural stiffness. This cross brace is also bolted to the lower edge of the body spare wheel well via a new bracket welded to the base of the spare wheel well.

Directly related to this subframe addition are two other TF body stiffening changes to the body: an 'X' type brace added behind the facia centre console and two bracing bars between the centre of the engine bay to boot bulkhead and the body panel above the engine. Both were useful additions to the overall body stiffness. All three

Fig. 2.118   The MGF used Hydragas suspension with the spherical Hydragas displacer fitted to the subframe.

Fig. 2.119   For the MG TF the suspension was altered to steel coil springs that demanded a design change to accommodate the new spring/damper unit. At the front there was not much difference other than the spring damper unit.

Fig. 2.120   At the rear there were substantial changes, including the rear lower arm (indicated), now twice the length and pivoting in the centre of the subframe.

Fig. 2.121   TF front subframes introduced a cross brace to add stiffness.

Fig. 2.122 Further stiffness to the centre part of the body was achieved by adding a triangular tubular brace behind the centre console between the cross brace tube and floor 'tunnel'.

Fig. 2.123 Two extra bars were added within the engine bay, here clearly visible behind the boot to engine bay grille.

braces can be bought as an upgrade kit for the MGF from Vehicle Handling Solutions (www.vehiclehandlingsolutions.com).

Minor Restoration and Protection (*in situ*)

While the actual body of the car is resistant to corrosion, unfortunately this doesn't apply equally to the subframes, as has been shown on some of the mountings. This is one area where the use of a Metro part is not favourable, since Metros are expected to have a fairly short life and the use of relatively unprotected steel in the subframes gives them a built-in obsolescence. As the subframes in the MGF and TF are of an identical construction, it follows that these are probably the parts most vulnerable to corrosion.

The weight of a subframe may give the impression that these can hardly be that vulnerable, but the march of corrosion is constant and it *will* destroy the subframes, starting with the front one

because it sits in the face of the weather and doesn't have engine heat or oil leaks to help protect it. Unless you get dirty and protect them, or pay someone else to get dirty, they will need to be replaced sooner than expected.

The only protection the subframes have is the black paint they received when the subframe was originally made. This will generally last for around five years before areas of the paint start to fall off. If you live near the sea or do higher than average mileages, that time scale will be shortened.

Long before it has given up it is common for the paint to look much better than it actually is, since rust will have crept underneath. Run around with a scraper and wire brush and you will probably be surprised at the extent of this hidden corrosion.

Obviously good access is needed to do this work when the subframe remains on the car, which will be how most owners come to deal with the problem. This doesn't give the best overall access but an adequate job can

be achieved if preventative maintenance is carried out early enough and refreshed periodically, say every couple of years for an MG in average use.

When preparing for any repaint or anti-rust treatment you need to remove all loose paint. Any deeper patches of rust and dirt need to be more vigorously cleaned to remove all dirt and as much corrosion as possible before applying a coating of rust convertor fluid/jelly. There is a wide choice of these available. Follow the individual product's instructions and then, as instructed, apply a coat of primer/paint.

Over nearly forty years, since I first bought a 1968 MGB, I have been a great believer in the benefits of Hammerite paints and Waxoyl anti-rust products. Smooth black Hammerite is much better than the original black paint applied to the subframes at manufacture.

Unless you treat the hidden areas of the subframe, however, the job will be only half completed and you will not get anywhere near the full benefits of your labours. This extra work involves

LEFT: Fig. 2.124 This rear subframe has fairly typical surface rusting.
ABOVE: Fig. 2.125 The rusting on front subframes is usually worse as there is no engine heat to quickly dry moisture.

Fig. 2.126   Once scrubbed down and given an anti-rust treatment the rear subframe is clearly improved.

Fig. 2.127   The full treatment does significantly more for the front subframe.

injecting anti-rust treatment inside the subframe. For this task compressed air injection is more of a necessity than a luxury. For some years, though, the compressors has been relatively inexpensive and investment in a small compressor brings benefits in the home and garden that extend well beyond checking and adjusting tyre pressures and various tasks during the rebuild of a car.

Using compressed air to inject Waxoyl, or your personal choice of anti-rust fluid, really atomizes the fluid so that it penetrates into the smallest corners inside the subframe members. Access is available through some of the gaps between welds along the underside of main members and through drain holes.

As well as being an anti-rust compound, Waxoyl is a good lubricator and this benefits the nuts, bolts and captive threads you find around the subframe. The lower suspension

mountings mean there are a number of well-hidden captive nuts within the members. I have hard-won experience of attempting to overcome sheared and seized solid captives inside Metro subframes that Waxoyl would have prevented. What applies to a Metro subframe also applies to the MGF and TF.

Indeed, to help reduce this problem you must check that there is a proper seal at the front curving up underside face of the subframes, where the 'window' to allow access to the front wishbone pivot bolt is located. In the early days this was a simple plastic bung, but cost savings in later years saw this deleted and replaced by adhesive cloth tape, which is far less robust.

Working On the Subframe Off the Car

So far attention to the subframes has been with everything *in situ,* but that does not allow access to all areas of the

subframe. In order to do as comprehensive a job as possible the subframe has to be removed from the car and all parts removed from the subframe. You then have a choice on how to deal with cleaning, one easy but more costly, and the other cheaper but so much more difficult and messy.

The simpler and costlier route, and probably the most effective, is to use a chemical dip process. The subframe is immersed in a chemical bath that strips paint, oil and all forms of built-up crud, before then being dipped in a neutralizing bath to clean and stabilize any stripping chemicals that remain inside the box sections. Once this is complete you have an almost perfect and clean bare metal subframe. If this is done early enough in its life, the subframe will need no welding repairs from corrosion, just painting or my preferred method, powder coating.

Remember to continue using Waxoyl (or similar) on the internal box sections

Fig. 2.128   The bungs removed during treatment to aid injection inside the subframe members are refitted to ensure the weather is kept out.

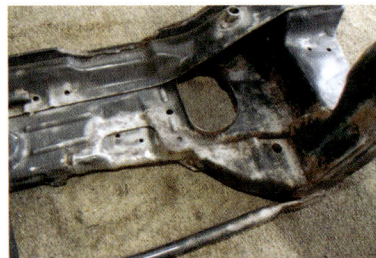

LEFT: Fig. 2.129   Once removed, areas such as the rear subframe are no longer inaccessible.

RIGHT: Fig. 2.130   The hard to reach areas of the front subframe can be fully derusted ready for painting or powder coating.

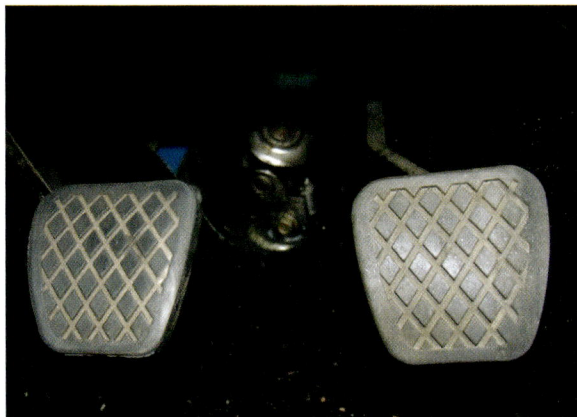

Fig. 2.131   The steering shaft universal joint, between and slightly above the pedals, has to be disconnected before the subframe can be dropped.

Fig. 2.132   MGF owners need to have use of a Hydrolastic pump to deal with routine and non-routine Hydragas suspension issues.

of the subframe to consolidate the protection for many years to come. A point worth noting is that having a slight surface covering of rust inside the box sections is actually beneficial in providing a good key to the surface, allowing the Waxoyl to stick better than it would to smooth rust-free steel

The DIY option is not as efficient and certainly not as fast, but definitely cheaper. It requires hours of scraping, wire brushing with hand or power tools, and even using a chemical paint stripper such as Nitromors, which will clean the surface more than adequately ready for final rubbing down and painting. With the facility of compressed air you can even consider grit blasting at home, but only if you have an outside space far away from house windows or neighbours' washing, as grit can find its way into the most unexpected places some distance from the working area, even when this is done in a temporary 'tent' to contain everything.

Front Subframe Removal

Up to this point I have glibly talked about cleaning the subframe off the car without mentioning how to get the subframe to that point. Buying second-hand is the simplest route, but at some stage the car's subframe has to be removed, so now is a good time to cover a few points beyond the workshop manual approach, which uses a vehicle lift.

Subframe removal is the same for both the MGF and TF, but the MGF has the added complication of Hydragas suspension, which uses interconnection pipes between front and rear suspension displacers, and dampers that have upper connections to the body. The TF, on the other hand, doesn't have Hydragas suspension, but conventional steel springs with integral dampers that sit in a subframe housing.

The front subframe is easier to remove. Remember that you need to have clear access to the four subframe mountings to the body and so the car has to have axle stands positioned under the body. I would suggest using the sill jacking points, as this will allow enough space for the subframe to be lowered from the car.

The job now starts with marking the two parts before disconnection of the steering column intermediate shaft at the steering rack pinion, a job that is done by crawling into the driver's footwell and removing the pinch bolt that clamps the intermediate shafts splined joint to the rack pinion spline. Lift the joint off the pinion spline and put it to the side.

Next the brake pipes are undone at the bracket where they connect to the flexible hoses. It is useful at this point to have already removed the brake master cylinder cap and stretched a piece of cling film or other thin plastic sheet over the top of the filler neck, then screw the cap back on. This will drastically reduce the fluid loss when the pipes are undone. It provides time for a suitable plastic cap to be pushed over the exposed end of the brake pipe to reduce fluid loss even further and prevent any debris entering. Remember the brake fluid used on the MGF and TF is damaging to paint and is also highly flammable.

While working with fluids, remove the two coolant hoses connecting the underfloor coolant pipes with the radiator. Before this is done the cooling system has to be drained, noting that the original hose clips are spring types that simply need a pair of grips to squeeze the ends together and slide the clip off. Time, and many previous owners, may have seen these changed for another type. If they are the worm drive types, check that the hoses haven't been damaged by overzealous tightening. In addition to the hose clips, note that each hose is held to the spare wheel well by a 'P' clip, which also needs to be removed.

On those cars that are fitted with air conditioning and automatic transmission, the additional pipes needed for these systems also have to be moved. Auto transmissions have oil cooler pipes, and there is an obvious oil loss when the two pipes are disconnected. Disconnecting air conditioning pipes is more involved and consideration has to be given to getting a professional to de-gas the air conditioning system, as it is irresponsible to simply vent gas refrigerant into the atmosphere. Tying small plastic bags over the exposed pipe ends should prevent dirt ingress and also catch further drips from any of the pipes.

The focus now moves to the suspension area. Unless the whole car is to be raised off the ground, I suggest inserting a couple of planks about 50mm thick under each rear tyre, so that when the suspension is depressurized the car does not drop down so far that the rear body makes contact with the ground when the front is raised.

Fig. 2.133   Attaching the Hydrolastic pump to the Hydragas system valve allows safe depressurization and afterwards the system can be pressurized once more.

Fig. 2.134   Once depressurized the pipe connection at the displacer can be disconnected.

Moving back to the MGF front subframe, you don't need blocks as you want the suspension to drop as far as it will go; this gives the best clearance for subframe removal with the least rise on the body. With the MGF you now need to remove the telescopic front dampers that have an upper fixing to the car's body. The TF has both spring and damper units on the subframe, so there is no connection to the body.

We now have to depressurize the MGF's suspension. Treat it with respect as it runs with a nominal fluid pressure of 400psi. I bought a Hydrolastic pump many years ago from Liquid Levers (www.liquid-levers.com), who make pumps for the professional motor trade. Despite hard and extensive use, it has been totally reliable with just a couple of seal changes and is recommended for all MGF owners to buy, beg or borrow.

Note that I describe this as a Hydrolastic pump, not a Hydragas pump. This is because the earlier Hydrolastic suspension system pump applies equally to the later Hydragas systems. Note also that you can buy alternative Hydrolastic pumps to the Liquid Lever types, but ideally you need a pump that not only provides the pumping facility but also has a vacuum facility that can draw air out of the systems before pressurizing. Air in these systems can create problems.

In the UK, at least, Hydrolastic fluid is still widely available in 5-litre containers at around £15 to £20, so it is not an expensive fluid. It is actually quite a simple mix of products: 49 per cent distilled water, 49 per cent alcohol, 1 per cent triethanolamine phosphate and 1 per cent sodium mercaptobenzthiazole.

I am aware that many owners have depressurized their suspensions simply by pressing the valve with a probe, but having a 400psi jet of Hydrolastic fluid in your face can be very damaging. Even wrapping the valve with a rag and pressing through it can still see pressurized fluid escape. The recommendation is clear: use the proper pump. Remember too that you will need to pump the suspension back up after the work is complete, and there is no way of driving the car to the pump without causing comprehensive damage to the front wings.

Once the system is depressurized you need to disconnect the Hydragas pipes at the junction immediately behind the valves and tie the pipes out of the way. Next remove the ABS sensor wires, if ABS brakes are fitted. Note that later cars with electronic speedometers have a single ABS sensor on the left rear wheel to provide road speed information. Remember that ABS sensors are expensive and may be damaged or broken when removing them from their fixing bracket on the hub. It is advised that they be given a soaking in a suitable penetrant such as Plus Gas or WD40, if possible for several days. Once the single fixing bolt has been removed they can then be carefully eased and rotated.

In fact, it is recommended that all underside nuts and bolts, especially the subframe mounting bolts, are pre-treated before it is necessary to remove them as there is a good chance they will be sticky or seized. Pre-treat as many nuts and bolts as you can reach several times in the couple of weeks before you start work.

You now need to remove the anti-roll bar-to-body fixings so that the bar is free to drop with the subframe. Also ensure that the brake servo hose is out of harm's way when the subframe lowers, as this is a rigid plastic hose that can easily be damaged by a wayward movement of the subframe. Finally, on the pre-2000 model year MGF it is time to remove the speedometer cable. These early models have a long three-piece speedo cable running from the gearbox to the speedo head under the car; later cars have an electronic speedometer.

Now is the time to drop the subframe. The best approach at home is to use a couple of trolley jacks. Check that all ten bolts fixing the subframe to the body – four front and six rear – are going to loosen; any that are tight should be dealt with before the subframe is hanging on that one stuck bolt.

I always suggest the use of single hex sockets as these offer far better fit on the hexagon heads of the bolts and much less chance of the head rounding off, which can be a real possibility with the more common tool sets using bi-hex sockets. The same advice applies when using ring spanners. If possible, always use a ring spanner rather than an open-ended spanner, as a bolt or nut that has been in place for many years is likely to round off when attacked. Rounded heads will make the job a real pain and often demand the use of more specialized tools to overcome a problem that a better tool initially would have avoided.

The usual professional way by which subframes are removed and refitted is to use a two post car lift and then simply lift the car, leaving the subframe sitting on the ground. While some of the illustrations here show a lift, I have more experience as a normal owner and working on the car on the home drive and in the garage, but with an excellent range of tools.

The pair of trolley jacks now come into play. Place one jack on the front of the subframe and the other at the rear, and gently press up on the subframe. This will then allow all ten subframe bolts to be removed and the subframe gently lowered using the jacks equally.

The overall weight of the front subframe is much less than a fully assembled rear subframe, so it is far easier to move it by hand, although still ideally by two people or more. This means that you do not need to raise the front of the car to anywhere near the height required to remove the rear subframe,

which has the considerable height of the engine to get under the rear of the car. Where additional height is needed at the front, you can easily jack up the front via the sill jacking points. I have even seen the front lifted by hand, as there is not much weight up front without the subframe, but this is not advised for obvious safety reasons.

Once out, the process of dismantling continues. Before doing this I always suggest it is a good policy to have a small digital camera to hand and take many images of the assembled subframe and fittings for reference when it is to be reassembled. You may think that you will remember, but it might be many weeks, or longer, before the reassembly commences, and there is usually something that doesn't seem right or you simply can't remember, and the available images really help.

As well as taking plenty of images during the dismantling, it is recommended that all the removed parts are laid out to give a 'plan view'. The items should then be separately boxed or bagged with appropriate labels iden-

tifying where these parts are from. The 'plan view' can be very useful to reproduce once all the parts have been cleaned and reconditioned prior to reassembly, as it makes this process simpler and immediately shows if you have lost any parts. Obviously, given the wonderful access presented by removing the subframe, it would be foolish not to make the best use of this and tidy up and refurbish as much as you can.

It is always easier for the home restorer to deal with one subframe at a time, since storing the parts of a dismantled car always seems to occupy a space about four times the size of the car. Refitting is really a case of going back the way you went to remove and dismantle the subframe. Some items, though, will be tighter going back in than when they came out because this time you are fighting gravity, so some added effort is to be expected.

Rear Subframe Removal

Removing the rear subframe is a much bigger and heavier task due to the bulk and weight of the engine, gearbox, drive shafts, suspension and brakes fitted into this subframe. There is also the added height needed to lift the body clear of the top of the engine, so here

Fig. 2.135 Lowering of the forward end of the front subframe is underway, as can be seen by the unbolted front mounting.

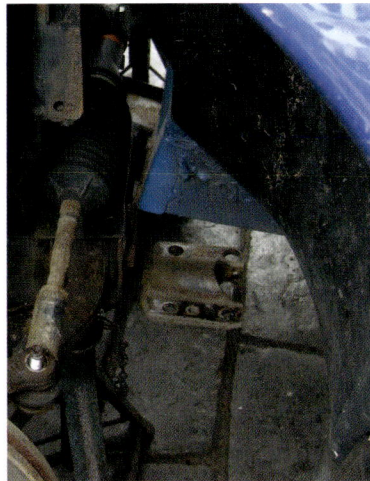

LEFT: Fig. 2.136 One of the rear subframe mountings is here shown in the lowered position.
BELOW LEFT: Fig. 2.137 Plan view of an MGF subframe removed and completely stripped for refurbishment.
BELOW RIGHT: Fig. 2.138 Here all the subordinate parts are displayed.

the basic concept will be to keep the wheels fitted and actually lift the body off the subframe using an engine crane, and then wheel the subframe out.

The work starts in a very similar mode to removing the front. Run around all the nuts and bolts and apply penetrant to help ensure all come apart as intended. There then starts a much longer list of tasks that include dismantling, in no specific order, the throttle, handbrake and gear change cables, tying them back out of the way.

Disconnect the battery, followed by the various electrical connections, including the engine loom where it connects to the main loom in the left rear of the engine bay, near to the engine management ECU. Some cars have the main power feed from the alternator passing through a fuse on the rear bulkhead and this will have to be disconnected. Also check for any non-standard previous owner additions.

Once the electrical connections are dealt with you can move on to the fluid connections, always including coolant connections, but cars with air conditioning or automatic transmission will need the same treatment described previously for the front subframe removal. The actual rear connections are simple bolt-together connections but it is critically important to ensure that these are kept spotlessly clean and that no debris enters if the system is to work again, so bag and seal as previously described.

When draining the cooling system, the best draining point is the rear junction of the underfloor coolant pipes to the engine hoses. Once drained the

Fig. 2.139 Later cars have quick-release heater hose connections.

hoses should be clipped back out of the way to prevent them becoming damaged. While under the car, remember that there are separate heater hoses that need to be detached. Later cars have quick-release connections but earlier cars have normal clips.

The oil in both the engine and the gearbox should be drained while you still have height to place receptacles under the drain points; this also helps remove a bit more weight. The later 160ps VVC engine cars have a coolant/oil heat exchanger bolted to the side of the block under the inlet manifold, but there is no need for any of the oil hoses to be disturbed at this time.

The fuel system has both fluid and vapour pipes and hoses between engine and car, which need to be disconnected and the lines moved out of the way. It is critical to ensure no naked flame heaters or other sources of ignition are anywhere near the car when dismantling the fuel system as vapours flow along the ground over huge

distances and, if ignited, travel right back to the source. Keep a couple of currently in-date fire extinguishers to hand in the garage, just in case.

The fuel feed and return use quick-release connections, but be aware that the system is designed to retain fuel pressure up to 3 bar in the feed line between fuel pump and the injectors, so when disconnecting this connection you should see a good spray of fuel. Prepare for this by having rags loosely wrapped around the quick-release joint to contain and soak up the spilt fuel.

The connection between the charcoal canister and the inlet manifold, near the throttle body, is a simple hose with spring clip and this has to be removed. The throttle cable removal also involves a simple clip, but don't forget to disconnect the throttle cable from the 'tidy' clip at the other end of the manifold from the throttle.

All cars have vacuum connections between the inlet manifold and the brake servo with a connection to the rear centre of the inlet plenum. Press the red collar in and hold while pulling out the pipe, which when free needs to be tied back. There are a couple of other oddities to consider. Pre-2001 model year MGF 1.8i models have a vacuum connection between the inlet manifold and the engine management ECU. Those early models also have a speedo cable that needs disconnecting.

Specific to TF 135 and TF 160 models made from the introduction of the TF in 2002, through 2003 to VIN RD631656 (during 2004), is that they have a further vacuum connection between the

Fig. 2.140 The orange pipe connector is the quick-release fuel feed connection. To release, press the black collar inwards towards the orange body. A second green connection a little below this one is for the fuel return.

Fig. 2.141 The exhaust system needs to be removed to access and remove the heat shield, which is usually very fragile.

TOP LEFT: *Fig. 2.142 Taking away the heat shield gives access when removing the anti-roll bar.*
TOP RIGHT: *Fig. 2.143 Sheared subframe mounting bolts are usually the smaller front side bolts.*

inlet manifold and an ECU controlled valve in the right-hand exhaust tailpipe. The operation and function of this is explained in Chapter 4, but if still fitted then there is an additional small bore vacuum hose connection to remove and tie back from the inlet plenum and from the actuator on the right-hand tailpipe.

The actual exhaust system is next on the list for removing and this should be done backwards from the manifold to the downpipe joint. This means the catalyst and rear silencer both have to be removed and this really does open up the space for better rear access. The heat shield above the exhaust silencer also has to be removed and it is reasonably certain that some of the fixing bolts will be rusted beyond recognition or turning. It should be your aim to remove the heat shield sufficiently intact to be reused, but do not be too annoyed if this isn't possible.

The last fluid disconnection is for the brakes. Once again this involves a simple removal of the brake pipe where it comes off the body to the subframe and connects to the flexible hose. The tip of wrapping cling film over the master cylinder neck, as described previously for the front subframe removal, should be followed, as well as the capping of the open ends of the removed pipes.

The subframe is almost ready to remove, but first the rear anti-roll bar-to-body mountings have to be disconnected. This is why you need the space afforded by removing the exhaust and

Fig. 2.144 Rear subframe mountings incorporate the mounting studs for the anti-roll bar. There are four bolt fixing positions to the body, but only three have ever been used.

its heat shield. Now the ten subframe bolts (four front and six rear) can be individually loosened and then tightened back up, just so you know they will all come out when you want them too. This is an area where problems may well be found with seized bolts, usually the fronts, so take whatever measures are to hand to loosen the individual bolts. If bolts do shear then you can deal with these when the subframe is out of the way.

There is one oddity that generates repeated questions. The rear subframe mounting to the body has the facility for four bolts, but only three are ever used. Quite why is not clear and this situation predates the MGF as it has been carried over directly from the Rover Metro. The probability is that two bolts would be acceptable and three provide more than enough security, so four would be overkill and saving a few pence on hundreds of thousands of bolts would soon add up.

Removing the subframe is best achieved with the wheels/tyres still fitted.

In the case of the MGF I also suggest that wide solid wooden planks about 50mm thick be placed under the front tyres so that the front bumper doesn't pivot into the ground when the rear is lifted. This is more acute than when removing the front subframe, as you need the rear to go much higher.

My own removal process now involves bringing in my trusty screw-type engine crane and using some old seat belt webbing, with one end attached to the crane and the other specifically used to provide a soft attachment to the car's body. The attachment point is inside the open boot and behind the panel that carries the boot latch metal loop.

The crane is lifted and tension created on the strap. The subframe bolts are then loosened and more crane tension applied to confirm that slight lifting of the body against the subframe occurs. Then the bolts can be removed and proper lifting commenced. As the body progressively is lifted off the subframe, check that no items are still connected

Fig. 2.145   Without the weight of the rear subframe, engine and other components, the body is actually quite light.

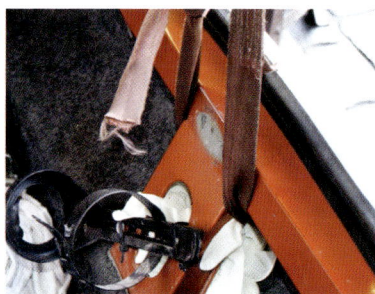

Fig. 2.146   Lifting with the engine crane, using an old seat belt strap attached to the body, is not the strain it may first appear.

between engine and body. Initially place a trolley jack under each rear sill jacking point and pump them up to follow the body lift, so that, should there be any need to adjust the crane, you do not have to return to floor level.

Once high enough the jacks should be changed for axle stands. As height is gained the axle stands are adjusted to keep their saddles close to the sill jacking points until the body is raised enough to allow the complete rear subframe to be wheeled out from behind. At an early point in the lift the common axle stands (lifts approx. 240mm to 400mm) will run out of height before the body has been raised sufficiently to allow the subframe to be wheeled out. The simple advice is always to beg, borrow, hire or buy bigger stands as safety is not worth compromising. In my case I also have bigger stands giving 300mm to 550mm, which was enough to provide the height needed.

Fig. 2.147   Once the body is high enough, substantial stands are placed under the sill jacking points.

Fig. 2.148   The crane is removed and the subframe moved out.

Once sufficient height has been reached to allow the subframe, engine and so on to be wheeled out, the body is then secured on the stands. Bear in mind that there is relatively little weight in the body once the subframe is removed. The crane is now removed to allow room for the subframe to be wheeled out. The crane will then be needed to lift the engine and gearbox from the subframe.

The high rear end stance is maintained as it is perfect for access for doing any rectification work that it is reasonable to expect, such as sheared subframe mounting bolts, corroded rear brake pipes and general cleaning. On this occasion a small degree of corrosion was found in the end 50mm or so of both sills, so with such good access this was repaired and the sequence of images gives an insight into what was done.

The subframe is then wheeled to a convenient spot where the stripping down process can begin. The wheels will have to come off, as the suspen-

Fig. 2.149 Removal of the rear subframe gives unprecedented access. The opportunity to deal with dirt, grime and worn parts should be grabbed with both hands.

Fig. 2.150 Brake pipe corrosion is commonly found around the junction shown here.

Fig. 2.151 Corrosion of the pipe under the 'shelf', though, was much worse.

Fig. 2.152 Once cleaning had been completed the transformation was significant, not least with the new copper brake pipes seen here.

Fig. 2.153 Although the heat shield and fan motor shown here appear to be new, they are original.

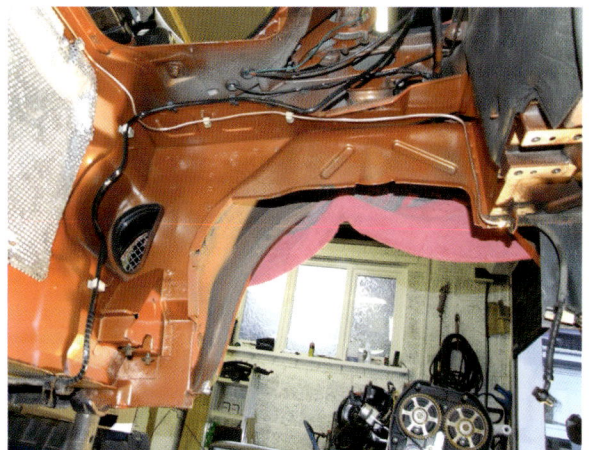

Fig. 2.154 The new brake pipe clipped under the shelf shows how moisture and dirt is thrown up from the tyres and why the originals corrode.

Fig. 2.155   Good access revealed a small degree of corrosion in this area of both sills.

sion needs to be at least partly dismantled in order that you can remove the drive shafts from the gearbox, before the engine and gearbox can be lifted out of the subframe with the crane. Once again I suggest taking plenty of photographs with the digital camera throughout the dismantling process, both to act as a reference during the future rebuild and for enhancing the value of the car if looking for an agreed insurance value – or, in what would be the worst scenario, if selling the car after all this work.

Laying all the components out on the ground and taking plan view images is really useful when approaching the rebuild as you can lay the pieces out like a jigsaw. It is then easier and quicker to identify and locate the parts correctly. The actual process of cleaning and treating the subframe is as previously covered for the front subframe.

Fig. 2.156   Removing the paint and underseal showed that the damage was much worse than initially thought.

Fig. 2.157   The corrosion was dealt with effectively by cutting it out and making up and shaping a repair plate.

Fig. 2.158   The repair plate is welded in place.

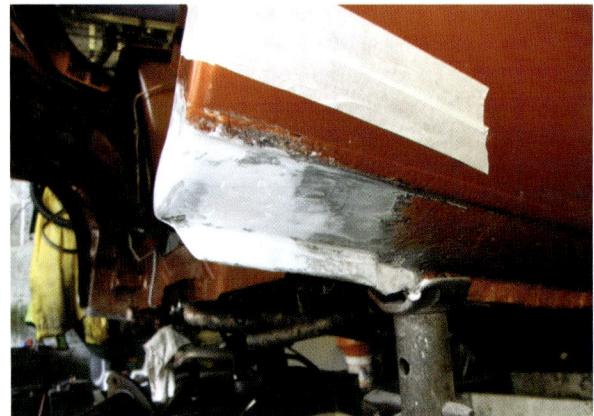

Fig. 2.159   Use a little filler to smooth the line.

Fig. 2.160   The repair plate is then painted.

Fig. 2.161   The rear of the repair was seam sealed before painting.

Replacement Subframes

If the car that you are working on did not display any odd handling quirks, or the results of a four-wheel laser alignment check came within tolerance, then this section will not apply. But if these showed that the car has a distorted/damaged subframe then the obvious solution is to replace it. Replacing with new should be a safe and secure route, but buying second-hand is slightly precarious as most subframes will have come from damaged cars being broken up for spares.

How do you check a subframe? The answer is to simply reject a subframe with any signs of collision damage. After this it is a little like checking the dimensions of a door or window frame before fitting to your house, measuring from corner to diagonal corner using common reference points. Alarm bells should sound if the bolt holes don't line up when offering the replacement subframe to the car. This is especially so if the car passed the four-wheel alignment check: in this case the suspicion is firmly with the replacement subframe.

I must add that the accuracy built into the subframes when first manufactured was not as good as we may have expected. Just one example of this from my own experience took place in early 2002, when I was following the build of my own TF 160 at Longbridge. The rear subframe build was nearly complete, with engine gearbox, suspension and brakes all fitted, when some final bolts would not align with their holes. This was due to a subframe manufacturing error, an occasional issue at that time. There followed the fastest subframe change I have ever seen as the production line was temporarily stopped, eight minutes as I recall.

Refitting Subframes

The refitting process is, in the traditional words of a workshop manual, 'a reversal of the removal process'. Since the overall weight of the front subframe is so much less than the rear, it is also easier to handle and move. Lifting it into place using trolley jacks and additional steadying by a couple of axle stands is quite realistic. Moving the subframe into position and getting it into the rather tight hole from

Fig. 2.162   Fine manoeuvring of the subframe was made easier by using a pair of MGF space-saver wheels and tyres, with the front of the subframe supported on a low line wheel trolley.

Fig. 2.163   The whole assembly was simply wheeled back under the car and carefully located before the engine crane was brought back to lower the body onto the subframe.

which it emerged does require a little levering and cajoling, but otherwise it is indeed a reversal of the removal process. Do make sure that none of the tied back parts have slipped and could get caught and damaged.

At the rear, because of the considerable extra weight of the fully built-up subframe, you need to reverse the removal process and now drop the car onto the subframe, which is again a reversal of the removal process. In more detail, the most important thing is to get the subframe really accurately positioned to start with, as there is little clearance to locate and fit the subframe to the body bolts when the car is dropped. You may want to use four much longer bolts, two front and two rear, which can be engaged much

earlier and so assist in the alignment while the drop is still underway, replacing the long bolts when standard bolts can be fitted in the other positions.

During the lowering process you need to feed the gear change and handbrake cables through to their approximate positions, as it is easier to do this while the subframe is being refitted than struggling to do so after it is back in place. Once the subframe is bolted back in, the rear of the car can once again be jacked up to provide the working space to refit the remaining components.

RAINWATER LEAKS

It is an unfortunate fact that hardly any soft-top cars are entirely rainproof.

51

Fig. 2.164   MGF and early MG TF heater air intakes used a big box (right); a more streamlined and watertight version (left) was introduced during 2003.

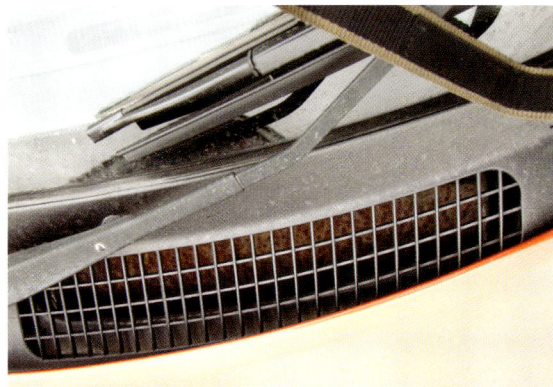

Fig. 2.165   Many of the earlier box-type airboxes are characterized by rust on the steel rain deflector, as seen here.

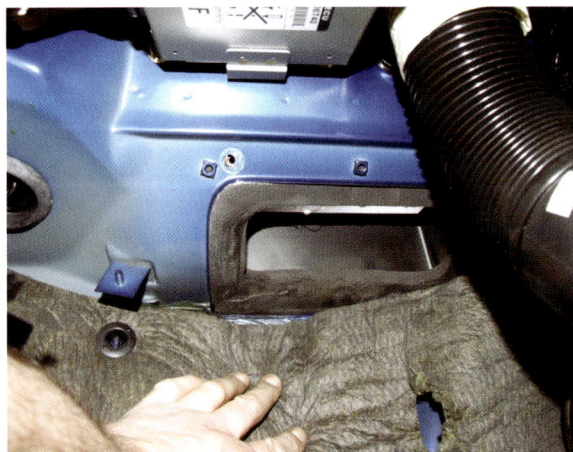

LEFT: Fig. 2.166 Looking up at the underside of the square airbox seal in its fitted position from the passenger footwell.

Fig. 2.167   Once the airbox is removed there were clear signs of staining caused by water leaking – and this was a good one.

More importantly, the MGF and TF are often some distance from the best performers. With both models there is a wide variation in the depth of problems reported by owners, but generally speaking more cars have problems than those that do not.

One common background factor is that most of the cars that are dry live in garages and, while they do come out in the wet, they are not often parked outside for long periods. The relevance of this is that most cars that get wet inside do so when parked, not when being driven, and that is why garaged cars suffer so much less.

There are several common entry points for rainwater and the major contributors are damaged or degraded seals. The commonest problem area is connected to the door glass and how it works with the hood/hardtop and windscreen seals; I will return later to this more complex problem.

When leaks occur it is more common for the passenger carpet to become wetter than the driver's side. The prime reason for this relates to the heater air intake design. On all MGFs and TF models up to mid-2003 (VIN RD612108), a large square-shaped plastic box will be

seen in front of the passenger side of the windscreen. You often see a rusty rain deflector shield below the grille area just in front of the windscreen, and poor performance of this, or the internal drain, will see rain collecting in this airbox and coming into the passenger side via the air intake.

The other weakness of this design is the seal between the airbox and the car's bulkhead. Over time this will fail, allowing water to leak past. This was worse on earlier MGFs, before an improved seal was applied about 1998, but a solution was not found until a new intake design was introduced in 2003.

The original airbox is secured to the body by four bolts and it appears that these are not able to apply even pressure to allow the seal to work effectively over longer periods. Many owners have resorted to applying silicone sealer around the box. By comparison the later air intake has six fixing bolts.

When the car is parked, one route for water draining off the windscreen is straight down behind the back edge of the bonnet, down the bulkhead and past the airbox. It should drain out through the open area behind the

spare wheel well, but some seeps past the seal.

The 2003 change saw an air intake of a completely different design used with more secure fixing to the body. Gone was the metal rain deflector that always rusted, replaced by the air intake end being doubled over on itself, so there was no access for water. This reduces the ram pressure effect to move air into the car without fan assistance, but this was never strong to start with. These later designs are easily fitted onto earlier cars but unfortunately these newer designs have become difficult to find new (part number JKA000120).

Heater Air Intake Replacement

Removal of the air box sees attention focused on the four fixings holding this box to the bulkhead, essentially one in each corner, and all are accessed from underneath. This means that you have to remove the glove box and heater air intake duct from the underside of the air intake to get at the back two – this is even more complex with air conditioning fitted – but the front two are accessed from the spare wheel area.

Fig. 2.168 The original heater airbox occupies all the space behind the brake servo, which traps it in that position.

this box. Rather than follow a workshop manual approach that would mean stripping half the braking system out just to get to this box, and as the new one is smaller and fits without stripping down the brake system, I decided to sacrifice the old box.

Looking at the shape seemed to show that a section of the front face would have to be cut away, or at least made flexible enough to be folded out of the way, thus allowing the box to be rolled over the brake servo and out. Rather than attempt to describe the position of the cut, just look at the image and the box *in situ* to get an understanding of the cuts that make a door-like section 'hinged' on the left side.

Years of inaccessibility means there was plenty of dirt. Here was a golden opportunity to have a good clean before fitting the new duct. There was also some excess seam sealer causing lumps where the seal fits, so these were trimmed flush to aid the life and efficiency of the new seal.

Compared with the removal of the original chamber, fitting the new TF air intake 'funnel' is a doddle. There are some differences beyond the obvious visual ones, notably the use of six fixings instead of four, so the clamping load is better spread, but four of these six fixing holes are in different positions. On cars from 1997 I have found that the fixing positions for the new bolts are already in place, including three with captive nuts.

The three new back fixing positions, where there are already captive nuts, require three M6 bolts of approximately 20mm length and three flat

The one nearest the vehicle centreline is not too bad as it can be reached with a ¼-inch long socket and driver, but the last one is somewhat concealed by the brake servo, master cylinder and associated assembly. (If air conditioning is fitted the evaporator has to be removed, which means the air con has to be de-gassed and other measures taken.)

I have found that by far the easiest way to gain access is to raise the front of the car off the ground and fit stands. Crawl underneath and, with a selection of extension bars to the ratchet and socket, feed these through the sub-frame, where fortunately there is an access hole. The last fixing bolt is then removed, but unfortunately this is only the easy bit done.

The box fills all the available space behind the brake servo and master cylinder: while it can be moved around a little it is still completely trapped by the brake assembly. There is just enough movement to allow those who have a leak past the seal to introduce some sealant and then refit it, if wished.

Since I had an example of the new air intake, my sole aim was to remove

Fig. 2.169 In order to avoid having to strip the braking system if you are replacing the airbox with the later design, cut a similar 'door' in the airbox with a hot knife or hacksaw blade. This allows the box to roll over the servo, which fits through the open door as the box is rolled out.

Fig. 2.170 Years of accumulated dirt can now be cleaned off.

Fig. 2.171 After cleaning the whole area is much more presentable.

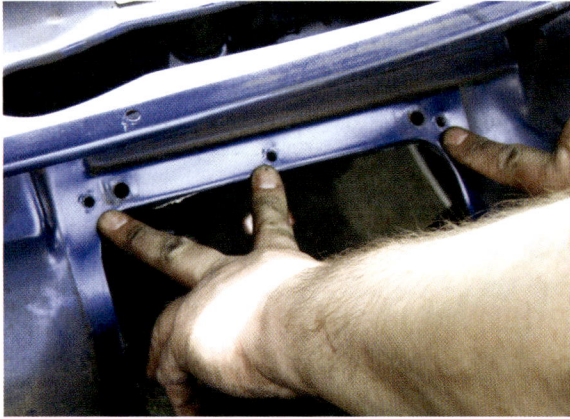

Fig. 2.172   The new intake has six fixings and three captive nuts are already in place, as indicated. Oddly, these are certainly present on cars as far back as 1997, six years before the improved intake was introduced.

Fig. 2.173   The new intake is a much more compact and tidy fit.

Fig. 2.174   The new intake also has a much better seal.

Fig. 2.175   The under bonnet plastic cover clips to it in the same way as it did to the old intake.

washers of approximately 20mm diameter to spread the clamping load. Some may prefer to use stainless fixings as this will look better and offer corrosion resistance. The front holes use two original holes and the third was already present, so again all that was needed were three new bolts, this time with three nuts as well as three pairs of washers.

With so much extra space, fitting the rear bolts is really simple, but the fronts remain a little restricted by the proximity of the servo, brake pipes and the flange of the leading edge of the bulkhead. Be careful not to overtighten these fixings, as that would distort the plastic base of the air intake. The end result is neater and simply a better design with a better seal against the body; the wonder is that it was not fitted earlier.

Door Mirror (Cheater) Leaks

The next common area for water leaks is the door 'cheater', the triangular mounting area for the door mirrors. It is common for owners to find small drops of water on top of the inner door trim panel in the area close to the 'cheater'. Close examination will often find traces of water having dribbled down the panel, across the speaker grille and then onto the carpet.

If there are cheater leaks as well as heater intake leaks the passenger side will soon get very wet, but feeling the

Fig. 2.176   Rainwater leaking past the door cheater (mirror mounting) leaves water sitting on top of the door trim and dribbles down the panel, but only when the car is parked.

carpet for wetness is rather ineffective as there has to be enough water to breed fish before the carpet feels wet rather than just damp, and the insulation under the carpet will be sodden.

An obvious sign of a problem appears in cooler winter conditions when internal misting of the windows takes an absolute age to clear, and the fan often has to be kept on setting two or higher to keep the windows clear. This would hint at higher internal air water content, fed from the reservoir under the carpet, and so deeper examination is called for. Fortunately, the often poorly fitting carpet around the sill area allows easy access for your hands to get under the carpet and feel the insulation. Obviously wet carpets or underlay demands drying out and this is really only possible by removing the carpets after the seats are taken out (*see* Chapter 3).

The cheater seal leak can be caused by the seal being old, hard and distorted. This is a reasonable possibility on older cars. The actual leak is a little more difficult to pin down, but in most cases the problem is where the top of the cheater finishes and the door glass begins. These two items butt against the windscreen seal and it is this contact that creates the weather seal. Often there is a distortion that creates a small gap through which the water will track and then find its way onto the inside of the glass and the door trim.

The fact that this leak is common only when the car is parked is the result of the route the water takes when draining off the front corners of the hood or hardtop. If you look at this when washing your car you will see that a trickle of water comes off the very front corner of

Fig. 2.177   When parked, the MGF and TF can suffer water ingress where the cheater and door glass edges meet.

Fig. 2.178   The correct closed position for the glass is critical: the transition edge from glass to cheater should be flat, as here.

LEFT: *Fig. 2.179   Stopping the door window rising too far involves a plastic stop that engages against a flange in the door. The three-piece design introduced about 1999 was not as liable to break as the earlier single-piece mouldings.*

RIGHT: *Fig. 2.180   The later window stop shown fitted in the door glass.*

Fig. 2.181   The inside face shows significant wearing on the contact face. Loosen the nut and turn this around 180 degrees to regain normal efficiency.

the hood/hardtop and then drops onto the top of the door glass. It then tracks down the glass to the seal contact area until it reaches the small gap mentioned above, when a small proportion of the water finds its way inside. When the car is being driven the airflow doesn't allow water to follow this route.

The amount of water entering the car when parked often depends on wind direction and strength, but one of the most influential factors is related to the position of the window relative to the cheater and screen seal, something dependent on the door glass stop.

Fig. 2.182   The old seal (left) shows clear indentation compared to the new seal on the right. Note that the old seal shown here is not as bad as they can become.

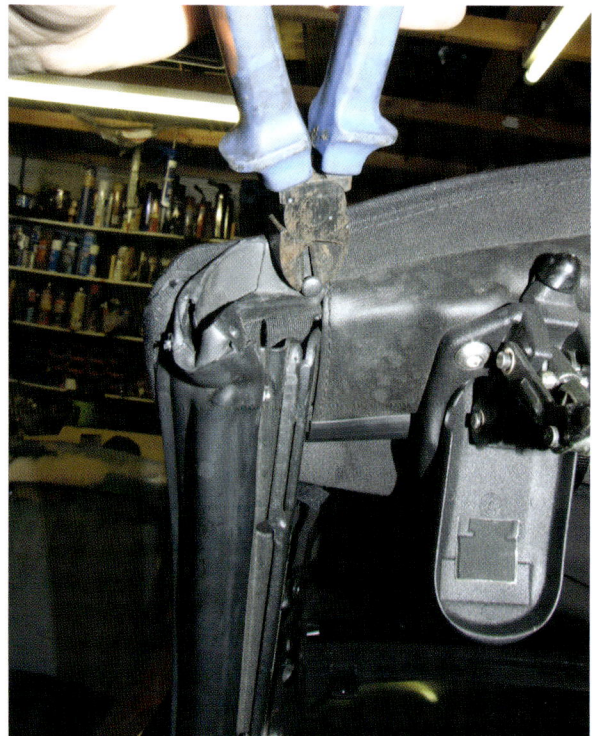

Fig. 2.184   Then the plastic scrivet needs to be removed carefully as you have to reuse this.

Fig. 2.183   Seal removal starts with removing the nylock nut from the threaded stud.

Fig. 2.185   Once the seal is peeled out, the stud has to be removed from the end and fitted into the new seal.

Inside the door there is a tongue of metal intended as a stop to prevent the door glass rising too far. What engages on this is a plastic foot, called the window stop, which is inserted into a hole in the door glass so that, when the two come into contact, it stops the glass rising further. The first two designs of window stop, found on cars made up to sometime during 1998, are single-piece mouldings that are clipped into the glass. If you find a broken bit of white plastic in the bottom of the door then this is the first type; if it is orange then it is the second style. Both were replaced with a third, more robust, type that resembles a top hat, with a square shaped rim, a separate plastic washer and stainless Allen bolt.

The first two types broke easily, allowing the window to rise too high, causing the screen and door seals to become distorted. If left for a long period the distortion on the seals becomes permanent: even if a new stop is fitted the distorted seal is less effective.

A common condition, and an immediate visual indicator that a window is rising too high, is that the top side of the door glass simply rests on the outside of the seal, rather than the top edge of the glass creating gentle pressure on the lower half of the seal, with the seal partially enveloping the top of the glass. Where the top of the glass does push into the seal, the seal actually holds on to the top of the glass making it noticeably more difficult to open the door. The best measure of a broken stop, however, is to look at where the door glass meets the cheater with the door open. You should be able to put a straight edge against the glass and it should align perfectly with the cheater without a step.

The top hat has an inner captive thread with an outer plastic body, and the rim of the hat is placed against the inside of the glass over the hole. The Allen bolt has a plastic washer slipped over it to protect the glass, and then both are inserted through the hole from the outer facing side and the screw tightened up to hold it in place.

That sounds easy, and with practise it is, but it is fiddly having to reach through the removed speaker hole in the door, with the glass raised up about 50mm from the bottom so you can both see what you're doing and get

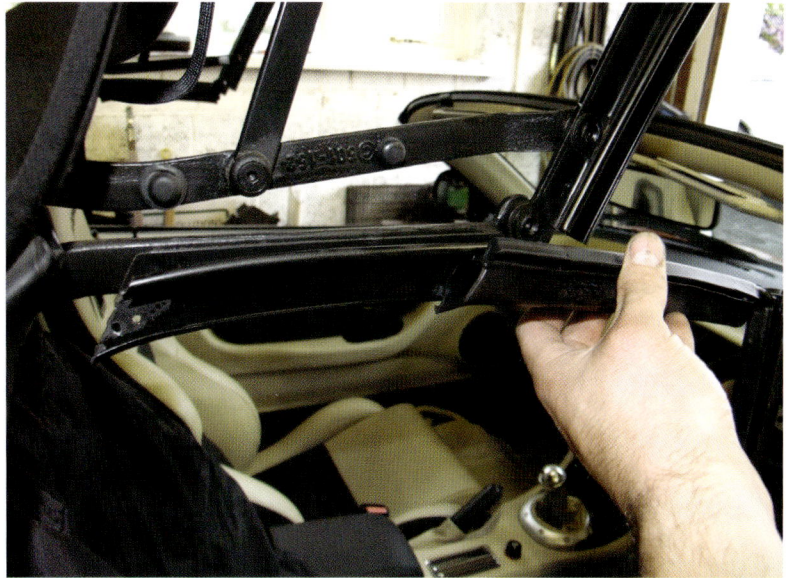

Fig. 2.186   Attempting to fit a new seal in the metal extrusions by sliding the moulded seal foot along, using some soapy solution, usually results in the seal sticking about a quarter of the way along.

Fig. 2.187   Feed one side of the foot into the back edge of the extrusion first, and then gently push the outer edge in a bit at a time.

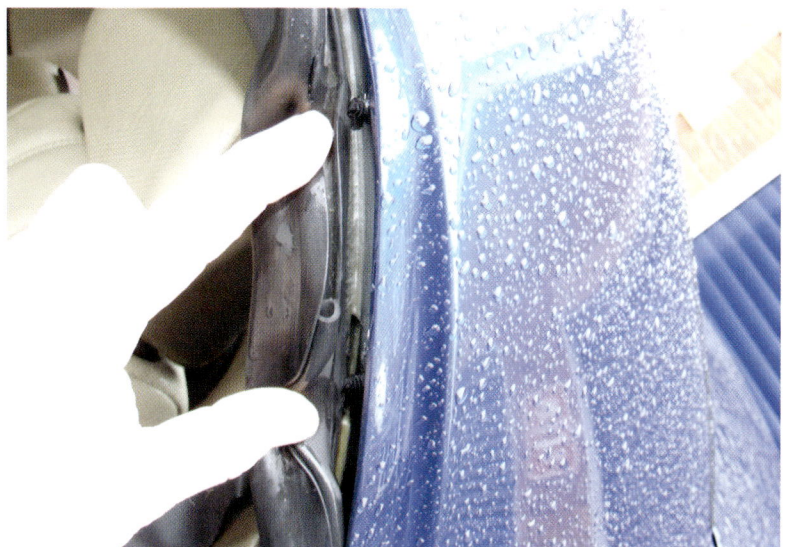

Fig. 2.188   Hardtop seals vary, depending on the top and when it was made. Some fit over an edge like the door frame seals, while others, like this Heritage top, have hidden plastic fir tree clips fitting into holes.

LOCATING AND MARKING THE POSITION FOR DRILLING HOLE FOR NEW SEAL CLIP

1. Remove old seal.
2. Remove any traces of adhesive or road debris from the A post area.
3. Apply a 50mm wide × 200mm long strip of masking tape to the lower A post as shown in illustration 1. Close door.
4. Using a tape measure and short steel rule, measure 210mm from the top of the cheater and make a pen mark on the adjacent masking tape (*see* illustration 2). Open door and continue mark into the underside of A post, ensuring that mark is kept parallel.
5. Using two rules, measure 12mm into the A post underside and make another pen mark where lines cross, this indicates position for the upper peg hole. Ensure that the rule being used as a straight edge rests on the flat portion of A post furthest away from the screen as shown in illustration 3.
6. From the first peg hole mark, measure down 50mm and mark with pen (*see* illustration 4). Using the same (two rule) method as before make another mark 12mm into the A post underside to indicate position of the second peg hole.
7. Protect inside of vehicle around door area from drilling debris. Using a 'sharp' drill, drill two 5mm holes in the A post underside in the marked positions (*see* illustration 5).
8. Remove masking tape and using a small scraper or file carefully remove any burrs from the inside edge of the hole (this is important to ensure that clips locate correctly). Apply a zinc-based primer to the holes and allow to dry. Finally, touch in with body colour paint and allow to dry.
9. Clean any drilling debris from area and fit new header seal ensuring that location pegs are pushed firmly into the pre-drilled holes and the existing hole at the base of the A post. Take care to align pegs carefully before insertion, failure to ensure this can damage the pegs which are not replaceable.

Fig. 2.189   New windscreen seals demand additional location peg holes and the procedure for positioning these holes was illustrated in an MG Rover bulletin. (Illustration 1) Placing masking tape on the screen pillar.

Fig. 2.190 (Illustration 2)   Measuring 210mm from the top of the cheater.

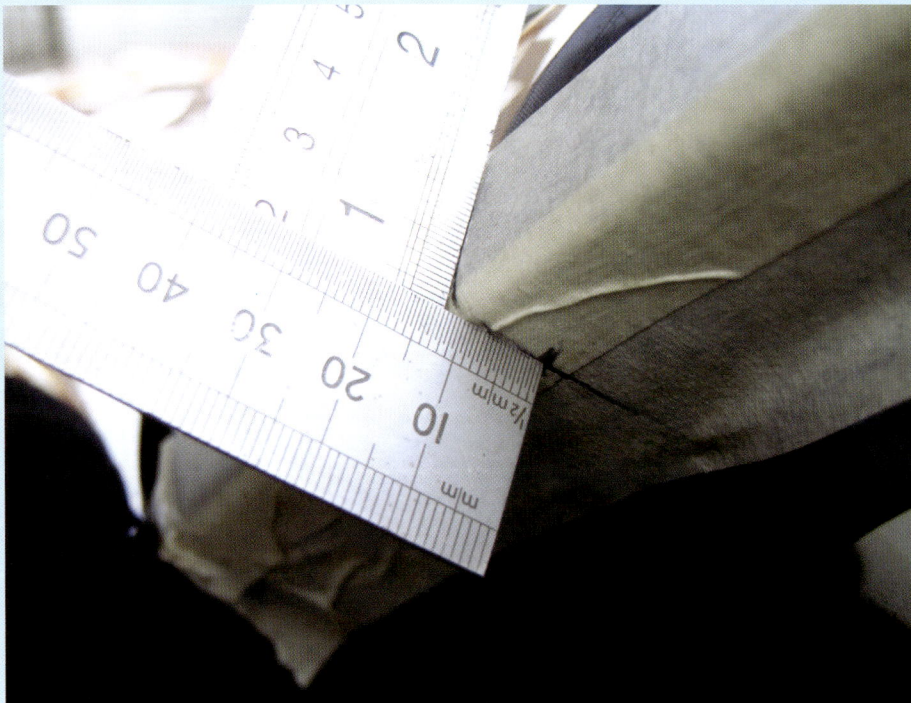

Fig. 2.191 (Illustration 3) Using two rules to accurately measure in 12mm to mark the upper peg hole.

Fig. 2.192 (Illustration 4)   Measuring 50mm down from the first hole mark to repeat the two rule positioning of the second hole position.

Fig. 2.193 (Illustration 5)   Drilling positions for the two holes.

Fig. 2.194   The two new 'fir tree' type pegs are here clearly seen.

Fig. 2.195   A new screen seal being fitted: the exposed metal of the newly drilled holes awaits treatment.

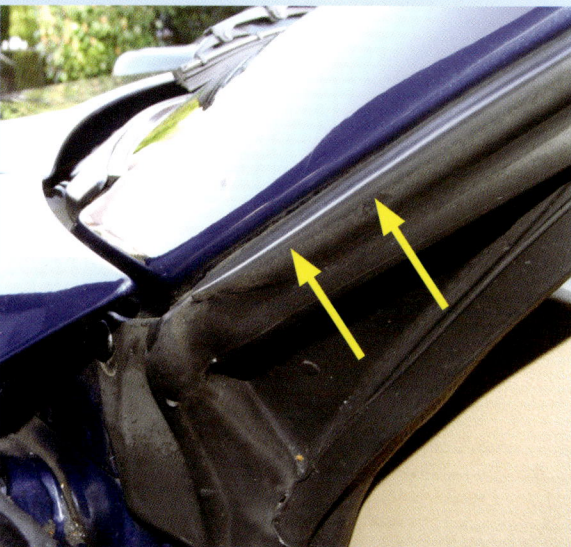

Fig. 2.196   The direction of pressure needed to fully engage the new seal locating pegs in the new holes.

Fig. 2.197   The new seal is here fully fitted, not forgetting the small plastic scrivet in the end under the wing edge.

your hand behind the glass to fit and tighten the bolt.

This design of window stop was unchanged all the way to the end of TF production in 2011. I have come across only a handful of cars with this later design that have given any problem, but one possibility can be quite severe, so it is worth mentioning both the symptoms and the cure.

Some cars may only see contact between the window stop and the metal flange in the door on their respective edges. As the plastic is softer than steel, it wears, and two resulting conditions have occurred. In the first the plastic wears on the edge and can ride up partially past the flange and jam. The window then neither lowers nor rises, although you can hear the motor trying to work and usually see some hint of movement. The other condition is where the window stop rides right past the flange: the tiny movement up and down that is visible indicates that the stop and flange are now working in reverse.

The cure for both conditions is the same. Remove the door trim to allow access to the inner steel door frame. Gentle force is needed to pull the door frame away from the glass and at the same time gently push the glass outwards to create and hold the gap, while the window is lowered by an assistant.

To help prevent the problem repeating, the steel flange has to be at 90 degrees to the glass and it may have been distorted slightly upwards. First, apply gentle pressure from above to restore its correct angle and then check that the inner steel face of the door is straight and has not been distorted inwards. If it has, gentle pressure is applied to the central area to restore the original position.

Additionally, if the plastic window stop has a chamfered edge, then loosen the clamping bolt and turn the 'top hat' 180 degrees to move the damaged area out of the contact zone. This will achieve just the same as a new window stop, but at no cost. (Fig. 2.181.)

Hood to Door Glass Seal Replacement

At some point this seal will have to be replaced owing to age and damage, but commonly this is premature

because it is window stop failure that has caused the seals to distort. Removal of the old seal is quite straightforward and starts with two mechanical fixings at the front (the header rail end). Firstly there is a threaded stud fitted within the front section of the seal and which projects through a hole in the back of the seal. When fitted to the hood frame this is pushed through the frame and a small nylock nut is seen on the inside face of the frame. Then there is a plastic scrivet holding the front flap of the seal in against the front face of the header rail' This has to be carefully eased out with a trim tool or with some side cutter pliers. New seals may or may not have these fixings, so always remove the existing fixing with care on the assumption they will need to be reused. (Figs 2.185 to 2.185.)

Fitting the new seal is not a difficult job, just involving some soapy solution to lubricate the new seal's moulded 'foot', which sits in the metal extrusion on the hood frame. Be aware, however, that what appears to be the simple way of fitting and sliding the moulded foot of the seal down the extrusion doesn't work, as it will bind about a quarter of the way down, and if you persist you can damage the seal. The best way is to feed the moulded foot into one side of the extrusion and then gently and progressively push the other side into the extrusion with a blunt screwdriver or wooden/plastic tool with a blunt flat blade.

Hardtop seals are supplied in one piece as they do not have to fold with the hood. Several different types of fixing are available, however, depending

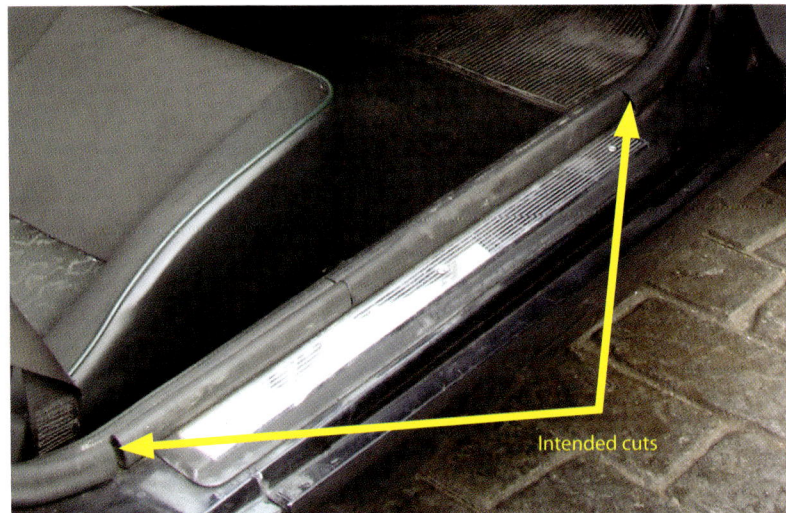

Fig. 2.198   The two cut sections of the seal were intended by MG to help stop water tracking inside the car.

Fig. 2.199   A later improved design featured a series of small holes.

on whether the hard-top is a factory one or an aftermarket design.

Windscreen Pillar Seal Replacement

This is actually quite a lengthy seal as it runs from halfway along the base of the door aperture, forward to the front vertical face of the door aperture, then up the screen pillar, across the top of the screen and down the other side, before ending halfway along the door aperture base.

Removal is quite simple as the seal has a common interference fit over a metal flange for most of the way. There are, however, two hidden rivets at the base of each side of the screen pillars, and the hood retaining clips and the sun visors, which have simple screw fittings, all have the be removed. A complication is that all MGFs and very early MG TFs (up to VIN RD602792) did not have the rivets at the base of each screen pillar; since all replacement seals come with these, two small 5mm holes have to be drilled, one per pillar. The approved MG Rover method is given in the accompanying description.

An oddity concerning the design of the seals along the lower edge of the door aperture is the very obvious 10mm sections of seal that have been cut out, one towards the front of the lower door aperture and one towards the rear, on the rear seal. These were

Fig. 2.200   *Rainwater leaks around the rear of the hood will show how good the insulation under the engine cover carpet is at holding water.*

Fig. 2.201   *Rainwater can cause serious corrosion to the engine cover.*

introduced to create 'drip edges', since water was found to track down the seals and could enter the car. Later seals featured a series of small holes rather than removed sections.

Hood Leaks

Generally this is not a problem where the hood is in good condition, but sometimes leaks can occur around the rear window. The scenario already seen in the passenger footwell can result, with apparently dry carpet on the rear deck covering soaking insulation underneath.

One additional consequence of this is that the removable engine cover and fuel pump covers will soon rust. This problem needs to be dealt with quickly. Cleaning the rust off, treating it and then painting with something like smooth Hammerite works well, but you do have to address the leak, which may require nothing more than re-proofing the hood, or possible replacing it.

Boot Leaks

My MGF was one of those that suffered from water leaking into the boot, requiring a pair of towels operating on a shift basis. The annoying thing

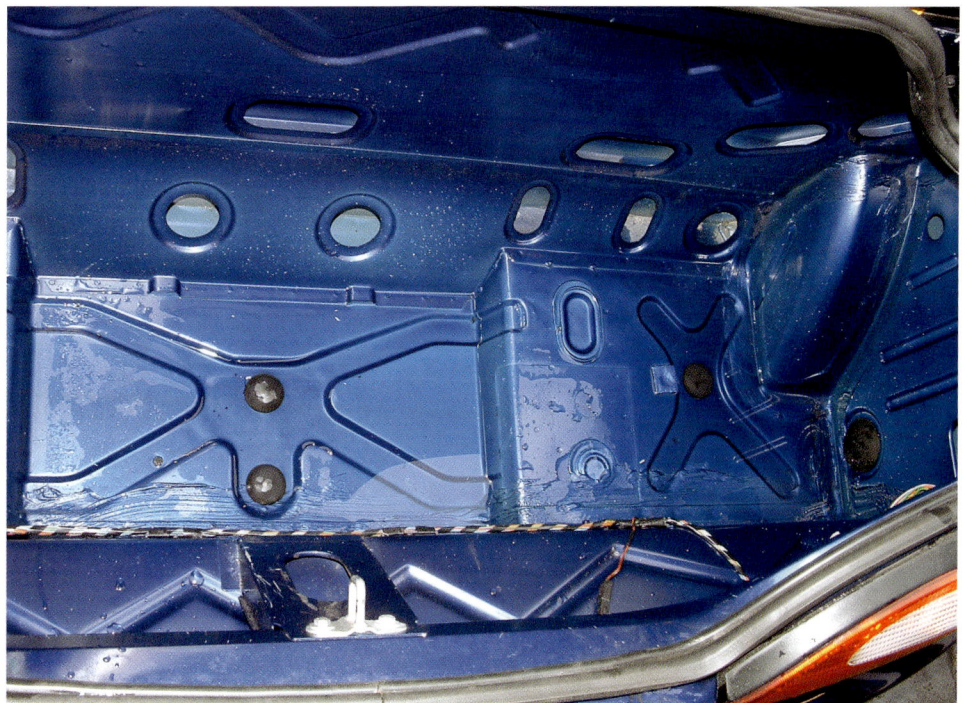

Fig. 2.202   *A water leak into the boot was collecting copious amounts of water.*

Fig. 2.203   After considerable testing the leak was found in a body join under a sealing strip.

Fig. 2.204   A short section of seam sealer had been missed out.

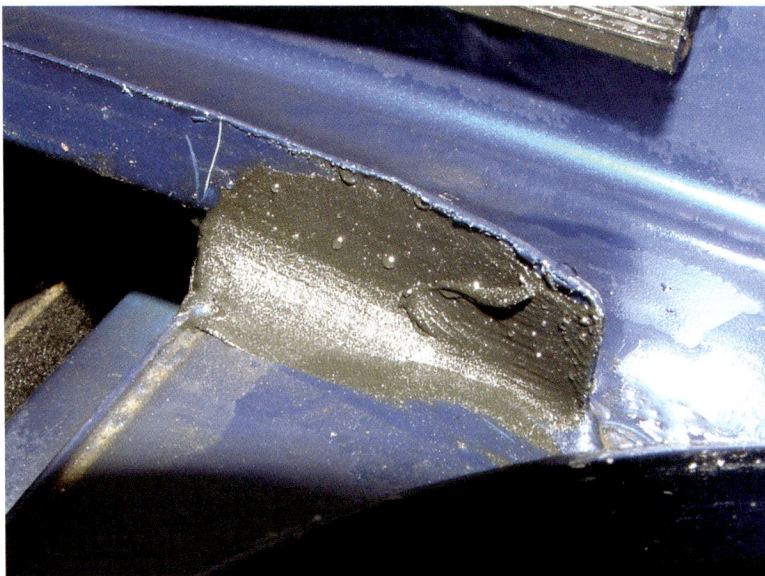

Fig. 2.205   After applying some fresh sealant the leak was cured.

was that there was no telltale water stain or wet tracks to point to the entry point. The most common leak point is always from behind the rear lamp assembly, caused by the failure of the seal between lamp and body to stop the water that is directed down the boot channels and on top of each lamp to then flow over and down to the ground. When the seal has failed there is a water streak inside the boot under the lamp. This can usually be detected without having to take the boot carpet out, but if the carpet is wet then it is logical to remove it to allow it to dry.

The next most common entry point can be from water tracking in via the boot vents that release hot air from the engine bay. Rain can sometimes enter the vents when the car is parked facing uphill on a slope. It does not pass straight through but tracks back towards the high-level brake light position and find its way into the boot. The manner by which the boot panels create a duct from the vent position to the high-level brake light position is not by chance, as the original design intended this as a duct for removing hot air from the engine bay, but it wasn't effective enough so boot vents were added.

It is worth mentioning that the problems anticipated with water ingress in the engine bay led to bad starting and misfiring problems on some pre-2001 MEMS 9 and 2J MGFs when the coil(s) got wet from water coming in through the vents.

Coming back to the wet boot problem, even without any obvious entry point and with the carpet removed, it is a typical situation to see a good depth of water. Fortunately there are several rubber bungs that open to the underside of the car, so the water can be quickly drained.

Once the excess water is removed the remnants are mopped up so that any fresh drops of water can easily be identified when the process of locating the source of the leak begins. This follows a logical approach of using a garden hose and spray nozzle to replicate rainfall onto the rear of the car (with the boot closed, of course). After a few seconds, pause and check inside for fresh water ingress. Here a couple of fresh dribbles are apparent in the right front corner. The position of the water indicates that it is somehow coming in from the wing to the boot external channel, so by gently trickling water into the channel the area may be narrowed down to the area above the bonnet release lever.

Once the channel trims were removed in this case, close examination located a small section between the panel join where seam sealer was missing. Pouring water directly at this section confirmed this as being the source of the leak. All that was needed was to dry the area before sealing it with some more seam sealant, a compound that sticks very well but doesn't fully harden and remains flexible. It can also be painted over, but in this case it was not needed.

BONNET RELEASE PROBLEMS

Problems with bonnet release cables are frequently enough encountered for it to be more practical to pre-empt them by dealing with the two main issues before having to resort to the fiddly method described below when there is no other way to open the bonnet.

The two main problems affecting the bonnet release mechanism are corrosion on the cable, leading to the inner cable stiffening and ultimately breaking, and free play in the system from a stretched cable. There is not a great deal that you can do to prevent corrosion, other than perhaps rubbing grease into the exposed areas of cable at the front of the car, so it is a matter of reacting to cable degradation before it leaves you with a problem.

When you pull the bonnet release lever in the boot you should expect to feel a smooth, even pressure (like operating pedal cycle brakes) and a clear clunk as the bonnet releases and jumps up. If there is any free play beyond about 5 per cent of the lever movement then this indicates there is potential for the inner cable to become detached at the bonnet end and pre-emptive attention is suggested.

There is a very simple hook on the bonnet release catch that fits onto a simple eye at the cable end, so it is not difficult to see how these can easily part company if there is slack in the system. Owners have found a number of ways to make this fixing more secure. I settled on using a small plastic cable

Fig. 2.206   The bonnet locking mechanism is susceptible to rust. The release cable comes in from the right side and has a simple loop over peg engagement that can drop off if the cable becomes loose.

Fig. 2.207   The addition of a small cable tie can add security (yellow arrow). Note too how the outer cable is only an interference fit and could slide out from the groove if worn (red arrow).

tie run through the eye and around the hook to simply hold the two parts together and so not allow any free play in the cable by which the eye can become loose on the hook.

You should also check, where the outer cable fits at the bonnet end, that the moulded plastic end of the outer cable has an interference fit into the U-shaped receiver bracket of the bonnet catch. If this is not a tight fit, or you feel the need to make the connection more secure, then you can use another cable tie to impart a slight tension on the cable to better hold it in place.

Use of cable ties is a cheap and effective option that allows very easy removal should you have a need to

dismantle any part of the system, then easily replace with another when it goes back together. They are also usefully resistant to corrosion.

If there is more than the described free play on the cable, corrosion, any roughness or clear drag, then the cable should be replaced sooner rather than later. Replacing the cable is not difficult, just a matter of accessing it as it runs along the right side of the under-bonnet area, under the lip of the wing, and through into the passenger compartment, where it is clipped along the right sill under the carpet together with the throttle cable, up and onto the hood deck and through into the engine bay, before finally passing through the

Fig. 2.208   If the bonnet cable fails, then you can only see the security cover plate from underneath. (The bonnet locking panel has been removed and upturned for clarity.)

engine bay to boot bulkhead, where it meets the release handle.

What should be done in the event that your bonnet no longer opens when the lever is pulled? First, if the cable is slack and you have not yet replaced it, check the cable at the boot handle and use a pair of pliers to give a direct pull on the inner cable to see if this releases the bonnet. If it does then don't assume that this will always happen, as I guarantee that this won't work for long. Rectify the problem while you have the chance.

When the bonnet remains firmly shut despite everything, then read on. I have given consideration to the security aspects, but it is such an awkward job that I doubt whether the usual lazy thief would have the inclination or opportunity to follow this route.

You will need a lever about 18in (450mm) long: I suggest a long pry bar or a similar heavy-duty flat-bladed screwdriver. The car needs to be raised quite high to give really good access to the underside of the car's front in order to insert and use the lever; hence the usual approach is a garage ramp. You will also need a willing helper.

The DIY approach is to safely raise the car and place it on stands. Then you move under to reach the gap behind the lower edge of the front bumper panel and in front of the body cross member that supports the radiator. If the car has

air conditioning, then expect the gap to be somewhat reduced and the prospects made more difficult.

You will be looking up to the underside of the bonnet locking platform around 15in (375mm) up from the gap you are looking through, which is the panel carrying the bonnet catch, but you will not see the mechanism as there is a simple but effective security cover bolted in place to prevent you doing what I am about to suggest. You can't remove the security plate as it bolts from the top, accessed only when the bonnet is open, but you can overcome this.

If you are really lucky (and in my experience the odds are only about one in twenty) then the tip of the arm that you need to move is just visible beyond the edge of the security plate. You might then get just enough purchase to move it towards the right-hand side of the car using the sharp edge of the pry bar or screwdriver. Study the images of the security plate to get a clearer idea of the layout, and then imagine looking up into the darkened area while on your back.

It is now the role of the helper to press down gently on the front edge of the bonnet, compressing the spring that is holding the bonnet tight in the catch. This light compression releases the tension from the release lever you're trying to move, making it very much easier for you. As you move the lever towards the right side of the car, shout to the helper to release the pressure on the bonnet: if you synchronize well enough the bonnet pops open.

On the remaining 95 per cent of cars, however, the security shield needs to be bent to provide access. The bigger the lever, the easier it is to bend, but you have to be very careful not to damage the radiator. The edge that needs to be bent is the corner of the plate on the side where the square hole is situated. Bend the corner back towards that square hole as far as is needed to access the lever, when the procedure described above then applies.

Once the bonnet is open, it is then a simple job to unbolt the bonnet locking platform from the body. This allows you to turn the panel to get easy access the security plate and remove it. You can then straighten it and deal with the cable.

Fig. 2.209   In most cases you have to bend the security cover to access the release lever. This then allows you to move it in the direction shown (towards the right side of the car) to open the bonnet.

Fig. 3.2   If it is not checked, permanent damage occurs. This is much worse with sporting seats like these XPower monogrammed rally Sparco seats.

Fig. 3.1   The most common form of seat degradation starts with the piping wearing thin on the edges of the side bolster.

Fig. 3.3   Here the leather bolster is collapsing because the foam inside is collapsing.

trim

When mentioning trim the immediate thought is just the soft materials found within the cabin, but I see this as just part of the passenger compartment, so all the plastics for the facia, the door liners, centre console, seats, carpets, seals and hood/hardtop come within the scope of this section. Then there is the boot area, the under-bonnet area and, to a lesser extent, various small bits and bobs on the outside of the body. Quite an extensive list can be drawn up.

Trim items are often at the very bottom of an owner's list of priorities. They are, however, the items that owners have most contact with, so many short change themselves by putting up with worn and dirty trim and adopt a 'round tuit' approach, which often means it is never done. Another problem is that many owners have no difficulty in throwing themselves headlong into mechanical and even body repairs, but shy clear of trim.

Start in the passenger compartment and look at the areas of weakness and wear on sensitive items. Here it is the signs of degradation on the driver's seat, the carpet and door card (the door's interior trim) that stand out – the usually pristine passenger side just glows by comparison.

SEATS AND CARPETS

Common wear will be found in the driver's seat outer bolster, the right side back support of the backrest part of the seat: wear here comes in two forms, the cover having been rubbed to an extent where holes are present, and/or the cushion in the backrest that gives the seat its shape may have collapsed.

Replacing the seat cushion is not that difficult, providing new cushions remain available, and not too expensive. If the damage is due to smoking, however, it usually means you need the services of a professional trimmer to do a repair, if it is viable.

Damage to bolsters is often found on cars used by shorter drivers, who pull the seat forward and closer to the steering wheel. By definition these drivers have less room to squeeze in and out, which means the bolster is compressed and rubbed more than is the case with taller drivers, who have the seat set further back.

Not that it is all one way, as taller drivers tend to be heavier and this puts more compression onto the seat base, leading to the driver's seat being more flattened and sunken than the less often used passenger seat. This additional stretching can also lead to the stitching on seats breaking.

Seat Foam Replacement

The seat shape has pronounced side bolsters that add a little support for the occupant but, as mentioned above, the outer bolsters can suffer. A collapsed driver's seat outer bolster, leaving the outer cover well ruffled, is actually relatively simple to correct. Many would consider that rectifying this problem is a professional job. Although I have no in-depth experience in trimming, the second MGF I bought second hand

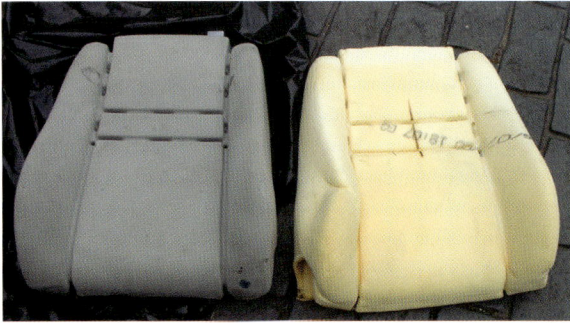

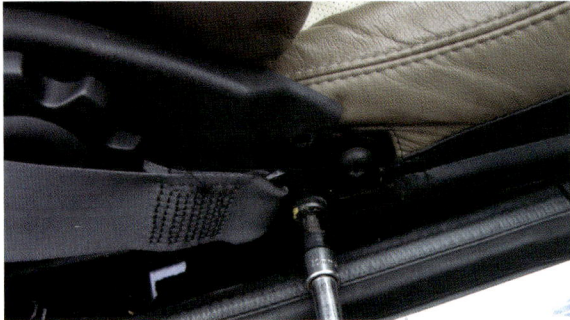

ABOVE LEFT: *Fig. 3.4   The light coloured foam (right) has a clearly collapsed bolster when compared with the new grey one.*

ABOVE RIGHT: *Fig. 3.5   Under each seat is the electrical plug for the SRS seat belt pre-tensioners that need to be disconnected before the seat can be removed from the car. Before working on any part of the SRS read the safety warning.*

LEFT: *Fig. 3.6   The seat belt anchors to the outer side of the seat frame. It is best to remove the right seat to floor bolts and loosen the left pair in order to lift the seat to get better access to unbolt the seat belt.*

SAFETY WARNING

Any work on the SRS system demands caution and disconnection of the battery, plus at least fifteen minutes of idle time to ensure all the residual power dissipates before touching any part of the system. Failure to observe this simple rule can lead to accidental activation of the system. Close proximity to an activated airbag can lead to serious injury or even death.

Do not mess with, poke, hit or drop an airbag. An airbag is rather like a wasp in that if you don't annoy it, it won't annoy you, but if you mistreat it then it stings. In the case of an air bag, though, the sting can be very dangerous.

had this problem and it seemed like a good time to explore the possibilities of a home repair – and if it went pear shaped I could pass it to a professional!

Changing the foam follows the same procedure needed for a cover replacement, so if a cover needs changing then

this process also applies. This specific job involved simply replacing the foam and I was able to buy a standard MG replacement foam at the surprisingly inexpensive price of less than £20. Trim is one area where a car manufacturer offers many variations and regular

RIGHT: *Fig. 3.7   The seat belt pretensioner is unbolted first, then the two bolts holding the backrest to the seat base are removed.*

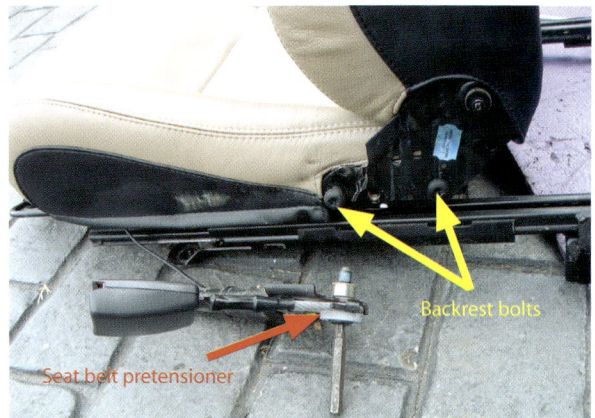

Fig. 3.8   One of the two backrest to base bolts is visible but the second is hidden by the trim cover. The adjuster knob has an interference fit to its shaft and is eased off.

Fig. 3.9   The cover has two hidden expanding clips. The two pegs show their positions as they are pushed flush when installed and have to be pushed all the way through to release the internal clips.

changes, so you can expect the demise of MG Rover to have left many of these original items unavailable more quickly than has been the case with mechanical parts.

The preformed shape of the new cushion confirmed that the bolster shape comes from the moulded shape of the foam cushion, which gives scope for a simpler repair. The repair option is to cut off the distorted bolster section and then get some foam of a similar density from a market or other source, trim it to shape and then use a suitable spray adhesive to stick the foam section to the original seat foam. This works remarkably well when the foam is inserted into the cover.

In order to remove the cushion for replacement or repair, the seat has to be removed from the car, which is simple enough using a size 50 six-sided Torx spline bit for the seat to floor bolts, although you first need to disconnect the seat belt pretensioner (red) plug under the seat.

You also have to remove the seat belt outer anchor bolt, using the same spline tool size, before you can remove the seat from the car. This is best done when the four anchor bolts holding the seat to the floor are removed, so you can lift up the right side of the seat that gives easier access to this bolt. Once disconnected, it is then just a careful fiddle to lift the seat up and remove it without damaging the trim or paint. This is much easier to do with the hood lowered.

Once outside, set the seat on an old blanket or similar to allow it to be rested in various positions without damaging the seat covers. Next the seat belt pretensioner is removed, along with the four retaining bolts holding the seat back to the base, and the backrest and base can be separated.

The head restraint is now removed. The spring clip retainers have to be pulled clear for each leg of the restraint before it will lift out. To access these, simply press down the seat material either side of the plastic seat back receptor, into which the legs slide, until the spring clip is visible.

The seat cover is then slowly and carefully 'peeled' off from the bottom, noting that it is best to turn the cover inside out as you go as this makes for better access to the numerous spring clips and easier refitting. The way the cover is retained against the foam is simple but quite fiddly, with a series of rings of bent wire that have to have their ends separated enough to allow removal, but not too much or the refit is more difficult. Just enough separation to allow the clip to be twisted off the wire with long nose pliers seems about right.

If working on the seat base, the cover and cushion are simpler to remove and come off as a pair. There are just a couple of clips towards the front corners and three plastic retainers, sewn to the cover material, that connect the flanges of the seat frame to unclip. Once off the foam and cover have a pair of through clips to disconnect, following which the two can be separated.

The relative simplicity of working on the seats, and the probable continuing reduction in available new parts, does mean that the use of second-hand components becomes more frequent. Here the fact that the covers and cushions are not handed (only the seat frames are), and the usual situation where the passenger seat gets relatively little use, means that it is viable to

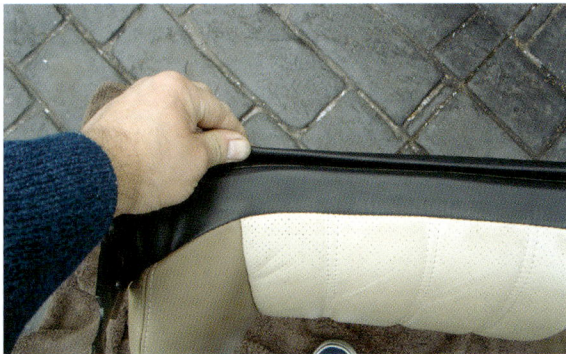

Fig. 3.10   The backrest seat cover is carefully unclipped from the bottom.

Fig. 3.11   Two spring lines have to be unclipped from the front side.

Fig. 3.12   The cover can then be peeled back.

Fig. 3.13   The other ends of the spring lines pass through the foam and have to be unclipped further up the seat frame.

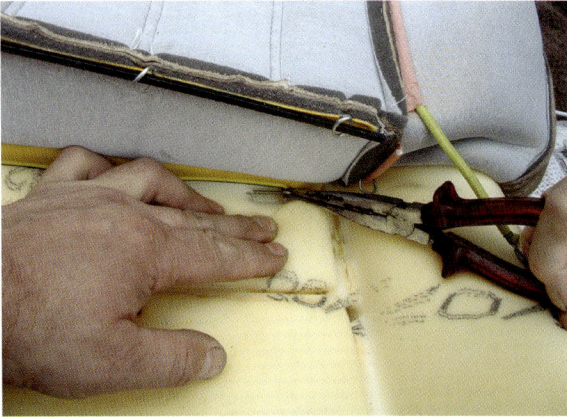

Fig. 3.14   A number of simple bent wire clips also have to be unclipped.

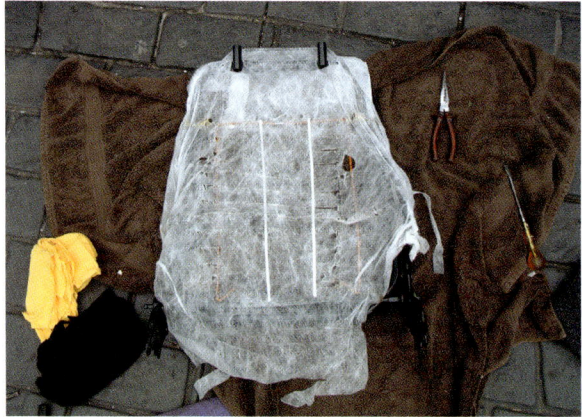

Fig. 3.15   The foam and cover may then be separated from the frame.

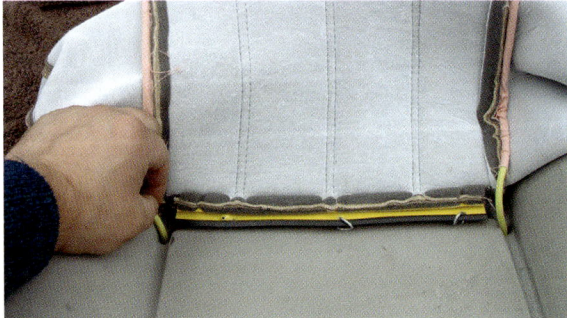

Fig. 3.16   Reassembly is very much the reversal of that dismantling process. It is much easier than words and pictures indicate.

RIGHT: Fig. 3.17   The refinished seat back ready to be refitted to the base.

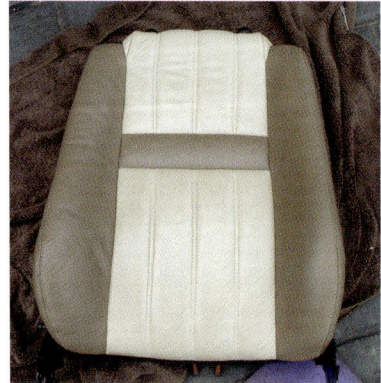

Fig. 3.18   The refurbished seat has suffered no repeat problems after 70,000 miles.

source passenger seat foams and covers in reasonable condition to repair worn driver's seats.

Once the seat is refitted there is a final check to make sure that the SRS warning lamp goes out when the engine starts. If it doesn't then the problem will usually be that the underseat connector is not making good contact, and so it needs to be separated and then firmly refitted together. Once again the

cautionary warning related to working on the SRS system applies: since it will have been electrically recharged, it will need the waiting time again.

Seat Lowering

One of the commonest observations made in recent years in respect of the MGF, and to a slightly lesser extent of the TF, is that you tend to sit 'on' rather

than 'in' the car. This refers to the seating position being perceived as too high. In strict terms this is somewhat unfair as shorter to average height drivers will say this is untrue, and those with experience of both the MGF and TF often commenting that they have a better view from an MGF seating position. Conversely tall drivers may find the seating a little high, leaving the tops of thighs close to the bottom of the steering wheel, and in some cases with their eyeline being uncomfortably close to the top of the windscreen.

In actual fact all the seats have the same basic frame and dimension, with seat height variations depending on the seat style and cushions used. The MGF 'Heritage Leather' seating of cars from the 1998 model year to the start of the 2000 model year does seem to be the highest when compared to most TF seats, showing that MG Rover reacted to seat height comments.

Where an owner feels the driver's seat (or passenger seat) is too high, there is a simple option to lower this by substituting small coil spring clips for the rigid wire clips that connect the seat frame to the seat diaphragm. In standard form the thick rubber diaphragm provides the spring medium, but adding these springs in place of the wire clips allows the seat base to sink around 10 to 12mm more when you sit in the seat. When there is no weight in the seat it will sit in the original normal position and so will not look any different.

Such a distance may not sound much, but it has a bigger impact than most would expect. Some, however, will find that this is still not sufficient and in these cases a modified seat frame will be needed. Modifying a seat frame is not an easy DIY operation as it carries the seat belt and tensioner, making it a highly critical, safety-oriented structural item. Vehicle Handling Solutions offers a modified seat frame that increases the lowering effect to approximately 20mm. Note that frames come in two forms; Mk1 (up to July 1999) and 2000 model year on (from July 1999), including the TF.

Fig. 3.19 Lowering your sitting position by 10–12mm is achieved by replacing the fixed wire ties that hold the seat base rubber diaphragm to the seat frame with these springs.

Fig. 3.20 The difference in quality between MGF and TF carpets is as marked as the colour difference here (the grey joined carpets are from the TF).

Carpets

Carpets in the MGF are not of a high quality, although those in the late TF are better, but both can wear quite noticeably on the driver's side. Many cars will have benefited from floor mats, which are of significant help in concentrating wear and dirt into the mat and not the carpet. The benefit, however, is only as good as the frequency of vacuuming out, as dirt and grit will soon get under the mat if it is not regularly removed and this acts as an effective abrasive between the underside of the mat and the carpet.

The MGF carpets use a thinner material and comprise separate left and right sides, while the late TF carpets have a thicker pile and backing, and come as a single-piece moulding with connections under the rear part of the tunnel. Certainly quality had improved quite noticeably by the time MG Rover went under, even though the only noted part change occurred for the start of the 2000 model year.

One common and lasting fault has been the abysmal fit of the standard carpets around the lower front sill and door aperture area. It is generally worse on the MGF than the TF, but both often see gaping gaps between the edge of the carpet and the door seal's moulded flap edge, which is supposed to go over

the carpet. The small strips of Velcro fitted to hold the carpet edges to the sill suffered from adhesive that was far too weak and the strips simply fell off when it dried. Even if you glue the carpets down, the fact that the moulded shape is not tight to the body always results in the carpet pulling away as soon as an occupant puts any weight into the footwell.

Fitting a late TF carpet into an MGF does make the interior look better and the thicker materials improve the sound deadening. It can be fitted intact, as on a TF, or cut to make installation simpler by not having to remove the centre console.

Replacing a carpet requires removing the seats, as described above for

seat cushion replacement. If you using a TF carpet for the replacement, and you want to keep the two parts joined, then you also need to remove the centre console assembly. This in turn means removal of the radio and the central console that carries the clock, oil temperature gauge and various switches, before the main centre console moulding can be unscrewed and lifted up to provide access for the cross sections of carpet.

There are a few obvious trim clips for some of the carpet edges, but otherwise it is a very simple change and one that allows a proper clean out, with the bonus that it usually reveals some loose change that has been lost over the years.

Fig. 3.21 One long-standing gripe has been the poor carpet fit, especially around the door sills.

Fig. 3.22 The standard adhesive Velcro strips stuck between the carpet and sill to try and prevent carpet movement were a complete waste of time. Most fall off when the adhesive dries.

Fig. 3.23   Carpet change starts with seat removal and recovering small change.

Fig. 3.24   The rear Tee bar has to be lifted to enable the centre console to be removed.

Fig. 3.25   The interior microwave security unit has to be taken out, followed by the rear console.

Fig. 3.26   The main console remains to be lifted. If you wish to save having to lift the console, the one-piece TF carpet may be cut into two separate sections.

Fig. 3.27   Main console removal starts with taking out the kick panels that hold the footwell illumination.

RIGHT: Fig. 3.28 Removing the kick panels exposes two front fixing screws either side of the console. Note the central console section has already been detached.

Fig. 3.29   There are two rear console screws to remove.

LEFT: Fig. 3.30   The three bolts of the driver's foot rest are removed.

Fig. 3.31 Once a selection of carpet fixings have been removed the original individual carpets can now be lifted.

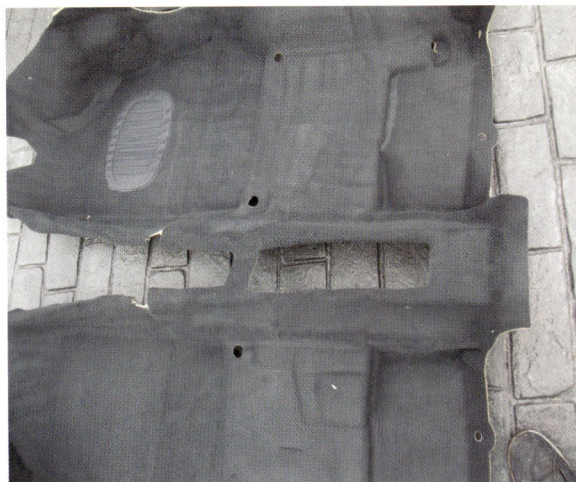

Fig. 3.32 The late TF carpet comes as a single piece and the joins are shown. The console has to be lifted to slide the carpet into place.

Fig. 3.33 The pre-mid 2003 cars used a separate window lift control, shown here covered with a spider's web of spray glue left over from an earlier attempt to hold the old carpet in place.

Fig. 3.34 The late TF did not have a window controller and so the carpet's insulation needs trimming.

Fig. 3.35 The original carpet insulation is used as a template so that the new insulation may be trimmed to fit over the control.

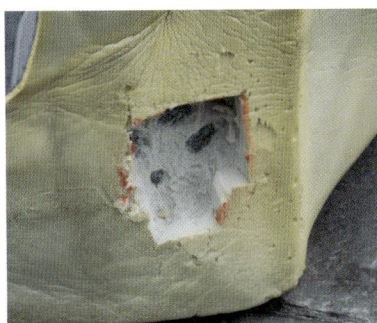

Fig. 3.36 The new carpet is fitted.

Fig. 3.37 The completed job.

CONTROLS AND FACIA

Driver Controls

While we are grovelling around the floor of the car it is pertinent to mention the rubbers on the brake and clutch pedals (the throttle is perforated metal). This is not a cosmetic issue but a safety one, as anyone who has got in a car with wet shoes and then slipped on a pedal without a rubber will testify. If your foot slips at low speed you will usually stall the car embarrassingly in the style of a learner's first lesson, but the consequences can be much more serious. Good availability of replaceable rubbers on the clutch and brake means this should not be overlooked.

The other main contact between driver and car is through the steering wheel. Here wear will often make the wheel uncomfortable and slippery to handle. This is more common with the leather trimmed wheels than the early standard MGF soft plastic wheel. Replacing a wheel is a job that has to be done with great care due to the presence of an airbag, but is otherwise straightforward.

A leather wheel in good condition gives a significant improvement over one that is worn or the plastic wheel. There is better control along with greater driving pleasure. There are many cosmetic options for standard leather wheels that cater for most applications, and when worn the wheel can be re-trimmed.

Facia Changes

Rarely should there be a need to

Fig. 3.38   Brake and clutch pedal rubbers need to be in good condition for safety reasons. These rubbers were standing up well after 90,000 miles.

remove or replace the facia unless damaged. In addition to the standard ash grey finish, four alternative colours were seen throughout MGF and TF production: walnut for the 2000 model year up until the end of MGF production; then light smokestone, grenadine and light tan for the TF.

I have owned cars with four out of the five options and have some experience driving cars with the fifth, so I feel I can pass comment. The ash grey was chosen for very sound reasons, as it is definitely more resilient to fading, but when the hood is raised the interior can feel dark and, in some conditions, depressing. Walnut, light tan and light smokestone provide a marked uplift in the same conditions, but fade more quickly than ash grey. Grenadine is a very strong colour making a specific statement, but like all red colours it can be more reactive to sunlight and so fading shows up more.

If looking to change the facia colour it is necessary to change the centre console, rear Tee bar and door cards to match. It is therefore logical to acquire a complete interior from another car, usually from a breaker's yard, or have your facia and other interior panels fully retrimmed.

Binnacle Cracking

Probably the most common problem encountered on the facia concerns the binnacle moulding breaking where it is held against the facia. The top of the facia has to withstand both direct sunlight and heat stress. The combination causes the plastic binnacle to crack around the screw fixings and eventually lift and rattle.

The official repair is to replace the whole facia. If this is done using a new moulding it can be very expensive: new facias are in short supply, partly owing to their bulk storage requirements and the number of different facias used over the production period of the MGF and TF.

After I noticed a crack develop in the lower edge of my MGF instrument

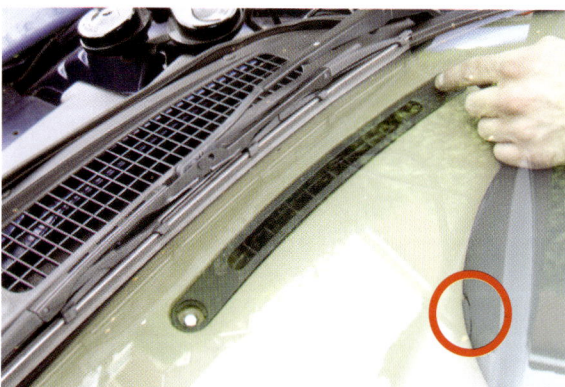

Fig. 3.39   The instrument binnacle base is screwed to the facia via three fixings that often break. Looking through the windscreen shows the small damage circled.

Fig. 3.40   Inside it can be seen that all three fixings are broken.

Fig. 3.41 Too many facia mouldings are poorly made. Continuous draughts are often due to poorly fitting ducting behind the main moulding, shown here by being able to slide a finger between duct and facia.

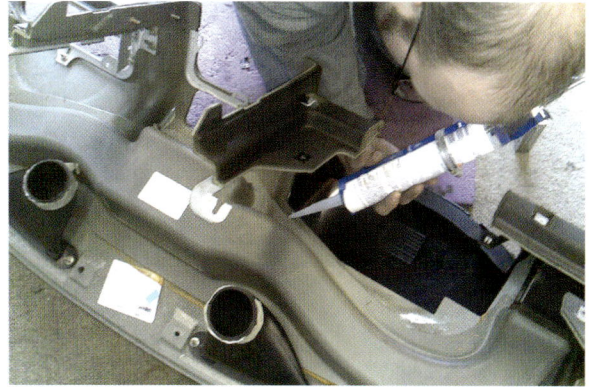

Fig. 3.42 The gap is rectified by adding silicone sealer.

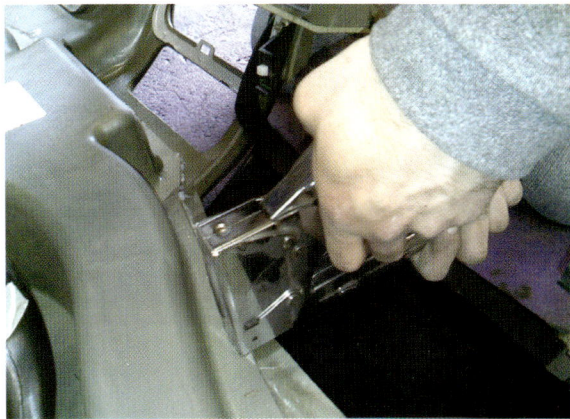

Fig. 3.43 The duct is then stapled to the facia.

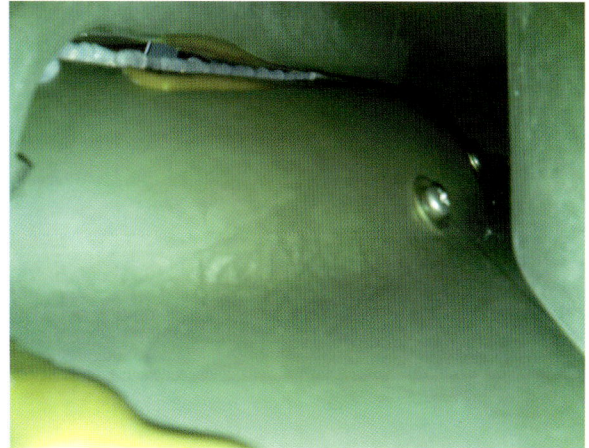

Fig. 3.44 Looking up the air duct, two of the three screws that hold the binnacle in place may be seen.

binnacle, I made a straw poll check on all the MGFs and TFs around the MG Owners Club headquarters on a normal weekday: five out of eleven cars had similar types of cracks to varying degrees. Time and usage will almost certainly guarantee that the proportion of cars affected will increase.

Logic would suggest that, as the binnacle is a separate part simply attached to the main facia, it ought to be possible to remove and replace it. Logic, unfortunately, doesn't work and the actual process is somewhat more complex. The main impediment to changing the binnacle in the same way it was originally fixed is the underlying construction of the facia, which demands a more imaginative approach.

The binnacle has a total of six fixing screws. The three screws around a supporting bracket that fits around the front edge present no problems. The three facia fixing screws, however, are fitted from under the facia up into the binnacle before the air ducting is glued to the back of the main facia moulding, so covering the screws.

A number of possible solutions may apply, depending on the condition of the various parts. If the problem is that the original screws have come loose and the binnacle is insecure, then a solution would be to wind out the screws so they drop into the air duct and allow the binnacle to be removed. Then fit plastic nut inserts into the vacated holes so that the screws can be refitted from the top, making removal in the future simpler.

In most cases, however, the binnacle is cracked around one or more fixings, and so it has to be replaced. Yet although the binnacle is clearly a separate part, it is not available as a new part and so replacement has to be with a second-hand unit.

While the use of nut inserts to allow the rear fixings to be top entry would avoid a facia removal, carrying out this operation would allow you to address the problem that many facias have poorly fitted air ducting. This is more likely to apply to older cars in which the main moulding has developed movement between the various

separate sub-mouldings behind the facia, resulting in the ducting pulling away from the facia and creating a permanent draught.

Removing the facia requires the removal or disconnection of battery, radio, centre console, heater controls, airbag(s), steering wheel, rotary coupler, steering column electrical switches and instruments. Before attempting any of this, refer once more to the safety warning about air bag removal that appears earlier in this chapter. The main element is to disconnect the battery and not do anything for at least fifteen minutes, so allowing time for any residual current to eek away to avoid inadvertent deployment of an airbag.

Lifting out and refitting the facia is a two-man job, so ensure a spare pair of hands are available for these operations. Otherwise it is a quite straightforward project for the average owner, and the illustrations give a flavour of what is involved.

Replacement of the binnacle sees removal of the supporting plastic frame, which has three screws fixing it to the

Fig. 3.45 As with all electrical work, the battery should be disconnected first, but make sure the key works the driver's door central locking to enable resynchronization of alarm fobs, and that any radio code is known.

Fig. 3.46 First take out the centre console.

Fig. 3.47 Next comes the instrument surround.

Fig. 3.48 This is followed by the instrument pack. (Note steering wheel also removed.)

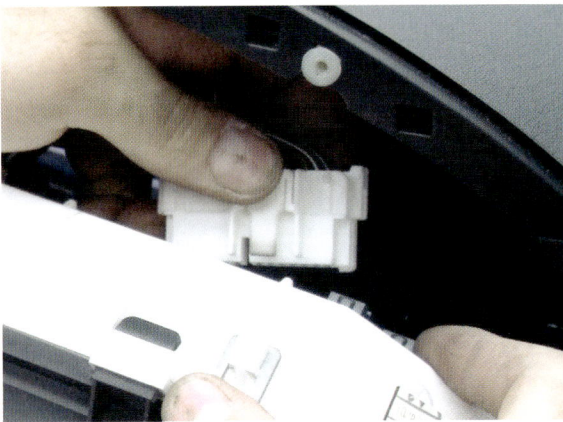

Fig. 3.49 The instrument pack can be moved out enough to disconnect the rear multi-plugs.

Fig. 3.50 Facia fixings start with the four bolts hidden under the caps at the ends of the demist vents. Half a turn with a washer in the slot releases the covers.

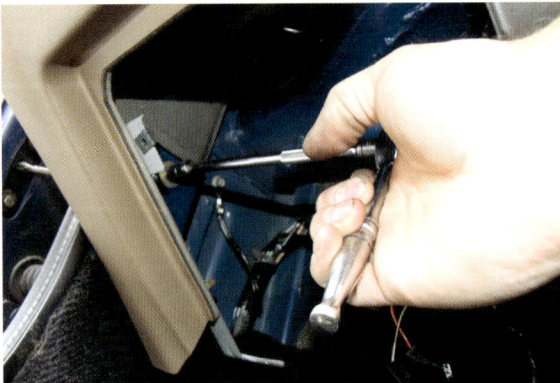

Fig. 3.51 The facia to body side fixings have to be removed.

Fig. 3.52 The four screws holding the heater controls to the facia come next.

Fig. 3.53   The facia can be eased out, preferably with a helper.

Fig. 3.54   The facia needs to be laid on some soft material so that the front binnacle fixings can be removed.

Fig. 3.55   Note that the small metal brackets are handed, so make a note of which way they come off.

Fig. 3.56   With the binnacle removed, the broken fixings are obvious. So is the effect of nine years of sunlight on the exposed sections.

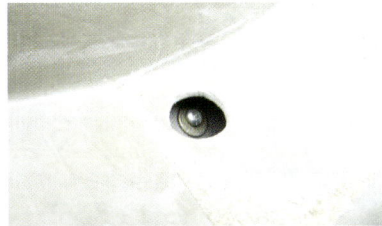

Fig. 3.57   20mm diameter holes were drilled to access the screws.

Fig. 3.58   Once the new binnacle was fitted the holes were filled with 20mm bungs on the flat section and a flexible rubber bung for the hole on the corner of the duct.

Fig. 3.59   The replacement was a reverse of the strip down.

curved front of the binnacle. Then at the bottom of each side of the binnacle front are two small metal brackets, each with two studs that sandwich the support frame and so need to be removed. Note that these brackets are handed, so make a visual note or stick on a bit of masking tape and write down which side is which.

In theory this leaves just the three screws holding the base of the binnacle to the facia. In my case, though, it turned out there was just one – and that was nearly cracked through. Moving it helped it fully break, leaving just the broken plastic stubs and the binnacle in the recycle bin.

I now moved to the underside of the facia and marked the approximate screw positions to cut access holes in the air duct. I chose to use a 20mm hole cutter to create a comfortable access hole that can be conveniently filled with 20mm bungs on completion. The resulting holes provided easy access to the screws and they were removed. The spire clips were swapped over to the new binnacle tabs, and the binnacle was fitted to the facia. Finally, the 20mm holes were plugged with bungs.

Refitting is very much a reversal of the removal process, but while the facia is out you have unrestricted access to the wiring and fittings that are normally hidden, such as the heater fan resistor. This is especially valuable if the car has air conditioning, as access to the resistor pack is otherwise impossible without first de-gassing the air con and removing the evaporator.

Sun Visor Droop

This may seem an unusual title, but it is a common problem where the

Fig. 3.60   The sun visors have an internal spring designed to push the visor up against the screen header when not in use, but if the spring is displaced the visor can sag.

Fig. 3.61   Repair is simple, starting with unclipping this plastic capping.

Fig. 3.62   The capping has been spot glued in the middle, so gently lever it up.

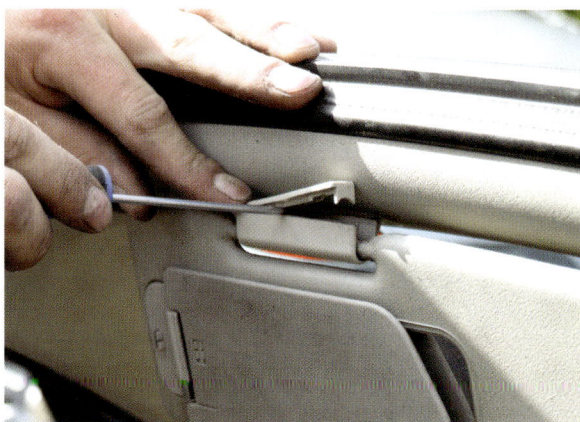

Fig. 3.63   Eventually the cap comes out.

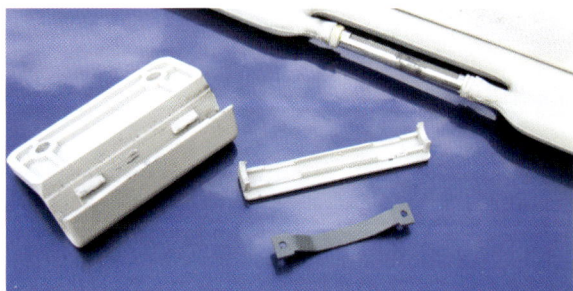

BOTTOM LEFT: Fig. 3.64   Leaving the visor in place held it steady to remove the cap, but now it can all be removed from the car ready for reassembly.
BOTTOM RIGHT: Fig. 3.65   The visor pivot rod is slid back into the plastic holder. The metal spring that will originally have been displaced then has to be fed in under the two plastic tags.

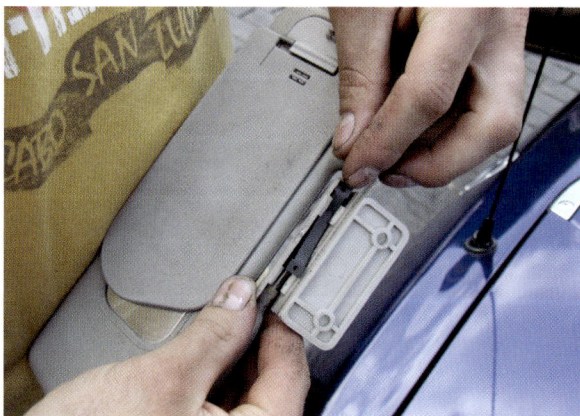

Fig. 3.66   This end is pushed under the other pair of plastic tags.

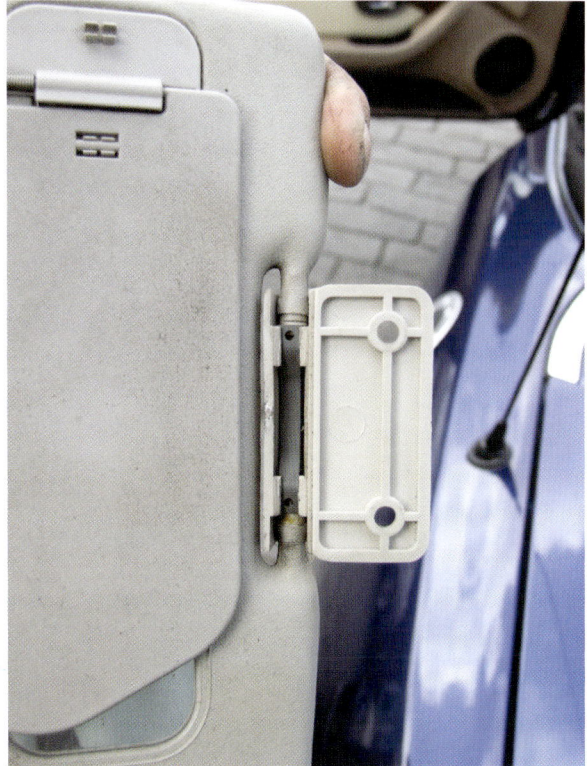

TOP RIGHT: Fig. 3.67   Once in position the end sits as shown.

ABOVE: Fig. 3.68   The plastic cap is refitted with just a spot of glue on either side at the centre point.

return spring within the sun visor base mounting has become displaced. To overcome this problem, the visor is removed and the cap, which was glued down during manufacture, is carefully cut open to reveal the spring and assembly. It is then simply reassembled and the top treated with a couple of dabs of superglue before being clipped back into place and held for the few seconds needed for the glue to go off.

The design of the visors is quite novel as it comes in a two-piece folding form, because a single-piece visor would conflict with the hood catches. It is more robust than it looks, but problems can arise with the small retaining clips that hold the folded sections together when not in use.

Hood Jamming

This is common and very frustrating for owners who do not know the simple temporary fix to prevent the jamming: gently pull backwards on the first hood cross spar rearwards of the header rail as the hood is lowered.

Fig. 3.69   The visor is then refitted to the car.

Fig. 3.70   It is common for MGF and TF hoods to jam when partially lowered.

Fig. 3.71   The first cross spar rearwards of the header rail is not being pulled back as the hood is lowered and locks the frame.

Fig. 3.72   Pull the hood back towards the screen enough to pull the cross spar rearwards and then lower the hood as normal.

There is also a permanent cure for this problem: fit a pair of additional elastic straps between each of the outer ends of the first and second cross spar of the hood frame. I say additional because, although there are elastic sections sewn into the longitudinally fitted hood webbing straps, this elastic is insufficient and also weakens too quickly.

Fitting the new additional straps is very simple in principle, but in practice it is a fiddle and the illustrations here are more effective than a bare description.

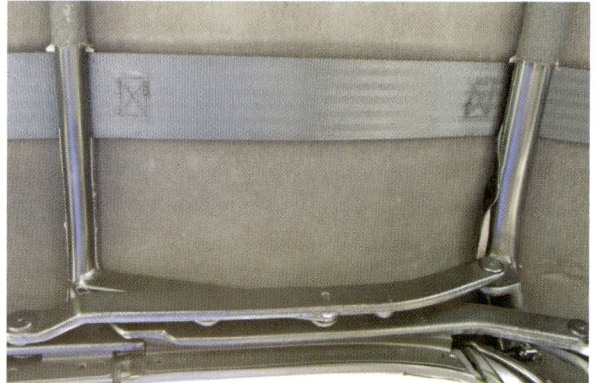

Fig. 3.73   The problem is that the elastic sewn into the strapping has weakened. The elastic sits between the strap and hood material and is not easily replaced.

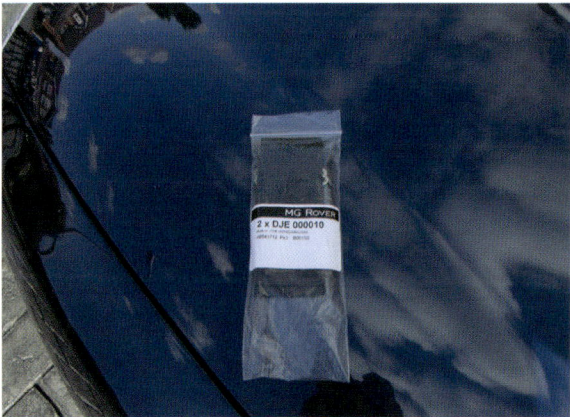

ABOVE: *Fig. 3.74   MG Rover developed a simple repair kit.*

MIDDLE RIGHT: *Fig. 3.75 The kit comprises two elastic straps.*

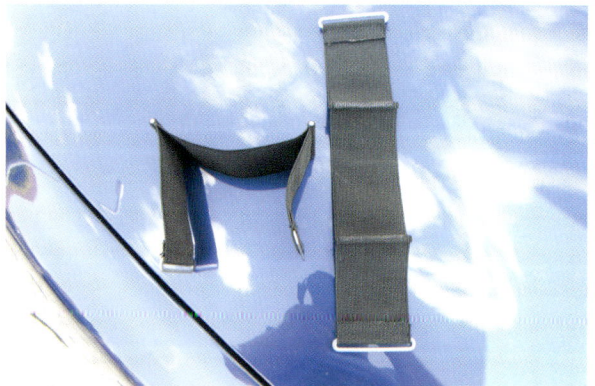

Fig. 3.76   A strap is fed around the first spar and fixed as shown (the steel pin has yet to be fully pushed home).

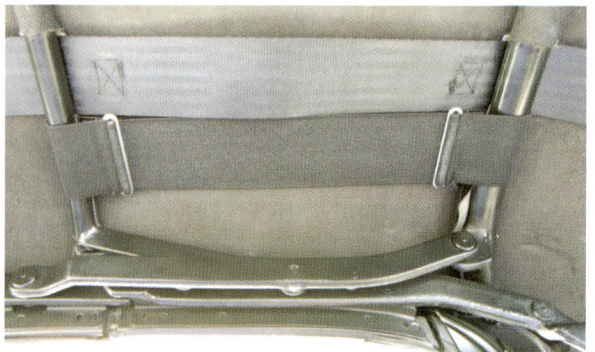

Fig. 3.77   The strap is then stretched to the second spar and fixed as shown. A second strap is used on the other side of the hood.

MG Rover's 'Project Drive'

Active cost-saving measures were introduced by MG Rover that effectively saw reductions in the equipment fitted to MG TFs from the end of 2002 to approximately the end of 2004, when some reversals of this process started. Obvious items removed were the plastic covers on the ends of the engine bay cover from the boot, the low note horn, the map pockets on the rear of the seats, the luggage net in the boot, and the standard supply of a hood cover.

Another item dropped with the introduction of the TF was the MGF's wheel arch edge protective strips, which help reduce paint damage on the lips of the arches. These are easily retrofitted, as are the second (high note) horn and the engine bay covers.

Fig. 3.78 MG Rover's 'Project Drive' saw equipment removed from the standard specification list, including the plastic ends from the grille covering the boot to engine bay aperture, here seen fitted on an MGF.

RIGHT: Fig. 3.79 The plastic ends are missing on this 2005 TF.

Fig. 3.80 One horn was also removed, but the wiring and plug remain.

Fig. 3.81 This makes it possible to retrofit the missing high tone horn.

Fig. 3.82 The MGF had a protective strip that slides over the edge of the wheel arch lip, but was deleted for the MG TF.

RIGHT: Fig. 3.83 The MGF items are easy and useful retrofits to the TF.

Fig. 4.1 Head gasket failures provide plenty of photo opportunities. Here elastomer sealing is lifting in the very common 'church windows' manner, so named because of the shape.

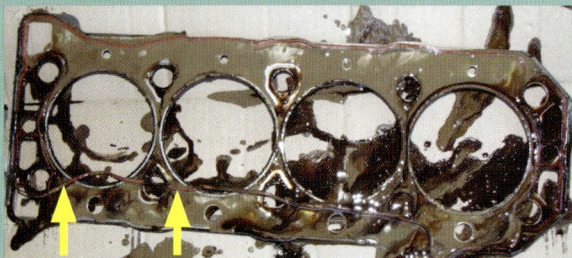

Fig. 4.3 This engine was used long after the driver should have stopped, which is by no means unusual.

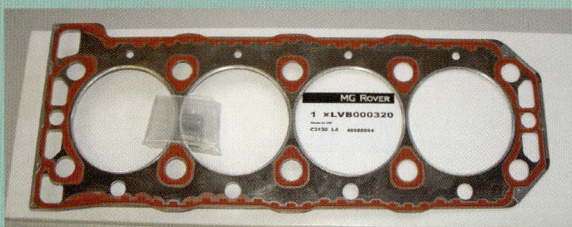

Fig. 4.4 An early 2005 specification MG Rover SLS gasket.

Fig. 4.2 Another failure on another engine in the same general area.

4

mechanical

ENGINE

K Series Engine: Synonymous with Head Gasket Failure (HGF)

It is an unfortunate fact that in general the public perception of the modern MGs is mostly related to 'weak engines', or simply that 'they all suffer from head gasket failures', something that Rover let develop in the late 1990s. Other manufacturers have had engines that suffer from similar reliability problems, but these were not usually allowed to reach epidemic proportions. In the case of the K series engine, however, the problem was aired twice on a prime time BBC TV consumer programme and this shows how high its profile reached.

The saying goes that there is no smoke without fire: this is quite true in respect of the K series engine, but not of all engines in the K series range. For a start the KV6 engines do not suffer a heavier rate of gasket failures than any other mainstream engines. The earlier 1989 to 1994 wet liner K series 4-cylinder engines also did not have the same depth of problems as the 'damp' liner 1600 and 1800cc engines that followed. The smaller 1400 and 1100 engines adopted the same block and liner changes, but didn't see the surge of HGF problems that affected the bigger capacity engines.

One variable influence on HGF characteristically affected all engines when new. This is that the full clamping force achieved within the engine was not seen until after the engine had experienced several full thermal cycles from reaching normal working temperature and then fully cooling off. This also saw some potential for the build-up of slightly different stress patterns within the engine that could add to the stress on the gasket and promote a slightly early HGF. Removing the head saw the clamping forces removed; when the engine was reassembled it would then be without any additional stress and nor would the engine see the thermal reaction of the new castings. (This is why many competition engine builders prefer used main engine castings to build their engines.)

Unfortunately I do not have access to factory records, which would give the best analysis of the HGF problem, but a good alternative comes from years of speaking with owners and collating their problems, together with a very healthy direct experience of replacing dozens of K series head gaskets on a range of K series-engined cars.

Further data comes from looking at a much larger number of suffering cars being dealt with workshops, including that of the MG Owners Club. I stopped counting some years ago after collecting the details of more than 1,200 cars, and this should provide a good sample from which to draw some general conclusions.

As most of these HGFs were with MGF and TFs, it is possible to deliver some focused facts. The main one is the type of failure, which in around 98 per cent of instances is the result of the degradation and displacement of the elastomer sealing strips that are bonded onto the original style head gaskets, known as the SLS gasket, a description I will expand on later.

The early MGFs were far more seriously affected than the later MGFs and TFs. Cars built up to 1999 would often see a first HGF occur between 20,000 and 30,000 miles from new, a wholly unacceptable situation. In those days of a twelve-month or 12,000 mile manufacturer's warranty, many failures fell outside the warranty, which caused heated disputes between owner and dealer, and also Rover. Although some owners were successful in gaining 'goodwill' from Rover where the car was shown to be not long out of warranty, had been dealer serviced and still had a low mileage, this failed to deal with the cause of the problem.

From the start of the 2000 model year the normal warranty period was increased to three years, which reflected Rover's belief that the problem was manageable and also brought many failures within warranty cover. My records indicate there was a useful reduction in the numbers of HGF, but the problem was far from eliminated.

In the spring of 2001 a small but significant change occurred with the use of steel dowels to locate the head onto the cylinder block, replacing nylon dowels. This reduced the potential for a condition known as 'head shuffle', where the movement of the head against the block would add extra stress on the head gasket. The use of nylon dowels may seem to have been an unwise one, but anyone with longer Rover engine experience will know how much of a problem steel dowels in alloy heads could potentially generate when the unlike metals chemically

Fig. 4.5   Steel dowels are not universal. These three pairs have all been supplied in gasket sets. Lengths and widths are fine, but the middle pair's inside diameter of 9mm makes them quite thin compared to the 7mm of the others. As they have chamfered ends, which make the fitting easier, the right pair is the ideal configuration.

bonded, sometimes leading to cylinder head damage requiring skimming or even replacement. Nylon, of course, suffered no such problems and its use in other Rover engines eliminated this problem completely and introduced no new issues.

On the K series, however, head shuffle was a more immediate problem than future sticking dowels, so the change to steel dowels extended that first failure mileage to the 40,000 plus mark. Another benefit of a steel dowel is that the front one also sees the cylinder head oil supply pass through the dowel, and the much tighter fitting steel dowel provided better oil sealing. With the nylon dowel instances of pressurized oil leaking were reported, occasionally causing elastomer failure. Steel dowels very quickly became the standard for all head gasket suppliers and new dowels are supplied in every head gasket kit I have seen since.

The MG TF arrived in January 2002 and with it came improved engine bay airflow, which reduced average temperatures in the engine bay by approximately 20 per cent (14°C), but this did not have a major impact on the average failure mileage for these early TFs compared to the last MGFs. In mid-2003 there was a significant change

from the original thermostat to what is called the Pressure Relief Thermostat (PRT; *see* 'Cooling Systems'). This change saw a noticeable drop in early failures and pushed the average mileage HGF closer to the 60,000 mile mark.

What is very important to understand is that the PRT is not a cure on its own, just a means of significantly delaying the earlier than expected failure that will occur when using the original style gasket. For the benefit of owners of 2003 registered TFs, the actual VIN number change point when the PRT was introduced is RD 622951, which relates on the production line to approximately June 2003. Instead of grovelling under the car to see if there is a PRT next to the exhaust manifold, just look at the VIN. If the listed number is higher than this, then it left Longbridge with a PRT.

This subject highlights an important check that should be done at service time. In order to ensure that exhaust heat has not damaged the nearest hose to the downpipes, and that the protective 'socks' wrapped around the hoses are intact, squeeze the hoses to see if they are in danger of cracking up. Replace crunchy hoses before they dump your coolant or cause more overheating damage.

Fig. 4.6   The positioning of the PRT means that hoses are close to the exhaust manifold and it is important to appreciate that heat damage is very possible. This is why the original hoses should have a protective 'sock' material around them for heat and abrasion protection. This car's sock can be seen to have heat damage.

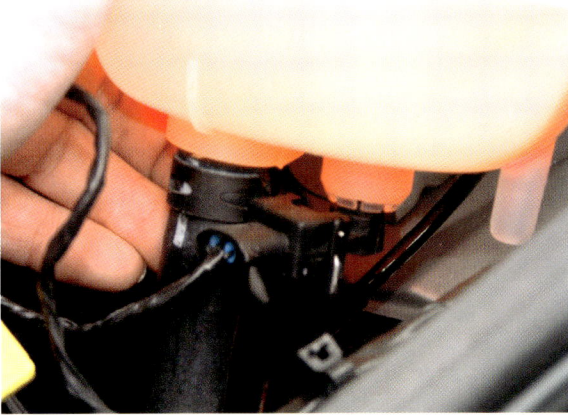

Fig. 4.7   2004 model year TFs gained a very useful low coolant warning system using a sensor in the expansion tank.

Fig. 4.8   Probably the biggest single step forward for K series reliability was the introduction of the Multi-Layer steel Shim (MLS) gasket.

Fig. 4.9   The MLS gasket comprises a single main shim and two subordinate shims either side, resulting in a five-layer gasket to which is added a further plain shim to go between the gasket and head face.

Fig. 4.10   Part of the Euro IV compliance programme included an uprated lower rail (top) to add stiffness to the engine 'sandwich'. This was made from tougher aluminium, 30 per cent heavier, and had a more robust layout.

The last specification change during the MG Rover period was made in mid-2004 when a coolant low level warning light was added to the standard dash warning lights. This was a useful addition that allows owners to be aware and react to coolant loss before overheating, potential HGF or worse occurs.

Before Powertrain Ltd went under as part of MG Rover's collapse, the company had set the specifications for the forthcoming Euro IV specification engines that would be required from the start of 2006, but would be introduced around six months before to ensure that all cars being sold at

Fig. 4.12   The new lower rail included stronger through bolts with flat ends and marked with 10.9 on the heads.

Fig. 4.13   The uprated bolts (right) are listed under part number WAM2293SLP, and the SLP is important as without that suffix code the old pattern bolts are supplied.

Fig. 4.11   The new lower rail has been fitted. (Austin Garages)

the start of the changed requirements would comply. Powertrain had already started production of these new Euro IV specification engines for the Land Rover Freelander and approximately 3,000 were reputedly delivered, which allowed Freelander production to continue for some months until nearly the end of 2005. This means that no MG or Rover production car ever saw the uprated engine, as they were still a few weeks away from introduction for the Longbridge cars.

We now jump forward more than three years from when the last MG Rover TFs were made to August 2008, which saw the restart of MG Motor TF production at Longbridge with the Euro IV specification engines, now officially labelled the N series, although this can be seen as an uprated K series. The changes made to comply with the Euro IV requirements are significant and include the introduction of the MLS gasket (Multi-Layer steel Shim). There was also an uprated lower rail, into which are screwed the long through bolts that hold the engine sandwich together, and new stretch bolts.

These changes were of great significance. The new gasket had a series of metal shims with an embossed pattern to replace the sealing functions of the elastomer material used on the SLS gasket. What this means in simple terms is that the item that accounts for around 98 per cent of all original SLS gasket failures was replaced with something that simply can't be degraded or displaced. No single element of change on its own should be seen as a one-stop cure, but to achieve the best reliability all these changes should be incorporated to mimic the final MG Motor specification.

How this benefits earlier engines is that these new parts are directly interchangeable with any K series engine made from 1989, so all earlier engines can benefit from these new parts in a simple one-for-one replacement of the old parts for new.

The Anatomy of HGF

To appreciate the benefits offered by the MLS gasket design, you first need to know the background to the failure of the original SLS gasket and a more detailed understanding of the design,

Fig. 4.14   The block and liners exposed to show the general layout and proximity of one liner to the next.

including its good points, as it is not a bad design in itself. The good points can be seen in race engines, where power outputs of up to 300bhp and up to 8,500rpm may be reached with reliability on the track. What is pertinent here is that race engines see quite regular rebuilds, meaning that the head gasket will be changed relatively frequently. While the gasket is clearly capable of absorbing such stresses, it is the slow and continuous degradation from longer exposure to heat that affects road cars.

Looking at the heat management of the engine helps to illustrate why these problems occur. First, the original wet liner engines made up to mid-1994 were available only in 1100 and 1400cc. In addition they were predominantly single cam, 8-valve engines, with the 16-valve versions confined to the sports models. The considerably reduced mass of the 8-valve head provides a better path to transfer heat out of the engine, significantly aided by these engine being less powerful and obviously producing less heat. It is no surprise to see 8-valve engines, especially the least powerful 1100cc versions, able to break the 100,000 mile barrier before HGF occurs. Conversely, the 1400cc twin cam 16-valve versions would fail perhaps 25,000 miles earlier.

The 1600cc K series appeared in mid-1994, followed by the 1800cc versions in the MGF. These larger displacements introduced a change from the wet liner configuration to a mix of wet and dry liner characteristics, so these later K series engines were described as 'damp' liner engines. The bore of the two larger capacity engines was

increased from 75mm to 80mm; to accommodate this increase, the liners when fitted into the block saw greatly reduced gaps between each liner for coolant flow than was available in the wet liner design. This change of liner design was also common to the 1100 and 1400cc engines. While the 75mm bore still applied to these smaller capacities, the external liner dimension, and so the reduced coolant flow around the liners, was common to all engines.

The coolant flow comes in via the water pump into the block's coolant gallery on the back (inlet side) of the engine, providing excellent coolant flow around the inlet side of all liners. Coolant then flows up into the cylinder head passages and some is intended to flow down into the block's coolant gallery on the exhaust side of the liners to assist the flow that can seep past the liners.

This results in slower heat extraction from the exhaust side of the engine and in turn this sees higher temperatures being seen around parts of the gasket. These are simply too hot for the elastomer to retain reliability over the long term, leading to slow progressive degradation until displacement and loss of seal occurs. Obviously the larger capacity engines produce more heat and this is why these engines generally suffer HGF earlier than smaller capacity engines.

The nature of the elastomer degradation is visually quite obvious on a failed gasket, with the exhaust side seeing a slightly darker colour than the unaffected elastomer on the inlet side (unless the engine has suffered

TOP LEFT: *Fig. 4.15   This engine shows how a huge mix of oil and coolant develop into a creamy mess instead of just coolant.*

BELOW LEFT: *Fig. 4.16   In some cases the mix comes through the breather system into the whole intake area. Here it is heavily contaminating the area from the air filter to throttle hose.*
BELOW RIGHT: *Fig. 4.17   More was found streaming through the inlet manifold.*

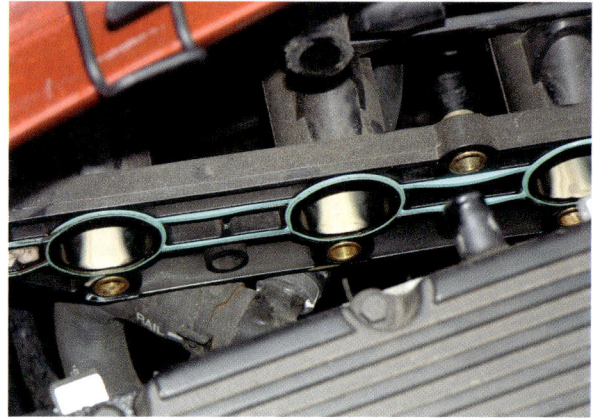

a serious overheat). In addition, the affected elastomer will feel 'mushy' compared to the firmer, unaffected sections, and in many areas simply feeling the elastomer will see it easily detach from the steel backing shim, if it is not already detached.

There are three common areas affected by the elastomer failure that is at the core of almost all HGFs. The first is on the exhaust side around what are known as 'church windows', a description that becomes obvious when you look at the shape of the elastomer around each hole through which a long through bolt passes (*see* Figs 4.1 and 4.2 above). This type of failure allows coolant to enter the sump and the characteristic sight of creamy mayonnaise spots on the dipstick, progressing to more consistent contamination. If left to develop further, it is not uncommon to see oil become a completely blended, creamy liquid.

Second, it is not unusual for oil to get into the cooling system, with the same creamy deposits appearing in the header tank. When these are fresh, indicating a current and developing problem, they are soft and sticky to touch as well as being light coloured. If they are a more golden to light brown colour and have a skin when touched, they are older and may be deposits not cleaned out following a previous head gasket replacement.

The last of the common elastomer failure variations is where the sealing strip on the outside edge of the gasket, on the exhaust side of course, fails and allows coolant to escape outside the engine. This type of failure can be slow and annoying in that weeping from the head/block area near the alternator occurs during warm-up, but then

Fig. 4.18   It made its way to the coolant in the header tank, before it was drained.

Fig. 4.19   And all the way through to the radiator, illustrated here on a Rover 218Vi with HGF.

Fig. 4.20   Head gasket failure is not always due to failed elastomer, but in this case head face damage/erosion under the fire ring of number one cylinder provided a leak path.

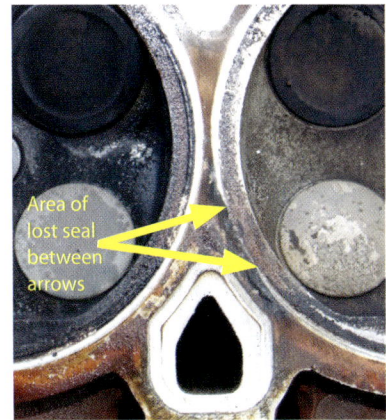

Area of lost seal between arrows

Fig. 4.21   The leak path can be seen more clearly in this image.

Fig. 4.22   Even when the head was cleaned it still showed as indented.

Fig. 4.23   Light skimming of the surface was required.

stops after about five minutes. This leads to a very slow coolant loss that many find difficult to locate, but the presence of dried antifreeze on the block face behind the exhaust manifold often gives a clue to the problem. Occasionally the failure can become quite spectacular as the displacement of the elastomer strip is usually quite sudden under pressure within the cooling system. This sees a jet of hot coolant sprayed onto a much hotter exhaust and the steam cloud generated often makes people assume the car is actually on fire. Indeed, calls to the fire brigade are not unknown.

I must also mention another form of cylinder seal failure, although this is not always a gasket failure, but sometimes a bypass of the gasket due to a head face defect. The result allows coolant to enter the combustion chamber. Initially it is seen as an engine that starts on three cylinders and usually clears to run on four after a few seconds. As the condition worsens the period of running on three cylinders gets longer and it can also develop into sudden overheating when combustion gases are able to enter the cooling system. This eventually creates an 'air lock' that stops coolant flow, followed by rapid overheating.

Fig. 4.24   Combustion gas in the cooling system can be tested with a professional test that uses a reactive fluid.

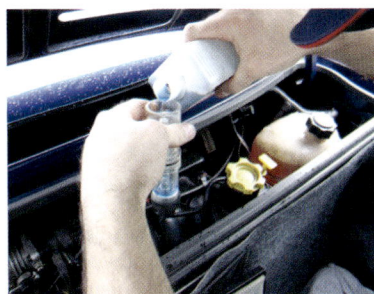

Fig. 4.25   The reactive fluid is poured into a special applicator placed on the open expansion tank.

Fig. 4.26   The gas/air is drawn from above the coolant. If the presence of combustion gases is detected the liquid turns from blue to amber/yellow.

Combustion gas in the cooling system should be detectable by professional 'sniffer tests'. The crudest is to get an exhaust gas analyser to 'sniff' the air above the coolant in the header tank, but that runs the risk of coolant being sucked up and damaging the analyser. The professional way involves a 'sniffer tool' that draws the air above the coolant through a reactive fluid, but this relies on the expansion tank not having been opened recently and letting these gases escape. The illustrations show how the test is done.

A bigger danger from this sort of fault, however, is for coolant to be able to enter the combustion chamber. This can create a hydraulic lock of the engine and give every indication that the starter motor is faulty and has lost the power to turn the engine. If the cause is indeed coolant in a cylinder, an owner who then looks to tow start his engine may well end up with a broken engine. The energy of a tow start can prove the principle that fluids can't be compressed: when the piston in the affected cylinder rises and is then stopped by the fluid, the energy has to go somewhere and that usually sees the liner shatter like a grenade and/or the con rod bends, sometimes causing piston damage. Note that when cylinders number one or four on an MPi engine with the plastic inlet manifold are the ones affected, then the ingress of coolant may be due to failure of the inlet to head seal (*see* the section on cooling systems below).

More recently, my MGF using an MLS gasket experienced a more unusual HGF failure after 41,000 miles: the fire ring edges on the underside of the gasket had eroded away to a point where combustion gas leaking into the cooling system caused air locks and loss of coolant flow.

Quite what caused this specific failure is unclear, but one of the engineers for the K series confirmed that erosion to the gasket fire rings was not something he had seen during their durability testing. Apparently during the hot testing that was part of the MLS development project, MLS-equipped engines were still failing the durability test after around 40 per cent of the test duration. Erosion damage was found on the head face, caused by localized boiling of coolant, so they added the additional steel shim between gasket and head to cure that. The boiling issue was due to too little coolant being in certain areas of the gasket. While it was damaging the alloy, I do wonder if the same condition was at the root of my gasket's damage.

The boiling issue was not present with the original SLS gasket because there is the thickness of just a single gasket shim in areas where the gasket is being sandwiched between head and block, leaving space for coolant flow between this shim and the block and head. When the MLS gasket is fitted there are five shim layers and this significantly reduces the space for coolant flow in these tight spots. This significantly reduced coolant volume is then more prone to boiling in hot spots.

Fig. 4.27 In extreme cases coolant leaks into cylinders can 'grenade' the cylinders affected.

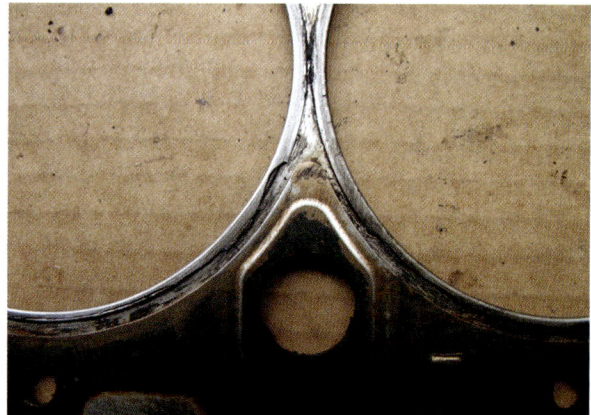

Fig. 4.28 A failed MLS gasket. Note specifically the fire rings that should be sealing the cylinders and the edges that resemble saw teeth.

Fig. 4.29 This was found on all fire rings on the underside of the gasket and contacting the liners.

Fig. 4.30 A look at a new gasket confirms the state of the damage.

This was not the whole story, however, as the reduced space for flow was being exacerbated by the lower coolant flow found with the original thermostat configuration. When the PRT was fitted, with its significantly increased flow on the bypass circuit and reaction to pressure changes, this increased flow in the tight spots completely cured the boiling issue.

He also mentioned that some of the main 'through' bolts to the original specification were not always reliable and would lose their elasticity after being fitted, and the clamping load would be lost with obvious consequences to head gasket performance. It is for this reason that the 10.9 specification bolts were introduced along with the MLS gasket when the MG Motor TF arrived.

Routes to a Reliable K Series Engine

Clearly there is a strong case to mimic the specification of the MG Motor TF for better reliability. While this is not always going to be possible, other measures can be taken to reduce the chances that you will be left stranded at the side of the road with a cooked engine. I must emphasize that it is very unusual for HGF to occur suddenly without prior warning, and the first signs may appear up to twelve months before the major failure. In nearly all cases there will be a continuing coolant loss, but this on its own is not conclusive of HGF, as leaks can occur elsewhere.

What is always needed is corroboration, and this most commonly comes from seeing the emulsification of coolant/oil mix in the oil on the dipstick, around the oil filler neck, although traces of emulsification in cars that are infrequently used or make journeys of less than five miles in winter can sometimes just be down to condensation. The next most common symptom is a clear external coolant leak from the exhaust side of the join line between head and block. When a HGF has been confirmed by the corroboration of at least two conditions, it is amazing that some owners still put off doing anything to correct the problem. Many only react when the engine fails in a big way, which usually involves significant overheating and damage.

In standard operation the K series can suffer annealing (softening) of the head face material due to the high temperatures that are seen on the exhaust side of the engine. What this means is that clear and very obvious half-moon shaped grooves appear on the exhaust side of the head face, caused by the gasket fire rings being pressed into the softened alloy. Very slight marking of a head face that you can run a fingernail across without it catching can be machined off and the engine may still usually give reasonable service, but where the grooves are deep enough to trip over then skimming on

Fig. 4.31   When HGF is allowed to develop to the point where the engine stops, the coolant turns to a light tar.

Fig. 4.32   The head gasket becomes a gooey mess.

Fig. 4.33   As well as the head face being covered in the tar, the gasket fire rings have sunk deep into the softened head face leaving deep grooves that scraps the head.

Fig. 4.34   This engine was run until it just stopped and all the plastics started to melt, with the cam cover reduced to a blob.

Fig. 4.35   The spark plug cover blended into the HT leads.

Fig. 4.36   The distributor cap was well on the way to joining the cam covers.

Fig. 4.37   Surprisingly, though, the plastic inlet manifold was just melting at the join onto the cylinder head.

Fig. 4.38   When a head anneals (softens) the gasket fire rings sink into the head material, always on the hotter exhaust side, leaving clear grooves. Skimming alone fails to solve this as it will recur as soon as the head is refitted.

its own is a waste of time as the new gasket fire rings will have created new grooves within the first fifty miles of use. It is a gamble whether the problem recurs within a few hundred miles or a few thousand. It is possible to have the head face treated to reinstate the appropriate hardness, but this is a very specialized process and access to this will normally be very limited.

The only long-term cure is to replace the head or use a Payen, Gosney or similar 'head saver shim', which come in various dimensions, commonly between 0.025in and 0.036in (0.6– 0.9mm) thick. The rigidity of these stainless steel shims spreads the loads coming from the gasket fire rings across the head face, so preventing any more damage. They can be used with either SLS or MLS gaskets.

Before looking at MLS gaskets in more detail, I have an observation relating to service life following replacement of an SLS gasket with another SLS gasket. When the job was done properly and there was no rapid repeat failure due to a fault being overlooked, it was common for the second gasket to last between 1½ times to twice the mileage that the engine covered before the first HGF.

The earlier mention of the MLS design has already described it as a series of steel layers. In the Land Rover, XPart and SAIC supplied parts, and most of the aftermarket alternatives. The construction consists of a main shim to which are attached two upper and two lower embossed subordinate shims (see Figs 4.8 and 4.9 above).

Since the MLS gaskets cannot suffer the same degradation and displacement to which the SLS gasket was prone, they would need to physically break up to achieve the same failure. That doesn't mean leakage is not impossible, and it has been reported on a few early MLS gaskets, but importantly it was not necessarily a gasket issue and this time the coolant loss is

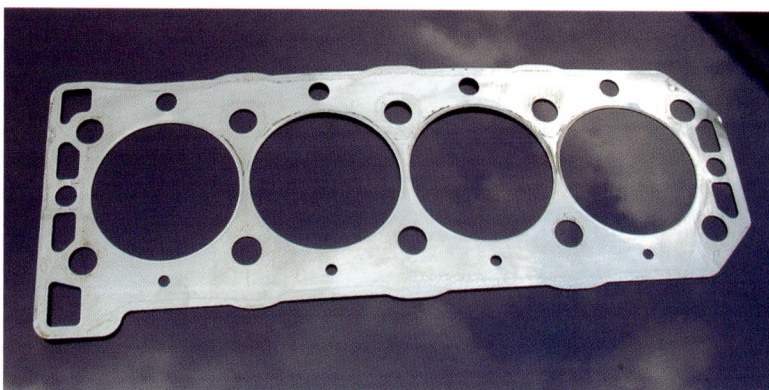

Fig. 4.39   A 'Head Saver Shim', like this one from Payen, is fitted as a solution.

more an annoying weep. When selecting specific MLS gaskets, I have not found fault with 'original factory' supplied gaskets from SAIC (MG Motor), Land Rover and Xpart, but I have with some aftermarket products.

Five years of experience with the MLS gaskets has given some insight into the characteristics of the design and how important it is to check the dimensions by which the liners stand proud and ensure they sit within the acceptable limits. Apart from this, the SLS gasket seems to have greater flexibility and gives a better seal, but if the dimensions are out the only advice is to correct it. Many will not fancy rebuilding the engine, however, and will often opt for the more palatable route of using another SLS gasket and replacing this when it fails again. Unfortunately many owners will see this as the cheapest route to get the car working properly again, at least for long enough to sell the car and leave the new owner facing the possible cost of a replacement engine.

On the brighter side, the majority of engines will work very well with the MLS gasket and, when the whole HGF repair is done properly, excellent long-term service should be achieved, much longer than with the SLS gasket. The MLS gasket, however, is not the only improvement that can be made to enhance an engine's long-term reliability.

Head Gasket Replacement

This is one of those jobs that has

Fig. 4.40   Contrary to a popular misconception, head removal is certainly possible with the engine still in an MGF or TF. (Austin Garages)

gained such a high profile and been so well covered in manuals, magazine features and within MG Club circles that there is no justification for repeating them here in a step by step guide. There are, however, some hints and tips that might be helpful.

The first comment to make is that, contrary to an all too common misconception, you can remove the cylinder head on an MGF or TF from the top and it doesn't require taking the engine out of the car. It is clearly not as simple or accessible as doing effectively the same job on an MG ZR, but it is the same job nevertheless: if you would consider tackling a head gasket on a ZR then there is nothing to stop you doing the same on an MGF or TF. The big difference is the reduced access: it takes twenty seconds to open the bonnet on

a front-wheel drive car, while accessing the engine bay on the MGF and TF takes twenty minutes!

Pre-work considerations should include thoughts on whether the time is right to replace the cambelt: I would always suggest that unless a belt has done less than 20,000 miles, or is less than two years old, it should be renewed even though the workshop manual guide states not to replace unless it has over 48,000 miles. If the belt is young enough, undamaged and not contaminated with oil you may allow it to be reused, marking the direction of rotation it has been working with chalk. Simply renew it if you have any doubt about it. Remember too that the belt tensioner must also be in tip-top condition, so for simplicity adopt the same principle of renewal.

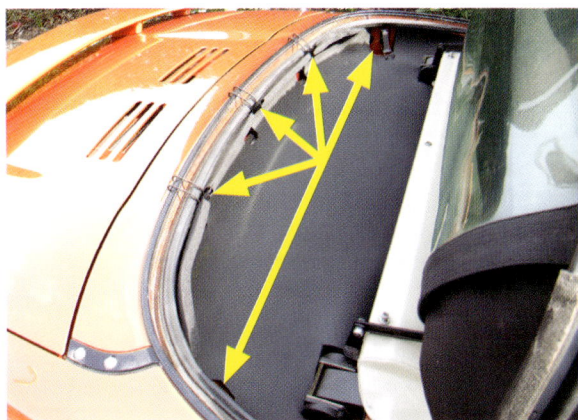

Fig. 4.41   Access to the engine bay starts by unclipping the hood from the windscreen to reduce tension. From the inside unclip the five spring clips that hold the hood to the rear deck. The rear of the hood is then lifted out of the rear deck channel.

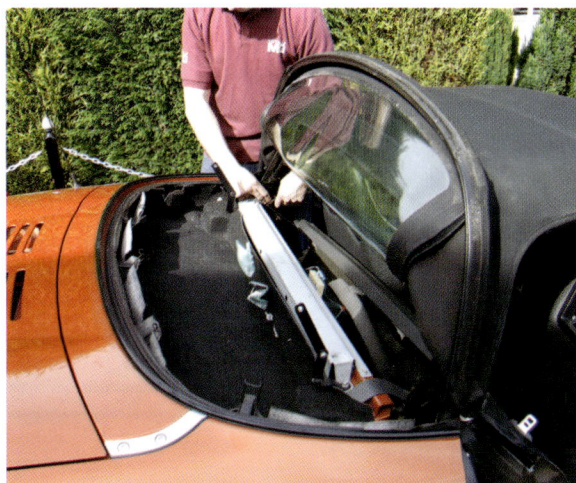

Fig. 4.42   If the weather is cold, unzip the rear plastic window; otherwise very carefully roll the window to avoid cracking.

Fig. 4.43   A 'bungee' strap is ideal to hold up the rear section.

Fig. 4.44   The rear engine cover carpet is exposed.

Fig. 4.45   Below the carpet is a layer of insulation.

Fig. 4.47   There are two extra 10mm headed bolts on TFs for the rear body bracing bars.

Fig. 4.46   The main engine cover and, just visible, the round fuel tank sender/pump access covers. Access to the MGF engine involves removing eleven 10mm headed bolts, three of which are hidden under the speaker box.

Fig. 4.48   Removing the bolts gives access to the top of the engine.

Fig. 4.49   If a belt tensioner fails then so does the cam timing, meaning valves and pistons make contact. A broken valve head means that a head is just scrap.

Fig. 4.50   A broken valve head loose in the cylinder soon trashes it.

Fig. 4.51   Bent valves are a less dramatic consequence of lost cam timing. All 16 valves shown here have been bent.

Fig. 4.52   Recovered bits of broken valve guide.

LEFT: Fig. 4.53   The source of the broken debris.

RIGHT: Fig. 4.54   Water pumps are prone to leaking at even quite low mileages. Since the cambelt drives the water pump, it is always best to renew the pump when the belt is changed. The clear pink antifreeze stains are from organic acid technology (OAT) coolant.

The manual tensioner (on all VVC engines and non-VVC engines to late 1998) has been known to suffer a failed bearing. If that happens the engine will be seriously damaged. On the other hand the non-VVC engine's auto tensioner, which was introduced in late 1998 and was then standard on all the non-VVC engines that followed, is much kinder to the belt and itself.

Another commonly forgotten aspect of the main cambelt is that it drives the water pump, so cambelt removal allows access to the pump. Since water pumps are well known for early leaks, it is an ideal time to simply replace it while the belt is off.

Head Removal

Looking at various ways of removing the head will dictate a different focus on what is removed and when. Looking at the non-VVC models using the plastic inlet manifold, it is a major fiddle to access the four 10mm headed bolts that hold the lower flanges of the inlet to the head, although the three upper nuts are much easier. It is quite possible to remove the head with the plastic inlet still fitted and this offers some relief from not just the removal of the manifold to head fixings, but even more so the fiddlier job of refitting them. The same basic approach applies to VVC and other engines with the alloy inlet, as the plenum can be removed separately. The two extra upper fixing bolts, used with the alloy inlet to help support its extra weight, are still easily accessed though.

Removing the head with either manifold requires the removal of a range of electrical plugs, throttle cable, vacuum lines and hoses (air and coolant), all of which are quite visible and accessible.

Three types of HT lead arrangements exist. The pre-2001 non-VVC distributor cap on the end of the inlet cam is best removed along with the rotor arm and HT leads, except for the king (HT) lead

from the coil, as this can simply be disconnected from the cap and laid out of the way. Then there is the pre-2001 VVC, which has four very long HT leads running down to two double output coils mounted way under the inlet manifold against the engine block. These should be labelled for easier identification later (if not already so labelled) and laid to one side.

Last, there are the 2001 and later set-ups that have two double output coils mounted on top of the engine/ Here you need to disconnect the two wiring plugs to remove these and the

cable from the head and lay them to one side. Note the coil at the front end of the engine has its electrical plug restricted by the cam cover, so the coil has to be removed before the plug can be detached, and then the coils are removed. Note also that these later spec engines also have a cam sensor and the main wiring loom connection at the gearbox end of the head has to be unplugged.

One simple pipe connection that seems to catch out many, leading to a broken sealing clip, is the removal of the brake servo plastic pipe from the

Fig. 4.55   MGF MEMS 1.9 systems use a distributor cap and rotor arm, clearly seen here with light blue HT leads.

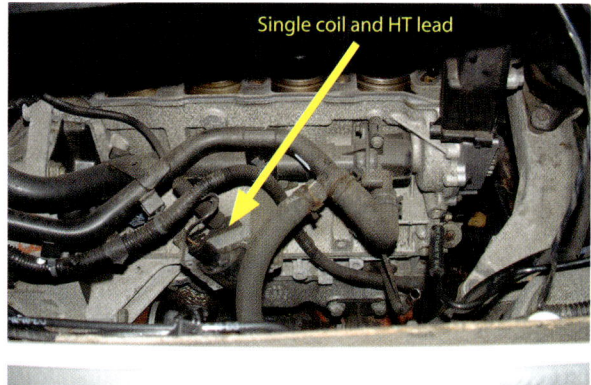

Fig. 4.56   The singe coil of the MGF MEMS 1.9 system is mounted to the block under the inlet manifold.

Fig. 4.57   MEMS 2J systems have two double output coils mounted, where the MEMS 1.9 system coil was mounted with four very long HT leads running to individual plugs. Here the four HT leads can be seen rising up at the end of the engine.

Fig. 4.58   The HT leads of a MEMS 2J system coil.

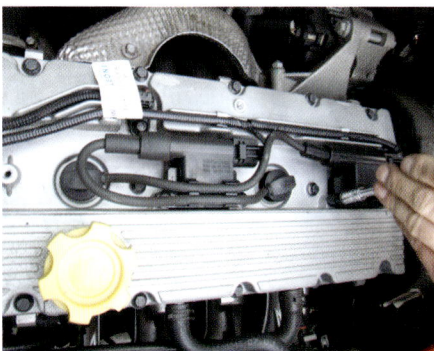

LEFT: Fig. 4.59   MEMS 3 also has two coils, but now each coil is mounted onto one spark plug and very short HT leads run from each coil to the other two plugs.

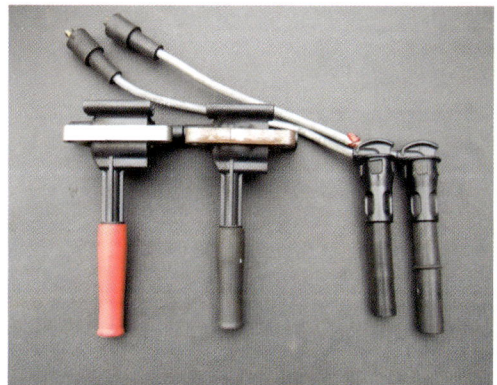

Fig. 4.60   A very important consideration with MEMS 3 coils and HT leads is that the VVC spark plugs are located slightly deeper into the cylinder head and need longer coils and HT leads. Coils are identified using red insulators.

Fig. 4.61 *Releasing the vacuum pipe holding the brake servo into the inlet plenum chamber requires simply pressing in the red clip. Hold it there as you draw the vacuum pipe out.*

Fig. 4.62 *The same sealing clip is used for the dipstick and oil filler neck where it joins the dipstick tube. In this case the clip is broken and there has been a minor oil leak.*

Fig. 4.63 *This cracking of the dipstick and oil filler neck support bracket is very common.*

Fig. 4.64 *A simple weld is needed to affect a cure for a reasonable period, although over time it may well crack again alongside the weld.*

the oil filler/dipstick to the manifold. Check the steel bracket as all too often these are cracked through fatigue, and I regularly find myself welding them up.

Even professionals can get mixed up when refitting the VVC actuator plugs. It does not help that there are two colour configurations, one for MEMS2J (up to 2000) and one for MEMS 3 (2001 on). The illustrations show the correct configuration of the two different types. Note that the 60-degree difference in the actuator plug positions is correct, as they must not be lined up.

At this point you will have removed the cambelt. Yes, the workshop manual is correct and you *do* need to remove both cam wheels and the M6 bolts holding the cambelt rear cover to the cylinder head before being able to lift the head. This is because the belt cover doesn't just attach to the head, but goes well below. Only when someone has previously taken to butchery and broken or cut the cambelt rear cover is this avoided, but I do not recommend

manifold: push in the red clip and then the pipe slides out, but force it and the clip breaks.

While removing the vacuum connections near the throttle body on the plastic inlet, take care as these moulded-in stubs are part of the

manifold and will easily break when you are trying to remove a hose stuck in place from years of being undisturbed.

As plastic inlets are so light they do not need the support leg required by the VVC's alloy inlet. You just have to remove the bolt and spacer holding

Fig. 4.65 *MEMS 2J VVC may use the same hardware, but the wiring plug connections vary. Note that the brown is on the HCU oil temp sensor and the black on the inboard VVC actuator.*

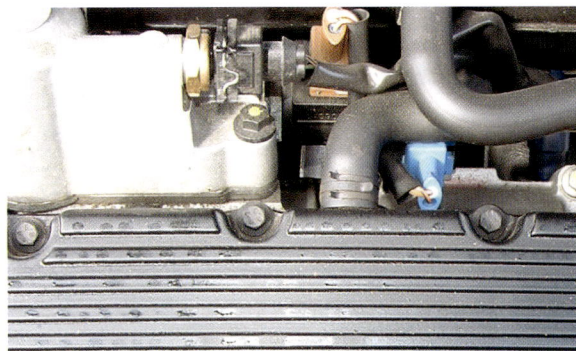

Fig. 4.66 *On the MEMS 3 VVC the plugs change places: the black now sits on the oil temperature sensor on the HCU and the brown moves to the inboard VVC actuator. Note that the VVC actuator plugs are at the correct angle of 60 degrees.*

Fig. 4.67   A cam wheel locking tool is a 'must have' gadget, preferably the blue metal one.

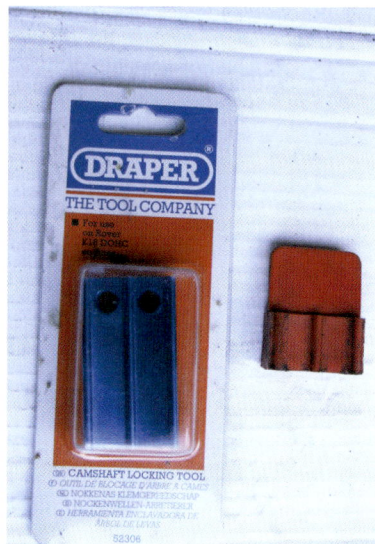

Fig. 4.68   A red plastic cam wheel locking tool is not recommended.

doing this if the cover is to remain intact. A metal cam wheel locking tool, rather than a plastic one, will be able to lock both wheels together while you loosen and remove the two cam wheel bolts.

Once the cambelt is disconnected and the cooling system and oil has been drained, the final steps towards head removal involve taking out the very long through bolts, often mistakenly called head bolts. These bolts are removed using a specific E12 splined socket needed to engage the heads. (Most good motor shops will be able to supply these sockets.) It is always best to remove the bolts in the opposite order than they are torqued up, and this should be done when the engine is cold.

Keep each bolt in the correct order so you know which hole it was taken from, unless you have decided to renew them. The simplest method of identifying them is to use a piece of card with ten holes and marked with their position in relation to the front of the engine. Bolts should only be reused if they pass the length test (*see* Fig. 4.82).

Once the bolts are out the head may be removed. It is critical that a K series head is never lifted upwards as there is a good chance that the movement will lift a liner and break the seal between liner and block. The way to remove a K series head is to rock it towards the front and rear of the engine so that any head gasket sticking is broken without lifting the liner. Once you have rocked it forward and back a couple of times it

will have started to lift anyway, so now you can lift the head clear of the block. Note that it really takes two people to allow proper control over the lift when easing the head and inlet manifold forward, up and out of the engine bay.

Lifting the head from the car is a messy exercise due to the volume of oil held within the camshaft area. As soon as you start to lift and move the head a significant quantity of this will leave the nooks and crannies it was sitting in, drain down the various bolt holes and dribble wherever you move the head. Prepare for this by taking appropriate steps to protect the part of the car you will be lifting the head over, usually the right rear wing area, by covering the body. Have a receptacle ready near to the car into which you can put the

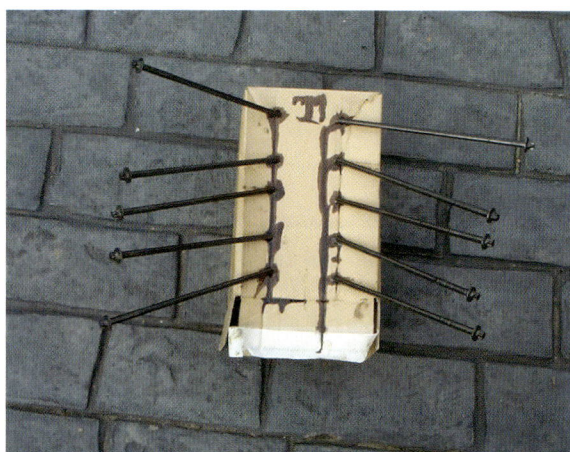

Fig. 4.69   If the main through bolts are to be used again after they have been removed and checked, they must be kept in order to make sure they go back into the holes they came from. Use a piece of card or as in this case an old box as a temporary store.

Fig. 4.70   When lifting the head off the engine there is a considerable volume of oil held within the head that will be lost when it is moved. Have a suitable tray to hand to put the removed head into to catch the residues.

TOP LEFT: Fig. 4.71 Once the through bolts have been removed you must never turn a K series engine over unless you have fitted liner clamps to stop the pistons lifting the liners of their seats in the block and breaking the seals. (Austin Garages)

TOP RIGHT: Fig. 4.72 A simple alternative to liner clamps can be made from steel tube and a series of washers.

head and catch all the fluids dripping out of it.

Do *not* turn the engine over unless you have first fitted the specific liner clamping tools, or made ones up yourself from tubing and larger flat washers, otherwise the care taken to remove the head without disturbing a liner will probably be undone as the piston movement upwards will lift the liner as well. Home-made ones need not have the shaped feet, just strong flat washers that are able to cover the tops of adjacent liners with a tube length of approximately 110mm.

It is now time to remove the inlet manifold to allow you to clean up the head so you can assess its condition, which is very important if the engine has suffered an overheating condition. The first area to check will be the head face. You are looking for half-moon indents into the head face on the exhaust side. If indents are present deeper than slight marks that you may catch a fingernail on, this is a clear indication of an annealed (softened) head material and skimming on its own will not alter this.

The 0.012in (0.3mm) thick addi-

tional shim with an MLS gasket set is designed to help reduce the spot loads through the compressed gasket fire rings, assuming the correct hardness of the head face. However, when there are clear signs of indentation this shim is very unlikely to be rigid enough to do anything beyond delaying further sinkage and loss of seal before another HGF. The shim is also designed to reduce the incidence of boiling coolant erosion.

In these cases the simplest solution aside from another head is to use the 'Head Saver Shim' (*see* Fig. 4.39), which

ABOVE: Fig. 4.73 If you find indentations where the gasket fire rings sat when removing the head, usually on the exhaust side, it is a sure sign the head has annealed (softened) and has officially become unserviceable. This head has clear indents all round as indicated.

RIGHT: Fig. 4.74 When looking to skim a head, or to check a newly acquired head, it is important to know the actual head thickness to assess if it has been skimmed before and by how much. The arrows indicate where that measurement should be done.

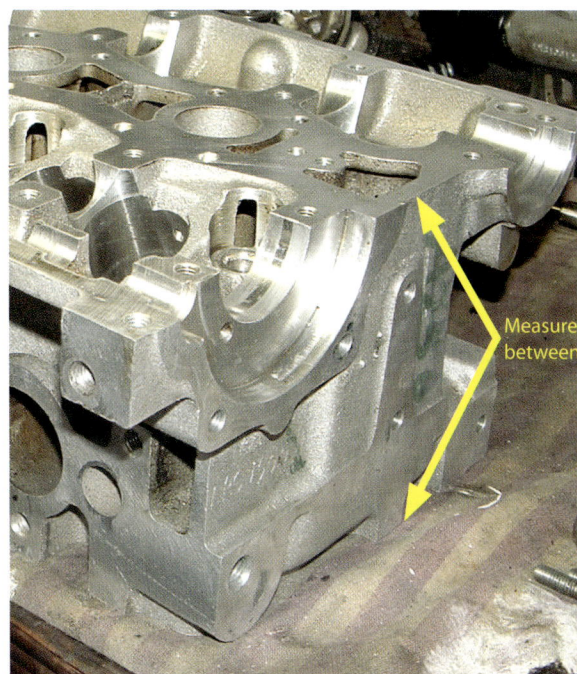

Measure between

will have enough rigidity to spread the clamping loads and provide long-term reliability from what in 'factory' eyes would have been a scrap head casting. Fitting a 'Saver Shim' is simple enough and replaces the extra shim of the MLS gasket kit after the head has been further skimmed. Before fitting, smear Wellseal gasket sealant over the whole surface in contact with the cylinder head, specifically noting that the 'Saver Shim' is always against the head.

The depth of additional skimming is calculated by measuring the current thickness of the head between the head face and the top face without the cam carrier, which in the original standard form was 119mm plus or minus 0.05mm. This will indicate if the head has been previously skimmed and by approximately how much. You now measure the thickness of the

'Saver Shim' and subtract the amount the head has been previously skimmed from the 'Saver Shim' thickness. This gives the final figure of the amount of metal needed to be removed from the head face.

In respect to general skimming of K series heads, there is a far too common approach that if the head is off, skim it – irrespective of whether the head needs skimming or not. Fortunately, most engineering shops have a sensible approach and skim as little as they can to 'clean' any marks off the head face, rather than remove a greater amount. As time passes and engines age, however, it becomes clear that the scenario of perhaps two or even three gasket replacements, each seeing a skim, is cumulatively going to remove a significant amount of material, way above the maximum normal skim limit.

A lesser-known concern, however, is that skimming can create more problems than it cures. This comes from the fact that factory skimming not only creates a flat clean surface, it also creates a non-porous surface. Skimming with a sharp tool cuts the surface of the head very cleanly, opens up the castings structure and can create porosity. If heads are to be skimmed, then in very basic terms this should be done with a 'blunt' tool as this then 'drags' material and in doing so creates a sealed (burnished) surface. The more accurate description of this cutting process is 'negative rake' with a single-point cutting tool.

Finally, on the skimming front are the practical restrictions that apply to VVC engines, as their valves are so much closer to the head face. As a result their practical skim limit is far less than an

Fig. 4.75   Valves are close to the head face that restricts the maximum skim limit and on this MPi head with small valves there is more scope for skimming.

Fig. 4.76   On VVC heads, where the bigger valves are much closer to the head face, skimming is more of a problem.

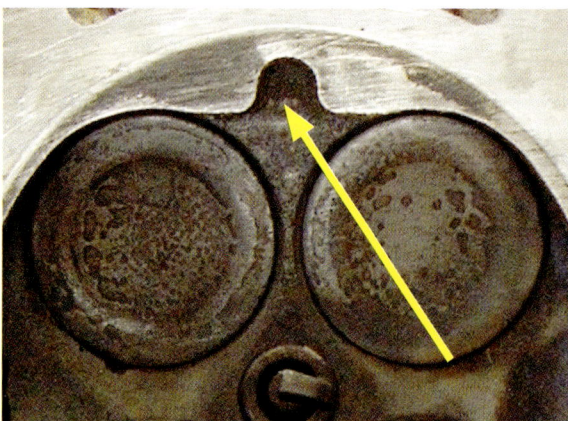

Fig. 4.77   An indication of previous skimming often comes from looking at the dimpled recess in the combustion chamber. This head has not been modified.

Fig. 4.78   A skimmed head looks like this. Some heads may even have seen the dimple completely skimmed away.

MPi head – yet another reason to only skim when there is a proven case for skimming. The illustrations here of a combustion chamber in detail provide a visual guide to previous skimming procedures.

Traditionally alloy heads have been regarded as being more susceptible to warping, but surprisingly the K series head is not that affected. Warping, however, may sometimes be encountered. The traditional method of checking for warping with a straight edge from corner to corner and across the centre is followed. The maximum warp permitted is 0.002in (0.05mm). Warping, though, would almost always be preceded by annealing and half-moon indents, as was the case with the two examples shown here.

Another area too often overlooked is the liner stand proud, which in very simple terms is the height the liner tops stick out above the block face. Officially this should be between 0.002in (0.051mm) and 0.003in (0.765mm). Critically all liners should be the same height or differ by no more than 0.001in (0.0254mm). In addition this stand proud has to be even all round each liner: this confirms that all liners are standing vertically and not 'leaning', which is unacceptable. You will rarely find that condition, however, except after a major overheat when heat degradation of the alloy block's engagement ledge can soften and lead to the same type of problem that occurs with the head face grooves.

In practical terms a good straight edge is placed across the top centre of the liners, which will immediately show any discrepancies in height. Since number four cylinder is often the one to suffer from heat-related problems, this one is most likely to show any sinkage. Sliding thin feeler blades between the straight edge and block face will confirm the stand proud. Move the straight edge either side of centre and measure again to check for uneven liners. Remember that these tolerances are necessarily tight and ignoring any discrepancy will mean an unreliable engine. If the liners are standing straight, but the heights are below the permitted range, then a MLS gasket may not seal properly but an SLS gasket may, as I have seen on a couple of 2004-built engines.

Fig. 4.79   Alloy heads have a reputation for warping, but K series engines anneal before warping. This seriously overheated engine has deep fire ring indentations.

Fig. 4.80   This engine was hot enough to melt plastic parts, but only showed annealing with deep fire ring grooves.

The next process can be skipped if new long through bolts are to be fitted, but old ones can be reused if they are up to specification. There is much discussion over whether these can be reused or should always be replaced. The manufacturer's advice is that the bolts can be reused if they are undamaged and within length tolerance, but if when checking you find that two or more bolts are out, then the whole set ought to be renewed.

The tolerance check is the length of the bolt in one of two specific checks. One check requires taking the lower rail out of the engine. For most this will be unsuitable, so I will refer to the more common one of winding the bolts back in the thread in the engine they came out of.

First, clean the bolt and lightly oil the threads, then in turn refit each bolt in the hole from which it came, using just finger pressure to screw the bolt

Fig. 4.81   Liner stand proud is a critical element for reliable operation. Although the distance by which the liners stick out of the block is minute, here you can just see an indication of this where the liners are against the block.

Fig. 4.82   It is critical to check the length of through bolts to see if they are can be reused. Here they are refitted by hand. When the bolt won't turn any more, measure between the block and the underside of the bolt head. Anything more than 97mm means a failure.

back in until it locks up. Now measure between the block face and the underside of the head of the bolt and note the measurement. If this is 97mm or less the bolt is serviceable, more than 97mm and it is *not* to be reused.

You may find that sometimes one or more of the three bolts on the exhaust side and nearest the gearbox end may lock out very close to 97mm, even when a new bolt is fitted, which should wind to the end of the thread. This may be because the bolt is making contact with the sump. There are two possible reasons: either the bolt specification was designed for an engine with the thin steel sump and when the alloy sump was designed its extra thickness took up the previous space; or the original bolts have a pointed end intended to aid bolt location during initial engine assembly. The SAIC uprated bolts have a flat end and the original bolt can have its point machined off to add clearance.

Since the demise of MG Rover, the engine has been in production in China for SAIC Motor group's MG and Roewe models, although with some changes to the design. The SAIC version of the engine benefited from the use of an uprated through bolt and this saw a change to the tightening procedure and values. This information, of course, is never going to be found in any workshop manual applicable to models of the MG Rover or Rover Group periods. The heads are identified by the '10.9' stamped into them and they are found under part number WAM2293SLP, the same basic part number as the standard bolts but with the SLP added (*see* Fig. 4.13).

The bolts are included in a specific Ultimate Head gasket set, sold by Xpart for all K series engines. The kit contains these bolts, the uprated lower rail, the MLS gasket and the shim. It is important to note here that the initial torque setting is the same as that for the original bolts, as is the follow-on 180-degree second stage. The third stage is now 135 degrees (and *not* 180 degrees as before). Let me stress that this amended process *only* applies to the uprated SAIC through bolts.

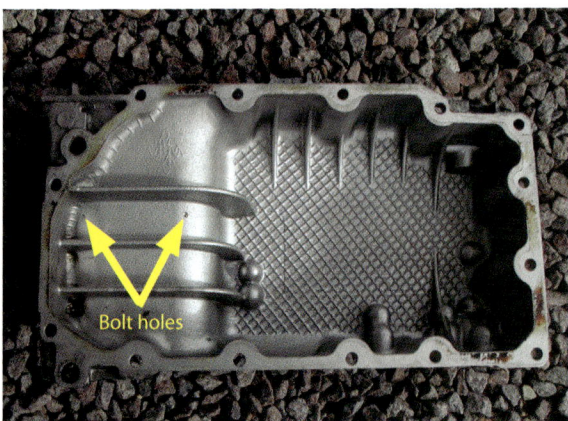

Fig. 4.83   Through bolts on the exhaust side and nearest the gearbox end can sometimes make contact with the sump.

Fig. 4.84   Contact between through bolts and sump shows more clearly in this close-up.

At this stage the uprated lower rail should be fitted to the bottom of the engine, should you decide to fit this. Land Rover insists that the uprated lower rail is always used with the MLS gasket and I would recommend that adding strength to the engine is something that is always worth doing.

Cylinder Head Rebuild

The non-VVC head is really quite simple as it uses two solid camshafts operating hydraulic followers, which in turn act on the valves. The VVC adds a significant degree of complexity to the operation of the inlet valves and needs a knowledgeable touch. In many respects the humorous term it has acquired, Very Very Complicated, is not without just cause. There are few professionals who can reliably deal with the VVC, and some areas of a VVC are not even covered in the workshop manual, so this is a subject I shall deal with later.

Before tackling specific aspects of the VVC, however, I will first deal with some basic features of both VVC and non-VVC heads that are very similar. Obviously this is covered by the workshop manual, but it should be emphasized that it is possibly a waste of time to avoid work on a head only to find an underlying problem after all.

Let me start with a general comment that actually applies to all K series cylinder heads: if you are coming to a K series from the familiar grounds of a classic MG, I guarantee that when taking the head to pieces you will start to wonder if you are dealing with a model engine, such are the generally small dimensions of valve train components, especially the valve collets. Those of you familiar with motorcycle engines will feel more at home with the small size of components.

The very first thing to consider when looking to do any reconditioning on a K series cylinder head is to ensure that the head casting is suitable for the work. Specifically, I want to stress the condition of the head face and that it has not annealed (gone soft), something I mentioned earlier in respect to head gasket replacement. Again I must labour the point that you should check for any indentation rings into the head, caused by the head gasket fire rings being compressed into the head face

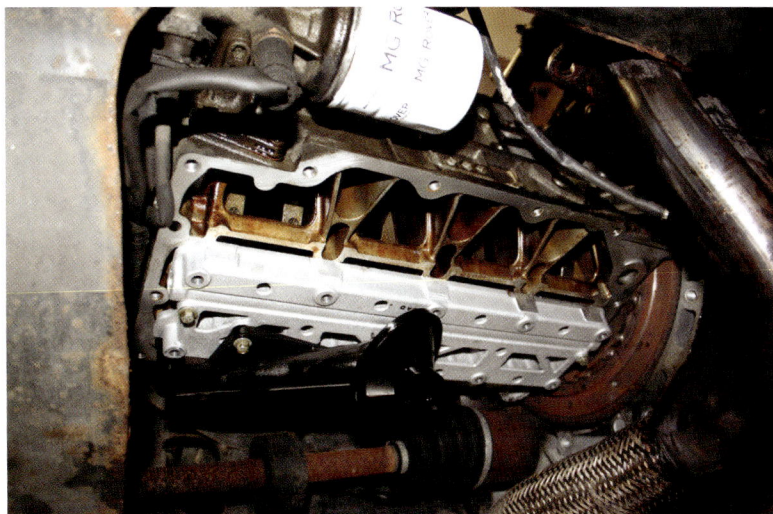

Fig. 4.85   It is only necessary to remove the lower rail in order to fit the shiny new uprated version.

(see Figs 4.38–4.73). Remember that simple head skimming will not provide a cure as it is the material that has gone soft. Only the use of a Head Saver shim will do the trick.

Marking of the head face without indentations is acceptable and this can be cleaned up easily with a block and very fine abrasive paper. Deeper marking or corrosion near coolant passages can be lightly skimmed. It is important, however, to know if the head has been previously skimmed. The methodology for dealing with this, both for establishing the measurement and for fitting a head saver shim, if required, is given above.

While head supply may not be a big problem today, it is certain that in a few years there will be a shortage of good cylinder head castings, because many will not have enough material left to allow a reface. The VVC heads will be the first to show this, as only about 110,000 VVC engines were made, as against approaching 3,000,000 other K series. Second, the larger valves of the VVC means that the valve seat inserts are not as deeply inset into the combustion chamber as the inserts on the non-VVC heads, and so there is far less material available to be skimmed before getting too close to the insert (see Fig. 4.75 and Fig. 4.76). The maximum official head reface skim limit is not set as low as 0.008in (0.2mm) without good reason and the VVC head shows why.

Both VVC and MPi heads are effectively the same once the cams are removed, so the strip down and wear/

damage assessment in the workshop manual applies to both. I have a tip aimed at those with comprehensive tool kits built up over years of owning overhead valve engines, whether operated by pushrods or an overhead camshaft. The valve spring compressors used on these engines will not work with a twin overhead cam engine like the K series and the earlier comment on the small size of the K series valve train parts means that often the older valve spring compressors are too big.

There is also the issue with the K series that the head casting has high side walls and so the top of the valve, even when fully relaxed, is still below the top of the casting wall.

Valve removal requires a valve spring compressor designed for modern twin cam 16-valve heads, but you should be wary that 'universal' tools may not be fully suitable for the K series due to its small dimensions, so make sure you buy correctly.

Stripping a head first requires that the cap and collets be separated. It is normal to find that when trying to compress the spring you experience a solid condition. Often the effort you can put into the lever of the valve spring compressor will not break the interference fit that has built up over however many years the engine has been running. The simple way to overcome this is to lay the head face down on a thick cloth. (I use an old bed sheet folded many times so it ends up around half an inch thick.) Then select a socket with a diameter that comfortably fits on the valve

Fig. 4.86   Plastic inlet manifold-to-head seals have a reputation for leaking, not aided by the availability of some poor-quality imitation green seals. The leakage point is usually at the cam belt end of the engine, as in this case, where the seal hardened and the leak points are clear.

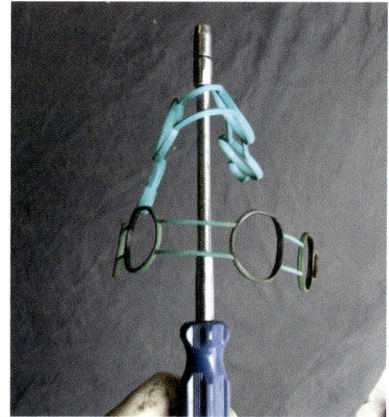

Fig. 4.87   A simple elasticity test demonstrates how a new seal can bend under its own weight.

Fig. 4.88   The benefits of the new seal are obvious once fitted.

spring cap, ideally a deep socket as it gives you more to hold.

Place the socket hex end on the top of the valve cap and give it a sharp tap with a hammer. The shock will break the seal between cap and collets, although you may be surprised by how hard a tap is needed. Don't imitate the bull in a china shop approach, so start this process with a light tap and increase the effort as needed. You will almost certainly find a few really tight ones that demand a much sharper tap. When the seal is broken the collets will come away and the cap and spring will be released.

This can be adopted as a strip-down approach and you can release all caps and collets this way: you just need to have a small stick magnet to poke into the cavities in the head to recover all the collets. Without the magnet it is a case of poking around and turning the head upside down to retrieve the collets. This does make the strip-down a simpler and quite quick operation by comparison to the individual removal using the spring compressor.

If you are reusing the removed components, it is advised to keep them in order to allow identification of which came from where on the head. This is because during your closer examination of valve seats, for example, you may find something that you want to cross-reference to see if the valve

shows any corresponding signs. In fact this applies both ways. It also allows valves and guides that have bedded in together to continue that relationship, although it is not anywhere near as critical as a piston-to-bore relationship.

Head Refit

Refitting of the head follows the instructions laid down in the workshop manual. I have a couple of comments to add to those instructions. Firstly you should decide if you are refitting the inlet manifold to the head before refitting the head to the engine, bearing in mind my comments before its removal regarding the difficulty of access to the lower fixing bolts.

In the case of plastic manifolds, always renew the flexible seal that sits in the moulded groove in the inlet face to head and which provides the seal between the two; note that the stiffer the seal the shorter life it will have before leaking. Indeed the original factory black seals had early life failures and so were replaced by a green seal that had a great deal more flexibility. Beware of poorer quality imitations, so preferably only buy genuine MG parts.

In the case of VVC engines, the two-piece alloy inlet manifold gives more options. Fitting the lower part to the head and leaving the refit of the upper part until after the head is replaced is a reasonable compromise not open to the plastic manifold. Just ensure that you have a new gasket for both upper and lower parts.

You should always use steel dowels to provide the location of head on block, but there is no need to replace

Fig. 4.89   Cylinder head location dowels changed to steel during 2001. To aid later removal I run an 8mm tap down new dowels, as shown here.

them if the engine is already fitted with them and they are not damaged. A downside of the steel dowel in the alloy engine is that steel and alloy will adhere to each other over time. To counter the anticipated difficulties in removing a dowel, I have adopted a simple modification to the dowels to allow easier future removal. The modification is to run a standard M8 tap down the dowel before fitting the dowels into the block. If the dowel has an inside diameter too big for the tap, then the dowel is cheap and of poor quality, so change them. The provision of this thread will allow a simple extraction tool to be made.

Refitting continues as described in the workshop manual, but when it comes to refitting the cambelt, and especially when fitting a new belt, the lack of flexibility in the belt often makes fitting difficult. When the belt has finally been engaged on both crank and cam pulleys, it often turns out that timing is a tooth out once full belt tension is achieved. To make correct alignment easier I suggest turning the crank half a crank wheel tooth anti-clockwise. To understand this better, refer to the images, where you will see on the front face of the pulley two dimples close together, which in the 'book' timed position will sit either side of a casting ridge, behind the oil pump body.

My suggestion is to align the casting ridge with the right dimple. This effectively shortens the distance between cam and crank pulley teeth, and it becomes easier to engage the timing belt teeth into the correct positions so that when the belt tensions and stretches it will move into correct alignment.

Another tip to help the refitting process is to select a well-used straight ring spanner, with a very smooth end from long-term handling, and insert this between the oil pump body casting web, which forms a lower belt guide, and the crank belt pulley. This doesn't impose any load on the belt but keeps

the belt and pulley teeth engaged. You can now concentrate on stretching the belt up and into engagement on the exhaust cam pulley (with the cam locking tool still fitted), and then around to the inlet cam pulley, around the water pump and finally around the tensioner.

From this point all should be plain sailing as far as the reassembly is concerned. Then we move on to refilling with oil and coolant. The former needs no comment, but coolant refilling on an MGF or TF involves, most importantly, bleeding of the cooling system as it is a complex system with a volume more than twice that of most K series-engined cars, due specifically to the engine being in the rear and the radiator and heater being towards the front of the car. This is why bleeding the cooling system is so important as the possibility of airlocks is so much more likely. Airlocks mean reduced coolant flow, which in turn means overheating and that can result in HGF, just what you are trying to avoid.

Cambelt Issues

The mention of broken cambelts raises the point that false information is still circulating that K series engines have a history of cambelt failures. What is fact is that the original K series engines (not VVC), with their original

LEFT: *Fig. 4.90   Cam belt refitting and correct alignment can be made easier by moving the bottom pulley back half a tooth, as described in the text. Here the timing marks are identified. (Note as shown timing is a tooth out.)*
ABOVE: *Fig. 4.91   When refitting a cam belt to stop the belt slipping on the bottom pulley while you negotiate the belt around the top pulleys, a well-used and smooth ring spanner acts as a loose fit simple lock to stop the belt moving.*

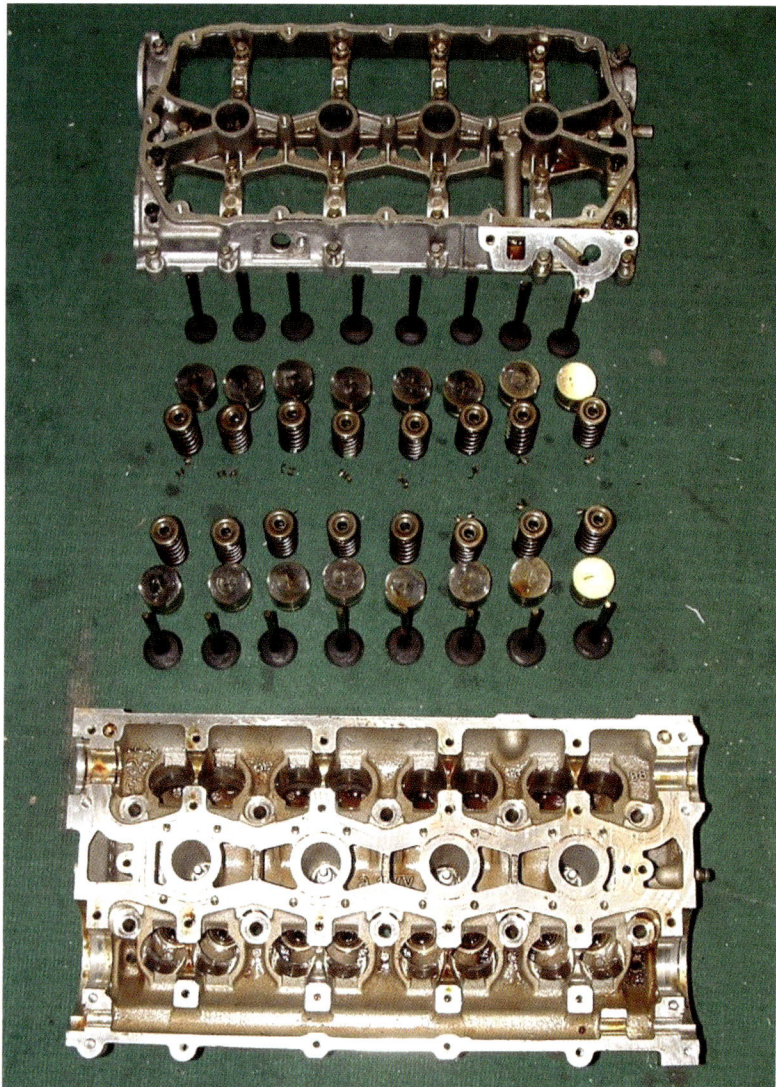

Fig. 4.92   *Keeping items in order so that they can be refitted from where they came is a good policy.*

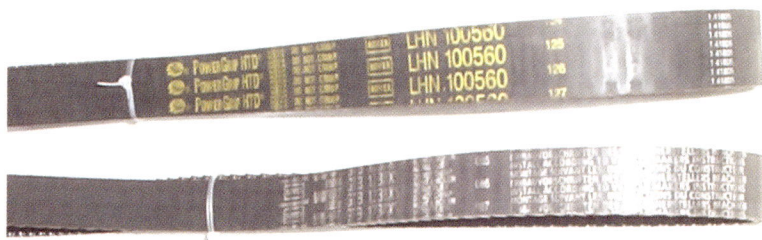

Fig. 4.93   *MPi cam belts were originally 23mm wide (lower), but were changed in late 1998 for the wider 26mm one.*

manual belt adjuster on a 23mm wide belt, initially had a belt change service interval of 96,000 miles or eight years, whichever came first. This can be found in a few early MGF handbooks, but soon this was changed to five years or 60,000 miles. (VVC engines, incidentally, use a different 26mm wide main front belt with the same manual tensioner and separate short rear belt.)

I have seen belt failures on 1.4 Rover 200s where the cars were well within eight years old but doing higher than average annual mileages and so were approaching the change point. The several failures I have seen were between 86,000 and 93,000 miles and the belt simply failed through fatigue. This is why the service change point was moved to 60,000 miles or five years, whichever arrived first.

Since that change there was a very significant development for the non-VVC engines when, at the end of 1998, a much softer operating auto-adjusting tensioner was fitted, along with a new 26mm wide belt, which is different to the VVC belt. The maximum mileage limit was never changed for the MGF or TF, but the maximum mileage change point for the FWD saloon MG and Rovers did move up to a 90,000 mile or six-year change, whichever comes first.

Mention of the more reliable wider belt and less harsh tensioner may have some thinking it would be nice to change their earlier MPi engine to the later set-up. Yes, this can be done, and the main pulleys are the same, but the head casting is different because the auto and manual tensioners have different anchor bolt positions and the head casting was changed to add material inside the head to accommodate the bolts' different positions.

VVC Cam Bolt 'Torque Relaxation'

There was also a specific VVC issue that affected some engines made up to the autumn of 1998 and the consequences would usually be catastrophic. The issue was that cam bolts could come loose in operation and the resulting chattering of cam wheel against bolt and locating dowel would lead to failure of one or both of these items. As soon as that occurred cam timing was lost and the inevitable valve to piston contact occurred. The result would require at least a new head, and in some cases a new engine.

The cause was publicly blamed on 'torque relaxation' in the cam bolts. The true cause, however, was that a torque wrench at one of the two stations in Powertrain where only VVC heads were assembled dropped out of calibration: when the bolts were being tightened the actual torque was below that which was required. Over a period of use the bolts could work loose. The lucky owners who heard a rattle or clatter, and then did not run the engine until the problem had been rectified, avoided the big problems. Many others only knew they had a major problem when the engine simply stopped.

This wasn't a problem that affected all engines, but since there was no way to trace the engines using heads

Fig. 4.94   VVC cam belt failures were essentially the loosening of the main centre bolt holding this cam wheel to the cam mechanism.

Fig. 4.95   On many occasions loosening would lead to damage like this.

shear torque for these bolts was not that far above the recommended setting. Consequently, MG specialists such as Mike Satur and Brown and Gammons offer uprated bolts with a much greater tensile strength.

I have tried to emulate bolt shearing on a spare head and gone considerably over the recommended torque without seeing the Rover bolt fail. Additionally, the 10mm sized factory fit bolts used were common to all 4-cylinder K series engines from approximately 1996, not just VVC, and to all T16 2.0 litre Rover engines from 1991 to the end of their production. I have noted that the part number has now changed, but the only difference was in the surface finish and everything else remained the same.

assembled with the faulty torque wrench, a notice was issued to all dealers to check the cam bolt tightening torques on all their customers' cars with VVC engines. This was in effect an internal recall and not a recall in the accepted sense of the word, where there are legal aspects. Therefore when searching for this under the (UK's) VOSA recall system, you won't find it as it is not a safety issue.

Between 1999 and 2003 I had many conversations with MGF owners from the UK, Europe, Australasia, Japan and a few more obscure locations whose engines had clearly suffered this problem. Encouragingly, these reports stopped and I do not recall one since about 2005.

The problem was so basic and the cure so simple, if it were caught in time. It was impossible to say whether any given engine had been assembled using the faulty torque wrench,

however, so the only safe approach once the problem was identified and became common knowledge was to assume the worst for all VVC engines in cars made up to late 1998. Many have extended this assumption to cover all later VVC engines, even though you can be sure that the same problem was not allowed to recur in Powertrain.

While it is fair to assume that any engine from the affected period that has covered more than 30,000 miles would have suffered before now if it had not been checked, and as dating a VVC engine in an MGF is not easy, it is simpler to routinely apply the solution unless service record information is present to confirm this has already been done.

The solution is to simply remove all four cam bolts in turn, apply a bead of thread lock fluid on each and refit, tightening them to 65Nm. Testing also produced some evidence that the

Remember that this problem is specific to the VVC, not the MPi engines. Additionally the early MGF 1.8i models used the earlier (roughly 1989 to 1995) K series 8mm sized specification bolt, which was clearly weaker but this wasn't an issue. Note that if the owner of an early spec engine wants to change to the 10mm bolt then this demands that both camshafts be changed too, but thread lock is equally viable on all cam bolts.

The VVC has two cam belts. When replacing the rear belt it is necessary to remove the rear exhaust pulley: this means the bolt has to be disturbed and there is the possibility that it might be tightened insufficiently or even overtightened. Given that all VVC engines should have had at least one belt change, and that some older engines will have had several changes,

Fig. 4.96   Applying thread lock to the cam wheel bolts is sound insurance against them coming loose in use.

Fig. 4.97 *VVC rear cambelt change always requires the exhaust cam pulley be removed, so applying thread lock to the bolt threads when refitting is advised.*

this disturbance may not have been done to the best practices. It is good practice to adopt a policy of removal and thread locking, or renewing the bolt and thread locking, using a known accurate torque wrench to set the correct torque.

Bent Valves, Broken Valve Guides and Related Piston Damage

When a valve contacts the piston and the valve bends, the bending forces will pivot on the point where the valve stem enters the cast iron valve guide and you end up with a section of the protruding part of the valve guide breaking off or being cracked. Obviously the guide has to be replaced, which is a job for an engineering shop or engine reconditioner. The valve seats then need to be re-cut, as this is not something you can normally overcome by lapping in the valve. The need for professional assistance is one of the main reasons why owners of cars suffering cambelt failure generally seek a good second-hand head or engine rather than look to rebuild the damaged head.

There is another aspect that must be considered when valves have contacted pistons, as the force needed to bend valves is focused on the top edge of the piston and the relatively soft alloy of the piston will yield under the pressure of the edge of the valve. This compression spreads down through the piston. Because it is near the edge, it is quite common to see the piston ring grooves close up, sometimes actually nips on the rings, or the piston land area can break. This will obviously have a serious impact on the engine's running, even with a new head. If there are valve imprints on the piston tops, the piston should be removed and examined for damage. If the imprinting has any measurable depth, then ring nipping and even broken piston lands is to be expected. This is why replacement engines are often advised by garages as a matter of routine.

Once all rectification engineering is complete and the valves are lapped in, then the time has come to reassemble the head. This is quite straightforward, but involves small, fiddly parts in an area with limited access. This is where it helps to have the better valve spring compressors with a wider access to insert collets. I have found that inserting collets is best achieved using a little grease in the valve collet groove, so that when the collet is inserted it has something to hold it in place. I then use a small flat-blade screwdriver with another dab of grease on the end, to which I stick a collet at a slight angle to align to the best insertion position.

As the collet is inserted into the collet groove, the grease in the groove is able to hold the collet as I gently twist the screwdriver to break the grip of the grease holding it to the collet. As access to insert the collets is limited, the first collet has to be gently eased around the collet groove in order to allow the second collet to be inserted in the same way. Once both collets are in place, gently release the spring compressor, while watching that the collets remain in place as the spring cap rises.

Fig. 4.98 *Another image showing how, when valves bend, the guide cracks off the lowest part of the guide.*

Fig. 4.99 *Broken piston land area between rings.*

VVC Heads

Before getting into the depths of the VVC, it is worth making the point that complex mechanical items will wear over time and miles. It is obviously important to have regular oil and filter changes if this wear is to be minimized. Unfortunately, most owners who face problems will probably be those who have recently bought a car with the VVC engine and are now facing the consequences of the previous owner's failure to follow the regular oil and filter change routine.

New VVC engines can be as quiet as non-VVC engines, but on average once more than 10,000 miles has been covered they do tend to gain a slightly harsh mechanical noise that is sometimes described as similar to a diesel engine. This tends only to be at idle and only a few hundred rpm higher, when the engine should smooth out quite noticeably.

An indication of excess wear within one or both of the VVC mechanisms is when you have a distinct 'tap, tap, tap' sound that is related to engine rpm and may at times be mistaken for a very noisy hydraulic tappet. As with all mechanical noises, try to locate where it is coming from by using an automotive stethoscope, if you have one. A length of wooden dowel, or even a long screwdriver, placed on various parts of the engine with the other end at your ear is almost as good at detecting the source of specific noises. If it is the VVC mechanism, then often it will be at the rear, gearbox, end, usually because it is at the end of the oil supply route.

Where a mechanism is noisy, it can be replaced by good second-hand parts without the cam section if desired, although it should be noted that the units are handed: if replacing a rear then the replacement has to be a rear. I have known the use of second-hand units to be a perfectly viable solution to a VVC problem. It is prudent to strip and properly clean and examine units to identify any issues before going to the trouble of fitting them, then finding a problem.

VVC Mechanisms – Strip and Rebuild

VVC mechanisms come with cams attached in a special tool holding the assembly together. The only information listed in the factory engine rebuild manual is limited to the removal or fitting and timing these to a cylinder head: there is nothing else in any other workshop manual publication. There is some information on the Internet about taking these items apart and putting them back together, but there does seem to be some variation on the information.

Here I want to cover the missing aspects where someone, without realizing the complexity of the system, takes things apart only to find the mechanisms drop to the floor like an exploding watch. The very nature of this process is one that words without imagery will simply bamboozle, so here the range of images take precedence and words will only assist.

Note that normal workshop manual processes should be observed, and only some of the required cleaning, application of sealant and oil seal replace-ment is mentioned in the following description.

Fig. 4.100   *VVC mechanisms come as an assembly held in a special tool that keeps correct timing ready for assembly.*

Removal and refit of the VVC mechanism can be done with the head still on the engine, although access in a MGF or TF is very restricted compared to that in a ZR160, which also uses the VVC engine. Where work is needed to deal with a valve or head face issue, then only items 1 to 6 below should be tackled this way: deeper work requires the head to be on the bench.

First the wiring, cam belts, covers, pulleys and cam cover are all removed. This leaves the mechanisms exposed ready for removal. The following numbered actions should be read and related to the images identified:

1. The two lower bolts holding the VVC mechanisms to the cylinder head are removed, while the two upper bolts holding the mechanism to the cam carrier are loosened a full turn, but no more (*see* Figs 4.101 and 4.102).

Fig. 4.101   *The two lower fixing bolts to the cylinder head are removed.*

Fig. 4.102   *The upper two fixing bolts are only loosened.*

Fig. 4.103 This allows enough movement to 'unstick' the mechanisms from the head/carrier.

Fig. 4.104 After the oil temperature sensor is removed from the HCU there is access to remove the one HCU fixing bolt.

Fig. 4.105 The HCU can then be lifted off.

Fig. 4.106 There are two cam carrier fixing bolts: one position is visible and the other is out of view, but its position is indicated.

Fig. 4.107 Lift the exhaust side of the cam carrier enough to break any seal and also ensure that the exhaust cam stays on the head. Then lift the carrier from the inlet side holding the VVC cams and mechanisms.

Fig. 4.108 Invert it and lay it on the bench.

2. Loosening only the upper two bolts allows a small degree of movement to pull the mechanism away from the head and cam carrier so that any sticking is released (*see* Fig. 4.103).

3. Remove the hydraulic control unit (HCU) oil temperature sensor to allow access to the end 10mm headed retaining bolt. Remove all three HCU securing bolts and lift off the HCU housing. Be aware that the HCU is full of oil and this will leak (*see* Fig. 4.104).

4. Turn the HCU lower plate, which carries the upper and lower oil seals, to provide access to the two cam cover bolts, then remove all the cam carrier bolts and break the seal holding the carrier to the cylinder head, but don't lift it at this stage (*see* Fig. 4.106).

5. Lift the exhaust side of the carrier up and ensure the exhaust cam is not lifting with the carrier. Ease it off as needed, otherwise it may drop out. Now lift the carrier off and ensure the inlet cams are not sticking to their cylinder head journals. Apply a little pressure to the ends of each mechanism to push it towards the carrier to help deter any unwanted cam movement (*see* Fig. 4.107).

6. Carefully invert the cam carrier (*see* Fig. 4.108).

7. Note that the screwdriver is pointing to a pair of slots in the rear mechanism. These are for alignment and are in the correct positions (*see* Fig. 4.109).

8. Moving to the front mechanism shows the two slots (top right) also correctly aligned. The screwdriver is now pointing to the correct orientation of the cross shaft gear with the mechanism's rack (*see* Fig. 4.110). Note that the alignment slot shown in the MG workshop manual is not in line.

9. The cross shaft and rack of the rear mechanism should be aligned as here (*see* Fig. 4.111).

10. Now remove the two bolts holding the mechanisms to the carrier and then ease the cam and mechanisms from the carrier, keeping gentle pressure to push the cam against the mechanisms to stop the cam falling out (*see* Figs 4.112 and 4.113).

Fig. 4.109   Note the correct alignment of the mechanism slots.

Fig. 4.110   The cross shaft to mechanism rack at the front is correctly aligned.

Fig. 4.111   And so is the rear mechanism.

Fig. 4.112   Remove the remaining two bolts holding the mechanism to the carrier and ease the cam and mechanism from the carrier.

Fig. 4.113   Maintain gentle pressure to hold the two together.

11. A long bolt is pushed through the front observation hole in the carrier (and the identical one in the rear) that is used to confirm the position of the two holes for checking alignment (*see* Figs 4.114 and 4.115).

12. Here the bolt is pointing to the slots in the assembled mechanism. Note that when the mechanisms are attached to the carrier you can insert a peg through these carrier holes and into the mechanisms to retain the correct alignment. This can be done any time the mechanisms are connected to the carrier (*see* Fig. 4.116).

13. Disassembly of the mechanisms starts by simply lifting the cams from the mechanism and then the inner parts of the mechanisms can be removed individually. Note that sometimes one of the square blocks can stick to the cam pins and then drop off when the cam is lifted, so take care not to lose this. Here the outer collar is removed and shows clear signs of poor maintenance, which was to be a common theme with this pair of VVC assemblies, leading to severe gumming up and jamming of internal parts from congealed oil (*see* Figs 4.117 and 4.118).

Fig. 4.114 Two holes are positioned in the top ends of the cam carrier to provide a means of viewing correct alignment of the mechanisms, or for inserting a peg to maintain that alignment. The bolt is passing through the front hole.

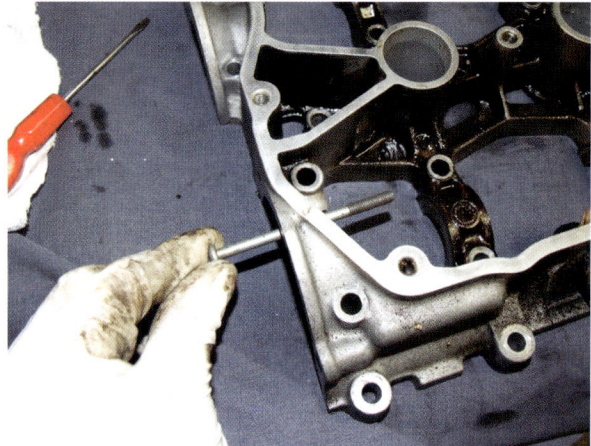

Fig. 4.115 The bolt is here seen passing through the rear hole.

Fig. 4.116 Here the bolt is showing the direction of engagement into the slot of the mechanism as it is fitted.

Fig. 4.117 The cam is lifted from the mechanism.

Fig. 4.118 The mechanism is dismantled with the main collar lifted out first.

14. All the parts that are simple to remove are laid out (*see* Figs 4.119 and 4.120). The inner bearing of the main case can also be removed but is a non-serviceable item, so if when reaching this point it feels that the bearing is rough or has excessive movement, then a replacement mechanism would be required (*see* Figs 4.121–4.124).

15. These parts were given only a brief clean and light oiling before being reassembled for illustrative purposes only. Deeper cleaning and parts checking would be done before

Fig. 4.119   All the parts removed are shown laid out.

Fig. 4.120   The stripped rear mechanism and cam below the still complete front mechanism and cam.

Fig. 4.121   The main mechanism bearing needs to be checked for wear and play.

Fig. 4.122   The bearing has been pressed out of the mechanism casting to show the front view where the cam wheel bolts.

Fig. 4.123   Rear view showing inside the mechanism.

Fig. 4.124   A side view showing the complexity of this bearing.

reusing. Here the inner collar is having the bearing slid over. Note this collar has its flange facing down into the mechanism (*see* Fig. 4.125).

16. The inner collar and bearing are placed into the body. Note the position of the machined cut-out relative to the internal pin (*see* Fig. 4.126).

17. The first of two spacer blocks is fitted over the pin. Note that the block has only two of the four faces machined to fit the slot. The other two sides can be seen to have a raised section (*see* Fig. 4.127).

18. The second block is fitted into the other end of the machined groove (*see* Fig. 4.128).

19. The outer collar is now fitted with its bearing: this time it is inverted to how the inner collar was fitted (*see* Fig. 4.129). Note that these collars have a wide range of letter markings seen in the upper recess, which may have had a function during the original assembly process at Longbridge, but there is no

Fig. 4.125   Assembly of the mechanism starts with placing a bearing onto a collar, lip downwards.

Fig. 4.126   The collar and bearing is placed in the mechanism.

Fig. 4.127   The first square block is placed onto the peg and into its slot.

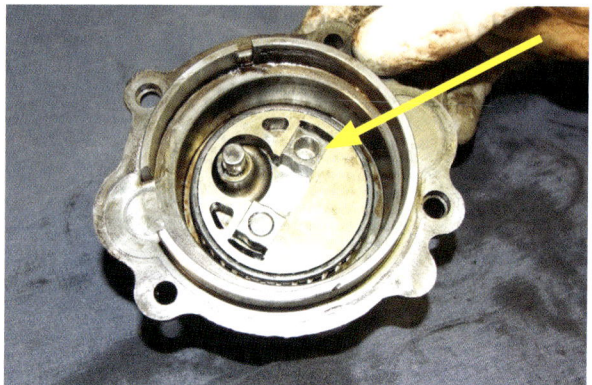

Fig. 4.128   The second block is placed so that it just sits into the slot.

Fig. 4.129   The second collar is placed onto its bearing, with the lip facing upwards.

Fig. 4.130   These collars have different letter identity codes, but this doesn't seem to have any impact on how we use them.

obvious impact if we change them or swap positions between inner and outer (*see* Fig. 4.130).

20. The outer collar is fitted within the case at 90 degrees to the inner collar so that it aligns with the pegs on the cam assembly end. Note that the front and rear cam and mechanism internal machining is handed, so no swap of these parts is possible (*see* Fig. 4.131).

21. Here the outer collar is placed in position (*see* Fig. 4.132).

22. One block is fitted over the peg and into the collar groove (*see* Fig. 4.133).

23. This is followed by the second block in the other end of the groove, ready for the cam peg to locate into once the outer sleeve is carefully slid over the bearings (*see* Fig. 4.134).

24. Note that there are two slots, here seen labelled A and B (*see* Fig. 4.136). The correct alignment is when the slot in position A leaves the rack teeth labelled C adjacent to the gap in the outer wall (labelled D in the image) where the cross shaft gear engages on the rack (*see* Fig. 4.136).

25. The cam is lowered into the mechanism and the pegs engaged into the holes in the vacant blocks. Keep

Fig. 4.131   The collar with bearing fitted is positioned so that the round cut-out is at 90 degrees to the first collar (note that the front mechanism is mirror imaged).

Fig. 4.132   Here the collar is seen in place.

Fig. 4.133   The next square block is fitted over the peg and into its slot.

Fig. 4.134   The second block is then fitted at the other end of that slot.

Fig. 4.135   The outer sleeve is now refitted over the assembled parts.

Fig. 4.136   When fully home the mechanism is aligned as shown.

Fig. 4.137   Here the cam is offered up.

Fig. 4.138   Ensure the pegs of the cam engage in the holes in the square blocks.

Fig. 4.139   Once correctly in place the cam looks like this.

Fig. 4.140   Use new mechanism to head oil seals to ensure oil tightness.

Fig. 4.141   The cam assemblies are then laid back onto the cam carrier and two bolts loosely fitted to hold the mechanisms to allow the cross shaft to be refitted.

Fig. 4.142   The HCU rack is slid back into place with a little upward pressure on the cross shaft.

Fig. 4.143   The HCU rack is aligned as indicated.

Fig. 4.144   The now refitted VVC assemblies are then fitted back on the head, onto which the exhaust cam has already been positioned.

the assembly in this orientation and somewhere secure so it can't fall over and come apart (*see* Figs 4.137–4.139)

26. Do not forget to fit a new oil seal that goes between the mechanisms and the cylinder head/cam carrier (*see* Fig. 4.140).

27. Before reassembly onto the cam carrier, check the correct alignment of the slots on the front and rear mechanisms. Once in place align and refit the two fixing bolts to the carrier per mechanism; as for the disassembly, leave them very slightly loose to allow flexibility to fit onto the head (*see* Fig. 4.102 above). Check the slot alignment has not been lost by moving the bodies until the bolts line up, adjusting as necesssary.

29. With the mechanisms still slightly loose, insert the cross shaft, followed by the HCU piston, and engage its rack with the cross shaft. This is made easier by applying gentle lifting pressure on the cross shaft, which allows the piston rack to pass the cross shaft gear (*see* Fig. 4.141 and Fig. 4.142). Remember to fit the HCU lower plate (and new labyrinth seals) by passing the piston through the hole in the plate, before pushing the piston rack into the carrier (*see* Fig. 4.106 above).

30. When the position is correct, the visible cross shaft gear tooth is seen to engage in the second gear tooth of the rack (*see* Fig. 4.143).

31. The reassembled unit is now refitted to the head. As described in the workshop manual, place a bead of sealant on head top face of the

Fig. 4.145   The completed job.

exhaust cam. Then lift the assembled carrier assembly, holding the cam mechanisms to prevent them jumping out, turn it over and place it on the head, taking care not to damage the new mechanism seals as you slide the assembly onto the head. Lightly fit the two lower bolts to head per mechanism, but do not tighten them until the cam carrier bolts have all been fitted (*see* Fig. 4.144 and Fig. 4.145).

Non-Restart, No Compression: All K Series

Occasionally a situation occurs when a reassembled engine is restarted and it spins on the starter apparently far too easily and quickly, almost as if there is no resistance. In effect this may be perfectly true and is a condition where the

hydraulic tappets have expanded during the period of relaxation from being compressed, and when the head is reassembled and refitted it holds some valves off their seats. This, of course, means it loses compression. This is easily confirmed with a compression test, but try this trick before you remove the head. If you tow start the car, the engine is being turned over at a rate that is probably six or eight times as fast as it would be by the starter motor at around 250rpm. This means there is less time for the compression to be lost and the engine will start and run if held at around 2,000rpm.

The engine should be warmed up at that rpm. Over the following ten to twenty minutes it will be possible to ease the throttle and let the rpms drop, and the engine will continue to run. Once the engine has been running for a while at the normal working temperature, it should now idle and restart normally after stopping.

What has happened is that the hydraulic tappets have 'pumped up', holding some of the valves off their seats. The period of use and the warmed engine's oil flow permits the tappets to readjust to their normal operation, allowing the valves to sit on their seats when the tappets are on the back of the cam lobes. It is far preferable to try this first before starting on parts that usually do not need removing.

Lubrication

A brief mention should be made of engine oil for the K series. The recommended types are shown in the handbook and the workshop manual. Since oil has an additional function within the control of the VVC, this type is more sensitive to the correct oil. Oil pressure is used to move the piston in the hydraulic control unit that controls the cam duration period. (VVC cam followers [lifters] also have a smaller oil hole, and so are more prone to clogging from oil residues.)

Oil viscosity changes with temperature and this will have an impact on the speed of operation of the VVC. There is a specific oil temperature sensor within the hydraulic control unit to monitor the oil temperature, so allowing the ECU to add corrective control. For these corrections to be accurate, however, you need to know the viscosity range of the oil at any given temperature. This is why 10W/40 oil is specified for the engines. This means that although the engine will apparently work fine

Fig. 4.146   *In the original MGF and TF up to 2003 the thermostat is fitted to the engine block and has 'O' rings to provide sealing (removed from this unit).*

with 15W/40 or 0W/60 oil, there will be small variations because the correction factor will not be as accurate.

COOLING SYSTEM

MGF and TF Cooling System Introduction

Some knowledge of the layout of the MGF and TF cooling system will help your understanding of why some of the issues arise. The cooling system is made up of three circuits: the bypass circuit, main radiator circuit and heater circuit.

In cars built before mid-2003 the coolant leaves the engine and passes into a 15mm bore rail (pipe) that runs around the back of the engine and empties into the thermostat housing, and specifically onto the thermostatic bulb of the stat, before entering the engine via the water pump. In these applications the thermostat is positioned in the coolant inlet (return) to the engine.

After mid-2003 the thermostat was changed to the Pressure Relief Ther-

mostat (PRT), which moved the stat from the coolant inlet to the front of the engine, close to the hot coolant outlet from the engine. The bypass is now controlled fully within the PRT and uses the main 30mm bore rail that runs alongside the smaller rail to return much greater volumes of coolant direct to the water pump. The smaller bore rail in this configuration is used for heater bleed return. The original thermostat is removed, but its outer rim section is retained. There are complications with the PRT set-up as there are different ones for manual (black) and automatic (natural) coloured stats. The operation is the same, although the opening temperatures and pressures vary slightly.

The benefits of the PRT come from the fact that, as the title indicates, the unit is sensitive to pressure as well as temperature. The pressure aspect of the PRT works to almost pre-empt a coolant temperature rise, so flow is opened to the radiator circuit before heat actually reaches the PRT. Pressure changes occur with water pump rpm changes. As the engine accelerates, so does the pump and that generates a higher pressure. This is immediately transmitted through to the PRT and generates the opening response. As engine rpm increases are tied to when greater heat is generated, this sees coolant flowing earlier so peak engine temperatures are kept lower.

The original thermostat is removed from its housing but is replaced by a blanking sleeve that is nothing more than a normal thermostat with the valve parts removed. This creates a slight restriction that enables better coolant flow than having nothing.

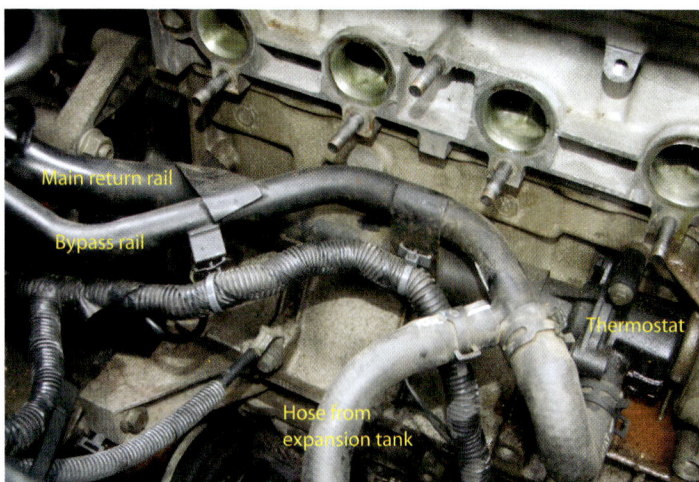

LEFT: *Fig. 4.147 Pre-2004 thermostat and coolant runs.*

Fig. 4.148   *The Pressure Relief Thermostat (PRT), introduced in June 2003, offers significant benefits to engine reliability. Shown here is the black (manual transmission) version.*

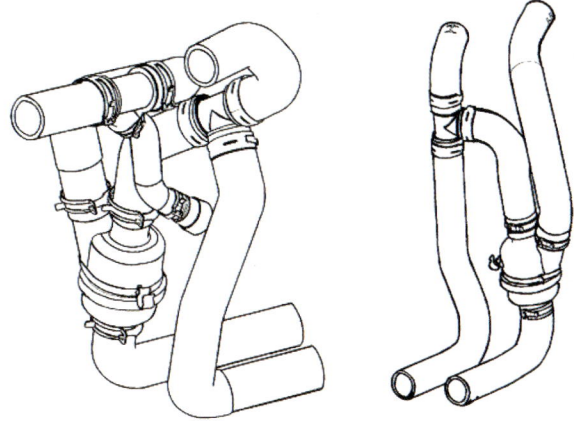

TOP LEFT: *Fig. 4.149   The black version in this MG Motor TF 135 is fitted close to the front of the engine and is not easy to see. This shows how close the return hose is to the single downpipe exhaust, although not quite as close as on the earlier MG Rover twin downpipe exhaust. Applying heat reflecting material would be a good move.   TOP CENTRE: Fig. 4.150   The general configuration of the manual PRT and its directly connected hoses. The heater return is part of this, but the heater feed is separate.   TOP RIGHT: Fig. 4.151   Automatic transmission PRT, showing that the heater feed and return are separate.*

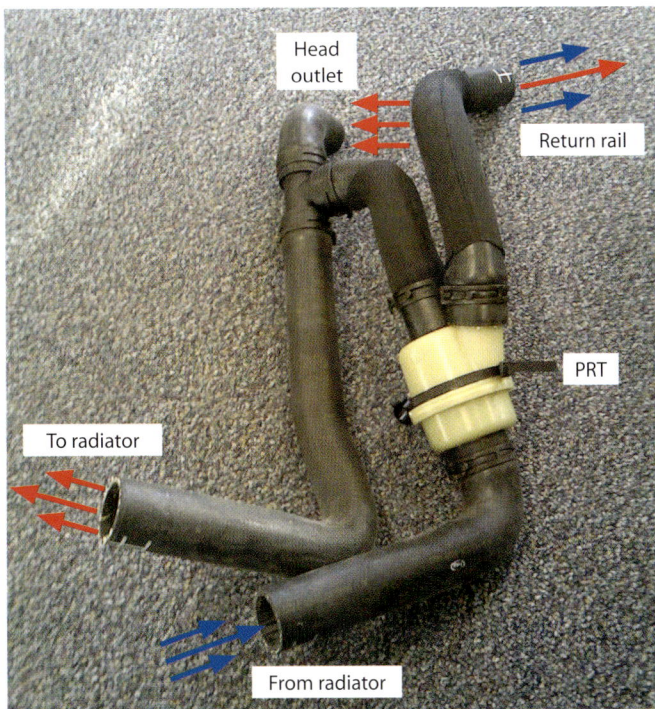

LEFT: *Fig. 4.152   The auto PRT comes as a complete assembly that is easy to retro-configure to an earlier manual or auto car when not all the original hoses are available new. The coolant flow is shown.*

ABOVE: *Fig. 4.153   PRT conversion carried out by Beech Hill Garage on a late MGF VVC using the auto PRT.*

Fig. 4.154   The conversion may not be as neat as the production set-up but worked.

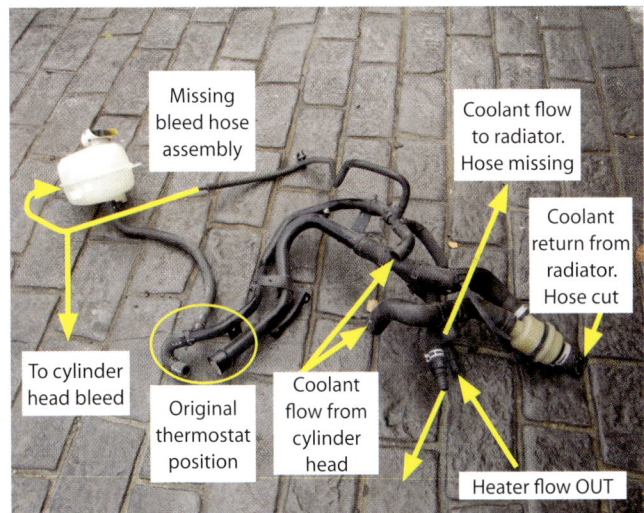

Fig. 4.155   A car being broken for spares can be a good source of most PRT hoses, such as this collection removed from a TF.

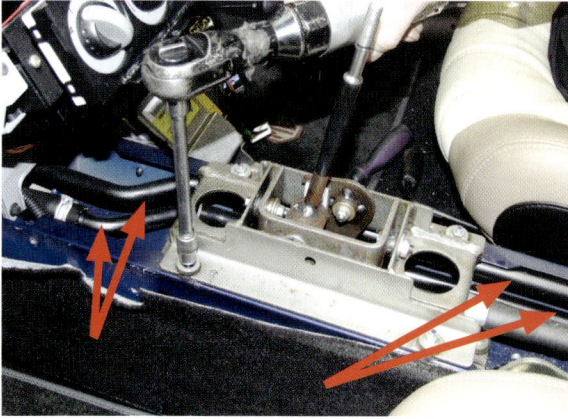

Fig. 4.156   Heater pipes (indicated) run in the 'tunnel' between the seats and under the gear change and centre console.

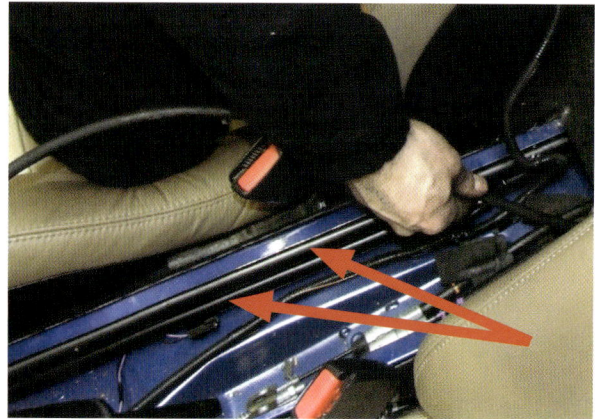

Fig. 4.157   Heater pipes run all the way to the back of the passenger compartment and into the engine bay.

The original bypass is a pipe half the diameter of the normal main coolant pipes and hoses, but with the PRT the bypass uses the main coolant pipe for much greater flow, although the original bypass remains for the heater return. As coolant warms the PRT it functions as a normal thermostat with the heating coolant passing over the thermostatic bulb. The thermostat will start to close the bypass and so create a restriction that diverts some coolant to the radiator.

The radiator circuit varies between pre- and post-PRT configurations with the earlier system seeing hot coolant exit the cylinder head into a main hose that connects to one of two under floor steel pipes that run towards the front of the car. These pipes end before the back of the front subframe and from there a hose carries coolant to one side of the radiator. Once coolant has passed through the radiator it returns to the engine via a second hose, using the other underfloor pipe before another hose connects to the 30mm metal return rail (pipe) that carries the coolant back into the engine via the water pump. Coolant only flows in this circuit if the thermostat is open.

Cars with the PRT see hot coolant exit the cylinder head and pass down to the closely located PRT. If coolant is below the temperature threshold for the stat to open, it is directed through the stat and into the main coolant return rail to be circulated back to the engine. If the temperature threshold is high enough the stat progressively redirects coolant flow from the bypass to the radiator.

The PRT was introduced into TF production in June 2003 (at VIN RD622591). It is fitted into a plastic moulded housing and has three hose connections: one from the engine, one to the return rail and one to the radiator return. The coolant temperature depends on the positioning of the internal thermostat valve, which dictates flow as indicated above, or a mix of the two.

The heater circuit sees some hot coolant exiting the cylinder head flowing through the heater circuit as long as the heater control is not set to 'cold'. This coolant travels along 15mm bore hoses to one of a pair of coolant pipes

Fig. 4.158   Auto air bleed within a plastic inlet manifold.

Fig. 4.159   An alloy inlet manifold has a similar air bleed.

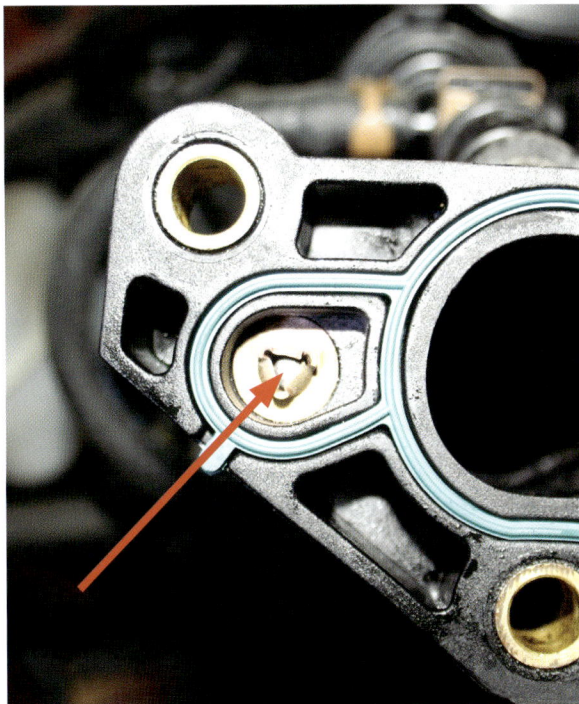

and rises, so closing off the path to the hose. If air or gas is present then the plastic pea falls to the bottom of the cage and the gas can pass into the hose and up to the expansion tank; as liquid coolant returns, it lifts the pea and the path is closed.

Sometimes this pea can block and permanently close the path and so gas remains trapped, but it is simple to check that it is free. In order to deal with any possible coolant loss, use a brake pipe clamp on the hose before removing and then immediately push on a length of similar hose. With the expansion cap removed, you can blow back into the engine through the new bit of hose to confirm the valve is working. This will often be enough to loosen a stuck pea.

A major point to note is that the total volume of the MGF and TF cooling system is 10.5 litres, whereas the average capacity of a FWD MG or Rover with the same engine is approximately 5.5 litres. This is a direct consequence of the engine being at the back of the car while the radiator remains at the front. This may not sound that significant, but it does mean there is nearly twice as much coolant to bring up to temperature and so this takes longer compared with the FWD cars. As a result there

set in the enclosed 'transmission tunnel' area inside the car. It then passes through the heater control valve and into the heater matrix, before returning via the other coolant pipe, then passing into the 15mm return rail and back into the engine.

At the front end of the inlet manifold on the engine is a small bore hose attached to a pipe stub on the inlet next to the number one inlet tract. This is an important auto air bleed where air that is trapped within the engine can automatically be purged into the expansion tank. It is in fact a very simple valve, essentially comprising a small plastic pea contained in a cage in the inlet manifold. The pea floats in liquid

Fig. 4.161 The development concept TF HPD 200 saw many aerodynamic changes, including the deletion of the open grilles between the headlamps to improve airflow through the radiator.

Fig. 4.162   Underfloor coolant pipes, which carry coolant between engine and radiator, have a reputation for corroding and leaking within about eight years. This image shows leaking original mild steel pipes (top) with the popular stainless steel replacement that have a much longer life. (Image credit Austin Garages)

Fig. 4.163   The full collection of underfloor pipes and cables only found on Auto MGFs (left to right): Hydragas suspension 1, brake vacuum, air con 1, air con 2, battery cable, coolant 1 and 2, oil cooler 1, oil cooler 2, brake hydraulic and Hydragas suspension 2. (Austin Garages)

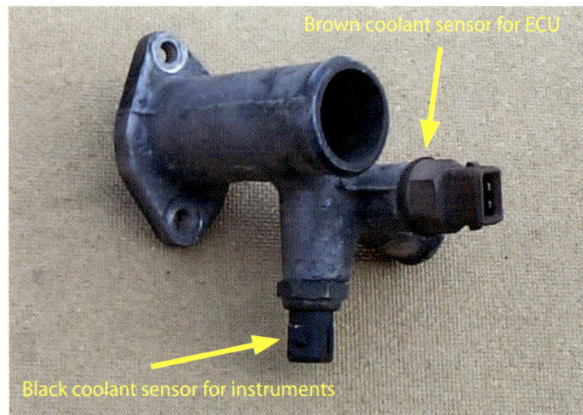

Fig. 4.164   Hot coolant leaves the cylinder head via this elbow, which has large and small bore outlets. The small bore has two temperature sensors attached, the horizontal for MEMS and the vertical one for the coolant gauge. MEMS 1.9 and 2J systems have sensors in these colours.

Fig. 4.165   MEMS 3 system uses these coloured sensors; aftermarket sensors can be any colour!

will be a longer period when there is a significant temperature difference between the bypass coolant and the return rail, so this can mean the engine sees more thermal variation.

As the coolant temperature rises it will reach a point where it acts on the temperature bulb of the thermostat and the thermostat valve starts to open, allowing cold coolant that is in the radiator circuit to enter the engine. When this flow becomes greater than the bypass flow, however, the overall temperature around the bulb will drop and so the thermostat closes. The return to just coolant from the bypass flowing over the bulb will mean that the thermostat then starts to open again and so this cycle continues. The pulsing of opening and closing results in the temperatures entering the engine cycling up and down more widely than would be the case in FWD cars with a smaller volume.

Many considered that the constant temperature change could aggravate a condition known as head shuffle, in which the head moves against the block through temperature changes, and that this would stress the elastomer sealing strips on the original SLS gasket. With PRT the bypass volume is much greater and so when colder coolant is being introduced there is less thermal variation.

One characteristic of the MGF and TF is that good airflow is only seen through the lower 20 to 30 per cent of the radiator, so much of the radiator is actually doing very little cooling. Indeed the upper bumper vents where the MG badge is fitted can see air coming back out rather than in. This has been confirmed by tests in the MIRA wind tunnel and explains why there are no vents here on the one-off TF 200HPD. This development car was able to use a much smaller radiator along with a vented bonnet to actually achieve better cooling. It is no coincidence that the part of the standard radiator doing the most work is also the part that is subject to the most corrosion.

To carry the coolant between front and rear there are two steel pipes connected together as a single assembly. Unfortunately, the original pipes are made from mild steel; even with protective processes they are known to be relatively vulnerable to corrosion and leaks can develop in less than five years. In response to this, alternative long-life stainless steel replacement pipes have been available for some years, except for auto models, and they have proved as effective as stainless steel has been to exhaust systems. Auto models have extra brackets for an oil cooler pipe, but can still use the manual version stainless pipes.

Another factor that influences coolant system performance is that the water pump is the same one used in the front-wheel drive saloons. A characteristic that can easily be observed in the expansion tank is that, when the engine has warmed, a jet of returning coolant comes in from the small bore hose that connects to the right side of the tank. At idle this stream of coolant will just about reach halfway across the tank, but between 1,400 and 1,800rpm there is a drastic increase in the flow that sees the jet hit the opposite wall inside the tank. Bearing in mind that the distance moved by the coolant in an MGF/TF is considerably greater than in any FWD saloon, it is obvious that any loss in water pump performance generates problems more quickly in the MGF and TF.

There are two coolant temperature sensors in the hot coolant outlet attached to the cylinder head next to the number 4 cylinder exhaust manifold runner. The one that passes information to the engine ECU points horizontally and is coloured brown on pre-2001 cars and black on 2001 and later cars. The one pointing down is for the temperature gauge in the instrument pack; it is black on pre-2001 cars, but this was changed to blue for later models. Additional confirmation comes from the fact that the engine ECU sensor has two wires in the two-

pin plug to the sensor, while the gauge sensor has only a single wire in its two-pin plug.

Cooling System Issues

Coolant hoses have a finite life. On a car more than ten years old it is reasonable to expect that it may be necessary to renew the hoses. Most are quite reliable and there are many cars with hoses that have given good service for fifteen years or more, but any with a moulded-in take-off are likely to be weaker. The main hose returning coolant from the underfloor pipe to the engine return rail also has a moulded-in connection for the heater return and these have been known to fail. Replacement hoses no longer have a moulded-in joint, and instead there is a plastic moulding for the junction.

The most common pump problem is that it will start to weep coolant from the mainshaft vent hole in the underside of the main body casting. I have seen this on infrequently used cars that have only just reached 30,000 miles from new. When a car is in regular use,

however, I would not normally expect a pump to show these signs until the 70 to 80,000 mile window on average. While the weeping rate is relatively low, once started it never gets any better and may develop into a steady trickle that soon lowers coolant levels to introduce overheating and all the maladies connected with that.

Always remember with the MGF and TF that, while there may be 10.5 litres of coolant in the system, only 2 litres of this is in the engine. Low coolant capacity within the engine is designed to allow fast warm-up from cold to aid efficiency, but this low level of coolant inside the engine also allows for overheating to develop very quickly. The 2004 model year and newer cars benefit from a very worthwhile low coolant sensing and warning system. Earlier cars can fit aftermarket warning systems to achieve the same peace of mind.

The K series water pump is a rather simple-looking pump with a small cast alloy body with a toothed wheel driven from the cam belt, and a pressed steel impellor, rather crude looking

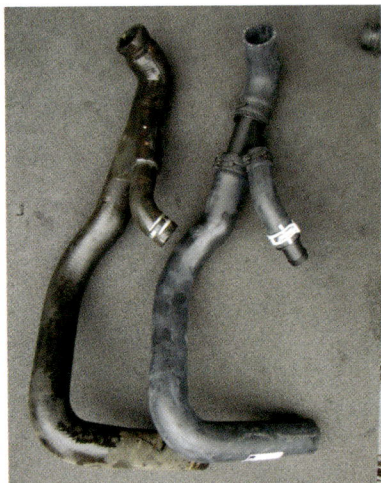

RIGHT: *Fig. 4.166 Pre-PRT cars use this hose for the main return flow from radiator to engine and the heater return feeds into it. Most, if not all, MGFs used a hose with a moulded connection and this can split, especially on older cars. The replacements have a more durable plastic moulded junction.*

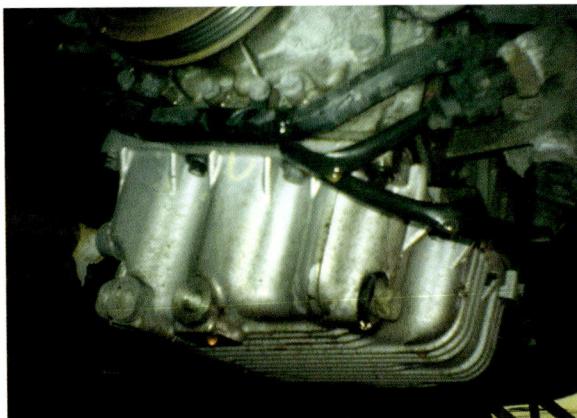

ABOVE: *Fig. 4.167 Another example of a weeping K series water pump.*
LEFT: *Fig. 4.168 Coolant is often found dripping from under the front pulley area and the front of the sump.*

LEFT: *Fig. 4.169   K series water pumps are simple castings with a pressed steel impellor.*

RIGHT: *Fig. 4.170   The impellor is driven by the cambelt.*

BELOW: *Fig. 4.171   Later pumps had an 'evaporation chamber', which may be described uncharitably as a means of hiding the pumps' failure to remain sealed.*

but effective enough, that is an interference fit onto the mainshaft. I have no depth of experience using the cast impellor type of pump, and no feedback from anyone who has used one, but there is no reason to suppose they perform any different.

The addition of what is called an 'evaporation chamber' on the K series water pump has raised unanswered questions. The chamber is nothing more than a small additional cast-in box above the lowest fixing bolt position, fitted with a little moulded rubber cap. As the positioning of the chamber is right in line with the dribbles that can escape past the water pump shaft seal, this may be intended to catch small dribbles and allow them to evaporate before reaching, and perhaps damaging, the cam belt. More serious leaks will soon bypass this chamber and show the telltale drips from the back of the crank pulley. In my view the water pump should be changed if there is any

sign of it leaking; a new water pump should also be fitted when a cambelt is changed.

I have also seen pump failures when the shaft bearing has worn, but fortunately this is rare as pumps usually leak well before this. On one such occasion the car's owner was the type who only responds to having maintenance work done when the car screams at them: having to top up the coolant twice a day was seen as inconvenient, but as

the car hadn't stopped it must be OK to continue to use! Quite how this hadn't resulted in a HGF or the belt jumping, as there was considerable slack in the cambelt, is beyond explanation.

Another, fortunately rare, cause of failure is where the impellor is not adequately pressed onto the mainshaft and comes loose. My first experience of this was with an HGF repair. When reaching the cooling system warm-up after bleeding the system, there was clear indication of warming up, but no circulation. Repeat bleeding made no difference and I had to stand back and consider the possibilities. Logic finally said to check the water pump, even though it was going to mean draining the cooling system and disconnecting the cambelt. It was still a surprise, though, as soon as I withdrew the pump, to hear a tinkling sound as the impellor fell off.

Fortunately, changing a pump on the K series is usually quick and simple once

Fig. 4.172   Water pumps occasionally fail when the impellor loosens on the mainshaft. This is more understandable on a pump that has done many miles, such as this one.

Fig. 4.173   Such a failure is not acceptable on a little used pump like this.

the cambelt is off. This is helped by the use of a separate 'O' ring seal that sits in the machined groove in the pump body: as it comes away cleanly there is no stuck gasket to have to chisel off, just a quick clean of the engine mating surface and the new pump can go on. You should only have problems where one or more of the six fixing bolts has seized, so go easy when undoing the bolts to avoid shearing them.

Detaching impellors is not a problem that only affects old and well-used pumps. I have seen the problem on a new pump fitted by an owner who couldn't understand why all was fine for a couple of days and then there was no circulation. Past experience of what can cause a lack of circulation made me suggest removing the pump, and once again the impellor was ready to fall off.

Steel Underfloor Coolant Pipes

The two main coolant pipes run in a recess along the centreline of the car. In standard form these pipes are painted steel and unfortunately their life is quite limited before corrosion causes coolant leaks. Often this may manifest itself in a small coolant leak that is difficult to trace, especially if the leak is one that projects coolant to the ground and leaves little telltale wet patches, so you may have to revisit the search process several times before it is found.

Just as stainless steel has become a favoured material to enhance the life of exhaust systems, so its use has done the same for these underfloor coolant pipes. Fitting these is a direct swap for the originals. Since they cost little more than the mild steel originals, the extra expense is well worth considering (*see* Fig. 4.162). The stainless steel replacements are fitted in exactly the same way as standard mild steel pipes, and the job is no more complicated than it appears, with the possible interference of a seized bolt or two on the main under passenger floor reinforcement tray, which is held to the body by no fewer than twenty two bolts.

All the underfloor coolant pipes for manual cars are common, so the stainless replacements are able to fit all. The automatic transmission cars (the Steptronic and Stepspeed models) have the same basic pipes but, because the auto cars have a front-mounted

Fig. 4.174   Underfloor main coolant pipes have a reputation for corroding. This example of weeping from corrosion where a fixing strap was welded occurred after nine years.

Fig. 4.175   This hole developed after only four years. Topping up a coolant leak every week diluted the antifreeze (and anti-corrosion) to the point where it accelerated the corrosion.

Fig. 4.176   Under the centre of the car there is a substantial bracing plate held on by no fewer than 22 bolts. This has to be removed when changing the underfloor pipes. This is a good time to treat the floor and bolt holes with underbody Waxoyl.

transmission oil cooler, they have an additional pair of oil pipes running to the front of the car, and there are extra mounting tags attached to the coolant pipes to allow mounting of one oil pipe.

Heater Pipes

The MGF and TF also have two steel heater pipes joined together in a similar way to the underfloor coolant pipes. These heater pipes run in the closed tunnel area between the seats, all the way to the engine bay. As this area is dry and well insulated from any weather, there should not be any corrosion occurring from the outside, but just as the main underfloor pipes can corrode from the inside out, there is always a risk that in time these may also develop a leak. Fortunately, to date this

has not been a common issue and only the occasional car has suffered, but it reinforces the need to ensure coolant is kept fresh and changed according to service schedules (*see* Figs 4.156 and 4.157). At the time of writing these pipes seem to be available only in the original painted mild steel, but if failures increase I am sure that one of the major MG spares suppliers will offer stainless steel versions.

The heater valve is located between the front of these pipes and the heater. Characteristically, with these valves there is often quite a variance between the setting selected and the heat delivered. Whereas you might expect the heat setting on the knob to deliver a specific level of heat in two different cars, this will only be true about half the time. It appears that the valve loses

efficiency as the cars accrue higher mileages. Trying to set a lower background heat level becomes a frustrating job of constant fiddling, and the only way to stop the annoyance is to replace the valve.

The valve available in 2011 was the third since the MGF first appeared. The one I had for replacement on my MGF was an older 'new' part bought online and I don't know whether the two superseded parts have seen any specification change or just supplier changes. Since then I have had another that doesn't seem to be any different.

Fitting a new heater valve is a matter of crawling into the right-hand footwell and pulling the carpet back. Brake hose clamps allow you to isolate the valve with a little coolant inside, but you still need to take precautions to catch about a cupful of coolant, and I suggest a good surrounding of old towels to catch any spills that are not contained in a small container.

Other than this the replacement is as described in the workshop manual, but do remember to bleed the radiator after the new valve is fitted and top up the expansion tank (*see* later in this section for more details). The amount of air that will get into the system is small and should not affect any other part of the cooling system, but it is far better to ensure none is present.

Engine Coolant Return Rail (Pipes)

There are also steel coolant pipes that run from above the gearbox clutch housing around the back of the engine under the inlet manifold. These consist of a large bore pipe, about 30mm in diameter, that carries the main coolant flow and a second pipe of about half that bore carrying the bypass flow. Most have a common design where the pipes are of almost equal length, but the 160ps VVC engines introduced an oil/coolant heat exchanger. The smaller bore return rail on these engines is much shorter to allow coolant hose fitting to the heat exchanger.

These pipes are made from mild steel and, being in the relatively kind environment of her engine bay, they do not normally rust on cars that are used reasonably frequently. External corrosion cannot be ruled out, however, on cars that are infrequently used.

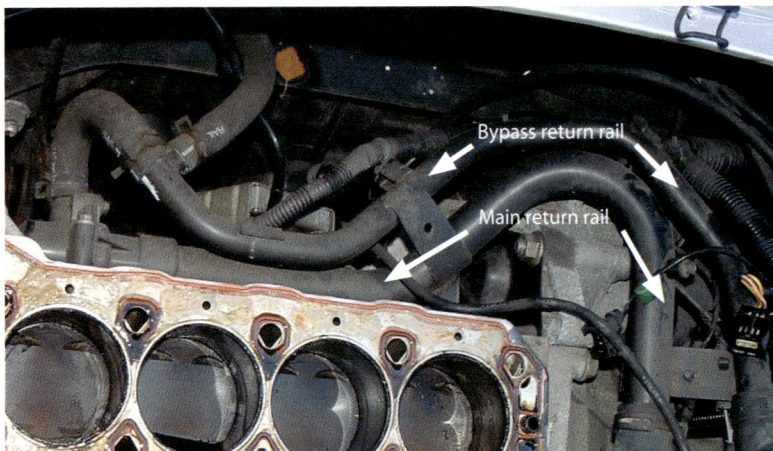

Fig. 4.177   Paired mild steel coolant pipes or rails return coolant to the engine from the radiator (large bore) and bypass (small bore). They are reasonably resistant to corrosion as long as the antifreeze mix is strong and the car is frequently used.

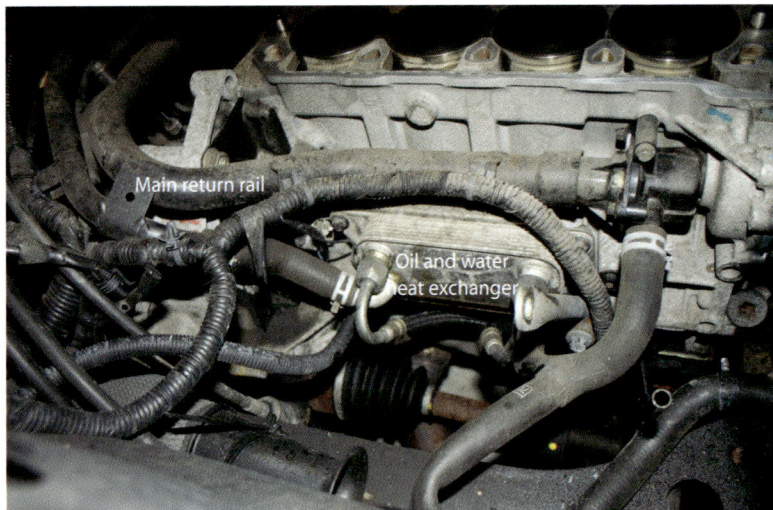

Fig. 4.178   160ps VVC engined cars also feature an oil/coolant heat exchanger, rather than a cooler, as it can transfer heat into the oil during warm-up as well as remove heat when the engine is used hard.

Stainless steel replacements for the common (not 160VVC) type are already available from some specialists.

The larger bore pipe has a sliding fit onto the end of the thermostat housing (whether there is a stat fitted or not) and sealing is by way of an 'O' ring. Removal is not an issue but refitting is: it is very easy to damage the 'O' ring and generate coolant leakage. It is advised to renew the 'O' ring if the pipe has to be disconnected or the thermostat housing has to be removed for any reason. Note that when the housing is removed there is another 'O' ring to seal the end that is inserted into the engine block.

Heating Problems on PRT Cars

PRT cars have a slightly different hose configuration to supply hot coolant to the heater. In order to ensure good flow to the heater, a plastic restrictor is inserted into the hose between the four-way junction and the smaller bore return rail. If this restrictor is missing, as in the accompanying view of a 2005 TF hose, then the heater performance should be markedly poorer, especially at low to medium rpms.

Restrictors are not available as a separate part. If it should be necessary to fit one to a car that is missing the restrictor, then the basic dimensions of the original inserted moulding are 17mm long, 10mm outer diameter and the centre hole inside diameter is 8mm. It appears that the item is not specifically made for this application but is a part from another component that achieves the desired end. It is only available as part of the whole hose assembly (PCH002792, which at the time of writing was £46.31 plus VAT). Some flow through the return rail is constantly needed and on 160Ps engines this flow is used to pass through the oil coolant heat exchanger.

Radiator

Radiators in an MGF seem to have a shorter life than those in a TF. Problems most commonly appear in the lower section, which can be viewed by kneeling down and looking into the lower air intake under the number plate. If it looks bad, you may be certain that it will be twice as bad in reality. It is not unknown for an MGF to go over an unseen speed bump far too fast and cause the radiator to collapse in a big cloud of steam. This rather unexpected result can be better appreciated as radiators sometimes fall apart as they are removed for replacement.

The workshop manual describes removing the front bumper panel to effect replacement, but there is a short cut that makes the job quite simple. You should first remove the four bolts holding the bonnet locking platform to the body (the panel between the headlamps that engages with the bonnet when it shuts), then the four bolts holding the upper radiator clamps. Also remove the five cross-headed screws that hold the top edge of the plastic front bumper to this panel.

You now need to remove the two 10mm headed nuts that are immediately forward of the bonnet catch. The bolts these nuts attach to are not captive and they will start to spin as soon as the tension is removed. This is where you need to lift the edge of the plastic bumper and squeeze a hand inside to hold the head of the bolt or, if the thread is really tight, then hold an 8mm spanner onto the head.

Once these last two fixings are removed the panel can be lifted up

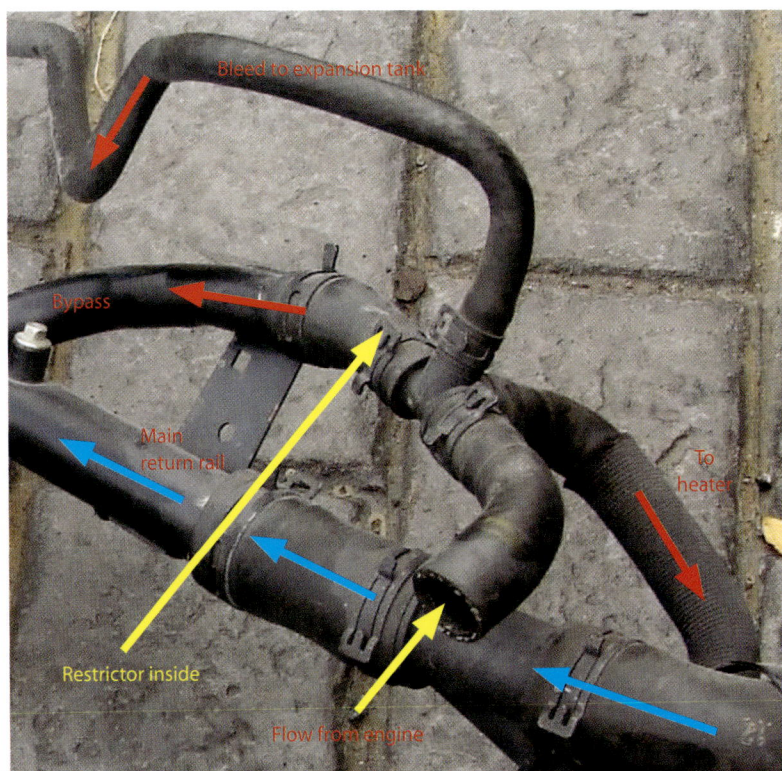

Fig. 4.179   Heater performance on PRT cars can often be poor at low engine rpms because the flow characteristics are different to the earlier cars. This schematic shows coolant flow and where the restrictor is fitted.

Fig. 4.180   The clearly open hose shows that this 2005 135 model is not fitted with a restrictor.

Fig. 4.181   The restrictor is a simple plastic moulding with an 8mm centre hole pushed into the hose.

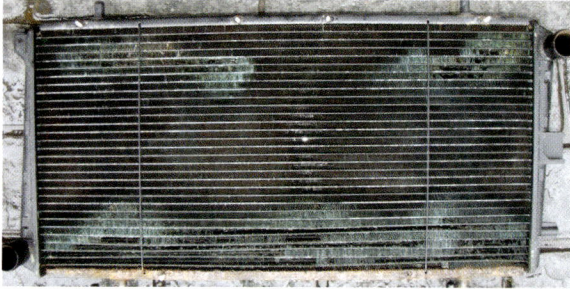

Fig. 4.182   MGF radiators often degrade more rapidly than those fitted to the TF. Corrosion, such as this on an eight-year-old MGF typically always looks better than it actually is.

Fig. 4.183   A significant amount of the radiator broke away when moved.

Fig. 4.184   Remove the bolts and the screws indicated.

Fig. 4.185   Remove the two nuts indicated here. Lift the bumper panel to access the loose bolts behind.

and placed into the spare wheel well area, as the bonnet release cable is still attached. (Take the opportunity to make sure the cable is tightly connected.) This panel also carries the two radiator upper mountings; these do not have to be removed separately as they simply lift off the radiator locating pins, but they are usually rusted and for that reason I include them as items to remove.

Now to simplify reassembly using the 'short cut' route, clean the threads of those two bolts and run their nuts up and down several times to confirm you can easily wind the nuts fully on the bolt threads with light finger effort, but do not add any lubricant. Now apply some silicone sealant, or other available adhesive, around the bolt head and refit it to the vertical strap. Allow some setting time before you come to reassemble them when there is usually enough adhesion achieved to make fitting the nuts back on and tightening them an easy job.

Those wishing to make a permanent modification can unbolt the strap's bottom two bolts to remove it from the car, noting that this may require bumper removal. Weld the bolts to the upper part of the strap, then rub down and repaint to restore corrosion protection before refitting.

Fig. 4.186   Once all the fixings are removed, lift the bonnet locking platform up and place it in the spare wheel well. The bolts behind the bumper panel have now been stuck to the panel with silicone sealant to make for easy refitting.

Radiator removal with the bonnet locking platform removed is really quite simple. Undo the hose clips and remove the hoses. Reach down and unclip the radiator fan electrical plug (there are two identical fans on air con-equipped cars and those for some export markets). The radiator is now ready to be lifted out with the fan(s). Do not be surprised if the radiator has the rigidity of a piece of stale bread, such is the commonality of corrosion.

If air conditioning is fitted the condenser radiator is rigidly mounted directly in front of the coolant radiator, so reducing the space to lift the coolant radiator and fans. In this case it will help to remove the fans from the radiator frame first. Expect the captive studs to be weaker than the grip between nut and studs, especially on the lower fixings, and for them to rip out. This is not an issue for the old radiator as you will be changing it, but you may need to recover the nuts, since they are a less common M5 size. In fact buying six new

Fig. 4.187   Radiator removal is quite straightforward: remove the hose connections and the fan's electrical plug.

Fig. 4.188   Lift out the radiator.

flange nuts, or plain nuts with washers, before refitting the radiator would avoid any delays.

Examine the two lower rubbers that sit in the lower body member and provide seating for the two radiator locating pegs. Corrosion from the radiator will usually contaminate these rubbers, requiring them to be cleaned up before fitting the new radiator into place, perhaps adding a smear of rubber lube if you have any. The two upper rubbers that sit in the mountings attached to the bonnet locking platform do not normally become contaminated and can usually be simply refitted, but once again a smear of rubber lube is helpful.

Refitting the radiator is now a reverse of the removal process, making sure that you remember to reconnect the fan electrical plug(s). Next refit the bonnet locking panel back into place and start by feeding the two bolts you stuck into the vertical strap earlier through the two holes in the platform. The previous work cleaning threads now comes into play in usually allowing the nuts to be spun on by hand tightly enough without having to squeeze your hand under the top edge of the bumper. Obviously welded bolts will be solidly fixed and offer no resistance to easy nut tightening.

If the coolant in the system was due for a change, before simply refilling the system with fresh coolant it is worth remembering that some old coolant residues will be present within the coolant passages. It is beneficial to refill the cooling system with fresh water and run the engine to dilute these residues, and then drain the system again. If changing from the earlier pre-2000 Ethylene Glycol coolant to the later OAT coolant (or another coolant such as Castrol 4Life), you need to remove as much of the old coolant as possible since the different coolants do not mix. It is a sensible move to repeat the flush, including running the engine to circulate the flushing water. Remember to ensure that the heater control is set to 'Hot' so that the heater circuit is flushed too.

Refill and Bleeding

Refilling and bleeding the cooling system is a critically important part of the job as airlocks restrict coolant flow, which in turn causes overheating that can damage the engine. Relatively new coolant can be reused as long as it is filtered, but the low cost of new coolant means it is usually best to renew. If using premixed coolant you can simply pour it into the cooling system, but if it needs to be diluted then make up a quantity of 50/50 mix of antifreeze and water. Bear in mind that the standard system capacity is 10.5 litres, but you will not be able to add this much. If refilling with the previously drained coolant, the volume that came out must go back in, usually allowing a bit extra to cater for what you spilt. If it doesn't, it will be because there are air locks.

When buying fresh coolant you must ensure that the correct type of coolant is used. In June 2000, at approximately VIN RD 520013, the coolant changed from the traditional non-organic antifreeze, which is usually identified by being blue or green in colour, to the new Organic Acid Technology (OAT) type of antifreeze, usually identified by being orange or pink in colour. The service change point for these two types of antifreeze also changed from two years for the non-organic type to four years for the OAT type.

Bleeding air from the system is such an important aspect and lay at the root of a significant number of HGF issues that occurred in the first five years of MGF production. Although it was never categorically proven in individual cases, the frequency of HGFs that followed very shortly after the first coolant change was too high not to have a common trigger – the coolant change. It is also one of the reasons behind MG Rover's recommendation to use the vacuum coolant drain and refill method rather than the manual bleed method, though it should be stressed that there should be no problem when the manual bleed is done properly.

There are three drain points and initially only two are used: the third only comes into play when bleeding by the first two doesn't clear all the air. The first bleed is on the radiator and accessed through a hole in the top panel next to the left-hand headlamp when the bonnet is open. That is opened until a steady stream of coolant is seen. The plug is a plastic threaded type with a 13mm hexagon head. These are quite weak and over time they can become brittle with many heating and cooling cycles. It is all too easy to either break them or strip the thread with over-

Fig. 4.189 Radiator bleed point.

Fig. 4.190 Heater bleed.

enthusiastic tightening. They need only be tight enough to stop coolant from leaking out, followed by a nip of perhaps a tenth of a turn to ensure it doesn't vibrate loose.

The second bleed is the heater bleed and looks identical to a brake caliper nipple sticking through the centre of the main front bulkhead. It can be accessed once the thin plastic cover behind the spare wheel is removed. Once again it is opened until a steady stream of coolant is seen. After these two bleed points have been attended to the coolant level is brought to the halfway seam line in the expansion tank and the engine started.

Ensure the heater is still turned to hot, open at least one dashboard air vent and set the fan to the second speed. In most cases the engine will warm up quickly and within a few minutes heat will quickly be felt coming through the open vent(s) into the car. Water pump efficiency and warm up is much better if the revs are held at around 1,500.

While the arrival of heat from the heater vents is fairly rapid, the volume of the cooling system means that, depending on the outside air temperature, it takes about twenty minutes in summer or forty minutes in winter to warm up the whole system. If the temperature gauge rises above halfway, this is a clear sign of an air lock and you should switch off and bleed the system again.

On pre-PRT cars the smaller bore return rail, which runs around the back of the engine under the inlet manifold, should start to heat up very quickly, as this is on the coolant heater and bypass circuit, and it soon becomes too hot to hold. It takes those twenty to forty minutes for the larger bore return rail to warm and eventually feel as hot as the smaller bore pipe. Not long after this the radiator cooling fan should come on, run for a couple of minutes and then switch off.

PRT cars will also see the smaller bore pipe warm up, as there is still bleed flow passing through it. Since the thermostat is close to the hot coolant outlet from the engine, however, and the main bypass flow uses the large bore return rail, this will get hot much faster and doesn't give the same indication that the whole system is circulating coolant. To verify this you need to go back to the front of the car, where the spare wheel and plastic cover will have been removed for access to the heater bleed, and you can now look through the hole behind the spare wheel well for the two coolant hoses that connect between the underfloor pipes and the radiator. You will feel one slowly get hot first, followed a few minutes later by the other one, indicating coolant flow.

The coolant gauge is very quick to rise during warm-up, but very slow to respond to any rise in temperatures beyond normal operation, so if the gauge rises beyond its normal reading it indicates an air lock is present and requires another bleed, but this time with the addition of the third bleed point. This third bleed point is actually just an 8mm headed bolt in the larger bore coolant rail, where it sits above the gearbox.

Normal operation is when the heater blows very hot air, the gauge reading remains static at the normal running position, the coolant pipes feel hot all around and the radiator fan has cut in and out at least twice. Even then I have found that some cars benefit from a subsequent bleed after a ten-mile drive, and it is common to see the expansion tank level settle by a few centimetres, but then not drop any further in subsequent use.

Fig. 4.191 Engine rail bleed.

Jiggle Valves

Another aspect of the pre-PRT cooling system on the MGF and early TF is that there are a couple of jiggle valves for internal air bleeding back to the header tank, whereas the PRT cars have just a single valve. It is worth checking them when a cooling system is drained. The common one for all engines is in the inlet manifold next to the number one inlet tract, as is clearly indicated by the small bore hose that connects to the pipe stub forming part of the manifold (*see* Figs 4.159 and 4.160).

The inlet manifold valve consists of a 'pea' in a cage. The pea moves with coolant flow and this covers the outlet port and restricts coolant flow. When an air/gas bubble arrives the pea 'drops' and the bubble is able to pass into the bleed hose, but as coolant follows the pea is moved back and closes off the path. The bubble then makes its way to the expansion tank and coolant replaces the bubble.

In the pre-PRT specification cars there is also a similar 'pea' jiggle valve within a plastic assembly. This sits at the top of a large bore hose forming part of the 'convoluted' hose that sits above the gearbox. This valve regulates the flow of coolant back to the expansion tank via the small bore hose connected to the right side of the tank, and its function can be viewed by looking at the flow from this return. At idle it is usual to see a stream of coolant inside the expansion tank that reaches approximately halfway across the tank. Raise the engine rpm to around 1,500 and the jet blasts the opposite inner wall of the tank. If you raise the rpm even higher, the flow will stop, indicating normal operation.

Both 'pea' valves can become stuck or blocked over time. This can certainly follow any HGF where the cooling system has suffered engine oil ingress and the oil and coolant mix has left a horrible light brown 'soup'. In these conditions you are likely to need more direct cleaning and use strong professional cooling system cleaning agents designed to deal with gummed-up cooling systems.

Where there is considerable oil contamination in the cooling system, it is of paramount importance that

Fig. 4.192   A jiggle valve is located here on pre-PRT cars to regulate coolant flow back to the expansion tank.

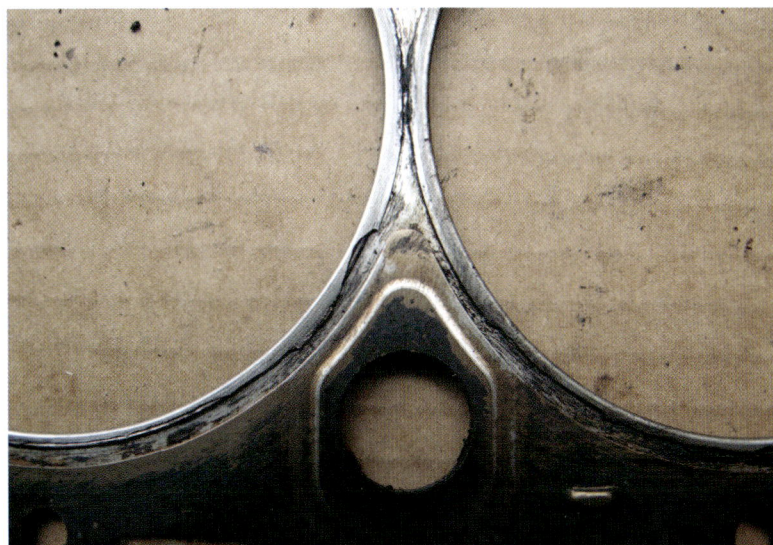

Fig. 4.193   This MLS gasket has suffered serious erosion of the fire rings in just over 40,000 miles.

Fig. 4.194   A new gasket demonstrates the extent of corrosion on the earlier example.

some coolant can flow through all the coolant passages if the additive is to have any cleaning effect. If, like me, you have taken on a car that had a HGF some considerable time before, and then stood immobile for some time before you bought it, then you can expect those oil/coolant deposits to have become a soft 'wax' demanding a more forceful cleaning approach. Usually the 30mm bore pipes and hoses will be clear enough, but the 15mm and smaller bore will very likely be blocked. I have found it necessary to use compressed air to clear them enough to allow the coolant to flow. In lieu of compressed air, mains water pressure may be enough; otherwise it is going to mean physical removal of all affected pipes and hoses to clear them individually.

Most cars will behave and the refill and bleed will be relatively painless. The task can be completed in less than two hours, but some cars will need repeated bleeding. In difficult cases raising the front of the car can provide some benefit.

A separate but related condition is when airlocks develop during normal use. This is indicated when unexpected early operation of the radiator fan is accompanied by a sudden rise of temperature gauge above normal, allied to a sudden drop in temperature from the heater. There is no issue when driving normally, but these conditions may occur when you come to a halt, for example at traffic lights. Interestingly they are almost instantly corrected by a sudden rev of the engine. No coolant loss is apparent but bleeding the system will show trapped air, and normal operation is restored when this is removed.

Logic says that airlocks don't just happen and the only place for air (gas) to come from is the combustion chamber. Over a period of several thousand miles this particular car started to see more frequent need for bleeding. Removing the head revealed some interesting erosion of the gasket fire rings on the underside (in contact with the liners), which was the source of the bad cylinder sealing. The MLS gasket was 3½ years old and had seen just over 40,000 miles (Figs 4.192 and 4.193).

Interestingly, the new radiator, just over 2½ years old and with less than 30,000 miles use, was also corroded and starting to weep. It was very much like the original radiator I replaced at eight years of age and well over twice the mileage, and at the time of writing the cause is unclear.

160 VVC Engine Blockages: Pre-PRT with Oil Cooler

The 160 VVC-engined cars have a standard coolant/oil heat exchanger (*see* Fig. 4.178) bolted to the engine block under the inlet manifold. Coolant uses the bypass rail pass through this before reaching the thermostatic bulb of the thermostat. Oil flow is taken from the oil filter housing and run around the engine via two steel braided hoses. It has been found on some engines that overheating may be caused by blockages within the coolant passages of this oil cooler. Therefore when dealing with cooling system issues with one of these engines, especially when oil has entered the cooling system, it is vital to ensure this is not blocked. On the PRT-equipped cars this specific issue can't arise.

Low Coolant Warning Systems

Coolant loss is almost a mandatory condition accompanying HGF, so having a low level warning system to provide early warning of such loss can provide that critically important opportunity to prevent overheating and potentially more serious engine damage. For all pre-2004 model year cars only a physical check of the expansion tank coolant level is provided; on the 2004 model year cars from VIN RD634868, however, a low level warning system was incorporated that provides a warning lamp on the instrument pack.

Cars from VIN RD632424 to RD634868 were fitted with the wiring, warning lamp and the SCU that controls this warning system, but they did not have the later expansion tank and sensor that clips to the underside of the tank. If these cars are fitted with the later tank and sensor, and are then run through the dealer pre-delivery check process to activate the system, they too can benefit from a very effective built-in low coolant sensing system (*see* Fig. 4.7).

Aftermarket conversions also exist, including one by MG specialist Brown and Gammons (B&G) that uses the MG Rover expansion tank and sensor as the basis of a stand-alone and very effective low coolant warning system. This system, which has an OE (Original Equipment) feel about it, has both a warning LED and a buzzer, and the self-check system operates each time the ignition is switched on.

A more basic and cheaper, but still effective, system is sold under the name of Lo-Larm. This uses the same sensing principles but achieves this with additions to the original expansion tank, including an internal float

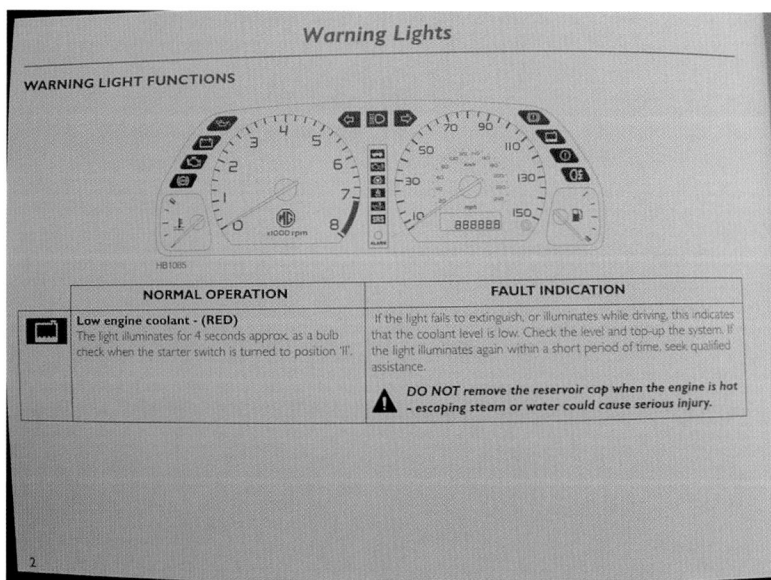

Fig. 4.195 Page from a 2004/5 TF handbook supplement identifying the standard low coolant level warning system fitted to these cars.

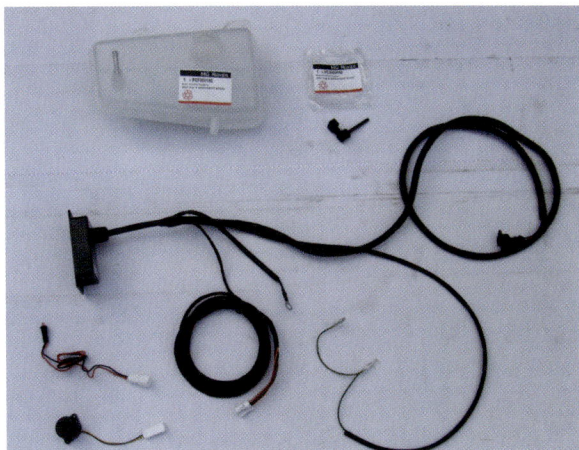

Fig. 4.196 Aftermarket low coolant level warning systems are available, such as this Brown and Gammons kit specifically designed for the MGF and pre-2004 model year TF with warning light and buzzer alarm. The kit is here being adapted to fit an MG ZS using that model's expansion tank.

Fig. 4.197 The Lo Larm aftermarket kit attaches a sensor and float to the existing expansion tank and has an audible alarm.

and an external sensor stuck to the underside of the expansion tank.

The MG and B&G systems have a built-in alarm delay, which means that a surge of coolant around the tank will not cause the alarm to activate during spirited driving or heavier braking.

Cooling Fan(s)

The radiator cooling fan(s) – two are fitted on cars with air conditioning or intended for some export markets – are controlled by the engine management system, which activates them at a relatively high 104°C (102°C on some early cars) and switches them off at 96°C. When fault finding or bleeding the cooling system, the fan should only operate when the coolant pipes, hoses and radiator are fully hot. If not, then this once again indicates an air lock. During normal cooling system operation when it is bled and

working properly, the fan comes in and out normally with no movement on the coolant gauge, even though the same temperature variation during warm-up shows more gauge movement.

If you are not sure whether the radiator cooling fan is functional, then removing the electrical plug from the engine management coolant sensor on the coolant outlet from the head (brown or black sensor, depending on the car's age) should enable the ECU to see a break in the circuit and put the fan on. If there is no operation, connect a paper clip between the two terminals in the plug. This allows a maximum voltage to pass, which the ECU will interpret as an overly hot engine and operate the fan. If you still get no fan operation, check the fuses and then the fan to find out why it doesn't work.

MGF and some early TFs had separate control for the radiator and engine

bay cooling fans (the fan in the right-hand side air vent), but on later TFs both fans were synchronized to operate together.

Heater Fan

The heater fan is generally very reliable. Only if moisture has entered while it has sat for long periods or when leaves have managed to get in will there be any untoward noise or failure to work. This can't be said for the resistor pack, which reduces voltage to provide the three slower fan speeds. The resistance is created using three small coils of wire of different thickness that each provides a different resistance. The greatest resistance is provided by the thinnest wire coil and this gives the slowest speed, with a slightly thicker wire for the second speed, and a thicker for the third speed. Maximum speed is where the motor sees full system voltage.

Fig. 4.198 Most MGFs and TFs have only a single fan in the right-hand position. Cars with air conditioning have two fans, as shown here. (Austin Garages).

Fig. 4.199 The heater fan speeds are governed by resistive coils in this unit; the small coil indicated is always the first to fail.

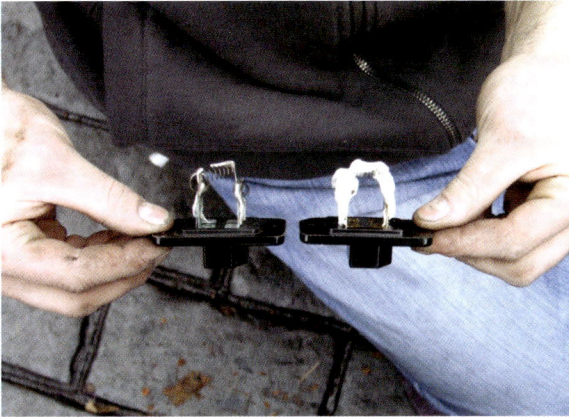

Fig. 4.200   Normally a complete new resistor pack is fitted to overcome coil failures, but cheaper aftermarket replacement coils can be soldered in place of damaged coils.

Fig. 4.201   Replacement of the resistor pack is simple on cars without air conditioning, but when it is fitted the evaporator, seen here sticking out below the glove box, is in the way. Removal demands degassing the air con.

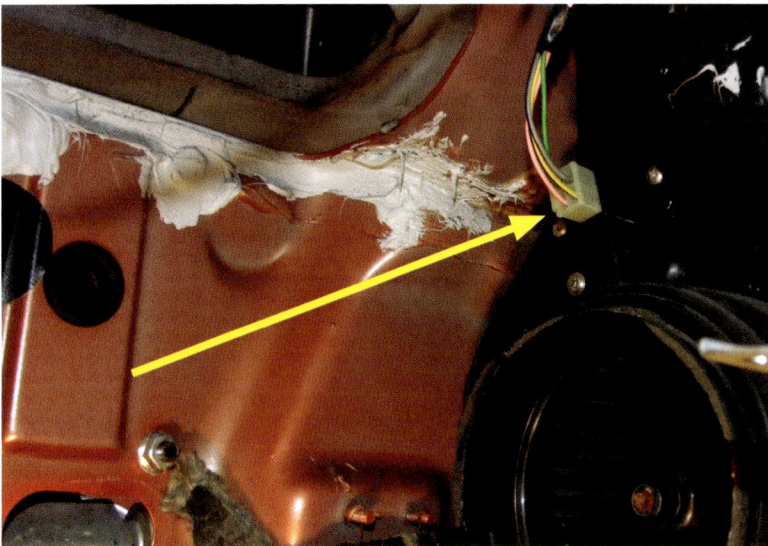

Fig. 4.202   Once removed, access to the resistor pack is wide open. Just one electrical plug and two screws have to be dealt with.

Creating this resistance also generates heat and this is why these resistor packs are mounted into the intake air duct so that airflow cools the coils. Even with this cooling, coils are regularly known to fail, starting usually with the first speed and then less often with the second. Rarely have I seen failure of the third speed coil, but then this is fairly logical since the first speed is often on for long periods as ram effect airflow is relatively poor on the MGF and TF. Second speed failure tends to occur on cars that have suffered a first speed failure and the resistor has not been replaced or repaired, so second speed now takes the burden and over time this also fails.

These resistor coils are mounted on a board with a single multi-wire plug for the electrical connection and a couple of screws to secure the module to the airbox of the heater assembly. Replacing this on cars without air conditioning is really quite simple and involves dropping the glove box for ease of access, then loosening the big jubilee clip holding the air duct from the air intake to the heater and the single anchor, so that the duct can be removed. The resistor pack can then be seen sitting on top of the heater air intake and it is a simple remove and replace with a new one.

If your car has air conditioning, however, then the simplicity of the process just described is turned completely on its head and it becomes a real pain. The issue is that the air con evaporator is fitted between the air intake and heater and completely blocks access to the resistor pack, unless either it or the facia is removed. Neither option is that attractive. Normally the evaporator assembly is removed, but this first demands that the refrigerant has to be professionally evacuated to allow removal of the air con. Once the resistor pack is changed, then refitting and refilling the air con makes the job costly.

A replacement resistor pack is a relatively expensive item at approximately £50. As a result, for some years enterprising individuals have created replacement coils that can be quite soldered in place of the failed originals. My experience is that they may not fully replicate the originals, but they are more than close enough to be regarded as a practical alternative, with the bonus of saving around £40. My experience of one under the name of Rezpax is very positive (www.rezpax.com).

Thermostats and Hose Clips

The subject of thermostats, and specifically the layout of the original pre-PRT specification, deserves further attention (*see* Fig. 4.146). Occasionally these may fail, as may be seen from how the bypass rail rapidly heats up, but the main coolant return rail will remain cold or at best only slightly warmed.

Thermostat replacement is quite straightforward for those with abnormally long fingers, or when the cylinder head is removed. The main problem for those of us with normal fingers is that access is very tight: while removing the return rail from the stat housing is simple, once the two fixing bolts to the block are removed, refitting is not.

Once the rail is out of the way and the other hose connection removed from the stat housing, it can be removed. The housing has an interference fit 'O' ring seal on the end inserted into the block and this has to be eased out. Once out it is a matter of undoing the bolts holding the two halves of the housing to access the stat. Note that the stat's dimensions are not the same as those of common stats, so you must make sure you get the correct application.

Refitting is obviously a reverse of the removal process, but ideally with new 'O' ring seals. Great care has to be taken when inserting the thermostat housing squarely back into the block to avoid damaging the 'O' ring seal. A little rubber lube helps considerably and the same care is also needed when sliding the metal return rail over the end of the stat housing. Lining up the return rail two anchor brackets to the holes in the block, in order to refit the bolts back in, is where ET's fingers might come in handy!

In an effort to reduce wide temperature fluctuations, many MGF owners tried various modifications, including drilling one or more holes in the flange of the thermostat. This trick has been used over many years on competition-based cars and it can certainly have an impact. What surprises most is the impact a hole as small as 3mm can have on the cooling system temperatures.

The intention of most MGF owners (noting that the practice dropped out of sight once PRT was introduced) was to reduce the temperature fluctuations seen with normal operation of the thermostat during warm-up. The hole allows some coolant flow all the time the engine is running. There is a downside, however, in that even a 3mm hole allows sufficient flow for the coolant temperature in the engine to drop to levels normally only seen during initial warm-up. When cruising on motorways or similar roads the heater can become cold. Naturally this is also going to hurt fuel economy and running colder adds to engine wear. I also doubt whether it helped reduce stress on the head gasket.

Before leaving the cooling system area, I have a few words about hose clips. The original clips with a simple spring fitting are actually very good, as they have a single clamping load that can't be overtightened. Replacement clips are commonly the screw type worm (Jubilee) clips, which can easily be overtightened. This practice often leads to damage to hoses. While it may not be immediately apparent, overtightening is sure to shorten the life of the hose being clamped and explains the original choice of spring clips.

The original hose clips may be very effective and long lived, but they cannot be described as visually attractive, so many will consider using stainless steel hose worm type clips for their aesthetic advantages (not that I see many visible hoses on an MGF or TF). There is nothing wrong with changing the hose clips to stainless ones if you wish, but just go easy when tightening up.

INLET AND EXHAUST SYSTEMS

There are only two induction configurations for engines fitted to the MGF and TF, but several detailed variations. These two configurations are the plastic inlet manifold, fitted to all non-VVC engines except the TF 135, and the alloy inlet fitted to the VVC engines and the TF 135.

On introduction the MGF 1.8i model used a plastic inlet manifold, a pattern that had been introduced to the K series engine range only the year before the MGF arrived. In addition to using plastic for the inlet manifold, the throttle body was also moulded from plastic. Plastic offers several advantages over the traditional cast alloy, including cost savings, lightness and ease of

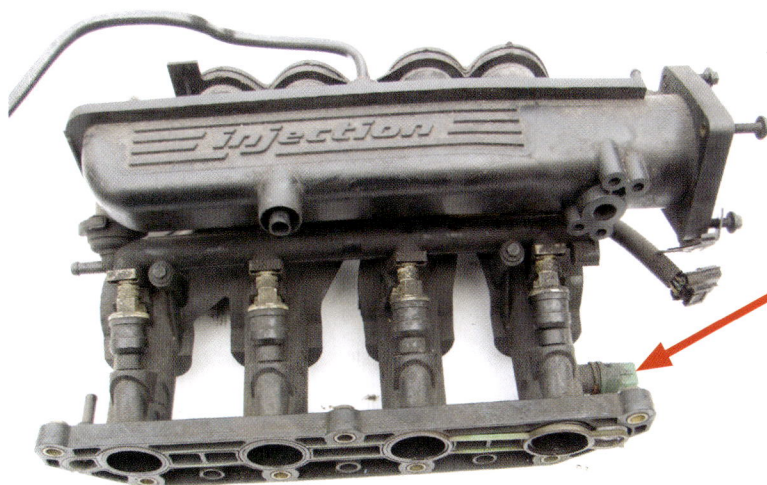

Fig. 4.203   Plastic manifolds for the MEMS 1.9 systems had a separate air temperature sensor.

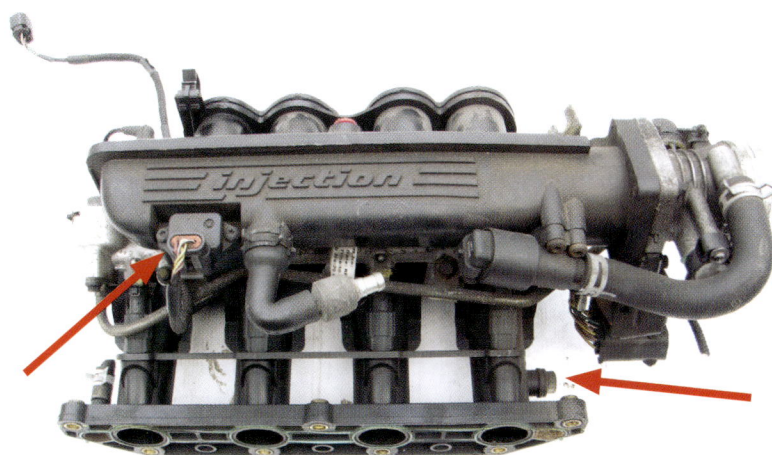

Fig. 4.204   MEMS 3 systems lose that air temperature sensor and the hole is filled with a bolt. The air temperature sensing function is incorporated into the new map sensor, which measures inlet air pressure as well. Note this manifold is from a 2T 1.8T turbo engine, although the manifold is also fitted to non-turbo models.

repeatedly creating accurate mould-ings. The biggest drawback to using plastic previously was the sensitivity of plastic to heat. Needless to say melt-ing manifolds has not been a problem, except during incidents of very severe engine overheating, but in those cir-cumstances other parts of the engine have also suffered severe damage, which shows that plastic manifolds are not weak (*see* Figs 4.34–4.37).

There are several small differences between the plastic inlet manifolds, depending on which version of MEMS engine management system they run with. Between 1995 and 2000 they used MEMS 1.9 and from 2001 on they used MEMS 3. The main differences between the two is that the earlier system has a vacuum connection between a stub on the neck of the manifold near the throttle body mounting and the ECU to measure engine load (MAP sensing), while the MEMS 3 system saw this func-tion moved to a separate MAP sensor mounted on the front top of the mani-fold plenum on a new recessed plinth.

The earlier system also had a sepa-rate inlet air temperature sensor, in

lurid bright green, mounted on the side of the number four inlet tract. This was discontinued with the MEMS 3 system, as the air temp function was included in the MAP sensor, but you may well find provision for the sensor in the inlet tract, now filled with a screw-in plug.

Alloy Inlet

The MGF VVC used a then unique alu-minium alloy inlet made in two halves: a lower manifold runner section and an upper plenum section. The need for this different design was said to be to match the higher airflow demands of the VVC engine at higher rpms with greater airflow potential, compared to the lower-powered MPi engine.

Like the plastic manifold, there are variations related to the specific engine management system used (MEMS 2J from 1996 to 2000, and then MEMS 3 from 2001). These differences are also related to pressure and temperature sensing, initially a three-wire MAP sen-sor mounted on a protruding boss at the opposite end of the plenum from the throttle, along with the same lurid

green air temp sensor as seen on the plastic inlet in the number 4 inlet tract.

MEMS 3 continued with this separate sensor arrangement for a short while, before combining the MAP and temp sensors on a reshaped and angled ple-num casting end opposite the throttle.

These alloy inlets are available in dif-ferent styles and finishes. Initially, as the alloy inlet was only intended for VVC engines, they featured a cosmetic ple-num with a specific VVC lettering and a double cam emblem as part of the casting. To ensure this was clearly visi-ble, the alloy inlets were coated in black and then the surface was machined flat to emphasize the VVC lettering and emblem.

During the latter half of the 1990s a healthy tuning industry developed for the K series engines. A common modifi-cation was to use the alloy inlet in con-junction with head and cam modifica-tions on non-VVC engines. Here there was no need for the VVC logo and so these were often machined off. With MG product planning indicating that the MGF's successor was going have a non-VVC version using the same

Fig. 4.205   The alloy inlet was initially fitted only to VVC engines (hence the VVC emblem). The MEMS 2J system ran separate MAP and air temperature sensors.

Fig. 4.206   On MEMS 3 systems a single sensor carried out both tasks. For the MEMS 3 sensor the casting was changed from a flat to a sloping end.

LEFT: Fig. 4.207   The MEMS 2J MAP sensor is a three-wire unit.

RIGHT: Fig. 4.208   The MEMS 3 combined MAP and air temperature sensor is larger than its predecessor.

TOP LEFT: *Fig. 4.209   Pre-2001 MGFs used the air filter (left) along with a resonator, while the 2001-on mainstream MGF and TF 115 and TF 120 used the filter on the right.*

TOP RIGHT: *Fig. 4.210   The MGF Trophy and MG TF 135 and 160 models all used a 'dual cold air intake' filter system, seen here from below during the car's assembly.*

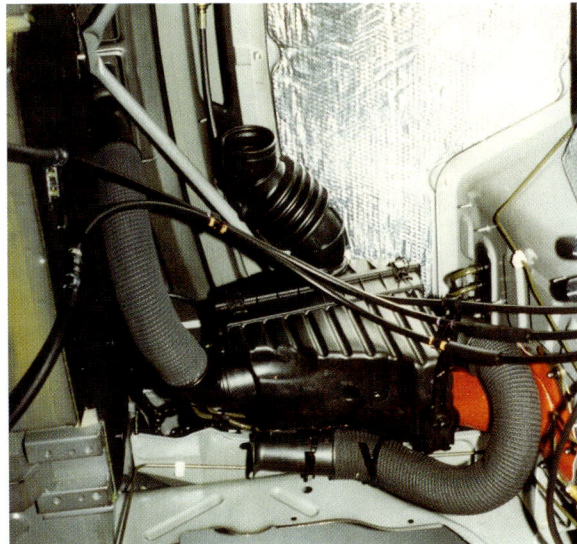

induction system as the VVC engine, a new plenum appeared with no cast-in identification and also no need for the additional expense of the black coating. There then followed a period when you could see black VVC plenums, plain black plenums and, finally, natural 'as cast' plenums.

Air Filters

The MGF and TF have seen three different configuration standard air filters and air induction systems feeding air to the throttle body with quite varied efficiency of airflow. All MGFs up to the 2001 model year changes at VIN RD522572 shared the same air filter assembly and a somewhat restrictive noise-reduction air resonator, through which air had to pass before reaching the filter. Air was collected from the central area by a single 'cold' air pipe strapped to the rear cross beam of the subframe. 'Cold' air is perhaps not quite accurate as intake air temperature was still influenced by the fact that the MGF engine bay normally runs quite hot.

A slightly larger filter was introduced from the start of the (EU3 spec) 2001 model year specification cars and the resonator was discontinued. No power gain was ever claimed, but these engines are normally a little sharper. Lastly, the introduction of the MGF Trophy 160 SE brought a new high-efficiency filter assembly that incorporated two 'cold' air pick-ups, one collecting from the same point as the other models and the second from the

side of the filter body, roughly where the old resonator sat.

The TF carried over the same air filters as the late MGF, the single 'cold' air inlet being used on TF115 and 120 models. The new 'performance' dual 'cold' air intake, first seen on the MGF Trophy 160 SE, was standard on the TF 135 and 160 models.

Throttle Body

The throttle is contained in a compact bolt-on assembly rather than have it integrated into the plenum part of the inlet manifold, saving money and also providing flexibility. As mentioned earlier, the original throttle body fitted to both 1.8i and VVC engines was a moulded plastic one and it fitted to

Fig. 4.211   Until the start of the 2001 model year, MGF engines used a plastic throttle body, but this was prone to sticking and distortion.

the end of either a plastic or alloy plenum by way of four small bolts; it has a diameter of 48mm.

The reliability of the plastic throttle body was not as good as the plastic inlet. Occasionally throttle bodies could suffer distortion, which would manifest itself as an uncontrolled high idle speed, simply caused by the throttle disc being unable to fully close. This problem could be significantly aggravated or indeed caused by the replacement of the original fixed tension hose clip that holds the air hose to the throttle by a worm type (Jubilee) clip.

The original clip is fitted using a special tool, but with judicial use of a pair of pliers you can squeeze the ends together and it will click back into the locked single fixed position. Overtightening of the worm type clip is a major contributor to distorting plastic throttle bodies. Worm type clips were also often associated with fitting non-original air filters.

Owing to continuing issues with distorted plastic throttle bodies, an alloy replacement was introduced for 2001, made by Dellorto in Italy. This added rigidity and immediately cured the problem of distorting bodies. The alloy throttle body carried over the same 48mm throttle size and, aside from the change in material, was a direct one for one replacement.

A version with a 52mm diameter throttle disc was also introduced, initially only for the MGF Trophy 160 engines. It was later common to all 160Ps engines in the TF and ZR, and also on the 136Ps engines in the TF

Fig. 4.212   The alloy versions that replaced these, still with 48mm diameter throttles, were made by Dellorto in Italy and cured those problems.

Fig. 4.213   A bigger 52mm diameter version was introduced for the 160ps VVC Trophy 160 MGF and carried over into MG TF 135 and 160 models. They can be identified by the cast-in '52' in a circle (48mm ones have no size marking).

Fig. 4.214   Throttles: (left) 48mm; (right) 52mm.

135. The 52mm throttle bodies are identified by a '52' in a circle cast into the top mounting flange of the body. This is worth noting since changing the 48mm throttle for a 52mm one is a common modification (*see* Chapter 6).

Anyone looking to replace their original plastic throttle body with an alloy one should note that there are other factory spec alloy throttle bodies with the same 48mm throttle disc, but with specific detail differences for other applications. These include the Turbo, with fewer breather connections, and another for the 84Ps spec 1.4 engines, which had a restricted opening throttle to hold back power from the common 103Ps to this 84Ps level on some Rover 25 variants.

Throttle bodies are often the subject of tuning discussions and some time will be spent on the subject in Chapter 6.

Injectors

Injectors are often taken for granted, yet they are very precise instruments for accurately metering fuel. Minor issues can have quite a marked impact on how the engine runs. How a car has previously been used and what mileage has been covered will have the biggest impact on what problems may develop and when, but it is almost totally safe to expect that at six-figure mileages there will usually be very clear benefits from exchanging the injectors for new, or having the existing ones cleaned ultrasonically and given new filter baskets and O rings. Indeed the benefits will often be found at much lower mileages, especially on cars that do shorter journeys rather than long motorway runs.

Injector accuracy is down to very precise control of the opening and closing that regulates the fuel flow. The ECU calculates and controls the time an injector is open to inject the precise volume of fuel needed for the next firing stroke. That calculation is based on the known fuel pressure and injector flow rates. Any changes will have an adverse effect on the correct and smooth running of the engine.

The injector cleaner that you can buy from your local motor shop generally has a strength that can periodically help reduce the onset of problems, but it is not strong enough to impact on longer standing deposits. Stronger injector cleaning fluids are available to the garage trade and these can deliver quite a marked improvement. For many years, though, I have considered ultrasonic injector cleaning as the most effective way to bring used injectors back to as-new performance. The positive results achieved by this method have made it widely available in the garage trade.

It is the nature of the deposits that have to be dealt with that makes this method better than just using strong (even the trade-only) cleaning fluids. Injectors are made to fine tolerances. This is especially true of the pintle (the tip where fuel emerges), which sits just inside the inlet tract and needs to be kept as clean as possible if it is to sit correctly on its seat and the fine conical spray pattern is not to be disturbed.

Every time the engine is switched off small amounts of fuel will be left on the end of the pintle and this will evaporate as engine heat transfers back up the inlet. Fuel is made up of a cocktail of compounds, some of which are solids in suspension with liquid elements, so not all fuel will evaporate. When the liquid elements evaporate these solids are left behind and

they will start to form a skin. This will largely be dissolved when the engine is next run, but over time and countless numbers of engine cycles these deposits build up. While the fresher deposits are more easily dissolved with cleaning agents, the removal of older deposits often needs a more aggressive approach.

Ultrasonic waves break up the hardened deposits and, by energizing the injector to allow volatile cleaning fluids to pass through, the broken deposits are easily dissolved and flushed. With this treatment the injector can be as good as new and there is a considerable cost advantage over new injectors.

More importantly for the future maintenance of any MGF or TF, except 2001 and newer VVC engines, their injectors are common to hundreds of thousands of Rovers, so the ability to obtain a spare set and get them checked and serviced should mean a total outlay of well under £100 and

keep your car on the road, just needing a relatively simple swap once you get the spare set back from cleaning. I am certain that the fuel efficiency savings that come from restoring correct operation will pay for the work relatively quickly.

All the earlier MGFs using the MEMS 1.9 and MEMS 2J (VVC models), that is up to the start of the 2001 model year cars, have the same injector made by Bosch, with a cream coloured upper band. MEMS 3 first arrived with the Steptronic auto model in 1999, but it was only with the start of the 2001 model year that the manual models also changed to MEMS 3. Different injectors were now used and there were two different specifications, one for the MPi engines (all black) and another for VVC (all blue). For reference there is another spec for the MG Motor TF, which has a red band.

Removal and replacement varies slightly between the models with plastic or alloy manifolds, but essentially

Fig. 4.215   Injectors used in the MEMS 1.9 and 2J systems were common and have a cream coloured upper band.

Fig. 4.216   Injectors for MEMS 3 cars come in two forms for MG Rover cars. The all black version is for 1.6 litre and basic 120ps 1.8 litre engines.

LEFT: *Fig. 4.217* The all blue injector is for the TF 135 and TF 160 models.

RIGHT: *Fig. 4.218* An injector with a red band made by another supplier for MG Motor TFs.

Fig. 4.219   The fuel pressure regulator is common to all engines.

Fig. 4.220   The fuel tank sits behind a bulkhead behind the seats. Here a TF is having its fuel tank fitted during production.

they all have an interference fit in the recesses in both the inlet and the fuel rail. This is where the 'O' rings fitted to the top and bottom of the injectors provide the interference fit, and with that the seal, so it is important to be easy with them or you might damage the 'O' rings. Apply a little rubber lube or other suitable lubricant to the 'O' rings before fitting and you will find the injectors slip in very easily.

Fuel Pump and Fuel Pressure

The fuel pump is a small part of a module that sits inside the fuel tank. It is accessed by removing the round access plate that sits next to the main engine cover on the deck under the hood rear window. It supplies fuel through a filter and onto the fuel rail into which the injectors are fitted. A fuel pressure regulator maintains a predetermined level and any excess pressure returns to the fuel tank.

The pump delivers a fairly constant 3.5 bar (51.5psi) at 13.5 volts, which is more than the operating pressure within the fuel rail. This is regulated down to a nominal 3 bar (44psi) by the fuel pressure regulator. I say nominal as there is a vacuum port connection from the regulator to the inlet plenum, so that when the engine is operating at a light or closed throttle a high manifold depression is seen inside the plenum and this is applied to a diaphragm within the regulator. This reduces the fuel pressure by up to 0.7 bar (10.3psi),

so that at these times the fuel pressure can drop to approximately 2.3 bar (33.8psi).

The fuel pressure regulator is a mechanical device and subject to production tolerance from new, and as it ages it will weaken. Therefore the operating 3.0 bar pressure is expected to vary and there is an official acceptable operating range of 2.8 to 3.2 bar (41.2–47psi). This does not mean those seeking more power can simply whack up the fuel pressure to 3.2 bar and expect to see more power. It doesn't work like this, and most of the time effects from variations in fuel pressure are adjusted out by the lambda sensors. It does mean, however, that if your pressure drops below 2.8 bar the engine will start to lose its edge, and power and smoothness will decline as the pressure drops.

As mileages increase it is reasonable to expect fuel pumps and pressure regulators will tire, resulting in the engine not running as well as it should. The easiest way to verify the general condition of this aspect of the fuel system is to check the fuel pressure. This is best done using a professional tool as you do not want fuel at 3 bar sprayed around. You can check the pressure range by having the vacuum hose connection to the plenum connected and disconnected.

There are three variations of tank to pump assembly. Because mixing and matching parts doesn t work, the new replacement is a kit of matching

pump and tank, with 'conversion' parts to match the pump to the car's wiring and the breather pipes. At the beginning of 2012 this cost more than £430 (£370 for the tank alone), and so most owners would probably head in the direction of second-hand if the need for replacement were to arise.

For around a third of the cost of a replacement assembly you can buy aftermarket pumps, many of which have good brand names and can be fitted in place of the original pump with little modification to the pump assembly. The delivery pressure on some of these replacement pumps is also higher and should give greater flexibility in standard cars, and even more so in modified cars.

Another point is that there is a rather large seal, available in two sizes, that fits between the top of the tank and the top of the pump assembly. The general factory advice is to renew this every time the unit is removed from the tank. There does seem to be a connection with owners reporting fuel smells after a pump assembly has been removed and refitted, so the factory advice has some substance.

Exhaust System

The exhaust on an MGF or TF is relatively short and compact due to the rear location of the engine and this demanded some clever packaging of the catalyst and exhaust system. Starting at the engine end, we have

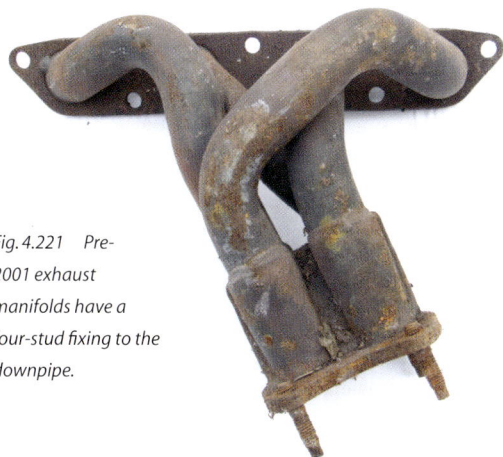

Fig. 4.221 Pre-2001 exhaust manifolds have a four-stud fixing to the downpipe.

Fig. 4.222 Exhaust manifolds from 2001 to 2005 have a cleaner design with a six-stud fixing to the downpipe.

a tubular steel exhaust manifold that comes in two designs: up to 2001 model year cars, and then the 2001 to 2005 cars. I will describe the MG Motor TF set-up separately. It is very easy to distinguish the two types as the earlier one has a four-stud downpipe connection, while the later design has a six-stud design. In performance terms they don't show significant differences, but on the six-stud design the holes in the flanges are bigger and the welds cleaner.

Lambda Sensor(s) and Catalyst

The early manifold also carried the lambda sensor above the downpipe flange and facing the engine block. This makes accessing the lambda sensor for changing a little difficult to say the least. Since it is close to the exhaust outlet from the engine, it is not uncommon for the sensor to effectively weld itself to the thread in the manifold, taking the thread with it when removed (often needing considerable force). That usually requires a replacement manifold and sensor. On the 2001 to 2005 manifold the lambda sensor is mounted further along the downpipe, instead of in the manifold section.

Both early and late downpipes have a twin pipe that turns under the engine before joining into a single pipe. This then runs through a flexible section turning 90 degrees to the catalyst mounting flange. Downpipes from 2001 on have a similar configuration, apart from the six-stud fixing and the 'upstream' lambda sensor mounted where the twin pipe section turns under the engine. Here it is much easier to access for removal, and being a little further down the exhaust, it is not subject to the really high temperature variations that cause the seizing problems of the earlier manifold and sensor.

MG Motor cars made between 2008 and 2011 have a combined manifold and pre-catalyst with the 'upstream' lambda sensor mounted before the catalyst section, all to help these cars comply with the Euro IV emission requirements. This type of exhaust manifold is termed a 'Manivertor': the downpipe connection is a single pipe that then follows the same route to the main catalyst as on earlier cars.

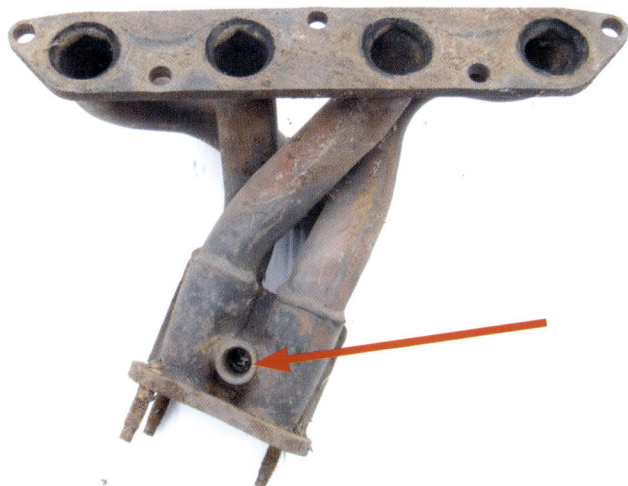

ABOVE: Fig. 4.223   Models up to 2001 had a single lambda sensor screwed into the exhaust manifold, 'upstream' of the catalyst.

RIGHT: Fig. 4.224   The 2001 to 2005 cars have two lambda sensors, the 'upstream' one in a boss welded between the two downpipes (indicated in yellow), with part of the sensor just visible (indicated in red).

Fig. 4.225   MG Motor TFs that had to comply with Euro IV emissions used a pre-cat manifold commonly called a Manivertor.

Fig. 4.226   The upstream lambda sensor of the Manivertor was mounted in the boss (centre) before the lower section containing the catalyst.

Catalysts are similar for all models apart from a major external difference that was introduced at the same time as changes were made to the manifold. Up to 2001 the exit of the catalyst has a mounting flange for connection to the remaining exhaust and silencer, but from 2001 on the flange is moved some distance towards the single silencer before joining it. The change was to allow the revised 'downstream' lambda sensor to be fitted within the catalyst section, which is less likely to need replacement than the silencer.

Silencer

The single large-capacity silencer is mounted across the underside of the boot area. This configuration is essentially identical for all models with just a variation to the flange position for mounting the catalyst. This means all have a common mounting arrangement and a twin tailpipe, one on each side of the car. This dictates some careful internal 'plumbing' inside the silencer to ensure the exhaust gas passes through silencing areas before being allowed to exit via the tailpipes.

This exhaust is generally very long lived, partly due to the relatively short run between engine and tailpipe, which tends to keep internal exhaust temperatures higher, and with that comes less condensing moisture that becomes acidic and eats the metal. It is not unusual for exhausts to last ten years, something quite unusual for exhausts unless they are made from stainless steel. In fact the system is made from a type of stainless steel, not the bright finish, high-grade stainless common for aftermarket systems, but a lower grade that still delivers the longevity.

What is certainly not as long lived, however, is a bracing strap that fits around the right side of the main silencer and then extends forward

Fig. 4.227   The single catalyst for cars built up to 2005, and the second catalyst for MG Motor TFs, is neatly packaged sitting next to the main silencer. The 'downstream' lambda sensor is in the exit side of the catalyst pipe leading to the main silencer for 2001+ cars.

Fig. 4.228 'Cat Saver Nuts' are tube nuts that protect the thread of the car studs from the severe corrosion they commonly suffer, so making removal in later years much simpler.

with a flange that bolts onto two of the three catalyst front flange studs. These straps fail much earlier than the rest of the silencer. Even though the strap has a function, many cars have run without them for long periods without an obvious problem.

Changing the silencer is a simple operation on paper, but it is almost certain the nuts and studs at the catalyst mounting flanges will have seriously corroded. You should expect to have to grind off the rusted remains of nuts and studs in order to release the various parts. As the studs are a permanent fixture to the catalyst flanges, you will invariably need to drill out the remains and replace with new nuts and bolts. Where the studs remain in a serviceable condition, it is very useful to replace the nuts with a long stainless steel tube nut that has been specifically made to encase the stud's thread and provide the required clamping load. These are usually sold under the name of Cat Saver Nuts and they offer a genuine long-term advantage.

Many exhaust silencers are changed not because the original has failed, but for stylistic or audible reasons. Both MGF and TF tailpipes are too bland in style for many (oval shape for MGF and round for TF) and there is no question that the mainstream MGF silencer delivered little in the way of a sporting exhaust sound. The TF was slightly better but was still strangled by drive-by noise restrictions the manufacturer

was obliged to meet.

MGF Trophy 160 had a one-off sportier-sounding silencer, but this did not comply sufficiently with the rules to be fitted on the production line, so each Trophy model was delivered to the dealer with a standard system fitted and the Trophy one was fitted by the dealer as a 'post-registration fit' to get around that legal hurdle.

Exhaust Noise Reduction Valve

The TF exhaust was better, but MG Rover considered that the emitted sound of the TF 135 and 160 models needed to be further toned down to pass the drive-by noise test. This

was achieved by creating what they termed the 'Dual Mode Silencer', which involved inserting an engine ECU-controlled valve in the right tailpipe. It resembles a turbo wastegate valve.

This system also contains an accumulator connected to the inlet manifold and an ECU-controlled, electrically operated valve that is connected to the accumulator and exhaust valve by a small bore pipe. When the ECU opens the valve, manifold vacuum reaches the exhaust valve and it closes off that tailpipe, diverting all exhaust gas out of the left-hand tailpipe. This explains why some owners think their exhaust is faulty when they can't see exhaust coming out of the right tailpipe on cold winter morning starts.

In June 2004 this system was deleted from production and from all replacement silencers for the 135 and 160 models. When fitting a new exhaust to a car originally fitted with an exhaust valve, it is important to leave electrical connections to the exhaust control valve, otherwise the engine ECU can throw up a fault. The rest of the system can be removed, if desired, and a plug fitted over the take-off stub on the inlet plenum.

Once you have overcome the common rusted nuts and studs when removing an original exhaust, you must take care when easing the silencer down as the tail pipes can damage the paint of the bumper. The best advice here is to wrap some rag around the ends of the tailpipe and secure it with masking tape. Two minutes spent

Fig. 4.229 From 2002 to 2004, TF 135 and 160 models were fitted with a 'Dual Mode Silencer', an ECU-controlled valve in the right-hand tail pipe to reduce noise.

doing this is much less than time spent rectifying scratched paint.

What can aggravate the potential for scratching is that the tailpipe lengths can vary. Genuine MG exhausts see the MGF tailpipe around 20mm shorter than the TF: aftermarket exhausts with fixed tailpipes usually sit somewhere between so they can fit either model.

FLYWHEEL AND CLUTCH

1.6-Litre Differences

Flywheels are specific to engine and gearbox. The Rover PG1 gearbox is fitted to all MGFs and TFs, but few are aware that two different flywheels and clutches are used. The 1600cc MGF 1.6i and the TF 115 use a 200mm diameter clutch with a matching flywheel, while all 1800cc cars use the 215mm clutch and matching flywheel. Uprating a 1.6-litre MGF or TF from the 200mm to the more common 215mm clutch requires the use of the 215 flywheel and clutch assembly, which simply bolts in.

Clutch Drag

Both the PG1 gearbox and the clutch system have been around since 1984 and pretty well everything is known about them. Two issues come to the fore: clutch drag, and corrosion and seizure of the clutch release arm.

Clutch drag has affected some cars while others never have a problem. The issue is especially obvious when trying to select reverse gear while the engine is running with constant crunching of the gear. If the engine is stopped and selection is no longer a problem, then this is a drag issue. The only cure is a new clutch. I have heard that slipping the clutch to 'burn' off any contamination or high spots can provide short-term relief, but don't blame me if you break your clutch completely.

Clutch Release Arm Seizure

This problem is more common on infrequently used cars and becomes obvious when the clutch pedal is depressed with a very heavy 'dead' feel. Release the pedal and the pedal moves back faster than the clutch engages or, worse still, the pedal comes back up through the pedal return spring, but the clutch doesn't engage.

If this occurs, then the problem is that the clutch release has seized on the upper bush that supports it in the clutch housing casting. Running the engine to introduce heat can ease the problem. Copious quantities of penetrating lubricant around the pivot arm where it enters the clutch housing can ease things further, as this bush is the main source of the seizure. If you are lucky, plenty of clutch pedal operation can restore sufficient freedom of movement to use the car normally. You should be aware, though, that once the problem has raised its head it will not get any better. Only very regular use can hope to maintain an adequate operation, and even then not always.

When the problem persists, the only solution is to separate the gearbox from the engine so you can access the clutch release fork's single 10mm bolt. Once removed, the arm can be eased up and out of the gearbox. Corrosion will be obvious and usually a clean and light rub of the steel arm with fine abrasive can achieve a surface that, with some grease, can return serviceability. The two bushes in the gearbox also need to be cleaned and greased before the arm is refitted.

Some of the accompanying images of a seized arm are off a front-wheel drive PG1 application, which may be identified as the release arm has a cable connection rather than the cup receiver for a hydraulic pushrod fitted to the MGF and TF, but the problem is exactly the same for all PG1 types.

The incidence of semi- and fully seized clutch release arms has been sufficient for several MG specialists to introduce a modified design of arm incorporating a grease nipple, which allows grease to be fed to the outer area of the shaft adjacent to the upper bush within the clutch housing. As this is the area where more corrosion usually occurs, this provides the facility to add a little grease at each annual service and that should provide greater protection against future seizure problems.

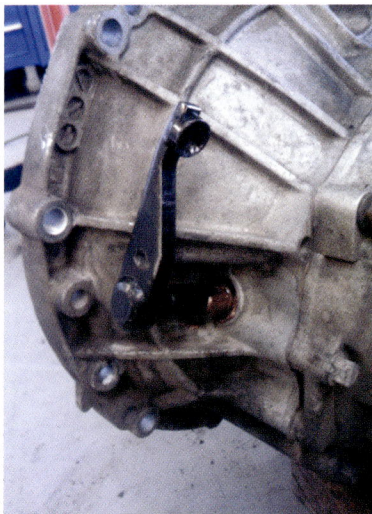

ABOVE LEFT: *Fig. 4.230 If the clutch pedal has been slow to return, then sticks to the floor and won't come back, and there is no drive, it may be because the clutch arm, seen here removed, has seized where the corrosion is visible in the upper bush area of the gearbox.*

ABOVE RIGHT: *Fig. 4.231 Removal of this arm needs the gearbox to be moved away from the engine, so if you are faced with this change the clutch as well.*

RIGHT: *Fig. 4.232 Once the arm and gearbox bush are cleaned up and reassembled using copper grease, the problem should not return in a hurry.*

GEARBOX

The same PG1 series gearbox is fitted to all MGF and TF models and has been the mainstay Rover Group manual gearbox for 1800cc and larger capacity saloons since 1984. It was originally a Honda design and was supplied by that company for the first three years, but from 1987 it was made under licence at the Powertrain factory at Cofton Hackett, next to the main Longbridge factory.

The gearbox comes in two basic formats, a higher spec gearbox rated at 240Nm, with bigger internal bearings, and a lower spec of 215Nm. These are the maximum input torque ratings when in a vehicle weighing 1,900kg, which means that in a lighter vehicle it can cope with more torque.

The lower 215Nm spec gearbox is used in the MGF and TF with the same set of intermediate gear ratios, but with a different final drive ratio. Non-VVC MGFs and the TF 115 use a 3.9 to 1 final drive and have a C6BP identification code. All VVC-engined cars and the TF 135 use a 4.2 to 1 final drive that effectively lowers the gearing by 10 per cent; the gearbox code is C4BP.

These gearboxes can be identified by a paper label with plain English lettering and numbering, together with a bar code. The main identifier is in the prefix, either C4BP or C6BP, followed

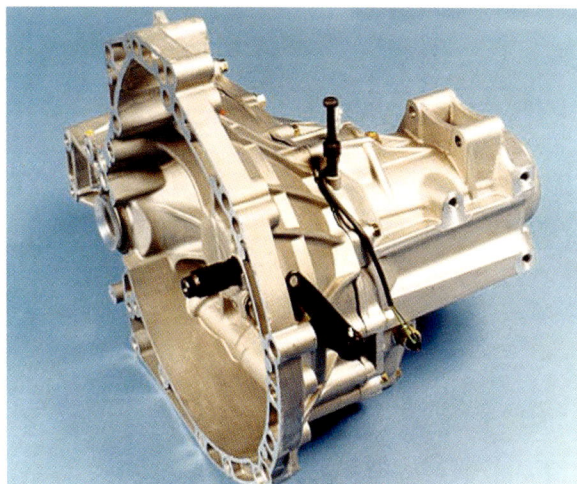

Fig. 4.233   The PG1 series gearbox is a well-proven and very robust gearbox. (MG Rover)

by a longer number, which is the individual gearbox number. These codes indicate the gear set, final drive ratio and differential type.

The PG1 generally has a very long life in MGFs and TFs. The power delivered by any of the standard engines does not put a huge stress on it and it can cope very well with higher outputs from modified engines. When a gearbox ages and wear reaches a point where refurbishment is needed, it is generally viable to simply replace the bearings and seals, as long as the gearbox hasn't been run for any length of time making constant whining noises.

The cost of these rebuild parts bought from dealers is going to exceed £330 (at 2011 prices), so bearing and seal kits made by transmission specialists at around £200 are more attractive. If you want to provide greater strength within the gearbox, I suggest that you replace the original nylon-caged bearings with steel-caged ones. Note that the bearings differ between the 215 and 240Nm specifications, so confirm the gearbox type before ordering parts.

Stripping these gearboxes down is not that difficult and is covered in the Factory PG1 gearbox overhaul manual. Anyone new to the strip-down will usually trip up, when trying to remove the outer case once the multiple bolts are removed from the outside, by not detaching the circlip that is accessed through the end hole in the gearbox when the end plug is unscrewed. Once off, the gearbox is very open and easy to further strip in sections and, in due course, rebuild.

When rebuilding it is important to ensure that, when the time comes to refit the case, it drops fully into place and doesn't need any force. Certainly the principle of tightening bolts to get the case to seat will always cause the case to be cracked. The case only needs to be hand 'wobbled' for final internal part alignment and it then drops into place, allowing the main circlip to be engaged, and then the numerous bolts can be correctly tightened.

Those wishing to buy a second-hand PG1 gearbox should be aware that there are different clutch housing cases depending on the engine it is to be fitted too. The list covers eight other Rover/Land Rover/MG Rover petrol and diesel engines in addition to the K series.

Fig. 4.234   The gearbox code identifies the use and internal gearing.

TOP LEFT: *Fig. 4.235   When stripping a PG1 gearbox, often the first hurdle is forgetting to disengage the circlip within the open hole that allows the main case to be lifted off.*

TOP RIGHT: *Fig. 4.236   Circlip pliers should be used.*

MIDDLE LEFT: *Fig. 4.237   This allows the main case to be lifted off.*

MIDDLE RIGHT: *Fig. 4.238   The parts can easily be dismantled and lifted off.*

Fig. 4.239   The internal arrangement of the gearbox is not overly complex.

Obviously for an MGF or TF you need an appropriate PG1 gearbox, but the specific nature of the clutch housing means that any PG1 fitted to a 4-cylinder K series engine will drop straight into the MGF. There are only three variations. Two of these mirror the MGF and TF options, where the same set of internal ratios are married to either a 3.9 or 4.2 to 1 final drive ratio, and then there is the rare Rover 200 BRM gearbox, which has a superb close ratio gear set and Torsen LSD (Limited Slip Differential). If you want to use a gearbox sourced from a FWD saloon, all you will have to change is the clutch release arm, simply removing one and refitting the other, as outlined previously in how to deal with a seized arm.

Lubrication

From introduction the PG1 gearbox used normal 10W/40 engine oil, but from the early to the mid-1990s this was changed to MTF94, in order to cater for the increasing power and torque levels of the engines the gearbox was being attached to. MTF94 therefore applies to all MGF and TF models, although there are good alternatives such as Castrol SMX-S 75W-85 fully synthetic fluid, now replaced by Syntrans Multivehicle 75W-90. I have good experience of using this in gearboxes attached to standard engines and also to turbo engines with Torsen limited slip differentials.

Changing the gearbox oil is an often forgotten service item. The change point is either side of the 100,000 mile mark, depending on the car's age and service schedule. It is also good policy, when buying a car without a service history, to change the gearbox oil as part of your initial main servicing to provide a reference point for all future servicing.

Gear Change Mechanism

The gearboxes are very robust and effective. In FWD applications the direct gear change rod linkage provides light and smooth gear changes. Transferring the gear change movement when moving the gearbox from the front to the rear of the car meant that rods were no longer viable and so a neat cable gear change was devised for the MGF, picking up on the standard

Fig. 4.240   This leaves essentially just the final drive and differential once parts seen in 4.238 are removed.

Fig. 4.241   The differential was here lifted out to change it for a Torsen Limited Slip Differential.

input selector shaft on the gearbox. The MGF and TF gear change is not as slick and this is evident when comparing a front wheel drive MG or Rover against an MGF or TF of similar mileage. You can still have a very acceptable change, however, as long as there is no wear in the system and the two cables are correctly adjusted.

The cables are called 'gear change' and 'crossgate' and these titles reflect the cable function: 'gear change' reflects the fore and aft movement; 'crossgate' reflects sideways movement of the gear lever. The cables follow the same route from the gear lever assembly until they enter the engine bay, where the shorter gear change cable goes under the gearbox while the longer crossgate cable rises up and over the gearbox.

At the gearbox end the inner cables connect to what is called a bell crank, which in turn is connected to the

TOP LEFT: *Fig. 4.242   Replacing gear change cables requires the centre console to be removed. If you are worried about damaging the seats these should also be taken out. Here the cables are seen running back from the gear change. Note the airbag controller (labelled in yellow) in front of the gear change. This also has to be removed, so the appropriate safety considerations must be observed.*

BELOW LEFT: Fig. 4.243   This image shows where the gear change cables emerge into the engine bay when the subframe is in place.

BELOW RIGHT: Fig. 4.244   Without the subframe and engine in place, the plate, two handbrake cables (left vertical pair), two gear change cables (right vertical pair) and the heater hoses are clear on this MGF.

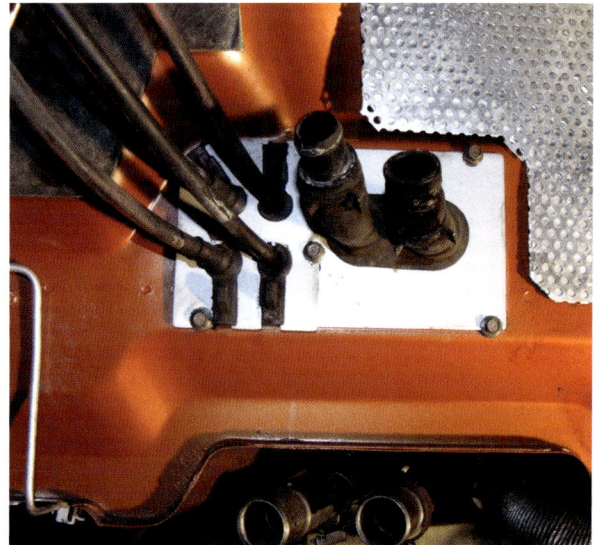

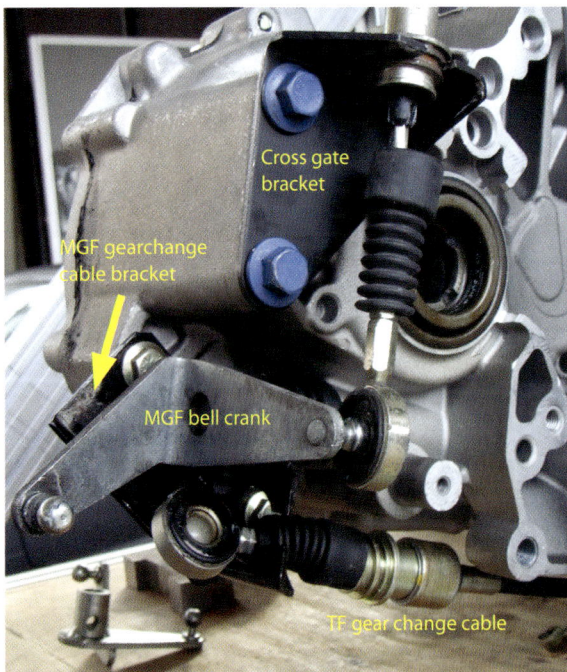

Fig. 4.245   Here, using an engineering module at Longbridge, are an MGF bell crank and cable bracket fitted to a gearbox, showing how much shorter the TF gear change cable is.

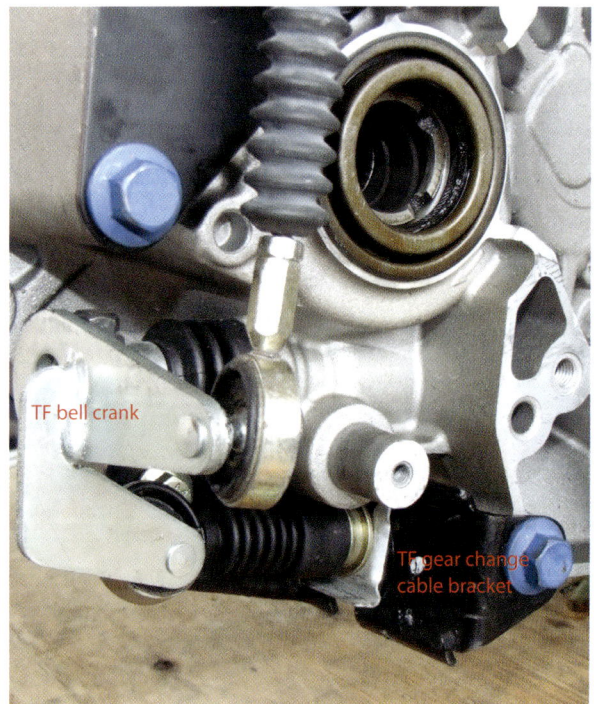

Fig. 4.246   When the TF bell crank and cable bracket is fitted everything lines up. Note that the crossgate cable is common to both.

gearbox selector input shaft. The outer cables are fixed to two anchor brackets that are bolted to the gearbox. It is worth noting that MGFs and TFs use a different gear change cable, gearbox gear change anchor bracket and bell crank. The TF gear change cable is around 3in (75mm) shorter than the MGF one, which I was told at the TF press launch was intended to make the TF change more precise than mainstream MGFs. The crossgate cable and its anchor bracket remained unchanged.

Most cars do not have any major issues with their gear change, though perhaps broken cables are the most common, but as time and miles pass it is not unusual to find general wear creating a significant degree of slop and this results in a far from expected 'sports car' driving experience.

Cable Changes

Cable breakage can be preceded by a stiffening of the gear change, usually caused when some inner cable strands have broken and are snagging on the inside lining of the outer cable as the cable moves. Other than this a break can come out of the blue. The usual cable to break is the gear change cable, leaving you stuck either in whatever gear you were or in neutral. If you are stuck with a box full of neutrals, a trick to help get you home, if you are prepared to grovel underneath, is to push the bell crank forward so the selector rod is pushed into the gearbox. As the natural rest position for the crossgate is in the third and fourth gear plane, pushing the bell crank forward will select third gear, which is a good compromise for being able to start from stationary and also to reach and maintain reasonable cruising speeds.

Replacing a cable is not one of the jobs I can gloss over when the workshop manual's instructions say to lower the front of the rear subframe, even though corroded subframe bolts are likely to shear, without considering the weights involved. Doing the job with the subframe *in situ*, the main problem is accessing the sealing plate that covers the aperture where the cables emerge. This is hidden behind the front cross beam of the rear subframe and access is a real pain with the

subframe still in place (*see* Figs 4.243 and 4.244).

The worst element is refitting the plate. If the seal is old it will be 'bloated' and difficult to refit. A new seal (part number AVJ100120, costing less than £10 at the time of writing) should be easier to fit. I can also well understand the alternative method owners and garages have followed in cutting the seal *in situ* and feeding the old cable out and new one in, often with some light lubrication, and then sealing the sliced seal with mastic.

My specific job was to retrofit the MG Motor TF gear change assembly to an MGF to confirm that the post-2008 MG Motor TF parts were backward compatible with earlier MG TFs and that some other parts were backward compatible with MGFs. Ironically, since there are so few MG Motor TFs, it is possible that in a few years they may need to use earlier parts, so this was a useful exercise in that respect too.

This job did not follow the workshop manual route of dropping the front of the rear subframe, although if the necessary facilities are available this small drop really exposes the plate where the cables – two gear change and two

handbrake – emerge into the engine bay. Completing the job without having to drop the subframe confirmed that the job is viable without this complication.

The rest of the process is as listed in the workshop manual. This involves having to remove the airbag control unit. Safety is a priority and this demands that the car's battery is disconnected. *Wait at least fifteen minutes before starting any work on disconnecting the airbag control unit.* This time lapse allows any residual power to dissipate, so the chance of accidentally activating the air bag(s) is removed.

Actually getting down to the air bag controller requires removing the rear Tee bar trim and cubby between the seats. The whole of the centre console may then be removed. Simply slide the electrical connector lock bar across to disengage the electrical plug and remove the screws to release it from its position over the front mountings of the gear change assembly (*see* Fig. 4.242).

Take precautions to cover the seats and interior trim or remove it. The gear change and cables are greased and it is so easy to contaminate the interior

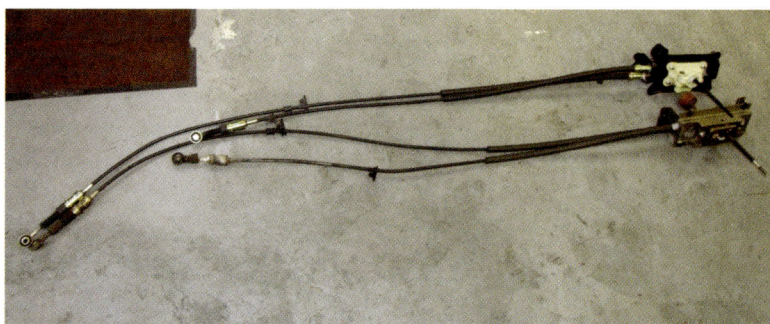

Fig. 4.247   Two different gear change assemblies with cables: (bottom) MGF and (top) an MG Motor TF, which has the same cable lengths as the MG Rover TF.

Fig. 4.248   The ends at the gear change are slightly different sizes, however, so cables will be individual to each. As complete assemblies, though, swaps are possible between pre- and post-2005 TFs, and with MGFs with the TF bell crank and gear change bracket.

Fig. 4.249   *It is worth adjusting the gearbox cable ends so that the socket and ball joint sit square to each other when at rest, not angled as is the case here.*

trim. Grease on cloth trim would be a disaster and any carelessness with the metal gear change's sharp edges will show no respect to even leather.

The standard MG Rover gear change cables for both MGF and TF have M6 threaded ends with 'pop on' socket joints that engage on ball joints on both ends of the gear change mechanism. This provides a reasonable range of adjustment but generally speaking most cables work as supplied, so simply fit the new cable and check selection, adjusting only if it is needed.

If adjustment is needed it will invariably be to centralize the gear lever at its rest position and also set the bell crank in a centralized rest position, so that accurate and smooth gear changes can be completed. If there is any oddity with the way the gears engage relative to the position of the gear lever, this will be an issue that requires adjustment of the cable lengths. Usually this will only affect the shorter 'gear change cable' and is a case of interpreting where it seems wrong on the car, taking corrective action at the more accessible gearbox end.

There is also a beneficial adjustment that helps precision and long-term reliability of the gearbox end cable joints as most joints rest with the joint at an angle to the ball joint on the bell crank. Ideally you should loosen the locknut and allow any retained twisting torque within the cable to settle out before

lining the joint at 90 degrees to the ball socket, then tightening the locknut.

The rear cable joints do appear to be very feeble and flexible. Although they are stronger than they look, they can be damaged through rough handling and inappropriate leverage when removing and refitting onto the ball sockets. Bear in mind that these are not separately available as MG parts, so care should be taken when working with them. It has been known for joints to separate, and if this happens several cable ties can make a temporary repair.

Fortunately like other small parts, such as door hinge pins, companies are starting to supply replacement gearbox end cable joints and the rubber boots, which are often in shreds or completely missing from many cars, plus complete and uprated gear change assemblies.

Excess Slop in the Gear Change Mechanism

One of the most common problems, especially in MGFs, is that there can be a huge degree of slop developing over time and miles. While the gear change remains quite light, much precision is lost. This slop is due to wear that develops in the system and it is something that you can go a considerable way to rectifying.

The first check has to be at the bell crank end, since even the smallest amount of free play developing where the roll pin engages the bell crank onto the selector shaft will always become a surprising degree of free play at the gear lever. As cars age they become subject to shoddy repairs, so do not be surprised if a nut and bolt has been fitted in place of the roll pin. This will always give lots of free play and the bolt thread chafes and wears the surrounding metal. When I have seen a nut and bolt approach it is the bell crank that suffers most and at least this is easily replaced.

While at the gearbox end, check the security of the cables into the anchor

Fig. 4.250   *If there is any play when fitting the roll pin that secures the bell crank to the gearbox selector shaft, this will massively amplify movement at the gear lever.*

Fig. 4.251   Up to 2005 the MGF and TF used the gear change shown on the left, but the MG Motor TF used the new design (right), which is generally smoother and quieter in operation.

bracket and the bolts holding these brackets into the gearbox, noting that the crossgate cable bracket securing bolts, which have a very fine and unusual thread, are coloured blue. The MGF gear change cable bracket uses normal metric threads, but the TF gear change cable bracket uses one standard threaded bolt and one fine-thread blue bolt (*see* Figs 4.245 and 4.246).

After the bell crank, the most common source of slop is within the actual gear change assembly inside the car. The original MGF and TF assemblies were made by one supplier and at the time MG Rover went under there were very advanced plans for a new assembly to be introduced. The design of this replacement assembly was later seen in the MG Motor TF. Whereas the original design is mainly constructed in steel with a small amount of nylon, the replacement is principally a series of nylon mouldings.

Wear and sometimes breakage of the nylon piece within the original design is known. Since these parts were only ever sold as complete assemblies, breakage or excess wear of small component parts can only be rectified by replacing the whole assembly or finding a good second-hand unit. Two slightly different assemblies were fitted, with the change coming after approximately 2000 TFs were built, but there is no obvious difference in use and anyway only the earlier item was listed as available in 2011.

Chinese-Made Gear Change

I have already mentioned the different gear change design on the MG Motor TFs and the fact it is carried over from what would have been fitted on the 2006 model year TFs if MG Rover had survived. Just after the relaunch of the MG Motor TF in September 2008 I fitted the Chinese-made gear change assembly on my 2001 spec MGF as a test to confirm backward compatibility for XPart. This also meant that I would be converting the MGF to a TF bell crank. As these were no longer available new, I had to source a second-hand one, but otherwise the fit was a direct replacement.

The first point to make is that the Chinese parts consist of a gear change and two cables and can directly replace the MG Rover period gear change assembly and cables. The Chinese parts can replace the gear change assembly and cables of an MGF, but you also need a TF bell crank, a gear change cable abutment bracket and the 'blue' fine thread bolt. Note also that you can't use the cables from the Chinese assembly with any earlier gear change assembly or vice versa, as the gear change assembly cable ends are different.

At the time of fitting the Chinese assembly my original MG Rover period gear change was still in good condition and well above average for its 57,000 miles covered. Since then, up to the time of writing, just over another 45,000 miles have been covered.

It was interesting to note how smooth, light and refined the new gear change was straight out of the box, and it remains that way. There was very little free play, but then my original displayed the same pleasurable tight and smooth operation not seen in enough cars. That lack of free play also helps provide a good level of precision, not quite the same as found with the FWD rod change, but very acceptable. The refinement bonus is small and clearly comes from the insulating effect of the comprehensive use of nylon instead of steel.

When I have driven MG Motor TFs I have noted the same insulating properties, but not all have been as sweet to operate, which may have more to do with the gearboxes being new or very low mileage. Certainly engineering cars I have driven with many more miles have been as sweet.

Steptronic and Stepspeed (Automatic) EM CVT Gearbox

In recent years the number of drivers in the UK restricted to automatic transmission cars has grown and, with congestion in urban areas increasing, many others are choosing cars equipped with automatic transmissions. Rover catered for this by introducing the Steptronic model, which uses a ZF VT1-32A series EM CVT (electronically managed - constantly variable transmission) only connected to the 120Ps specification 1796cc engine.

Within a year, though, BMW had departed and taken with it the registered name of Steptronic. The now nameless automatic MGF was given the title of Stepspeed, which was also applied to the automatic Rover 25/MG ZR and 4-cylinder 45/ZS siblings. The BMW Mini from 2001 to 2006 also had a model using an almost identical version of this gearbox, the VT1-27T series. In time this is probably going to be a bonus as the BMW connection should provide a longer period of spares availability and general know-how than would have been the case if the gearbox had only been used in the MG and Rover ranges.

With relatively few MGFs and TFs equipped with this gearbox, it is only occasionally that problems are seen to occur and many were in the early days shortly after the introduction. It seems that the most common problem is the use of the wrong transmission fluid and the lack of the two-year service oil changes. Failure to change the transmission fluid will lead to rough gearbox

Fig. 4.252 The Steptronic/Stepspeed models are rare and interior views are even rarer. Here are the variable diameter pulleys and the steel drive belt.

Fig. 4.253 Inside the inner casing.

Fig. 4.254 The oil flow control system resembles a maze.

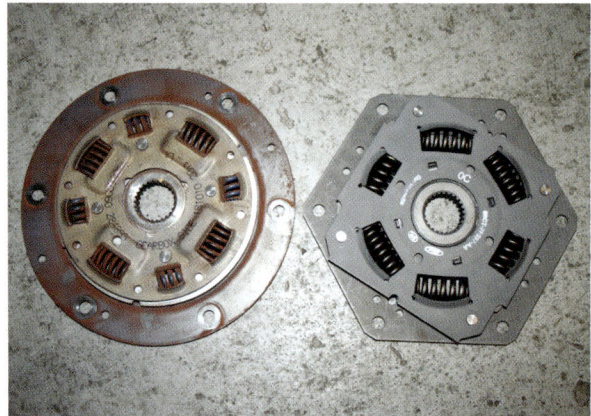

Fig. 4.255 The standard torsional vibration damper (left) and an uprated one (right). Note that this has a Ford logo stamped on it.

operation, loss of drive, or delayed or refusal to change gear when cold.

Some more serious problems that have occurred can be laid firmly at the door of incorrect fluid. An MG Rover bulletin was issued in March 2004 to emphasize that the only transmission fluid approved for use with these EM CVT gearboxes was Esso EZL799; the use of any other oil, and they specifically highlighted Unipart CVT (GUL 1201/5), could lead to transmission failure. The correct fluid is available from XPart in containers from 1 litre to 20 litres, and of course the Mini uses the same fluid.

When problems occur through component failure or general wear it has been found that there is little knowledge or skills in the mainstream MG specialist world. This tends to generate a short circuit straight to 'you need a new gearbox, mate'. A new gearbox used to be £3,000 before fitting, but the availability of new items has dried

up and only rebuilt units remain listed on the XPart parts lists at around half the price of a new unit, with a £500 surcharge pending the return of your old gearbox in a 'reconditionable' condi-

tion. Since few models were made, finding second-hand is going to be difficult.

Some general hints and tips regarding these auto gearboxes should be useful:

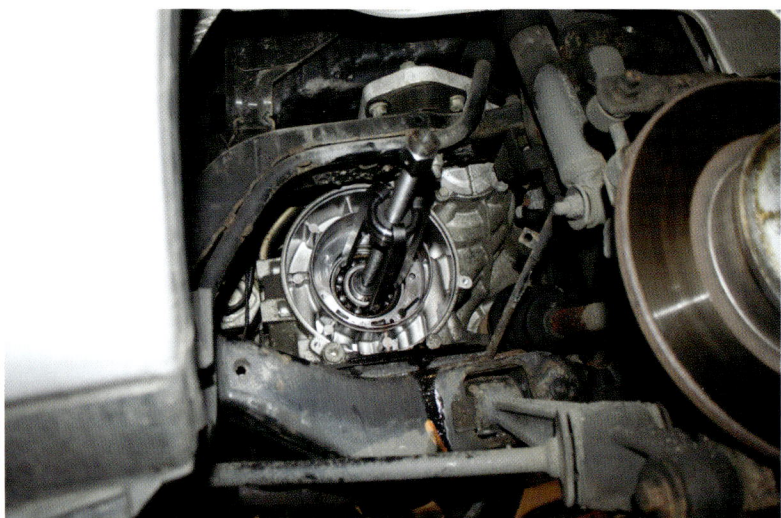

Fig. 4.256 The primary bearing is known to fail and become noisy. Here it is being replaced without removing the gearbox. (Austin Garages)

◆ A very loud bearing sound in D and R from 2 mph upwards, consistent with engine speed, may indicate a primary gear bearing failure. This does not require an expensive rebuild or gearbox removal, since by using special tools issued by MG it is an *in situ* repair.

◆ An EM CVT ECU software update is available via the TF diagnostic disc. This official software update was issued for the TF and, as there is no specific software update for MGF autos, the TF software can be applied to MGF, often with better results than on TF. The update improves cold-start rough running and transmission drivability. Note that this improved software was never officially listed as an upgrade and so is often overlooked. Positive owner feedback has been received from those whose cars have had this software update.

◆ Most EM CVT faults are electrical and not a mechanical fault with the transmission. The most common indications that it is an electrical fault are the transmission warning lamp illuminating or the PRND disappearing from the odometer display. Electrical faults of this nature are best diagnosed with dealer diagnostics, although you can always go through all the electrical connections you can and ensure they are clean and electrically sound.

Fig. 4.257   The auto-selected gear position (PRND123456) is displayed in the speedo odometer window, here in Drive.

SUSPENSION

MGF Suspension

The MGF uses many Rover Metro parts because heavy use of the parts bins for existing Rover cars was critical in enabling the business case to be made to actually get the MGF to market. The MG TF uses more individual parts, especially in the suspension areas, as the healthy MGF sales figures made it easier for the company to justify the investment.

Before starting any actual hands-on work to improve the suspension, I would advise that the car should first be checked out on a four wheel laser alignment rig to highlight any serious errors in the suspension geometry. This check is available from MG dealers, MG specialists, tyre specialists and often at local garages as this type of test equipment is both quite common and very accurate.

The point of the check is very simple: to help highlight errors in the overall suspension geometry that may be caused by worn suspension parts or, in more serious cases, body or subframe

Fig. 4.259   The sensor units are connected to a computer that displays the way the car is set up, badly in this case after a steering rack and suspension arm replacement.

Fig. 4.258   Four wheel laser alignment is an accurate way of checking and setting suspension geometry and should be done after any suspension/steering work. One of these units is fitted to each wheel.

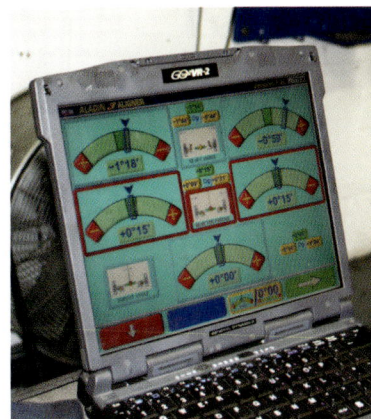

Fig. 4.260   With adjustment the car's handling is soon back to being acceptable to good.

damage from previous owner 'incidents'. If errors show up that point to body or subframe damage, then this is the time to identify them. Don't waste time, effort and money on something to which you have to apply a different approach and change what appear to be unrelated items.

The importance of having a straight car can't be overstressed as the MGF and TF handle brilliantly when set up properly … and 'set up properly' is the critical wording – with errors in the geometry they can't offer anything but poor handling! This all goes back to the time when you bought the car and shows how important it is to get a car that drives straight and handles safely.

Hydragas

The MGF comes with the Hydragas gas-over-fluid suspension that replaces steel springs, developed from the Rover Metro system that uses very similar displacers. This system was itself developed from the Hydrolastic suspension first introduced in the 1959 Mini, and you will find references to Hydrolastic in relation to the suspension fluid and service pump as they are common to both systems.

What would be spring units on a normal car are replaced by displacers. In simple terms a displacer is a metal canister with a waistline indicating that there are two internal chambers, one on top of the other. Inside the upper round chamber is a flexible diaphragm and above this is contained nitrogen at a nominal pressure of 300psi. This normally takes up most of the upper chamber space, but below the diaphragm the chamber is filled with Hydrolastic

Fig. 4.261   The MGF uses Hydragas suspension. The two rear displacers, shown here, look the same as those for the front, but there are different internal settings.

Fig. 4.262   MGF suspension connection points for the Hydrolastic pump to service the suspension. The pump is actually connected to the left valve in this image.

fluid at a nominal 400psi. Hydrolastic fluid is also found in the upper part of the lower chamber and is contained by a second lower diaphragm. In between the two chambers is a valve that regulates the transfer of fluid between the upper and lower chambers and provides a degree of damping action.

Suspension movement is transmitted into the lower chamber via a piston rod connected to the suspension's top arm, the shape and dimensions of the end of the piston varying to apply different characteristics on the lower diaphragm depending on application. When the piston is moved upwards it displaces fluid up into the upper chamber through the valve, which slows that flow. This influx of fluid increases the internal pressure within that upper chamber and, since fluids will not compress, it is the function of the nitrogen contained within the upper chamber to compress and so provide the 'spring' medium.

Additionally all displacers for all applications have an external port from the lower chamber to allow for evacuation and recharging of the fluid to cater for servicing and repairs. In the MGF the front and rear displacers on the same side are interconnected by way of a high-pressure pipe and a single high-pressure Schrader type valve for those servicing functions is fitted in that line. With this interconnection not only do you see fluid displaced from the lower chamber into

the upper chamber when the suspension compresses, but some fluid will be displaced to the other displacer, which causes that unit to raise the car slightly and the MGF's fine ride characteristics are derived from this principle.

There are a number of problems that can affect displacers and, put simply, these units are not serviceable, so when problems occur you are faced with replacing the affected displacer. One major current problem at the time of writing is that stocks of new displacers have run out, other than the occasional dusty shelf find at a dealer's parts department. This means that owners with failing displacers have to look for second-hand replacements, a situation that will get worse over time as the available second-hand numbers shrink.

How this will come to a head in the future for mainstream MGF owners is clear from the current experience of Trophy 160 SE owners. Even now there are Trophy cars 'off the road' due to a failed displacer and, because they are of an individual specification, there are rarely any second-hand units available.

Solutions for the Trophy owner can come from the use of standard MGF displacers and to swap the piston of the Trophy into the replacement standard displacer, which will provide the correct ride height and, because there is a slight difference between the Trophy and standard MGF head size and shape, introduce some of the Trophy characteristics.

Fig. 4.263   These displacers are standard MGF on the left and Trophy 160 on the right. The alloy Trophy piston is clearly shorter and this is where the 20mm lowered ride height is achieved.

Fig. 4.264   Detailed differences in the shape and dimension of the piston: (left to right) standard MGF, Metro front and Metro rear.

In 2011, a long-term solution arrived in the new and innovative replacement steel spring suspension for the MGF produced by the long-established major German spring manufacturer Suplex. (For more information on this conversion *see* Chapter 6.)

The common problems that can affect displacers start with a simple fluid leak. This becomes obvious as the Hydrolastic fluid used in Hydragas and earlier Hydrolastic equipped cars is a bright green in colour and has a degree of luminescence, so you often see drips hanging from the suspension. Drips on garage floors are often mistakenly diagnosed as coolant, which is understandable as Hydrolastic fluid is predominately a mix of water and antifreeze. However, once the wheel nearest to the residue location is removed

you can quickly look up at the underside of the displacer and see if the fluid is leaking from there. The lucky ones may see the leak coming from the outside and possibly it may only be that the pipe connection to the displacer needs tightening, but most will not be that lucky.

Usually when there is a loss great enough to leave traces on the garage floor, there will be some obvious settlement of the suspension on the affected side when you look at the car parked on level ground. It may not be quite as clear on cars that have serious settlement over a long period of time, but soon any leak will see the car down on its bump stops, and at that level it becomes unsafe to drive for two reasons. One is the obvious impact the lack of any suspension, apart from the compressed

rubber bump stops, will have on steering and stability. The second is that the tyres will come into contact with the front wing on the settled side, even with small steering movements. This will seriously distort the wing and the sharp edge can easily slice into the tyre.

The other common displacer failure is when the nitrogen gas leaks out and you then have a very hard-riding car with a slightly lower ride height on the affected corner. Some intrepid individuals have tried to recharge the nitrogen gas by fitting an additional valve into the top chamber of the displacer, but I am not convinced this would be successful beyond the short term as the basic questions remain: where did the leak originally come from, and what will stop the fresh nitrogen from leaking out the same way?

Fig. 4.265   Hydrolastic fluid leaking from this displacer is evident from the wetness and green 'hue'.

Fig. 4.266   When removed, the failure on this displacer was obvious.

Fig. 4.267   When the suspension deflates on an MGF, you must not drive it as the front tyres will damage the wing edges with even the smallest steering movement.

Fig. 4.268   Looking at the Metro displacer (left), corrosion will become an issue in the future and has already started on the MGF displacer (right).

One last issue that has not yet affected MGFs to any degree, but experience with older Austin/MG and Rover Metros suggests will definitely arise, is corrosion in the steel displacer body. Usually this will be concentrated on the lower edge or skirt of the displacer. The nature of the construction of the displacer means that there is a little leeway before corrosion starts to impinge on the effective operation of the displacer, but to catch this in time demands that periodic checks are made to check displacers or that some preventative treatment and paint is applied to supplement the original surface treatment of the displacer. While general surface corrosion can be quite extensive when it starts to eat the lower skirt edge, leaving a jagged edge that ruins a weather seal fitting, that is the time when failure is much closer.

Replacing a displacer is a simple job, except for the need for a Hydrolastic pump (*see* Figs 2.132 and 2.133). Safety comes first here and I have to remind you that the fluid pressure inside the displacers and interconnection lines is nominally 400psi. A spray of fluid at that pressure in the eyes and other sensitive places will do you damage! Therefore it is advised to use the professional tool to depressurize and ideally vacuum out the system before any spanner touches the displacer connection nut.

Remember that the suspension is connected between front and rear on the same side, so if you need to jack the car up, unless the suspension has

already collapsed, then you should do this first as you will not get a jack under the collapsed side. You have to start on the other side and lift it sufficiently to be able to block it or slide a jack partly across the other side until it is lifted enough to get a jack under a suitable hard point.

Hydragas suspension uses the earlier Hydrolastic suspension pump and fluid. While these tools are still readily available from the manufacturer (www.liquid-levers.com) and from some Classic Mini specialists, they are costly. When looking at a comprehensive MGF repair or restoration, this is a tool purchase that can be justified over the longer term. While you can find some home-made alternatives, usually made from a higher quality grease gun, that may be acceptable for limited uses such as on race cars in the paddock, I do not see them as suitable for any restoration or major work.

View the purchase of a pump for the MGF as equivalent to buying welding equipment for the classic MG. The classic MG always needs extensive welding during restoration, but even the earliest MGFs seem to be resistant to structural corrosion, so spend that money on a pump.

The Hydrolastic pump I bought in 1999 has been invaluable for maintaining the suspension at the correct height over many years and for various jobs where the suspension has to be disturbed, all without the hassle of involving others and the delays and costs incurred every time it is needed.

On top of this you become every other MGF owner's best friend! At the time of writing Hydrolastic fluid is still readily available from most motor factors, at least in the UK, in 5-litre containers at a similar cost to engine oil.

Using the Hydrolastic Pump

The MGF has a single connection point each side via a Schrader-style valve that is visually very similar to a tyre valve, but to a higher pressure specification. These are located under the front bonnet area and behind the thin removable plastic cover that is behind the spare wheel well and covers the bulkhead (*see* Fig. 4.262).

Look at the Hydrolastic pump union at the end of the pipe that screws onto the valve on the car. Note that there is a T-shaped screw attachment into the top of the adapter. This must be unscrewed before the adapter is fitted onto the Schrader valve on the car, and the hexagon collar screwed on and nipped up with the spanner.

Set the pump to the 'Pressurize' position and then fully screw in the T-shaped screw. This releases suspension pressure into the pump's fluid pipe, but no further. To depressurize the system it is simply a matter of moving the pump control lever to the 'Depressurized' position, and this allows suspension pressure to be vented into the pump that collects the displaced fluid. Once the pressure has drained off you can then move the control to 'Vacuum' (if the pump is one that has the vacuum

Fig. 4.269   Close-up of the Hydrolastic pump connection to the car's suspension valve.

Fig. 4.270   Removal of the rear displacer is easiest by lifting it out like this.

function) and evacuate as much fluid as possible, as indicated by the lowest reading on the vacuum gauge. The suspension is now fully depressurized, making suspension dismantling quite simple.

In this condition removal and refitting of a displacer is very simple at the front. It is only the need to ease the displacer out and upwards, rather than straight out, that makes the procedure more difficult at the rear. Please note that, even when you have vac-uumed out the system to the maximum degree, when you are removing the displacer and compress the piston, as you surely

will at some stage, there will be a jet of fluid projected from the hose connection point. Once the displacer is out, to avoid further jets of Hydrolastic fluid I normally invert the displacer over a bowl and pump the piston several times to remove the majority of fluid. As I have the use of a Hydrolastic pump with a vacuum facility, I have no worries about removing the air that will replace the fluid. I will shortly describe how to do this without the vacuum facility.

Refitting a displacer is as straightforward, but you do need to ensure that the piston engages fully into the 'roller foot joint', the correct description for

what most refer to as the 'knuckle joint'. This may not fully happen until you start to pressurize the system, so it is a point to check several times during the pressurization stage. In addition you need to ensure that the 'knuckle joint' is fully seated into its recess in the top suspension arm.

A professional Hydrolastic pump with a vacuum facility comes into its own at this point by removing as much air as possible. Air will seriously hamper the correct operation of the displacer. If you only have a Hydrolastic pump with no vacuum facility, then the best way of removing air from the system is

Fig. 4.271   The rear displacer can also be fiddled out through the wheel arch, just as the front one is removed.

Fig. 4.272   The 'knuckle joint' is the vertical pin and hidden joint under the rubber boot that sits in a cup in the upper suspension arm. This joint is correctly seated, but if the boot is displaced then check the joint is sitting correctly. The spacer being moved is a standard item and should be retained.

to pump the suspension up to 500psi, which of course means you need a pressure gauge – another advantage of the professional type pump – and then let the pressure down to 200psi. Repeat the cycle from 500 to 200psi, before pumping up again to 400psi, the nominal working pressure for the MGF suspension.

This should have seen air removed from that part of the system and allows you to provisionally set the ride height, which is something I will mention next as it deserves attention. Deal with the other side of the car in the same way and then fine trimming of the ride height can be carried out.

Setting the MGF Ride Height

The MGF has always had an issue with the suspension ride height. It always settles over a period of time and requires what is in simple parlance a 'pump up'. The trouble with that description is that it oversimplifies the process. While you can invariably get away with such a simplified and rough and ready approach for a Metro, this approach usually bites back if it is applied to an MGF. Generally speaking the settlement of the suspension without any fluid leaks will see a need for the suspension to be reset every two to three years. To return to the nominal 368mm measured between the front wheel centre and wheel arch lip above. I recommend this be done by someone well versed with MGF suspension.

General Suspension Wear Points

By creating superb handling and grip for the MGF and TF, the many Metro-based suspension parts are placed under more stress and in some cases wear out more quickly. The additional grip from the much wider wheels and tyres is an obvious difference, so if a car is habitually driven hard then earlier failure from general wear can be expected.

As most owners tend to treat their MG with far more respect and love than the average Metro owner, the actual lifespan of components isn't that different. The common failure points for Metro can be seen as the same for the MGF and, where applicable, for the TF too. This means that most owners of a car with more than 75,000 miles can expect to have to change the upper and lower ball joints sooner or later.

Upper Ball Joints

One advantage of having parts derived from the Metro, which mainly applies to the MGF, is that obtaining new replacement parts is straightforward and not hugely expensive owing to the wide availability generated from the Metro's huge former market penetration. The upper ball joint for both front and rear on the MGF suspension is just one example, with the same joint as the Metro used. It should be noted that, while the TF has many parts carried over from the MGF, the upper ball

joints are not among them: not only are TF joints different to MGF, the front and rear ones also differ, although the process of replacement is the same for all cars.

Fitting a replacement can be quite simple and for once the workshop manual adopts the simple approach. This is to jack up the corner needing attention, then place it on a stand. Move the jack under the lower arm/hub of that side's suspension and jack it up until the car starts to lift off the stand. If this is at the front of the car, then expect to open the bonnet and push down on the inner wing above the suspension to generate more suspension compression. Note that I say the inner wing: the outer wing is not as rigid and dents in that wing do not look good.

Now remove the suspension rebound rubber that sits on the subframe under the upper arm, and then insert a cold chisel or similar between the upper suspension arm and the subframe. Lower the jack. As the suspension drops and the axle stand takes the car's weight, the upper arm can't drop as far as it would normally and so the suspension is no longer under tension. This allows for simpler ball joint removal. The ball joint lock tabs are knocked back and the upper nut removed. The ball pin taper seal into the upper suspension arm is released, usually employing a suitable ball joint splitter (mechanics often break the seal with a few sharp hammer taps to the end of the upper arm).

Fig. 4.273 The upper arm 'rebound rubber' being replaced. Replacing upper ball joints is much easier if you remove this rubber and insert a cold chisel or similar while the car's weight is still through the suspension.

Fig. 4.274 Upper ball joint removal is simple, but it is important to have the correct socket to undo and refit the ball joint.

The lack of suspension tension then allows the lower arm and hub to be pushed downwards to disengage the ball pin from the upper arm. It is now free to allow the tab ends to be tapped flat and the ball joint socket to be fitted over. The use of the correct ball joint socket is really quite important as the ball joint hexagon is a massive $1^{13}\!/_{16}$ in size and, as can be seen in the accompanying images, there is next to no depth, so it is very easy to damage the hexagon if trying to improvise with tools such as adjustable wrenches that only grip two flats. Removing and replacing the ball joint is a quick and easy job with the right tool. These specific sockets are readily available, because of the Metro connection, and the cost is normally around £15. When refitting, don't forget to knock the tab washers over for both top and bottom parts of the ball joint.

FRONT LOWER ARMS AND BALL JOINTS

The lower front arms on the Rover Metro were carried over to the MGF and TF with small changes in the ball joint and in the way the anti-roll bar is connected, with the MGF having an additional support plate riveted to the arm for connecting to the anti-roll bar. The TF carries over the MGF design with minor differences focused on the inner pivot bush specification, and further reinforcement for the anti-roll bar fixing on the MG Motor TF 85th Anniversary cars.

The general construction of the lower arm comprises two steel mirror image pressings that are then welded together to create a rigid assembly. They are handed because the lower ball joint, which is riveted between the two welded plates, is angled and the specification of the front and rear pivot bushes differ, not by much but enough to create a suspension imbalance if the incorrect specification arm is fitted.

At present original specification MGF lower arms are no longer available as official MG parts and have been superseded as replacements by TF lower arms, although the bush differences dictate they are fitted as a matching pair. The MGF Trophy spec lower arms are also shown as different, but again it

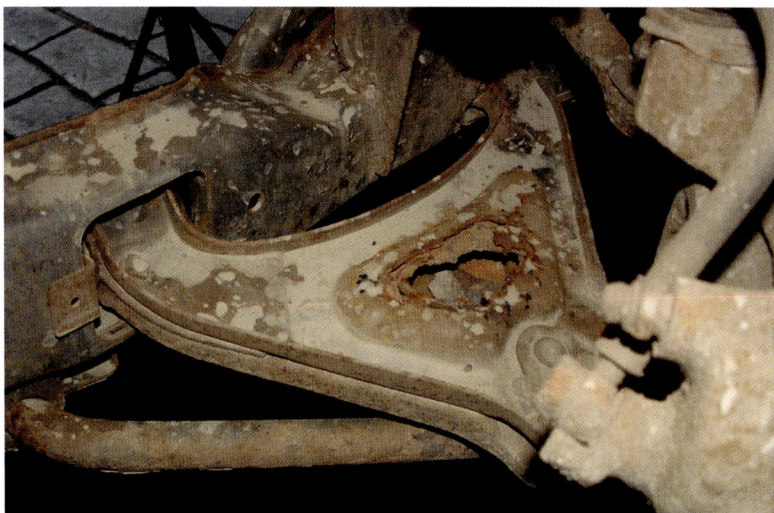

Fig. 4.275   Front lower arm corrosion is not unusual and can be worse than this.

is a bush difference, with the rear bush simply fitted at 90 degrees to the way it is fitted for the mainstream MGF. I would suggest that few will consider disturbing bushes unless replacing them with Poly types, which offer better performance, equal comfort and longer life.

There are usually three reasons driving the need to change a lower arm on either an MGF or a TF: severe corrosion on the upper main body section of the arm, which often manifests itself in a big hole; the inner pivot bushes have worn or softened; or the lower ball joint becomes worn.

If the ball joint fails, you can replace just the ball joint. This involves carefully drilling out the three rivets without elongating the holes in the lower arm. The new joint is then inserted and held by three new nuts, washers and bolts. It is fair to say that the money saved by buying just the joint is more than offset by the time taken to remove the old joint, which usually demands removal of the arm from the car anyway.

Wheel Bearings and Drive Flanges

Anyone with memories of the first MG Maestro and Montego models will recall the dreadfully short service life that the two-piece front wheel bearings on the early models delivered with 7,000 to 8,000 miles not unusual for the pre-1986 models. The original bearings were replaced with a much bigger single-piece ball bearing assembly that helped considerably, but the problem did not go away until a much stronger

taper roller bearing was introduced in 1989.

The reason why I mention this bit of history in relation to the MGF and TF is simple: the taper bearing adopted for the Rover Metro from 1989 was directly carried over into the MGF and TF, both front and rear. The benefit for the MGs is that the bearing was stronger than needed for the other applications and so this is a bonus for MGF and TF.

One issue that has come to light is that many diagnosed wheel bearing failures may not be the failure of the bearing or just the bearing, but may involve the drive flange, the bit that carries the wheel studs. Most bearing failures generate a characteristic whine at between 45 and 55mph coming from the affected hub, which is a good indicator that the bearing in that hub is worn. Corroboration comes when that wheel is raised off the ground and you can feel sideways play that vanishes when the footbrake is applied.

When there is no whine, however, and an MOT tester diagnoses a worn bearing through movement, then this may not be the bearing or the bearing on its own, but wear on the shaft of the drive flange that passes through the middle of the bearing. In essence the excess wheel movement will be a worn drive flange shaft and that will also need to be replaced as well as the bearing.

The change of a wheel bearing is straightforward and the job is well documented in the workshop manual. I will just add a comment on how to complete the job without a number of special tools, especially a hydraulic press. The job can be much easier if you have a friendly garage within convenient striking distance and transport to take the removed parts there for them to press out the old bearing and press in the new. Indeed, if you suffer from a well-seized CV joint to hub spline, which is more common on the rear, where the drive torque tends to see things tighten up over the years, then that press can often be the only route to separate the driveshaft CV from the hub.

A quick test should be done to see if the splines are free or not, as if it is solid you will have to take the whole hub, including the driveshaft if it is a rear assembly, to the garage with the press – or the whole car for them to do the job. Rear driveshaft removal also means the gearbox oil has to be drained before the shaft is removed, so making the job much more involved.

The first job is to raise the car, remove the wheel and knock out the bent-in part of the staked driveshaft nut to allow easier unscrewing of the hub nut. Then remove the centre 'MG' cap from the wheel, refit it to the car and lower it to the ground. You now have access to the 32mm hub nut. With the weight of the car and handbrake fully applied, you can now loosen the nut with a long 'Tommy bar', though in some cases you may still need an assistant to stand on the brakes.

If you have compressed air and high torque air tools then this fuss can be avoided, as the nut can easily be removed without the wheel off and with just the assistant on the brakes. With the hub nut partially wound out so that the end of the nut is level with the end of the shaft, which gives a larger contact area for the next part, you then give the hub nut a sharp tap or two with a soft-headed hammer (or steel hammer and wood insert) to see if the drive shaft moves on the splines. If it moves easily you can feel confident that a major headache is not present, but if the spline seems solid after several impacts and the end of the nut starts to distort, then you may well need the assistance of that hydraulic press.

On a 1998 MGF, for example, nearly 30 tonnes of pressure was needed before the corrosion seal between the splines gave up and allowed the driveshaft to be disconnected, with a bang! The problem was that such pressure crushed the threaded end of the outer CV joint, so this needed to be renewed too.

With a free spline, simply follow the workshop manual for removing the hub from the car. There are various differences between front and rear and between MGF and MG TF, including the need to split ball joints; on the MGF, for example, removal is easier when the suspension is lifted and a wedge placed between upper arm and subframe, as mentioned previously. Brake calipers need to be removed and hung out of the way with wire or cable ties so the hydraulic lines are not stressed.

An impact driver is also usually needed to loosen the screws that hold the brake disc onto the drive flange. Corrosion on the edge of the drive flange to inner bell of the disc will often make easy removal a distant dream. Some effort will then be needed to remove the brake disc: use a soft metal (lead or copper) hammer to hit the exposed disc, turning it 180 degrees between hits. In the absence of a suitable hammer, use a piece of wood to soften the blows of a steel hammer. Some discs are solidly corroded in place and may be damaged during removal. If they suffer damage they *must* be replaced. *Always wear eye and hand protection with this and other hammering aspects.*

ABS sensors are a pain as they are fragile and often become stuck in the hub. Ideally, several days before work is planned the area around the sensor should be pre-treated with some WD40 or Plus Gas penetrant. The sensors are only held in place with a single locking bolt, but you need to be careful in twisting the sensor body back and forth with further lubrication to ease them out in one piece. If one breaks then a replacement in 2011 was £78.38 (with VAT).

Once the hub and drive flange are removed from the car, suspend the hub on a couple of wooden blocks. This allows you to drift out (hammer) the drive flange from the hub and it will come out with half the inner bearing race firmly attached to the shaft of the drive flange. Removal is covered a little later.

The other half of the inner race will still be in the hub and can now be tapped out towards the rear of the hub, leaving just the outer race locked into the hub. There is now the fiddly job of removing the circlips, which may also be rusted in, so tapping around the edges with a cold chisel helps to loosen them. Lever the one edge with a small flat-blade screwdriver, and then use a second small screwdriver to lift it out in a peeling fashion. Repeat for the second locking ring at the other end of the bearing race. The main bearing race is then ready to be removed. Note that the ends of the locking ring have angled cuts, so you can only get behind one end.

Once the circlips are removed, you need to carefully tap out the outer bearing race. This needs small taps with a cold chisel or similar on the ledge

Fig. 4.276 Loosening the hub nut and checking that the inner joint is not corroded solid to the drive flange spline confirms that a hydraulic press will not be needed to separate them.

that the tapered bearings sat against. Alternate your taps 180 degrees, so the force is evenly applied, and slowly it will ease out. Standing the hub on wooden blocks gives the clearance needed to remove the race.

Now I have a use for this scrap race, employing the trick on a variety of bearings over the years. Very simply, with an angle grinder I cut through the race so that I can use it as a drift. It is the ideal size to transfer impact energy direct to the end of the new bearing and will not damage the bearing. The bonus is that the cut in your old race means it will not get stuck.

At this point it is very important to check the drive flange using the new

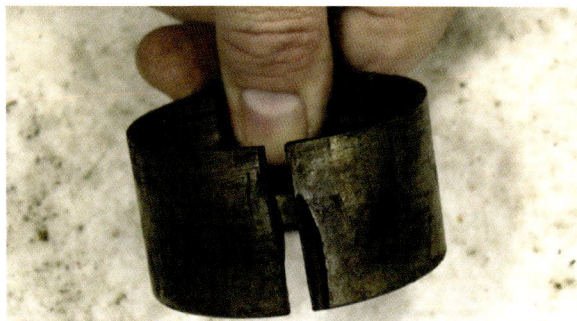

Fig. 4.277   The outer race of old bearings is very useful for making a 'drift' by cutting through the race. This can be used to knock out old bearings and, more importantly, tap in new bearings without damage and without the drift becoming jammed.

Fig. 4.278   Knocking out an old bearing using a race.

ABOVE LEFT: Fig. 4.279   Wheel bearing failure may be due to a worn drive flange shaft, as the corrosion here shows.

LEFT: Fig. 4.280   The diagnosis is confirmed with a simple check of whether the new bearing slides on. If it does, this confirms the wear is unacceptable.

ABOVE RIGHT: Fig. 4.281   Fitting the flange normally needs the services of a press.

BOTTOM LEFT: Fig. 4.282   When the drive flange is serviceable, half a bearing will still be firmly attached.

BOTTOM RIGHT: Fig. 4.283   The bearings need to be removed, leaving just the inner race, which has a convenient ledge to tap.

Fig. 4.284   An old jack handle through the flange holds it far enough off the ground to let the race pass.

Fig. 4.285   The inner race is tapped off.

bearing. This will be a final confirmation (if needed) of drive flange shaft wear. If the new bearing simply falls onto the drive flange shaft, then the drive flange needs replacement as it should be a tight interference fit, and this is why a press is often used.

If the new bearing won't slide onto the exposed part of the drive flange shaft, then it is reasonable to reuse this flange, which means you now have to remove the remaining inner race of the old bearing. Once again the taper bearing leaves a convenient edge to engage a chisel and alternating impacts at 180 degrees will move the race down the shaft.

However, you will need to hold the flange in a position where the race can move down without being blocked.

I have found that an old jack handle passed through the inside of the drive flange and then placed on a solid surface does a fine job in holding the flange at an angle that allows the inner race to be tapped off.

Using the 'Home-Made' Wheel Bearing Drift Tool

Clean up everything to be reused, especially the locking ring grooves, before applying a little copper grease in the circlip grooves. Good quality bearing kits come with two new circlips and a new hub nut. If your kit doesn't have these, then your removed parts would have to be in very good condition before I would suggest they can be reused.

First, fit a new circlip in the rearmost groove and tap it into the groove to ensure complete engagement. With the hub on wooden blocks, place the new bearing on top of the hub as square to the hub as possible and then use the split race drift tool and tap the bearing into place. Tapping alternately at 180 degree angles from side to side may still see the bearing go off line initially, so you need to keep a close eye on the position of the bearing and when it is off line then concentrate your tapping to the 'high' side to correct the bearing's path (Figs 4.277 and 4.278).

Once the bearing is around halfway in it will not easily go off line again and so progress becomes faster. When the bearing reaches the circlip the sound of the tapping will change to a more solid thud and you know it is fully engaged. This will be confirmed by being able to see the outer circlip groove. This circlip can now be fitted, followed by a few gentle taps on the circlip edges to ensure full engagement.

Next find a socket with the same diameter as the inner bearing race. Place this on a block of wood of sufficient size that, when you very accurately place the hub onto the socket, the inner bearing race rests on the socket. (Having a helper hold this in place is an advantage.) It is very important to place the hub accurately so that the inner bearing race and the socket are in direct contact. This is because you are about to tap the drive flange through the bearing and that inside inner race would pop out if it were not blocked in.

This is followed by general reassembly, noting that the splines of the CV joint and drive flange should slide easily together and should have a little copper grease to help prevent future corrosion. If the original discs are to be refitted, then clean the inner bell where it contacts the outer edge of the drive flange. With original or new discs give that edge a smear of copper grease.

Before leaving this section I include some views of a car that suffered a wheel bearing failure but had been driven for a while before the owner was forced to respond. Words do not convey what the pictures do and so I will leave you to ponder the irresponsibility of some fellow drivers.

Fig. 4.286 It sometimes beggars belief that people can drive their cars with such dangerous faults. No MOT examination is needed to confirm the wheel bearing has failed.

Fig. 4.287 The ABS ring did an extensive machining job on the inside of the hub.

MGF Dampers

MGF damper rates are quite unusual in that they have virtually no resistance on the compression (bump) side, but much more on the rebound. This often throws the unfamiliar off balance when they diagnose the MGF dampers as defective from this lack of compression damping. The reason for this low level setting comes back to the inbuilt damping action within the displacers.

This split damping is also reflected in the way the dampers are mounted to the car's body. The body mountings for the dampers are relatively weak. While there are no reports of problems when using standard dampers, the

Fig. 4.288 Ironically the drive flange was not worn, as can be seen since the bearing inner races are still attached.

use of non-original sporting dampers set hard and aggressive driving has seen some damage occur around the damper body mounts. The MGF Cup race cars and other competition cars had welded-in strengthening plates to cope with the much higher rated dampers and hard use on these cars.

Fig. 4.289 MGF damper mountings on the body are fine for standard and mildly stiffer dampers, but significantly stiffer dampers can damage the body.

Fig. 4.290 The very stiff MGF Cup race cars had strengthened damper mountings.

Fig. 4.291   An MG Rover built TF could have a standard ride height or it could be fitted with 'Sportpack 1' lowered suspension. One way to confirm which is fitted is to measure between the two (yellow) arrow points: 73mm equals Sportpack 1, and 78mm equals normal ride height.

MG TF Suspension

Beyond the headline differences between the MGF's Hydragas and TF's steel coil springs there was a huge raft of changes. One of the most important is that the TF subframe now took on board all the suspension functions as the MGF had its upper damper mounts on the body. TF incorporates the spring and damper into a single assembly and all the suspension loads are contained within modified subframes.

A simple glance at the rear suspension shows that there are bigger differences between an MGF and a TF than there are between, say, a Ford and a Toyota. When TF arrived most observers failed to appreciate how radical the changes to the suspension were and the long-term benefits this would provide. Most understandably focused on the rather harsh ride characteristics and at that time longevity was somewhat irrelevant.

In fairness the ride was very hard for all TFs. The criticism was justified but it was not connected to MG Rover creating hard-riding MGs as a contrast to their soft-riding Rovers contemporaries. The TF didn't have a Rover equivalent to be separated from, only the obvious rivals from other manufacturers and the MGF itself, so why did all the TF range have such a hard ride that was

so different to the MGF, apart from the Trophy 160 SE?

The answer is actually quite simple. Originally the TF was planned to have two suspension systems: the mainstream models would keep the Hydragas system from the MGF, while a new steel spring conversion was specifically developed as a sports suspension. Apparently what happened to change this was that Dunlop significantly increased the Hydragas unit costs in relation to the projected small volumes. From Dunlop's position it was an understandable situation, as they had produced a significant volume up to 1998, with both the Rover 100 and MGF in full production, but once the Rover 100 went out of production there was a significant reduction in the number of displacers required.

With MG Rover constrained by time, they decided to use the newly developed steel spring sports suspension on all TFs. To differentiate between the sports and standard suspension, however, they raised the ride height of mainstream models by 10mm (358/353mm front/rear), leaving the 'Sportpack 1' lowered suspension at 348/343mm, the same as the MGF Trophy 160 SE.

The best way to identify the two different suspensions is to measure between the underside of the lower

spring platform and the centre of the lower bolt holding the damper to the upper arm: if it is 73mm it is a lowered 'Sportpack 1' specification, and if it is 78mm then it is a standard-ride height car. If the parts are original MG ones than there is also a part number stamped on the lower front edge of the damper. It should be possible to read it with a little rust removal: RND000700 is a 'Sportpack 1' lower ride height damper and RND000270 is a standard-ride height damper.

TF Softer Ride

The hard ride hurt sales as many MGF owners looking to trade up a new TF found it too uncomfortable and so either kept their MGF or moved to a competitor. MG Rover responded to feedback from many sources with a softer ride for the ZT models within twelve months of the model range's introduction. The TF, though, was ignored until the very short-lived 2005 model year cars arrived on 17 January 2005; production stopped effectively on 6 April after only 631 examples had been made. The MG Motor TF continued with the 2005 models' suspension, aside from the 85th Anniversary models.

Not that owners or potential buyers of 2002–2005 hard-riding TFs have to put up with that hard ride as there is the obvious route of trying to use 2005 model year suspension parts. Included in the long list of changes made for that model were springs that were significantly softer than the original 2002–2005 models, some 20 per cent softer at the front and 30 per cent softer at the rear. Unfortunately, there is a considerable number of different parts between this and the earlier suspension spec and to change them all would have been very expensive, as I found when I stopped pricing the parts once they had passed the £1,000 mark, which didn't allow for fitting.

Today there are several replacement suspension kits aimed at delivering an MGF level of comfort while still retaining great handling. I was involved with creating the first back in 2005 and the story of how it evolved and how it has more recently been incorporated into a production MG Motor TF is interesting. (The conversion itself is covered in Chapter 6.)

Following the closure of MG Rover in April 2005 and the redundancy of most of the employees, several of the former chassis team created their own company, Vehicle Handling Solutions (www.vehiclehandlingsolutions.com), to sell their considerable expertise, especially that relating to MG and Rover cars. I asked whether there was a simple route to replicating the ride handling balance of MGF and was surprised to receive an immediate 'yes', as that route had previously been developed but the MG Rover 'bean counters' had rejected this on the grounds of cost. Ironically their chosen route demanded many more changes and I doubt whether there was a cost saving.

The rejected route was to use a special Bilstein damper, which had significantly enhanced capabilities over the normal dampers. Bilstein is a highly respected name in the damper world and many MG models were developed using Bilstein prototype units, but that 'bean counter' influence meant that only the MG ZT 260 and the Rover 75 V8 saw the use of Bilstein dampers in production cars. The fact that the TF had been developed using Bilstein prototype dampers to create a superb ride and handling compromise was a real bonus as prototype dampers could be configured very quickly and fitted to a suitable car for evaluation.

The Bilstein set-up was tested and the dampers compared on a 2004 TF 160 driven over the former MG Rover test route in Leicestershire, which had been carefully selected to offer plenty of variation for useful data gathering. The testing showed very significant improvements even though the original springs were retained. The

Fig. 4.292   Vehicle Handling Solutions was a company set up by former MG Rover chassis experts Andy Kitson, Alan Phillips and Wayne Nation to develop and sell improved suspension products for MG and Rover cars. Here Wayne (left) and Alan are in front of their test TF 160 during 'Comfort Kit' testing.

improvement was such that MGOC Spares commissioned VHS to build the kit, which became the now well-known and respected TF Comfort Handling Kit, sold by MGOC Spares and VHS.

The story does not finish there, however, as two of the three VHS team were drawn back into their former roles in the new SMTC (SAIC Motor Technical Centre) at Longbridge, designing and developing the suspensions and steering system of new MG and Roewe models. They also created the limited production TF 85th Anniversary model, which arrived in 2009.

All MG Motor TF models carried over the 2005 model year softer springs. For the 85th these springs were married to the Bilstein dampers, with some small

internal detail changes. Significantly thicker front and rear anti-roll bars were used and, for the first time, different width wheels, 6.5 × 16in on the front and 7.5 × 16in at the rear. The original 195/45 × 16 front and 215/40 R16 rear tyres were retained. This combination delivers what I consider to be the best combination of ride and handling characteristics of any standard MGF or TF for the road environment.

TF Suspension Problems

The many differences between MGF and TF suspensions mean that different problems arise, but let's look at the common problems first, starting at the front of the car. As the lower

LEFT: Fig. 4.293 TF rear suspension lower front arms were originally adjustable.

RIGHT: Fig. 4.294 In 2004 they were changed to a 'cheaper' solid bar.

Fig. 4.295   When compared to the new one, the lower arm is clearly seen to be bent, caused by striking a kerb.

suspension arms are almost identical, in time they will exhibit the same problems – rusted out upper sections, worn ball joints and pivot bushes – all of which can be dealt with as on an MGF. While the upper ball joints are different, they too will suffer wear over time and need to be changed. Again the same approach applies.

MGF and TF rear suspensions share a similar design of upper suspension arm, while the MGF's lower arms

consist of a substantial cast front arm and a steel rod for the rearmost arm. The TF, on the other hand, has a pair of the steel rod lower arms, the rear one being of considerable length, and a complex 'A' shaped trailing arm. While the two cars' rear lower arms are obviously very different, they share similar joints and so similar problems will arise with wear on the outer ball joints and the inner pivot bushes that will dictate replacement of these arms.

It is worth mentioning that the 2004 model year TF saw the front lower arm of the rear suspension changed from an adjustable bar to a solid bar on the grounds of cost saving, although there is no huge difference in the replacement cost to owners: at the time of writing, indeed, the solid bar was priced some 11 per cent more than the adjustable one. Both arms are fully interchangeable and the added adjustability that the earlier bar gives is an advantage, so fitting the earlier adjustable bar is recommended.

I have seen instances of TF bent lower arms due to cars sliding into kerbs, which seems bad in one way but the reality is that replacing a bent arm is simpler than replacing some other components that would otherwise take the impact energy.

The 'A' shaped trailing rear arm that is a signature part of the TF rear suspension has a focal point at its front mounting where the separate bracket carries a large bush. This bush will wear and when sufficiently worn you will detect a knock coming from the back

ABOVE: Fig. 4.296   The TF's front 'A' shaped trailing arm front mounting bush becomes visible when the arm is removed.

RIGHT: Fig. 4.297   Here the same bush is seen from above through the open engine bay.

ABOVE: Fig. 4.298   The front mounting bush seen from below (indicated in red). The yellow arrow is highlighting a sheared subframe mounting bolt and there is also one on the other side.

RIGHT: Fig. 4.299   To ease the lowering of the front of the subframe, two much longer bolts for each rear subframe mounting were used to lower the rear around 30mm.

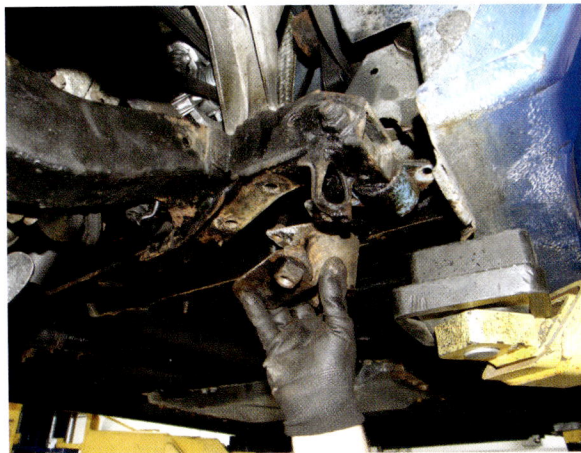
Fig. 4.300   Once the two securing bolts per mounting were removed, the front of the subframe was lowered to allow the old bushes to be removed.

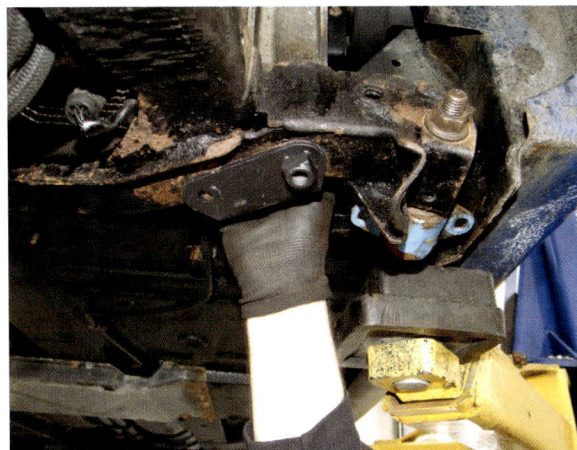
Fig. 4.301   New bushes were then fitted.

of the car while driving. Checking is a matter of inserting a lever between the subframe and trailing arm and levering to check for movement. If movement is present then this will be the most likely source of the knock. While it is likely to affect just one side, the process of replacement is one where the work involved makes it advisable to replace both and save on later cost.

The process is covered in the workshop manual but it is one of those jobs that seems at first to be relatively simple, but then degenerates into an 'I wish I hadn't started this' situation. Removing the trailing arm is no problem, but then the bush and its bracket are bolted through the subframe and the engine and gearbox support arms use the same bolts and sit on top of the bracket. When these are loosened you can't get the bush and bracket out without lowering the subframe, and I have found this includes lowering the rear of the subframe to allow enough movement at the front to get the bracket and bushes out. A helpful hint here is to replace two rear subframe-to-body mounting bolts per mounting with longer bolts, which then allows a much greater controlled drop of the rear of the subframe.

Another point to note is that, while these subframe rear mountings have four bolt positions each side, only three bolts are actually used. This doesn't stop you adding a fourth bolt, however, as I have known MOT testers erroneously fail cars for lack of the fourth bolt!

Lowering the front of the subframe is complex enough without the usual

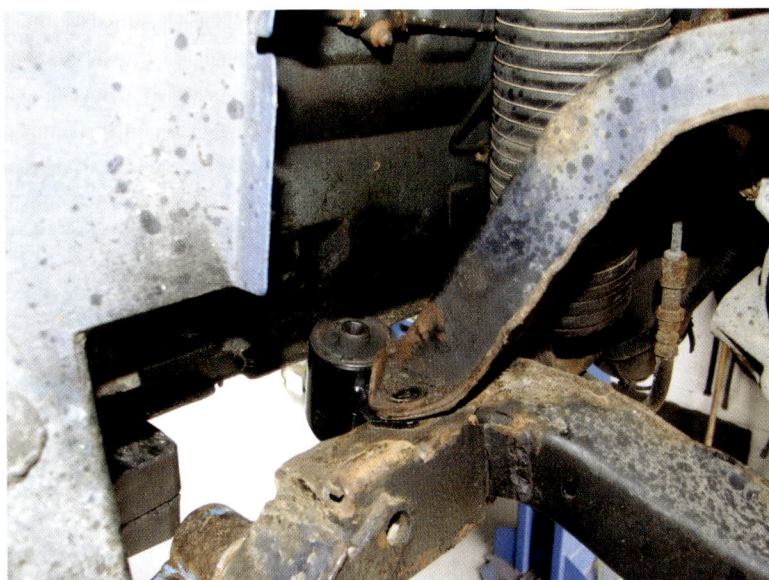
Fig. 4.302   A view of the top of the new bush fitted.

issues of rusted-in front subframe-to-body bolts (*see* Chapter 2). The long bolts don't help here as it seems the exposed section of bolt thread is able to corrode away; once you come to remove them they seize when this corroded section winds into the captive thread as you start to undo the bolts. Accessing the rear bolts also means the exhaust and catalyst, exhaust heat shield and rear anti-roll bar have to be removed. During reassembly, liberal use of copper grease was used to coat metal surfaces, especially the subframe bolt threads, to help prevent future seizure.

It is also worth noting that there is a replacement 'Poly' bush for the original bushes, but it is not the complete ready to bolt-in configuration of the original MG bush. With the 'Poly' type replace-

ment you need to remove the original bush from the case of the original part and then fit the 'Poly' bush in its place. If following this route, the original bracket has to be in a serviceable condition, aside from the fact it will always need derusting and painting before reuse.

STEERING

Steering is a relatively simple subject area with only a few variations between the MGF and TF and the Rover Metro from which it was derived. The steering rack used on both MGF and TF is a manual item: cars with power assistance (most MGF and all TFs) get assistance via an ECU-controlled electric motor mounted within the steering column, hence the description of EPAS (Electric Power Assisted Steering).

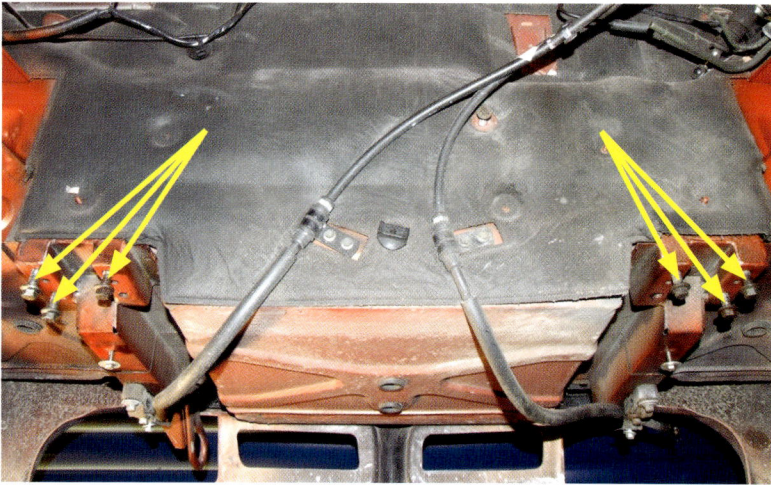

Fig. 4.303   Rear mountings on both front and rear subframes have provision for four bolt fixings, but only three are ever used.

EPAS was an option for the MGF 1.8i until 1997, when it was standardized; it was, though, standard on all VVC models from their introduction. It operates by taking inputs from the tachometer (rev counter) for engine rpm, speedometer for road speed and a simple potentiometer on the steering column for the effort being applied into steering by the driver. The ECU then calculates the degree of assistance that should be applied and provides an appropriate voltage to the motor and appropriate engagement of the clutch to transfer the motors energy into the steering column.

If things do not operate according to the ECU's mapping, it will automatically disconnect the motor and suspend any power steering assistance, plus illuminate the warning lamp with the steering wheel motif on the instrument pack. There are a number of fault conditions that can generate disconnection, but the common ones are loss of engine or road speed signals, often accompanied by the loss of the reading from the tachometer or speedometer. As the pre-2000 model year cars use a long three-piece speedometer cable, it is not unusual for a separation between two sections or a cable failure to generate this problem.

An EPAS fault condition can also be generated from holding engine rpms above around 1,800rpm when station-ary for more than a minute, such as when trying to see a faster warm-up on cold winter days. This is generated because the EPAS ECU is programmed to see a higher rpm for more than around a minute with no road speed input as a fault. Resetting is simply achieved by turning the ignition off for at least thirty seconds for the system to shut down, and then start up and drive off. Within a few metres the system will see road speed information and restore normal operation.

MGF and TF steering racks have different ratios, as does the Metro, and a common upgrade is for the TF rack to be fitted to the MGF as it has a better 2.8 turns lock to lock against the MGFs 3.1 turns. Identification of the different racks *can be* by way of a coloured band around the inner part of one rack gaiter – red for TF and yellow for MGF – but the red ones can take on an orange hue. This method of identification is not foolproof, as later new TF racks didn't have this ID and neither did the Metro rack, so do not rely on this method and measuring the total number of turns on the pinion shaft. Changing a rack is a straightforward job, although it is a little fiddly negotiating the rack through a relatively small space between subframe and body.

Steering Bias Fault

A common EPAS issue that develops over time is for the steering to acquire a left-turn bias: a greater assistance level when turning left and reduced assistance turning right. There is also a natural left pull to the steering when travelling straight, something that can easily be confirmed by raising the front of the car off the ground, ensuring enough clearance so the steering can be turned freely from lock to lock. Set the steering in the straight ahead position and, without touching the steering wheel, start the engine. If the bias condition is present then the steering will steer to full left lock: if centred or turned to full right lock, once released the steering wheel will self-turn to full left lock again.

This is an issue with the setting of the potentiometer on the steering column and is something that develops over time. Correcting this is officially seen as needing replacement of the steering

Fig. 4.304   The red band (here seen looking slightly orange) is shown around the steering rack on this TF 160.

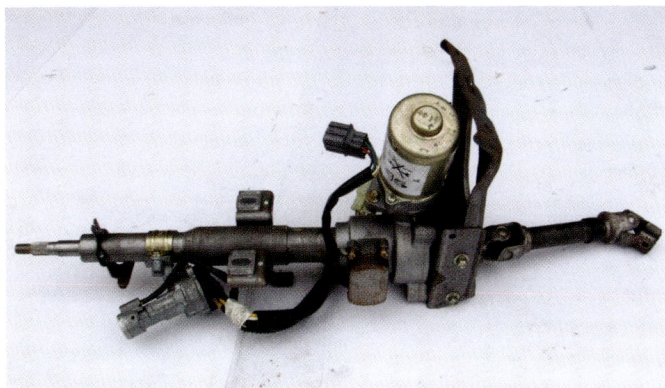

Fig. 4.305   *The MGF and TF EPAS is self-contained within the steering column, including a potentiometer to measure the steering loads to allow calculation of the assistance required.*

Fig. 4.306   *The potentiometer is covered by a security plate held in place by 'security Torx' T25 screws.*

Fig. 4.307   *The potentiometer is also held in by T25 security Torx screws. If the EPAS needs to have an 'assistance bias' adjusted out, the resin indicated by the screwdriver has to be partially cleaned out.*

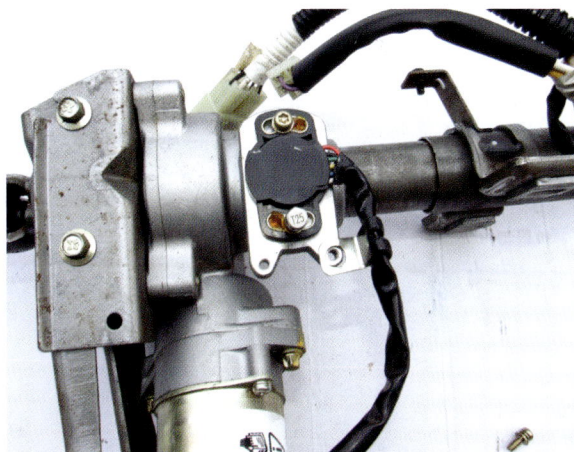

Fig. 4.308   *There should be a very small amount of movement of the potentiometer when the screws are slightly loosened. Note that there is a T25 security tool bit in one screw (see text).*

column assembly (with fitting, a new steering column costs more than £1,000). It is not the only route, however, and unless there is some major additional fault you just need to recalibrate the potentiometer.

The potentiometer is located under a protective steel cover secured to the column by two security Torx screws, which are screws that have a built-in pin in the centre of the star pattern in the screw head preventing a normal Torx bit from engaging. The security Torx has a centre hole drilled to allow it to slide over the security pin. It is difficult to access these screws when the steering column is fitted into the car and ideally the column needs to be lowered.

A more brutal approach I have seen is to lever the cover up and out of the way. This is not a very elegant approach and there is always the risk of accidentally damaging other parts, so I prefer the column lowering method,

even though it makes the job more involved.

Once the pressed steel protective cover is removed this gives access to the potentiometer, which is secured by two similar security Torx screws and a 'resin' filling the adjustment slot. The resetting process requires the resin to be dug out to allow slight movement of the potentiometer once the two T25 Torx retaining screws have been loosened slightly, but not removed, just enough to be able to move the potentiometer and for it to stay in the new position.

The process of resetting is now one of trial and error, still with the front of the car raised off the ground. Very small movements of the potentiometer will have quite significant effects on the steering. You are looking to judge how much you have to move it from where it is currently set until you start to see the opposite steering bias. Noting that position and the original position, you

then reset to the mid-position, when you should find the steering no longer has any bias or desire to self-steer to either lock.

You then retighten both lock screws a little at a time on each. The system is so sensitive that simply locking up one screw can see the steering drop back into a self-steer mode. Small, even tightening of the two screws will allow any compression movement in the potentiometer when turning one screw to be cancelled out by the same movement on the other screw. There is no need to apply any resin as was seen in the original set-up, unless you wish.

Steering Wheel Changes

Even though it is covered in the workshop manual, I will mention this here as it is something that many owners will want to do for various reasons, but be aware that this means dealing with an airbag. These have to be given

Fig. 4.309   With the steering wheel removed the 'rotary coupler' is visible, as is the yellow air bag lead and plastic shroud where the horn and Steptronic electrical connections are housed.

Fig. 4.310   The 2005 model year TF included a pair of spacer washers between the steering arm and hub. These are specifically required to go with that model year's suspension changes.

the utmost respect as they are a form of explosive. If you are too close if it is accidentally triggered, then injury or worse can result.

The golden rule is to follow the workshop manual guidance to the letter. The main element of this is to disconnect the vehicle battery and allow at least fifteen minutes for any residual current held in the system to dissipate as it might still trigger the airbag. Better still, disconnect the battery and go and have a cup of tea, coming back after twenty minutes.

Removal of an air bag is quite simple. There are two Torx headed long screws accessed via deep holes through the back of the steering wheel. The airbag can then be lifted from the wheel centre and the single plug wire connection is withdrawn. Carefully place the airbag module somewhere safe.

The wheel is next removed, first ensuring the front wheels are in the straight ahead position to allow correct refitting. Loosen the centre securing bolt but don't remove it. With the bolt still in place, but loosened a few turns, there is enough free space for the wheel to be loosened but not pulled from the column. The wheel can be actually released from the column by gripping the wheel at the three and 9 o'clock positions and pulling the sides alternately towards you. The twisting motion helps to release any bond between wheel and column spline.

Refitting is simple enough but do take care to locate the free-moving plastic connector part of the 'rotary coupler' (*see* Chapter 5) through the slightly offset oblong hole in the wheel and to engage the splines so the wheel is accurately aligned.

2005 on Model Year Steering Oddity

A small point that has been the subject of questions from TF enthusiasts relates to 2005 model year on cars that have the softer suspension set-up (not 2005 cars with Sportpack 1). This concerns two obvious packing washers that are fitted between the front hubs and the steering arms that bolt to the hubs. These were added specifically for these softer suspended cars and have an important role in correcting the steering geometry.

BRAKES

The braking system for the MGF was a collection of braking parts from other Rover models and it provides safe, reliable braking for the performance levels of which the car is capable. The system was made up of 240mm diameter vented front discs that first appeared on the 2-litre Montego in 1984 and, with a different single-piston slider caliper, was adopted for the Rover Metro GTi models in 1990. The GTi set-up was carried over to the MGF for the front, but rather than use a drum brake that was common to the previous applications, a 240mm solid disc was used at the rear clamped by a Rover 800 rear caliper, which has an inbuilt handbrake mechanism. The Bosch ABS (antilock braking system) was an extra cost option for the 1.8i models but standard on the VVC.

By modern standards these brake dimensions are only modest, but they provided more than adequate braking for these original MGF models, and this performance was aided by the mid-engine layout, which maintained more weight at the rear so the rear brakes were working harder than FWD saloon rear brakes. Good fade resistance was aided by the very open wheel design of both initial MGF wheel designs, which allowed a greater airflow through the wheel to cool the brakes.

Even with great cooling and adequate braking performance, the 240mm diameter discs was not able to meet the projected Track Day required

Fig. 4.311   MGF and TF brakes have a common size for rear brakes but there are two sizes for front brakes. This image has the 304mm diameter front discs (left) and standard 240mm discs (right). In the middle is a common 280mm conversion.

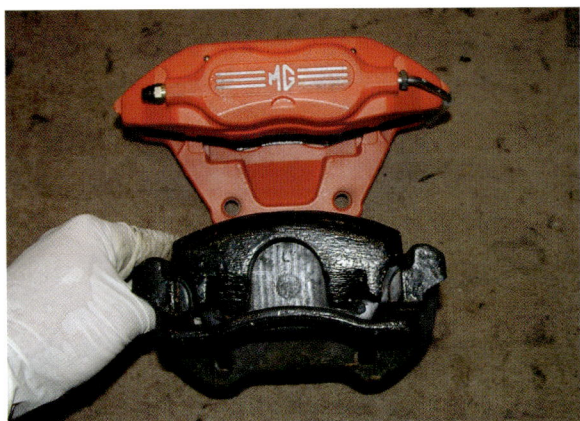

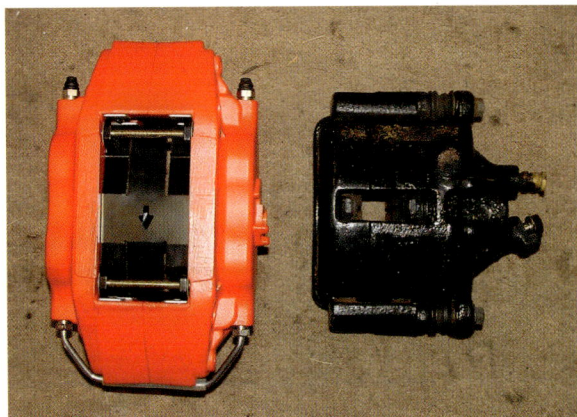

LEFT: Fig. 4.312   Standard 240mm slider caliper bottom and 304mm four pot side-on view.

BELOW LEFT: Fig. 4.313   The view from end on shows how much bigger the four pots really are.

BELOW RIGHT: Fig. 4.314   VVC models, auto models and all late models came with ABS as standard; others had it as an option.

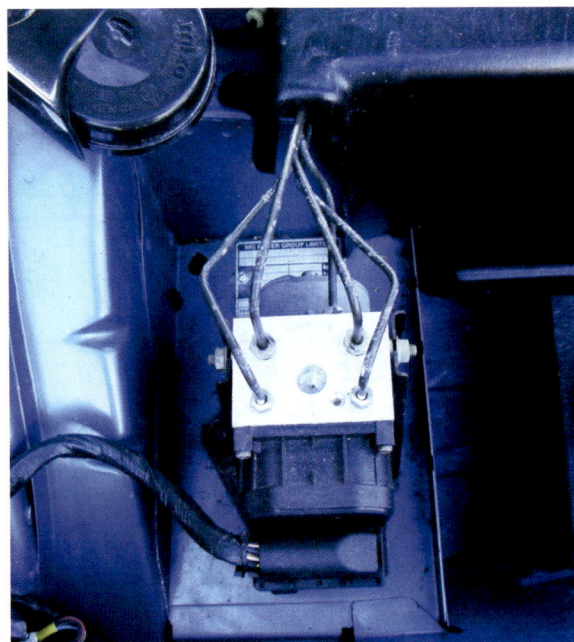

Fig. 4.315   Just before MG Rover collapsed, they were about to introduce a 'cheaper two pot' MG-branded AP Racing caliper to replace the 'four' common to the TF 160, along with wider use of the 304mm discs. This view shows the two types side on.

Fig. 4.316   An end-on view shows that the pads would have had a smaller surface area.

braking performance of the Trophy 160 SE model of 2001. With greater performance and targeted at track day enthusiasts, it would clearly have left the car short in braking terms. Taking a leaf out of the MGF Cup race cars, which used bigger front discs clamped by AP Racing four-pot (piston) calipers, the Trophy model followed suit with 304mm diameter vented discs and MG-branded AP Racing four-pot calipers.

For owners stepping up from a standard MGF to a Trophy for the first time, the braking efficiency was hugely better and many commented that they felt they would 'bend their nose against the windscreen', such was the massive increase in braking power. It was somewhat surprising, though, that the Trophy models did not come with ABS and it was not an available option, but this was less of a concern.

Both braking systems were carried over when the TF arrived, except there was wider availability for the big AP Racing brakes, which were standard on TF 160 and optional on TF 135 and TF 120; when fitted they also came with standard ABS. When the MG Motor TF was reintroduced it had just the one braking system, the larger AP racing type system with standard ABS. It retained the same 240mm rear brakes and caliper fitted to all other MGF and TF models.

MG Rover came very close to introducing an alternative front brake caliper as a standard feature for all TFs using the 304mm discs. Even the last 2005 TF brochures stated this change, which was a move to a cheaper two-pot (piston) AP racing caliper, still painted red and using a smaller pad. Some of these calipers have found

their way out into the wider world and some ex-MG Rover cars fitted with them were sold by the Administrators; replacement brake pads for these cars are listed under Mintex MDB1890 or EBC DP2197/2.

ABS

Many cars have ABS supplied by Bosch. The ABS system is essentially an ECU-controlled valve placed between the driver's foot and the brake on each wheel. There is a wheel speed sensor on each wheel that feeds the ECU with a series of pulses that equates to the speed of that wheel. Under normal braking conditions the ABS does nothing and all the effort the driver imparts into the brake pedal is transferred to each wheel to provide braking.

Fig. 4.317   ABS front wheel sensor and toothed ring.

Fig. 4.318   ABS rear wheel sensor being removed.

During braking, if any individual wheel speed is detected as being more than approximately 20 per cent slower than the other wheels, the ECU interprets that this slowing wheel is about to lock. It then invokes the first control stage, which is to close a valve, which prevents any more fluid pressure from the master cylinder reaching that specific brake.

If this fails to restore a more even wheel speed situation, the ECU then opens a second valve, which allows some of the trapped fluid pressure between the valve and brake to be relieved. The braking effort will be reduced and this allows that wheel's speed to increase. Once this is achieved the ECU returns the valves to their off position and normal braking is resumed.

This process is completed in a very short space of time. When the braking is returned to normal, and the wheel speed once more drops below that threshold, the cycle repeats but now there is a situation in which repeated relief would see the brake pedal sink to the floor, as only a small amount of fluid is contained in front of the brake master cylinder piston.

To overcome this there is a high-pressure pump in the system, which then feeds fluid back into the system between the master cylinder and ABS cut-off valve so that the brake pedal never goes to the floor. The driver feels this fluid introduction through the brake pedal pulsing as surges of fluid are introduced. The whole process keeps repeating until the wheel lock issue stops.

ABS is an extremely reliable system and problems are almost exclusively confined to the wheel speed sensors, which are quite fragile and often get broken when work is being completed, as the sensors can seize in the hub. The sensor works by being mounted close to a toothed ring, which is a shrink fit on the outer CV joint of the rear driveshaft or the part CV joint that is used on the front.

The clearance between the ABS sensor and the toothed ring is very small. It is worth noting that if a wheel bearing starts to fail and give off its characteristic hum at various speeds, you should look into replacing it as soon as possible, otherwise free play can see the

Fig. 4.319   Excess wheel bearing movement can damage ABS sensors, but this is extreme.

toothed ring contact and damage the sensor tip.

An ABS sensor can be tested with a quality multi-meter with a low level AV voltage and resistance scale. First, check the voltage by disconnecting the ABS sensor plug and insert the meter probes into the sensor wiring. Rotate the wheel and you should see a pulsing voltage generated. If nothing is seen then check the resistance through the sensor. If it shows an open circuit then the sensor is defective, otherwise around 1,500 ohms should equate to a good sensor. Fault checking should include making sure the ABS sensor hasn't lost the retaining bolt and moved too far from the toothed ring to detect movement, or that a previous owner hasn't replaced the CV joint with a non-ABS one without a toothed ring.

General Braking Faults

The MGF and TF (foot) brakes are no different to other cars' and can suffer the normal range of problems that any modern car suffers. Usually the problems are related to two categories of driving style. There are the 'light brakers', who tend to generate glazed and/or corroded discs, seized and semi-seized caliper pistons and sliders. Then there are the 'heavy brakers', who predominantly generate rapid pad and disc wear, but tend to suffer far fewer longer-term problems. Many cars also suffer from poor maintenance.

Periodic servicing should involve pad removal to clean off brake dust, check that the pads are still free to move, that there is no uneven wear

and that the pads' friction material has not started to separate from the steel backing. This condition will seriously reduce the efficiency of the brakes and lead to overheating of the pads as heat will not be dissipated efficiently. The caliper should be checked for free piston and caliper sliders, at the same time visually checking both disc swept faces for wear, scoring and corrosion. The routine change of brake fluid is often missed and is advised if there is no service history.

Handbrake problems are not so variable according to driving style, but the heavier user generates more heat and tends to keep the rear caliper internals free for longer, so only external caliper linkage and cable issues arise. One common sticking point is the connection between the end of the cable and the caliper lever, where semi- and full seizure of this pivot is quite common.

Cable issues are usually confined to ageing and stretching, which can be felt when operating the lever with a solid and dead feel rather than a quite springy feel. The spring in the cable is what actually provides the energy to hold the handbrake on, so this springy feel is generally a good sign. The point at which handbrake cables need to be replaced is not seen at any specific age or mileage, but judged by the dead feel and running out of cable adjustment, which will usually attract an MOT fail.

Most cars will need a rear caliper replacement much sooner than a front caliper change, and a 'soft braker' will certainly find the internal mechanisms seizing earlier. While it is possible to remove and strip a caliper and clean

Fig. 4.320 *Rear brake caliper pistons need to be screwed back in when changing pads. There are four cut-outs to enable tool engagement, although suitable pliers often work well.*

it up enough to provide a form of first aid repair, a more comprehensive rebuild replacing all the seals and rubbers, together with any other worn or corroded items, is usually the only way to restore long-term reliability. Sourcing all the parts that may be needed is usually not as cost-effective as buying a reconditioned caliper, or better still a pair to keep brake balance.

Brake Pad Changes

A pad is really a very basic item to change. Because of that many will leap in and get on with the job, yet some difficulties can arise. The biggest problems usually come from fitting rear pads, as the internal auto adjuster has to be wound back in by turning the caliper piston, which has cut-outs for the appropriate caliper wind back tool. The tool is not always needed if the piston is free to rotate, as you can often insert long-nosed pliers into the cut-outs.

In the event of the piston failing to rotate, stronger persuasion using a big pair of grips will usually move the piston, but great care is needed not to damage the piston or seal. Once movement has started, and with a little light lubrication (WD40) around the seal edge, rock the piston back and forth to ease movement into it. Then it is a case of slowly and carefully winding it back, but if it remains stiff it may be necessary to wind it in and back out a couple of times to ease it more. If this fails then it is indicative that the caliper is in need of full refurbishment or, an easier operation, replacement.

Replacing the front pads is much less complicated as there is no internal caliper adjustment mechanism, but there are two quite different designs of caliper to deal with. The common one is the simple slider caliper with a single large piston used with the mainstream 240mm diameter disc brakes. There is also the distinctive red MG-branded AP

Racing caliper, which has four small pistons in two opposed pairs, from which the slang term 'four pots' is derived.

The 240mm brakes' slider caliper can suffer from the main piston sticking, but far more likely is that the slider mechanism seizes up. This is an area to check and ensure it doesn't become contaminated due to the rubber boot becoming damaged, with water and dirt getting inside and causing the pin to corrode and seize. When an issue of semi-seizure is developing it will often be felt when braking lightly, with a hint of an initial pull to one side. The side the car pulls to is usually the affected side as the sticking brake will often have a little bit of drag on that side, which will pre-warm the disc and pad so the initial bite will be stronger.

Dealing with sticking brakes is usually not difficult and it is worth trying cleaning before replacing the calipers. First, remove one pad and insert a piece of wood the thickness of the pad's steel backing. Operate the brakes to push the piston out to expose a large part of it for cleaning. While this can be done with a sensitive helper pushing the pedal down, obvious care has to be taken not to push it so far that it pops out and gives you a much bigger job. The inserted wood is intended to provide a stop for the pistons to prevent them coming out.

Once the piston is exposed, the use of a proprietary brake cleaning fluid will be ideal. If needed you can create some 6in strips of rag that can be wetted with cleaning fluid, wrapped around the piston, then pulled back and forth to clean the piston. If the piston is corroded then this will not work and caliper refurbishment or replacement is necessary.

The 'four pot' MG-branded AP Racing calipers, specifically designed for the MGF and TF, have just four smaller diameter pistons and no slider in sight. If a piston or pistons becomes sticky or seizes in this caliper then there is less working room, but the same method of cleaning applies. Here though an additional piece of wood that only allows one piston out at a time helps access. Once out the piston can be cleaned and 'exercised' in and out a few times if sticky, and when pressing it back in it is very easy to feel it easing. Indeed this minor exercise process is useful to

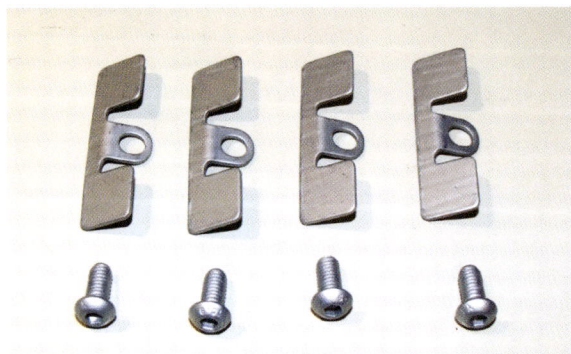

Fig. 4.321 *Pad guide plates that screwfit to the four-pot caliper are available from MG specialists.*

do as routine maintenance with these 'four pot' brakes, as they are more likely to become sticky through insufficiently hard use.

Both types of calipers have stainless steel pad guide plates for the pad edges to sit on. While those of the slider caliper type are not readily available as separate parts, the ones bolted into the four pot calipers are available from some MGF and TF specialists. The latter type allows for smoother operation and movement of the pads in the caliper. They often become heavily contaminated with brake dust residues and this needs to be cleaned off periodically, with the pad edges given a light smear of copper grease.

Brake Squeal

A negative aspect of modern braking materials is the tendency for them to make more noise during operation, although I prefer this to being contaminated by asbestos residues, which were legal in brake and clutch friction materials up to the beginning of September 1999 (in the UK). The recipes for brake friction materials in use since then have included more metallic elements and this led to an increase in brake noise, although this has eased as brake companies have refined their materials. Even so it is not unusual for some materials on some discs to squeal, which may be an issue, not just with the pad material but also the disc, especially if it is glazed.

The first suggestion to overcome this is to use an anti-squeal shim, which came with the standard MG pads. These are metal shims glued to the back of the pads; if they are not found on the replacement pads, they can be carefully removed from the old pads and fitted to the new. Second, the traditional application of copper grease onto the back of the pad can still work in cases of minor noise, but this is not so effective for more pronounced squeal.

Last, effective universal anti-squeal kits are widely available, employing adhesive-backed pads of a bitumastic like material that you cut to the size of the disc pad back and then stick it on. The nature of this material, about ¼in (6mm) in thickness, is that the caliper piston sinks into the material on first application and that then becomes a sink for any vibration generated during braking.

The vast difference in the two standard front braking set-ups on the MGF and TF does lead many of those with the mainstream braking system to want to upgrade to the bigger four-pot brakes (for this and a number of other options, *see* Chapter 6).

WHEELS AND TYRES

The MGF and TF have always come with alloy wheels. Since their 95.25mm pitch circle diameter (PCD), the diameter of a circle drawn through all four of the wheel studs, is so unusual when compared to most other mainstream cars, there is not a huge choice for alternative wheels. There is, however, a good choice of standard wheels that satisfies most tastes.

When introduced the MGF had a single style of six-spoke alloy wheel for the 1.8i models and a five-spoke design with a higher quality finish for the VVC.

These wheels were all 6in wide with a 15in diameter and the same Goodyear Eagle NCT3 tyre was fitted to all, but with a 185/55 R15 size for the front and 205/50 R15 size rear. This tyre mismatch was deliberate and is all to do with the MGF's mid-engined configuration, where 55 per cent of the weight was at the rear. There is also a significant element in the tyres' stiff construction, especially needed at the rear.

Due to the oddity of these tyre sizes, the spare wheel and tyre was different again and officially designated as a 'Temporary' spare wheel, meaning in simple terms that it was legal to run at a maximum of 50mph for 50 miles. In the UK (and I suspect in most other MG markets) tyre legislation makes it illegal to use different sized tyres on the same axle, except when using a 'Temporary' spare wheel and tyre. Different sizes between front and rear axle are fine, but that means that to have normal legal use at all times two spare wheels would be needed to cater for punctures, one for the front and one for the rear. That is obviously impractical for most cars and certainly for a car the size of the MGF, hence the adoption of the 'Temporary' spare wheel, which interestingly is a Maestro 5.5 × 14 steel rim and 175/65 R14 tyre.

In 1998 the first wheel variation arrived with the 'rounded' six spoke 7 × 16in design wheel fitted with 215/40 R16 Goodyear Eagle F1 GSD2 tyres for the Abingdon LE model. Here we see the same size of tyre fitted front and rear and this was to feature on all MGFs using a 16in wheel, except for the MGF Trophy 160 SE.

Fig. 4.322   Original six-spoke 6 × 15in MGF alloy wheel.

RIGHT: Fig. 4.323 Original five-spoke 6 × 15in MGF VVC alloy wheel. (The Rover wheel centre reflects the fact that this wheel was fitted to a modified Rover Metro.)

Fig. 4.324   Common temporary spare wheel in 5.5 × 14in steel.

Fig. 4.325   The Abingdon 7 × 16in six-spoke alloy was the first 16in wheel introduced.

Fig. 4.326   Multispoke 72 × 16in alloy wheel introduced with the 75th Anniversary model.

Fig. 4.327   Standard 6 × 15in alloy wheel for a 2000 model year 1.8i MGF.

Fig. 4.328   The Steptronic model had this 6 × 15in six square spoke alloy wheel.

Fig. 4.329   2000 model year VVC introduced this 7 × 16in six square spoke alloy wheel.

Fig. 4.330   The Trophy 160 SE model introduced this 7 × 16in eleven-spoke alloy wheel with a design to fit around the new MG-branded AP Racing four pot front brakes.

Fig. 4.331   This 7 × 16in Ultra Lightweight alloy wheel was a very expensive option .

The 16in wheels were popular and many cars were retrofitted, a practice that continues. One small modification was specified to the MGF front suspension bump stop area when 16in wheels and tyres were used. This has caused discussion among owners for years and is discussed in Chapter 6. The 75th Anniversary model of 1999 introduced another new 16in wheel design, still with the same 7 × 16in dimension and carrying the same tyres, but now with a 'multispoke' design.

The 2000 model year upgrades saw 1.8i manual models with a new eight 'round spoke' design 15in wheel, and the Steptronic (auto) model featured a new six 'square spoke' 15in design, both with the same rim dimension and tyre sizes as previous models. VVC models moved up to 16in as the standard size with a six 'square spoke' design replacing the original five-spoke 15in design. Rim and tyre sizes were the same as other 16in fitments.

The final variation for MGF wheels came with the Trophy 160SE. This was much more than a simple cosmetic change. The model introduced the MG-branded AP Racing 'four pot' calipers with 304mm discs and previous 16in wheel designs would not fit over those calipers. The mainstream Trophy wheel was a new eleven-spoke design in which the spokes were quite prominent to allow enough room behind for the big caliper. The projection of the spokes on these wheels means they are vulnerable to careless parking against kerbs, so be warned. A new front tyre size, 195/45 R16, was also introduced just for the Trophy models.

At the same time a very expensive wheel was added as an option (£1,525 extra on a new car), finished in gunmetal grey. This Ultra Lightweight wheel, still the same 7 × 16in size, used the new Trophy tyre sizes 195/45 R16 front and 215/40 R16 rear, but that additional cost over the already exclusive Trophy 11 spoke alloys guaranteed that few took up the option.

The 'lightweight' description of these wheels is perfectly accurate and they are around half the weight of a standard MGF alloy rim. All this seems to be for nothing when you then pick up a tyre and find it is so much heavier than the rim. When comparing the weights of rims with fitted tyres the startling difference felt with just the rims is almost lost. Certainly having a couple of sets of these Ultra Lightweight wheels allows comparison and they don't show any major differences in the steering or handling.

Spare Wheel No Longer Fits ...

The move to big brakes also created problems for the spare wheel. If the earlier standard 16in wheels do not fit over those big brakes, then clearly neither will the 15in wheels nor the 14in steel temporary spare wheels. To overcome this MG Rover introduced the IMS (Instant Mobility System). This was quite a good system comprising a small suitcase filled with a 12V compressor with gauge, a bottle of tyre sealant, goggles and gloves, and was much better than the ITR (Instant Tyre Repair) aerosol cans, aptly nicknamed 'Spray and Goo', that replaced IMS.

The problem with both these instant repair systems is that they can't cope with anything more than a small sharp object penetration, so any cut or tear leaves you waiting for recovery. In fairness to MG Rover these systems were being widely introduced by many motor manufacturers, but at the root it was a cost-cutting move.

The suitcase type IMS system does at least give the opportunity to add the sealant and, if the tyre fails to inflate, you can rotate the wheel/tyre to spread the sealant and continue to use the compressor to add air. The ITR, on the other hand, injects the sealant using the propellant in the can and that propellant is also the medium for reinflating the tyre, so you only get one shot at it. Additionally, assuming you are successful in reinflating the tyre with the compressor, you can read when the correct pressure is reached, unlike the ITR, where you can generally assume that you will probably not reach the optimum pressure.

Clearly the IMS and ITR systems have shortcomings as a replacement for a spare wheel and tools, so I would immediately advise any owner of a car

Fig. 4.332 The Trophy introduced the IMS (Instant Mobility System) 12V compressor and tyre sealing fluid in place of a full-sized spare, which became an option at extra cost.

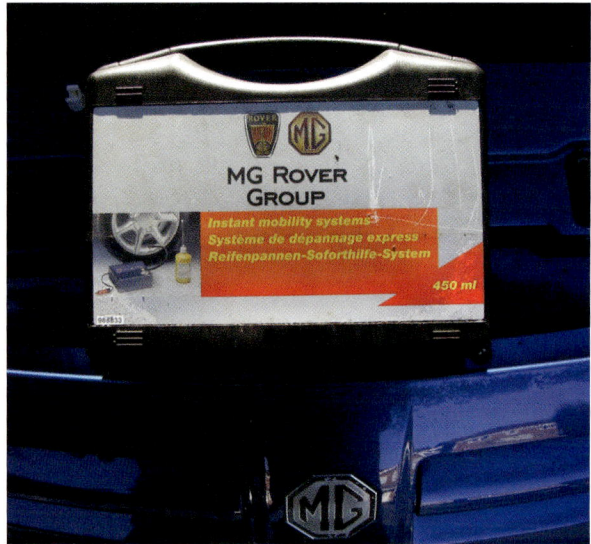

Fig. 4.333 The IMS came in a neat MG Rover plastic suitcase.

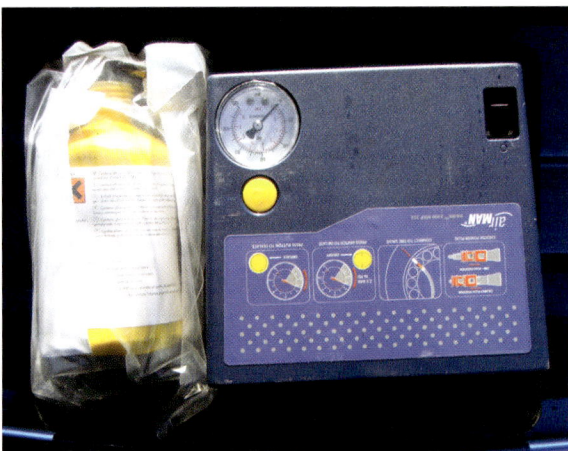

Fig. 4.334 The case contained a bottle of sealing fluid, 12V compressor with pressure gauge, goggles and gloves.

Fig. 4.335 Cost cutting later saw the IMS replaced by an aerosol can with sealing fluid.

with an IMS or ITR system to source a spare wheel, the wheel securing bolt and tools. Most cars with the 'Instant' systems are the MGF Trophy 160, TF 160 and other TFs that adopted 'Sportpack 2' (big brakes and related 16in wheels). A full-sized spare wheel was always an optional extra for these cars and when chosen this was a full-sized wheel fitted with a 195/45 R16 Goodyear Eagle F1 GSD2, as found as standard on the front wheels.

To make it very obviously a 'temporary use' spare, the Trophy rim was painted a bright yellow, while TF rims were painted matt black. The full-sized spare fits in the front of the MGF or TF, although it is a bit tight between the tyre and nose of the brake servo. A deflated 215/40 R16 tyre occupies around the same space as an inflated 195/45 tyre, but an inflated 215/40 R16 tyre is a much tighter fit in the spare

wheel well. Note too that the retaining bolt used for a full-sized spare wheel is longer than the commonly used one for the steel temporary spare wheel.

As previously mentioned, MGF Trophy 160 model introduced the problem that even the temporary steel spare wheel would not fit over the front

brakes. To overcome this, MG Rover introduced a full-size spare wheel with a normal 195/45 × 16 tyre, which was still classed as a temporary spare. This was because it could not be a legal fit on the rear with the 215/40 × 16 tyres, and if the tyre used was the directional Goodyear OE fit tyres, then that would

Fig. 4.336 When a full-sized spare wheel was bought the longer stud spare wheel retaining bolt (right) was needed as the steel spare wheel bolt (left) was too short.

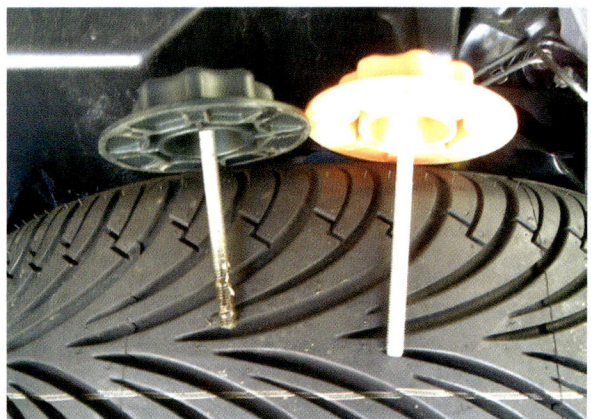

TOP LEFT: Fig. 4.337   The first full-sized spare wheel was a bright yellow so that its intended use was obvious.

TOP RIGHT: Fig. 4.338   The spare wheel had this sticker on it.

MIDDLE RIGHT: Fig. 4.339   Later full-sized spare wheels were black. This made them different to all the wheel colours available, until black became an option for wheels on the MG Motor TF LE500.

BELOW LEFT: Fig. 4.340   When the TF arrived the top models came with a slightly different eleven-spoke alloy wheel design to that of the Trophy wheels, still with dimensions to clear the big brakes and still the same 7 × 16in size.

BELOW RIGHT: Fig. 4.341   A shadow chrome-coloured version came with the limited TF 80th Anniversary cars.

only be rotating the correct way on one side at the front. Temporary spare wheels are allowed to be different sizes and rotate incorrectly in order to get you to the garage or tyre depot on the legal basis of a maximum of 50 miles at no more than 50mph in the UK.

Initially full-sized spare wheels were painted yellow, then orange, and then black, confusingly the normal wheel colour for many MG Motor TF LE500 models, and finally they would be standard colours just with the temporary use sticker.

The arrival of the TF saw the MGF eight round spoke 15in rim design carried over for the mainstream 115 models, while the six square spoke 15in style previously used on the Steptronic/Stepspeed models continued for the TF Stepspeed and for the new TF

Fig. 4.342   The 2005 model year TF 135 introduced a new V spoke 6 × 15in alloy wheel, which was the last design to appear before the company went bust.

Fig. 4.343   MG Motor TF LE500, introduced in September 2008, mainly used black versions of the previous TF eleven-spoke alloy wheel, which had seen service previously in this colour only as a spare wheel.

Fig. 4.344   The following year a 16in version of the 2005 model year's V spoke wheel appeared in the common 7 × 16in size.

Fig. 4.345   MG Motor's final fling was the sculptural 85th Anniversary alloy wheels, which also introduced a new pair of sizes, 6.5 × 16in front and 7.5 × 16in rear.

135, when 'Sportpack 2' was not fitted. The TF 160 introduced a new eleven-spoke design, similar to the outgoing MGF Trophy 160SE; this also catered for the 304mm AP Racing front brakes, which were also carried over for the TF 160. The TF 160 eleven-spoke wheels were also used when the AP Racing front brakes were specified for TF 120 Stepspeed and 135 models. Several of the previous 16in wheel designs were carried over as extra cost options for all models *not* using the AP Racing front brakes, and the Ultra Lightweight option was available for all cars, including those with the AP Racing brakes.

For 2005, the eight-spoke round 15in design was dropped and TF115 adopt-ed the six square spoke design, while the 120 Stepspeed and 135 models adopted a new 'V' spoke 15in design, still the standard 6 × 15in. All other wheel fits and options remained the same.

The MG Motor TF wheel options were simple and when relaunched the TF carried on with the TF 160 eleven-spoke design in silver or black, depending on body colour. There was also a limited run of cars with a new 16in version of the 2005 'V' spoke, still the same 7 × 16in.

Finally, the TF 85th Anniversary model introduced the 'Twist of Pepper' wheel design, which, aside from being strikingly different to any previous design, for the first time featured different sizes for the front and rear axles. The front wheel was reduced by half an inch to 6.5 × 16in and the rears gained half an inch to 7.5 × 16in. Tyres for all MG Motor TFs were the same Goodyear Eagle F1 GSD2 with 195/45 R16 at the front and 215/40 R16 at the rear.

Wheel Security

All MGF and TF models came with locking wheel nuts as standard. Until 2004 these were the relatively simple rounded nut with two slots fitted at different points around the circular edge of the nut. A corresponding locking tool with protrusions at the same points would

Fig. 4.346 *Standard wheel locking nuts until 2004 used this simple design with two pegs matching two recesses around a circular nut and tool.*

Fig. 4.347 *From 2004 the locking nuts were changed to McGard, which have a higher security level with their recessed 'flower' pattern in the head face of the nut. The nuts in this image are cracked.*

lock into the slots to undo and tighten the nut. A bright trim cover fits over the nuts once fitted.

These locking wheel nuts are relatively weak in both security and physical strength. They are very easy to remove without the tool, which is actually fortunate as it is usually owners who have the problem of removing the locking nuts after the protrusions on the tool break away. This breakage is almost always due to excess torque being applied when the nuts are tightened, so demanding excessive torque to undo them. While you can buy replacement locking tools against the stamped-in number on the original tool (MG spares specialists such as MGOC Spares carry a wide range), they don't provide significant security as there are widely available tools that mimic the locking tool and make removal of the locking nuts almost as simple as using the tool.

MG Rover recognized this security shortcoming and in 2004 introduced McGard security nuts, which are identified by being a bright finish, single-piece nut with no additional trim cover, and with an indented groove in the face in what is best described as a 'flower' pattern. The removing tool carries the same 'flower' pattern in mirror form and engages into the recessed groove nut, allowing removal and refitting.

This design provides enhanced security but can still be damaged from the use of excess torque. This is especially so if air tools are used and the tool is not fully engaged onto the nut: if only partially engaged the two can slip apart, damaging the edges of the 'flower'.

I have seen McGard nuts with cracks in the 'flower' pattern and even with

Fig. 4.348 *These are even more badly cracked. This is not a McGard failing, but the result of using a nut intended for a Ford application and 7mm shorter than the MG application. When tightened the MG stud will be forced against the internal end of the locking nut and breaks the top off.*

the top of the nuts broken away. The reason is because the wrong security nuts have been fitted, usually Ford applications that have the same thread and washer profile but are too short inside. The proper McGard nuts for the MGF and TF have an internal depth of 30mm, while the Ford ones have a depth of 23mm. The result is that, when tightened, the length of the MG stud comes into contact with the inside end of the McGard nut and quite literally cracks the top off.

MGF and TF Tyre Requirements

If there is one area that really needs to be stressed in terms of driving safety, it has to be related to tyres. Many have scoffed at the warnings that are widely circulated and found to their cost that there is a genuine issue with the choice of tyres for any MGF or TF. Get that choice wrong and you will have a much better chance of leaving the road unexpectedly.

A mid-engined car like the MGF and TF is designed to provide excellent handling characteristics. When well set up it will do just that, but the contrast between a well set-up MGF and TF and one that isn't can be vast and the biggest single influence on set-up is tyre choice. With a 45/55 per cent weight split front to rear, there is a need for the rear tyres especially to have a stiff carcase construction to support that rear weight bias. Having a tyre at the rear with a softer construction is a recipe for problems.

If you fail to observe this general principle, the consequence will be that, once your speed rises above around 55 to 60mph, the rear of the car will become quite 'loose' and very similar to the conditions experienced with a tyre that is deflating. If the speed rises above that threshold when you are entering a bend, the likelihood of an off-road excursion becomes quite possible.

The first principle is to use only the tyres that have been approved by the manufacturer. As MG Rover no longer exists, however, and the official approved 15in tyres have gone

MG ROVER GROUP

TECHNICAL BULLETIN

Model/Derivative:		No:	TB0129　Issue 2
MG TF		Date:	28.07.2004
MGF		Section:	TYRES

Title:

GOODYEAR TYRE 'EAGLE F1' GSD2 16" – CLARIFICATION

Affected range:

Applies to MG TF / MGF range with **16"** tyres fitted.

Description:

The recommended Goodyear GSD2 **16"** tyre specification is unchanged. Goodyear have **NOT** discontinued this tyre.

*Note: For information relating to **15"** tyres, refer to Technical Bulletin TB0128 dated 28.06.2004.*

Re-issue information:

- **Correction to MG TF front tyre load index and speed rating.**
- **Addition to Caution note.**

Action required:

16" tyre specification:

MG TF
- Front – 195/45 R16 80W Goodyear Eagle F1 - **GSD2** – part number RTB000460
- Rear – 215/40 R16 82W Goodyear Eagle F1 - **GSD2** – part number RTB103120

MGF
- Front & Rear – 215/40 R16 82W Goodyear Eagle F1 - **GSD2** – part number RTB103120

For tyre pressures refer to the owners handbook.

Important notes:
- **Not all Goodyear Eagle F1 tyres are of the same construction. Only the GSD2 tyre has been developed to match the MG TF & MGF handling characteristics. Use of other tyre sizes, brands and inflation pressures may adversely affect the vehicle performance. If in doubt, always contact the tyre manufacturer for advice.**

- **All tyres are directional i.e. they must only be fitted one way. The tyre wall indicates the correct orientation.**

⚠ **DO NOT FIT GOODYEAR 'EAGLE F1' - GSD3 16" SPECIFICATION OR ANY OTHER MAKE OF TYRE THAT IS NOT APPROVED BY MG ROVER FOR THE MGF & MG TF.**

Parts information:

Not applicable.

Warranty information:

Not applicable.

out of production, there is no longer an approved replacement. MG Motor can't help as they have only used the 16in wheels and tyres and have no obligation to support any TF owner other than their customers.

The original approved tyre for 15in wheels on the MGF was the Goodyear Eagle NCT3. This was replaced in the Goodyear range by the NCT5, which has a softer construction type that is not suitable for the MGF and TF. Instead the NCT3 was replaced by the Continental Contact Premium tyre, which was first seen on the TF.

The Continental Premium Contact has itself been replaced by the Continental Premium Contact 2, and a third generation is likely to replace the 2 in the not too distant future. Fortunately cars with 15in wheels/tyres do not suffer quite the depth of sensitivity found with 16in wheels/tyres. The basic advice remains, however, that you should ensure that all tyres are the same make, model and sub-model, as keeping a balance on each wheel is a prerequisite to stability. *Never mix tyres.*

Fitting a known brand of tyre on all wheels is the very minimum that should be done. Even if these tyres do not provide the best grip and handling they should provide stability. Ideally a stiff construction tyre should be chosen to eliminate any remaining waywardness at speeds over 60mph. MG Clubs, such as the MG Owners Club, and other focused owners' groups can often come forward with more detailed tyre suggestions.

For the 16in wheel fit there have only ever been two official approved tyres, the Goodyear Eagle F1 GSD2 and, for a short period around 2001, the Yokohama A539, in both 195/45 R16 and 215/40 R16 sizes. In 2004 MG Rover encountered a problem when Goodyear replaced their mainstream F1 tyre with the GSD3. This small title change hid a massive change in handling on the MGF and TF, and a wave of handling problems were reported. This led to MG Rover issuing a technical bulletin highlighting that all Goodyear Eagle F1 tyres are not the same and that the GSD3 was *not* recommended.

In essence Goodyear had 'softened' the construction of the GSD3 tyre to aid comfort and this is just the wrong direction for the MGF and TF. Still worse was that, since rear tyres commonly wear out first, many cars were having worn GSD2 rear tyres replaced innocently by easier to find GSD3s, leading to seriously upset handling and loss of stability.

After the approved Goodyear Eagle F1 GSD2 16in tyre ceased production, two further tyres, the Falken ZE912 and Toyo Proxes T1R, were tested and approved. These are expected to remain in production until approximately 2013/14 at the earliest.

In February 2011, I was fortunate enough to be involved with the testing carried out by MG Motor to find a replacement for the Goodyear GSD2 tyre. Quite a number of different tyres were selected for testing on the basis of availability in the two MG TF 16in sizes, and a commitment by the tyre makers involved that these tyres would be in production for a reasonable number of years to come. These two parameters eliminated quite a number of tyre brands at the first cut but still left a large selection. The list was then whittled down with road testing to a shortlist of five to test to extremes at the extensive facilities of MIRA (Motor Industry Research Association).

As a result of that testing two tyres came away with an MG Motor recommendation, but note this is for full sets only, with no mixing. First was the Falken ZE912 and second was the Toyo Proxes T1R, using standard sizes and pressures. The MG Motor recommendation is specifically for MG Motor TFs, but it is just as useful for earlier TFs and MGFs with 16in wheels, as I can confirm from having both on my own MGF and TF.

Tyre Pressures

Correct tyre pressures are a simple but critically important element to ensure stability. It should be noted that there are some significant differences between MGF and TF and also some variations in published data. The pressures listed here are taken from the last Technical Bulletin, issued a month before MG Rover collapsed, together with information provided by MG Motor to complete the picture for cars from 2008.

AUTHORIZED TYRE PRESSURES

MGF Front

185/55 R15	=	26psi (1.8bar) mainstream MGF
195/45 R16	=	24psi (1.7bar) Trophy 160 SE
215/40 R16	=	24psi (1.7bar) mainstream MGF with 16in wheels

MGF Rear

205/50 R15	=	28psi (1.9bar) mainstream MGF
215/40 R16	=	28psi (1.9bar) mainstream MGF with 16in wheels
215/40 R16	=	36psi (2.5bar) Trophy 160 SE

MG TF Front

185/55 R15	=	26psi (1.8bar) Mainstream TF
195/45 R16	=	26psi (1.8bar) Mainstream TF with 16in wheels, including MG Motor TF

except

195/45 R16	=	30psi (2.1bar) MG Motor's 85th Anniversary TF

MG TF Rear

205/50 R15	=	36psi (2.5bar) mainstream TF

except 2005 model year (soft suspension)

205/50 R15	=	30psi (2.1bar) 2005 model year TF from RD639634 on
215/40 R16	=	36psi (2.5 bar) Mainstream TF with 16in wheels, including *all* MG Motor TFs

Fig. 4.349   *This view from an MGF is not what you want to be driving through in any MGF or TF with wide, low-profile summer tyres.*

The list shows similar front pressures between all cars aside from the MG Motor 85th Anniversary cars, but a deliberately wide range of rear pressures. Some ill-informed owners and mechanics have a feeling that 36psi is too high and then unilaterally lower the pressures. They are wrong and poor handling will often arise. The pressures have been arrived at after extensive testing in a wide variety of conditions, using technology and the judgement of highly skilled testers. These pressures are allied to the use of the approved tyres. While they generally apply to all tyres, there is some scope for owners to try small variations of pressure to suit different tyres such as some softer winter tyres, which may demand slightly higher pressures for normal dry and wet road conditions, and perhaps lower for snow.

Winter Tyre Considerations

Very little thought is given to winter driving outside those countries

Fig. 4.350   *Cars with standard 15in wheels and tyres can only use snow chains on the rear. (Roger Martin)*

Fig. 4.351   *Covers commonly called 'snow socks' may be used at the front and for cars with 16in wheels and tyres. These are simple covers for the tyres that are light, relatively easy to fit and take little room when not in use.*

Fig. 4.352   Snow tyres are a very good step towards coping adequately with snow conditions, as well as any other weather conditions below around 7°C. The Toyo Snowprox sized 215/40 × 16 on this MGF have worked so much better than summer tyres, especially in both fresh and hard-packed snow.

that have a defined winter and where drivers usually have to change to winter tyres. The wide, low-profile summer tyres of the MGF and TF perform more like a sledge than a car in snow. The car's weight is spread over a wide surface area, so it acts more like a snow shoe and does not cut through to the road surface underneath. The summer characteristics are also completely unsuitable for snow.

Snow chains have been an available Rover option since the early days of MGF, but only for cars with 15in wheels and only for the rear tyres, since there is simply not enough clearance between the front tyre and the wheel arch liner/body of the car. With 16in wheels the rear clearance is also insufficient, and so chains can't be used at the rear either.

Snow Socks, however, which have recently been introduced, do not need the same clearances and most certainly can be used. Feedback indicates that they are very effective, take up no space in the boot and are quickly fitted.

In the UK snow is not normally a long-term winter hazard, but frost and ice are much more regular visitors and so the concept of using winter tyres is worthy of serious consideration. Following longer periods of snow and ice during the winters of 2009/2010 and 2010/2011 there is a much better availability of winter tyres made in MGF and TF sizes. Winter tyres are better once

temperatures fall below 7°C, as their tyre compound does not harden in the same way as normal summer tyres.

They also have a different tread design to provide improved grip on both wet and snow-covered roads. I have experience with these in conditions of fresh and hard-packed snow and ice. The improvement has been marked, as I found when caught behind a small 4 × 4 on summer tyres struggling to climb a long, steady hill! As with any tyre choice for the MGF and TF, I stress the need to have the same make, model and sub-model of tyre on all wheels, to keep a balance.

Another aspect of winter driving is the need to keep the car clean after periods of freezing weather when the roads will have been salted. It is important to hose down the car, including the wheel arches and the underside, to remove as much salt as possible. This is the main accelerator to corrosion that will affect the subframes. When spring comes a more comprehensive spring clean is advised. Remove the front underwing shields and you may be surprised how much mud has collected in the rear lower edge; if left this have an adverse effect over the long term.

Fig. 4.353   The front wheel arch mudtrap needs regular cleaning.

Fig. 4.354   One three-month winter period saw this collection of debris accumulate.

Fig. 5.1   Multi Function Unit of a pre-2004 model year car.

Fig. 5.2   The MFU (indicated) in position attached to the rear of the passenger compartment fuse box. (Austin Garages).

5

MGF and TF electrical systems

This is an area that many owners dread, as there is a perception of the black arts about the electrical systems of modern cars. In fact the MGF and TF are not that modern in electrical terms, although if you come from the direction of an MGB I grant there is some justification in thinking the MGF and TF have modern systems.

Take the MGF and early TF (to 2004 model year). There is a degree of simplicity about the electrical control systems in that the three control units – MFU (Multi Function Unit), Lucas 5AS Alarm/central locking, and window lift – are known to be very reliable and there is not an over-complexity that demands deep dealer-only diagnostic gear to do anything. Occasionally diagnostic interface is needed, but this is widely available, certainly in the UK, and also in many countries where MG and Rover cars were widely sold. More recently, diagnostic equipment has become available for the keen owner, which makes those more difficult aspects much simpler to deal with.

The situation for cars for the 2004 model year on is more complex. The functions of the three control units were incorporated into one, the Security Control Unit (SCU), and the security levels surrounding this were significantly increased. This created many more problems for the later cars, which I will cover in more detail later. Simple identification of whether the car has an SCU comes from the type of fob on the key ring, which is now round with an MG badge in the centre.

CHARGING AND STARTING

All cars have a simple basic electrical system with an 85 amp alternator feeding the battery. For early cars there were two different specifications: a 405 CCA (cold cranking amps) for cars without EPAS (electric power steering) and a 480 CCA version for cars with EPAS. The difference is important as anyone who has suffered an alternator failure while driving will know that even a well-

Fig. 5.3   Pre-2004 model year car's Lucas 5AS alarm and central locking control.

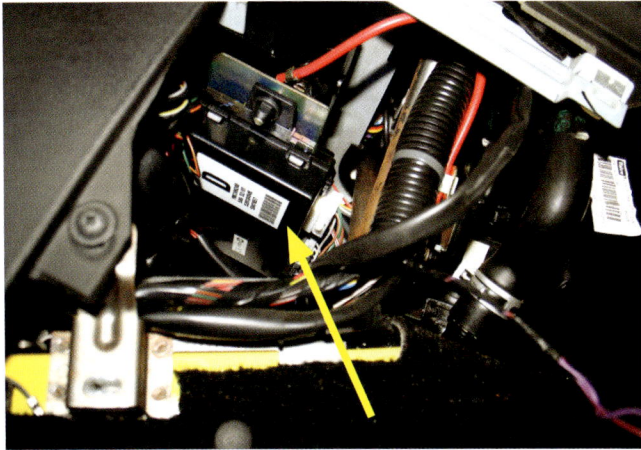

Fig. 5.4   The Lucas 5AS is fitted under the heater controls in the centre console, seen here viewed from the right footwell. (Image credit Austin Garages)

Fig. 5.5   Cars made in 2003 span the change from 2003 to 2004 model years. To confirm whether the 5AS system is fitted, check the remote fob on the key ring. This design is for the 5AS systems, round ones with an MG badge are for SCU.

ROVER GROUP

YWC-106170

Window Lift ECU

A-0531G02   C0802

Fig. 5.6   Pre-2004 model year window lift control.

Fig. 5.7   Window lift control mounted in the driver's footwell under the carpet.

charged battery will have been drained by the EPAS within around five miles. If your ignition warning light comes on and you have a few miles to drive, stop and remove the 40 amp EPAS fuse located near the under-bonnet fuse box behind the battery location.

An '027' series battery, which comes with a nominal 550 to 570 CCA rating, is commonly fitted and recommended today for all MGF and TFs, since only a relatively few 1.8i cars from 1995 to 1997 did not come with EPAS. I mention this straight off as the choice of battery has often been the subject of discussion after some were sold spurious batteries with a lower rating. These might be fine for the early 1.8i cars not specified with EPAS, but having the higher-rated battery will give you much better reserve and, from experience, a longer life too.

The other consideration is that the battery is mounted at the front of the car, while the engine and starter are at

the rear, so just like MGA and MGB there is a long battery cable run under the car. This can lead to some voltage drop, another reason for having a higher-rated battery rather than a lower.

There have also been several starter motors fitted to the MGF and TF. While

there is some conflict in official documentation as to what was fitted, when and to which model, the main point is that all are interchangeable, aside from the starter for the Steptronic/Step-speed auto transmission models. Differences surrounding the starters on

Fig. 5.8   2004 and later model year cars moved to the Security Control Unit (SCU), which absorbed the functions of all three previous control units and was mounted in the same place as the 5AS. The SCU is identified by the fob used.

Fig. 5.9   The 027 series battery used on MGF and TF is relatively heavy duty because of the electric power steering.

the manual transmission cars revolve mainly around the different suppliers involved with some minor differences in the power outputs, which are variously reported at 1.0 to 1.4kW. It appears that from the start of the 2001 model year (RD522572) all manual cars used the same starter.

Another oddity is that all later MGFs and all TFs have a protective line fuse on the alternator to starter solenoid (battery) feed on the rear engine bay bulkhead. If a car seems to have a duff alternator, check that the fuse hasn't popped. This check becomes more pertinent if a new alternator has been fitted or work has been done in the engine bay, especially if this involved removing the alternator. In order to save unnecessary expense, it is worth checking the fuse before committing to a new alternator if the loss of charging is sudden.

Fault Finding

The MGF and MG TF charging and starting circuits are generally reliable, but on the odd occasions issues occur, it is usually quite simple to identify and deal with. First, a new and fully charged 027 battery will normally retain sufficient power to start the car after a lay-up of five to six weeks. Once that period drops to less than two weeks after charging it is an indication that the battery is dying. At this time a new battery is advised, but if the battery is relatively new or the period of time needed to drain the battery has suddenly shortened, then consider an electrical fault rather than a duff battery.

The first check should be the alternator output, for which a simple series of voltage checks with a voltmeter is usually sufficient. Connect it to a convenient part of the electrical system. The simplest way is to connect the meter to the battery and read the voltage, but if the battery has been on charge or the engine recently run then give it thirty minutes for the voltages to settle. A fully charged battery will show around 12.5 volts, dropping to below 12 volts with a battery with a very poor charge level.

Next the engine is started and run at around 1,500–2,000rpm with no electrical loads other than what is needed to run the engine. After a few seconds stabilizing time the voltage level should be around 14 volts plus or minus 0.5 volts. Next apply some electrical loads, such as headlights, the heater fan on maximum and wipers. That sort of load should not see any substantial drop in voltage, certainly no lower than 13.2 or 13.3 volts, but if the voltage plunges below 13 volts then the safe conclusion is that the alternator performance is very poor; if the voltage drops below 12.5 volts then the alternator is effectively dead.

Most of the time the ignition warning light is a trustworthy indicator of whether the alternator is charging, but occasionally you may encounter odd behaviour that may not see the light come on, even though a discharge situation has developed. The first indication of such an event may be the low glimmer of the dashboard warning lights, followed by the ABS warning lamp coming on (if ABS is fitted) or the engine hiccuping when operating indicators. The engine may even stop when switching on a heavier electrical load, such as headlamps. If these conditions occur, find a safe stopping place as you may only have a couple of miles left before the engine stops.

Changing an alternator is simple and the subject is well covered in the workshop manual, but space is a little tight. Don't try to be clever by not disconnecting the battery: it is all too easy to short a loose wire to ground and create problems far deeper than issues following battery disconnection.

Fig. 5.10   Alternators have a separate screw-on main output cable and clip-on subordinate plug. These are usually easier to access for removal/refit when the alternator is partially removed.

Fig. 5.11   It is not unknown for the fine adjuster thread to seize. Since access is limited, it can be easier to remove the adjuster bar pivot bolt at the engine end (indicated), and then remove the alternator and bar together before separating them off the car.

Fig. 5.12   Never be surprised by some previous owners' 'repairs'. Here the alternator is sitting at a funny angle because the main pivot bolt had been replaced with a smaller diameter bolt, allowing the alternator to twist when under belt tension.

Fig. 5.13   The same 'repair' also created fatigue problems for the belt.

Fig. 5.14   It even caused the adjustment bracket to crack (note the rust line near the hole).

The method of belt tensioning on cars without air conditioning can be confusing. Essentially there is a bracket with a long groove, but instead of using a lever to tension the belt before tightening the bolt that locks up the alternator foot to the bracket and holds the tension, there is a second threaded adjuster that allows much finer control of the belt tension, and only when this is set at the desired tension is the locknut tightened. Air con cars have a much longer belt that drives the air con compressor as well as the alternator, so a different (simpler) tensioner is used.

When changing an alternator the adjuster may be seized. In that case it is often easier to remove the adjuster bracket bolt, where it attaches at the engine, and then remove the alternator with the bracket and deal with it off the car. Don't lose the main long pivot bolt, as this can have a bigger impact

ABOVE: Fig. 5.15   The alternator, belt and crank pulley are all protected from road dirt by a cover: fibre for the MGF (right) and a much better plastic moulding for TF (left).

RIGHT: Fig. 5.16   The TF plastic moulding is easily fitted to an MGF.

than at first appears. The car in Fig. 5.12 had been fitted with a thinner alternative pivot bolt, which allowed the alternator to twist when the belt was tensioned. This quickly ruined the belt and also stressed the adjuster bracket to cracking.

A critical part often found missing is the alternator and drive belt shield. This can lead to rapid wear of the pulleys and drive belt, which is even worse on cars with air con, and result in failure. On rare occasions, this belt can smash its way through the timing belt cover. The MGF had a fibre cover in this location; the TF had a better moulded plastic cover, which can be retrofitted to the MGF. The part number for this is CLK000020, but at the time of writing this had been on back order for some time, so a used one may be the only option.

The starter motor is of the pre-engaged design. Problems are quite rare in the starter itself, but common with the solenoid trigger wire connection. The issue is usually just a dirty and/or loosened connection, which normally only requires cleaning of the terminals and tightening up of the spade connector. Occasionally there is corrosion and the required solution depends on the depth of corrosion.

Problems in the ignition/starter switch can also be the cause of failure to start. MG TF ignition switches (the type where the wiring plugs directly into the switch) have known problems. Not cranking the engine is the most common, but there is also intermittent EPAS failure. The switch is not listed as a separate part and so officially a lock set must be purchased. However, the same

switch is available separately for the MG ZR under part number YXB100350A.

Engine Electrics

The space needed to fully cover the systems that control the MGF and MG TF would require a book in its own right, but a general tour around the system and where problems may lie should reveal at least some hidden aspects.

Injection operation is by way of fuel being maintained at a given pressure. The ECU then opens and closes the injector by controlling the injector's earth path for a given time that dictates the amount of fuel injected. The time calculated is based on a three-dimensional map (engine load against engine rpm) held in the ECU memory, and the time chosen is dependent on a series of inputs from various sensors around the engine. At the same time the ECU is also calculating the appropriate time for the HT spark to be generated, at which time the ECU makes and breaks the earth connection for the coil(s).

Three engine management systems have been fitted to MGF and TF models, all different versions of the Rover MEMS (Modular Engine Management System) family. The MGF 1.8i used the MEMS 1.9 system up to the start of 2001 model year cars (VIN RD 522572).

The original MGF VVC models used a more powerful MEMS 2J system, again up to the same VIN point, when both these MEMS systems were replaced by the MEMS 3 system.

MEMS 1.9 is a multipoint injection, meaning it has an injector per inlet

port that operates 'grouped' injection, which means injectors one and four are pulsed together at a different time to injectors two and three. Naturally this means that only one injector at a time will be spraying fuel into the inlet when the inlet valves are open, but the required fuel is injected in two parts, one part per engine revolution. Remember that the complete engine cycle takes two revolutions of the engine to complete, so injecting in two parts makes engine operation more even. All injectors have a common power feed (useful for diagnostics) and it is only the earth path wires to the ECU that split into the two pairs.

On the ignition side there is a distributor cap and rotor arm on the end of the inlet camshaft, as MEMS 1.9 operates a single coil. This sees a traditional single HT lead (the King lead) transfer the HT current generated by the coil to the distributor cap and the rotor arm distributes the HT current to the appropriate HT lead to the spark plugs.

This is a well-proven system, but it also has known weaknesses in the form of degradation of the cap and rotor arm. Experience says that renewing them either every three years or at 30,000 miles, if that comes sooner, is a good way of avoiding non-starts on cold and damp winter mornings. HT cables also benefit from routine replacement, but this can be extended to every five years or 50,000 miles.

It should be noted that the mounting position for the single output coil is on the rear of the engine block, below the inlet manifold. This keeps it out of direct heat, but the downside is that,

Fig. 5.17   MEMS 1.9 ECU.

Fig. 5.18   MEMS 2J ECU.

depending on the angle the car may be parked, rainwater can find its way through the boot vents and down onto the coil, creating or aggravating starting issues.

MEMS 2J is similar to the previous system, but is more powerful and also controls VVC operation. The extra computing power needed to control the VVC operation is complemented by having 'sequential' fuel injection and wasted spark ignition.

This is still a multipoint injection system, but sequential means that each injector is controlled individually to ensure that it injects precisely the fuel calculated as being required immediately before the inlet valves for that cylinder are opened. This precision aids emissions and fuel economy.

Having each injector controlled separately means that there is still a common power feed to all injectors, but then each injector has a separate earth path wire back to the ECU. To be able to provide sequential injection the engine is fitted with a cam sensor, so that it knows which of the two pistons that are always rising towards TDC (Top Dead Centre) is actually on the compression stroke rather than the exhaust.

If that cam sensor were to fail during engine operation then the engine continues without change until it is stopped, but if the cam sensor is faulty before the engine is started then the engine is run with 'grouped' injectors as the MEMS 1.9 system. You may not detect the engine operating in this reduced efficiency mode until you find the rev limit is held back to around

Fig. 5.19   MEMS 3 ECU.

the 5,500rpm to 5,800rpm level, rather than the normal limit of more than 7,000rpm.

On the ignition side there are two separate coils, each with two HT connection points from which four extremely long HT leads connect between the coils and the spark plugs. When the ECU fires each coil, two spark plugs receive a spark as one cylinder is approaching TDC on its firing stroke while the other is approaching TDC on the exhaust stroke. Only one spark is actually needed, but the provision of another doesn't cause any problem; this is the origin of the description 'wasted spark'.

MEMS 3 replaced both of the earlier systems for all 4-cylinder K series engine variants. While externally visually identical, internally there are significant hardware differences, depending on application. These ECUs have greater

processing power and were designed to cater for the EOBD 3 (European On Board Diagnostics 3rd generation) requirements, which became mandatory from 2001. The MGF Steptronic and Stepspeed had MEMS 3 from their introduction in July 1999, initially to the earlier EOBD 2 requirements, before changing to the 2001 specification.

MEMS 3 refined the fuel injection operation and introduced sequential injection to all applications. Injectors were different to either of the two previous systems and now two different injectors were used: black ones for all non-VVC applications and blue for VVC and for TF 135 engines. The flow rates for the two injectors are massively different, so swapping injectors is ill advised, unless accompanied by mapping changes to suit.

The ignition system is very similar to the MEMS 2J system, being a wasted spark system. A big difference was the

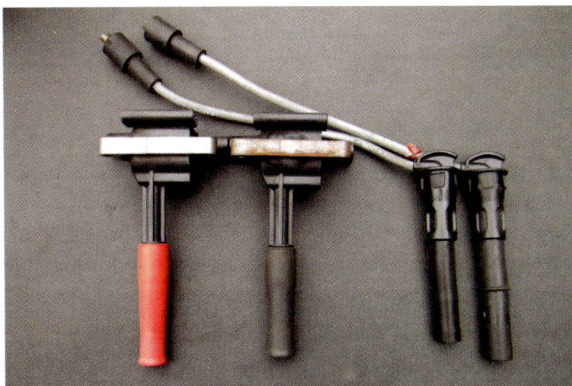

Fig. 5.20   The same coil is common to MEMS 3 MPi and VVC engines. Spark plugs are deeper in VVC heads, so the coils need longer HT connections, which are colour coded red. The additional HT leads are also different lengths.

RIGHT: *Fig. 5.21   MG Motor TFs used a different coil with a different connection to the plugs. These are only interchangeable with non-VVC engines.*

removal of the Achilles heel of the 2J system, the very long HT leads and somewhat exposed coil mounting position. These were replaced by two double output coils mounted on top of the engine with a direct feed to one spark plug and a very much shorter additional HT lead to the second spark plug. This required a new cam cover for the new coils to be mounted on and an additional plastic cover.

Coils have different HT sections to connect to the plugs depending whether they are MPi or VVC, as the VVC has a deeper spark plug cavity. Identification of the two types is made easy as VVC insulators are red, while MPi ones are black. The same depth difference applies to the separate HT leads. Most aftermarket leads are made to the VVC length and so the tops of the moulded ends sit a little high on MPi engines, but this is not an issue.

Universal System Aspects

A clever feature of MEMS systems is that they are adaptive: as the engine runs, the ECU 'learns' the requirements of the engine. This is an on-going process, as the engine wears so the ECU adapts further. This is something you do not notice normally, except when the engine has run with a fault for some time and has 'adapted' to it. When that fault is corrected, the engine may run rough for a while until the engine adapts back. This process may take a few hundred miles, but to shorten this time there is a facility in the dealer diagnostics that allows the return to the original mapping under the title of 'Reset Adaptions'.

In the event that a replacement second-hand engine ECU is needed for any of the MEMS systems, the replacement ECU will have to be of the same type and from the same engine. Unfortunately ECU part numbers are not always specific to MGF or TF applications and are often universal to many models, but with slightly different mapping. For example, cooling fan control on the MGF and TF has a secondary engine bay fan: if a saloon ECU is fitted, the engine bay fan operates continuously while the ignition is switched on. Any new ECU that is obtained will need to be given final programming via the dealer level diagnostic equipment.

Category 1	Combined alarm and immobilizers
Category 2	Electronic/electromechanical immobilizers
Category 3	Mechanical immobilizers
Category 4	Wheel locking devices
Category 5	After-theft systems for vehicle recovery
Category 6	Stolen vehicle tracking systems
Category 7	Stolen vehicle location system

VEHICLE SECURITY

MGF and TF models have security that meets with the UK insurance industry requirements and for most of the production period for MGF and TF that means Thatcham Category 2, or Category 1 certification only for late cars. Thatcham refers to the Motor Insurance Repair Research Centre, an insurance industry-funded research and testing centre based at Thatcham, Berkshire, which is well known in the UK for testing security systems on cars and confirming they meet certain minimum standards.

Today they are involved in much more than car security rating, but a brief look at the different security categories applicable at the beginning of 2012 (above) will give more clarity.

The whole purpose of this system is to reduce vehicle crime, which has traditionally been high in the UK, and finding effective systems to recover a vehicle quickly in the event of it being stolen. Some insurers may demand upgrading of the standard security on vehicles before they accept a theft-risk aspect of any policy. While this is not something yet experienced with MGFs and TFs, it could be raised if the

car were kept or used in certain crime hot spots.

The MGF gained Thatcham Category 2 certification with effect from July 1997. The cars made before that date and delivered from September 1995 used the same security system, the Lucas 5AS system, but were built to the previously applicable insurance industry standards.

The level of security was further improved with the introduction of the Pektron-made SCU in TFs made from June 2003 (VIN 620549) (*see* Fig. 5.8). The two systems are easily identified by their different remote fobs 'plips' on the key ring. The older 5AS system uses square-shaped, plain two-button fobs, while the SCU system has round fobs with a central MG badge and buttons that curve around the badge (*see* Figs 5.5 and 5.8). SCU equipped cars have the bonus of Thatcham Category 1 certification.

Security System Issues: Lucas 5AS Systems

The 5AS system is a reliable standalone security system that only features control of the central locking, in addition to the alarm and immobilization

Fig. 5.22   Lucas 5AS alarm and central locking controller.

Fig. 5.23 The inside of the Lucas 5AS remote fob showing the large round CR2032 battery in its docking position.

functions. It has a relatively 'relaxed' approach to security that gives a much greater degree of flexibility than modern security systems, and this is where its security levels let it down. However, it still maintains an adequate level of security to beat the casual thief and a reasonable delay to the determined one.

System operation is actually more complex than many give the system credit for. Most problems are easy to deal with, but often aggravated by owners who do not respond to fault conditions, or do not understand the system and realize that there is a fault. Inactivity can easily leave a car immobilized in the wild and needing to be recovered.

Every car was supplied with two keys and two fobs to remotely operate the alarm and central locking (if fitted). These fobs have two buttons for arm (lock) and disarm (unlock). When new there is a clear padlock symbol moulded into the lock button, which is always the one on the right when holding the fob at the key ring end.

The alarm and immobilizer are activated with a single press of the lock button. This is confirmed by a single long flash of the indicators and a short period of rapid flashing of the alarm LED in the instrument pack. On MGF and TF models with remote central locking there is a secondary arming level available called Superlocking, which is the internal disconnection of the locking mechanism to the door sill buttons (pins), activated by a further quick double press of the lock button.

Superlocked means that if you pull up the sill buttons that would normally unlock the door, it will not now have any effect and the doors remain locked until the fob unlock button is pressed or the key is used in the driver's door to unlock the car. Superlocking is confirmed by a secondary double clunk and three additional flashes of the indicators.

If there is no confirmation flash of the indicators when first arming the system, or the LED in the instrument pack doesn't flash rapidly, then it is indicative that part of the system is faulty, or if there is a warning beep from the horns as well, then a door, boot or bonnet is not fully closed. In these conditions superlocking will not operate.

The most common problems that arise are when a fob is lost or broken when you are out, or if you do not notice the fob battery is weakening.

Fob batteries last up to about three years, depending on degree of use. A failing battery is always signalled by the alarm LED flashing rapidly after remotely unlocking the car and until a door is opened, so this can be used as a check method.

In addition you should also note a reduction in the range a fob button works from. If it fails you will still be able to get access to the car via the key, but not get the car started unless you have your Emergency Key Access code (EKA). You also need to fit a new CR2032 series battery and resynchronize the fob as described below, which is easier if you are close to shops than trying to enter the EKA.

If the fob has become damaged, the built-in EKA, a four-digit number unique to the car supplied to the first

Fig. 5.24 The security card issued by the dealers to the first customer of every new MG or Rover shows the radio serial number and security code (if applicable) on the front.

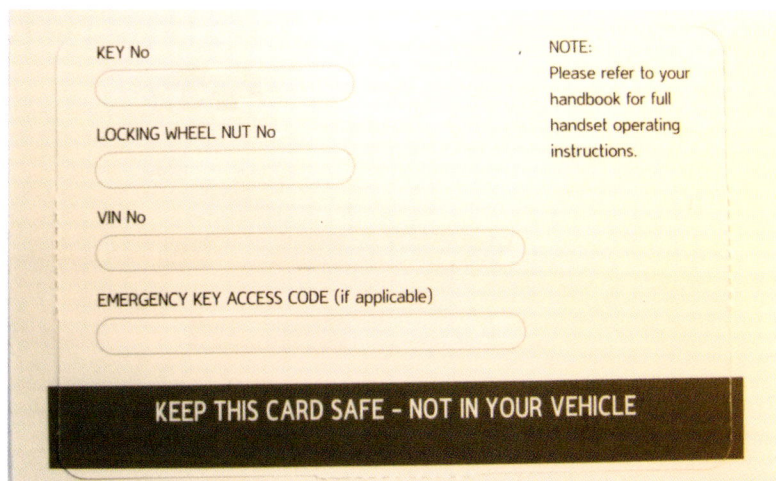

Fig. 5.25 The key number, locking wheel nut number, VIN and EKA code are on the reverse of the security card. First owners usually take heed of the 'don't leave this card in the car' warning. When the car is sold, they often forget to pass the card on or it has been lost.

Locks & Alarm

ENGINE IMMOBILISATION OVERRIDE
(Emergency key access code)

If the handset is lost or fails to operate and the key is, therefore, the only means of unlocking the car, the engine can be re-mobilised by using the starter key to enter the four digit key access code (this is recorded on the Security Information card).

Enter the code as follows:

1) Using the key, turn the driver's door lock (clockwise), to the LOCK position and hold in this position for at least 5 seconds. Then return the key to the centre position.

It is now possible to use the key to enter the numerical value of the four digits of the emergency key access code, as follows:

2) Enter the FIRST digit of the code

If the first digit is 4, turn the key to the UNLOCK position 4 times. Ensure the key is FULLY returned to the centre position after each turn of the key.

3) Enter the SECOND digit of the code

If the second digit is 3, turn the key to the LOCK position 3 times. Remember, the key must be FULLY returned to the centre position after each turn of the key.

4) Enter the THIRD digit of the code

If the third digit is 2, turn the key to the UNLOCK position twice, ensuring that the key is returned to the centre position after each turn of the key.

5) Enter the FOURTH digit of the code

If the fourth digit is 1, turn the key to the LOCK position once. Ensure the key is FULLY returned to the centre position afterwards.

6) Finally, turn the key to the UNLOCK position one more time; this will re-mobilise the engine.

If the correct code has been entered: the alarm indicator light will stop flashing and the engine can be started.

If an incorrect code has been entered: a warning bleep will sound when the key is turned to the final unlocked position. In this case, open and close the door (this will cancel the error), and enter the code again.

After three incorrect entries, a ten minute delay period is invoked during which the security system will not accept any further attempts to enter a code.

Entering the key access code deactivates the engine immobiliser. Once deactivated, the engine immobiliser will remain inactive until the handset is next used to lock the car.

WARNING!

- *NEVER leave the Security Information card in the car.*
- *Memorise the key access code or keep the Security Information card on your person in case of emergencies (a damaged handset for example).*

Fig. 5.26   *MGF handbook explanation of how to enter the EKA code. (MG Rover).*

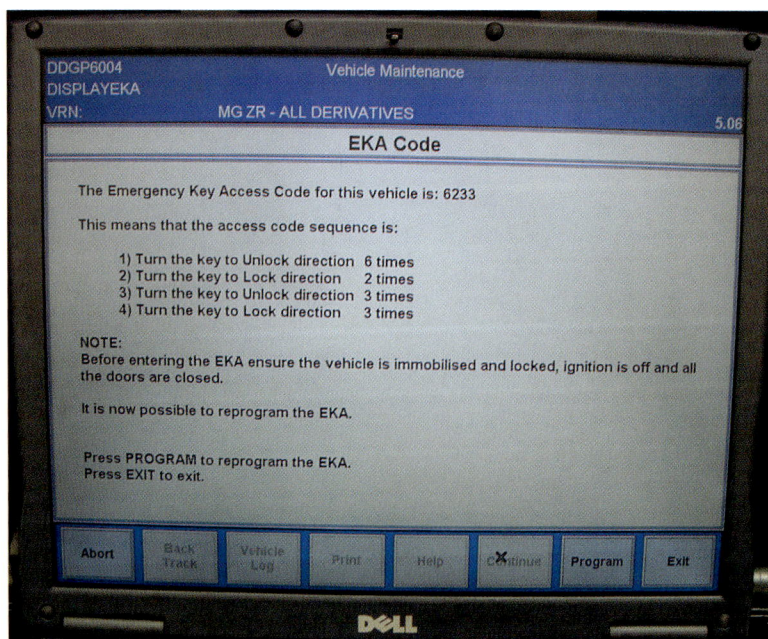

Fig. 5.27   *Dealer T4 diagnostics can read and reprogram the EKA code. Here a ZR was connected to T4, but the 5AS on MGF and TF operates in the same way.*

owner written on a credit card-sized 'security card', comes into its own as a way of bypassing the normal methods of disabling the immobilizer and allowing the car to be driven. Under normal fob operation the immobilizer should automatically reset when the engine is stopped and the ignition left off for more than thirty seconds, but when the EKA is used the immobilzser should remain inactive until the alarm is next set using the fob, which of course means a lower level of security.

The method of entering the EKA is explained in the handbook. Insert the key into the driver's door lock, turn the key to the lock position and hold it there for at least five seconds, then back to the vertical entry position. Turn the key to the unlock position and back to the vertical entry position the number of times that relate to the first number. The second digit is entered by turning the key between the vertical entry point and lock position the number of times that relate to the second number, then back to the unlock position and vertical entry position the number of times for the third digit, and then to the lock position and vertical entry position the number of times for the fourth digit.

Once the final digit has been entered and the alarm ECU has recognized the correct code, the alarm LED will stop flashing. If it is not entered correctly or the EKA is wrong, then horns will emit a quick beep. Once the correct number has been entered you can unlock the car and drive normally.

Problems found when inputting the EKA have led to a modified approach. The commonest involves excess free play in the linkages between the key lock and the lock/latch assembly in the door in which is located the micro switch that generates the signal seen by the 5AS. When returning the key to the vertical entry point this play sometimes causes insufficient movement to trigger the micro switch and register that digit. To overcome this you need to turn the key back a little further, to approximately the 11 o'clock or 1 o'clock positions as appropriate. Note that if three consecutive incorrect entries are made, the system locks you out from trying again for ten minutes.

Another problem is that if the 5AS has been changed then the EKA code may have been changed with it, something that would need the car connected to diagnostic equipment to check the number that is recorded in the 5AS memory.

You can obtain the original EKA code from Rover/MG Rover records via dealers or the company officially set up with authority from the MG Rover Administrators, MGR CC Services (www.mgrcc-services.com). However, records are not complete for cars before 1998. This means the only way to be certain of confirming the EKA code is to plug into diagnostics and read the EKA recorded. Keep the EKA code safe. I also suggest that you try entering the code to confirm it works. Note that if the central locking doesn't respond or the alarm is not disarmed when you turn the key in the driver's door, then you have an electrical fault and no communication with the alarm ECU.

Resynchronizing After Battery Change

The alarm fobs operate by transmitting several bits of data every time a button is pressed. Part of that is an individual rolling code and any interruption to the power supply of either a fob or the car's battery will immediately lose that synchronization.

When either the car's battery or a fob battery is disconnected on Lucas 5AS equipped cars, the rolling code synchronization between fob(s) and car should be lost. The method of resynchronizing involves turning the key in the driver's door to the unlock position and then immediately pressing the lock button on the fob rapidly several times. After three to five presses the car should remotely lock. If the car battery is ever disconnected or goes completely flat, then this will demand the same resynchronizing operation for both fobs. If the central locking or alarm switching does not operate when turning the key then there is no communication to the alarm ECU, and so resynchronizing won't work.

As the youngest MGF is around ten years old at the time of writing, the fobs will have seen considerable use. Often cars will have only a single working fob, which is rather like walking on thin ice as you can never be sure when it will crack and drop you in it. One of

Fig. 5.28 Moulded into the rear of the Lucas 5AS remote fob is the fob series number. The newest and best fob series to get for any car with the 5AS system is the 17TN.

the weaker security aspects of the 5AS system, even though an owner-friendly feature, is that it is simple to use working second-hand parts from other MGF/TF 200/25/ZR and 400/45/ZS models, as long as they were made before June 2003 and use the 5AS system. There is also some crossover to Land-Rover and other makes that used the 5AS system, but with so much availability from the MG and Rover ranges, plus the alternative but identically operating aftermarket fobs, there should be no need to look further afield.

When looking for a replacement or additional used fob you will see many that seem to be identical, but they are not. The ideal fob to get is one from the 17TN series; this number is moulded into the rear of the fob. Earlier MGF fobs will normally carry 3TXA and 3TXB: if your working fob is also of this type these will be compatible to your

system. The 17TN, however, is much better all round and compatible with all earlier systems, whereas early fobs won't work with the later 5AS systems from about 2000.

The remote alarms for cars for the UK and most European markets transmit on 433.9 MHz, while Japan, Australia and North America use 315 MHz. You should be aware that a fair number of MGFs sold in Japan have been returned to the UK, or other countries, as a result of the Japanese domestic legislation. These cars will be operating at 315 MHz and so replacement fobs will be harder to come by. A complete change to a UK specification 433.9 MHz 5AS and fobs is probably simpler and cheaper.

If you wish to avoid the need for diagnostics, then find a car of like model year and model in a breakers yard and buy the 5AS, ideally with two fobs that are already coded to that 5AS, and the matching engine ECU, which

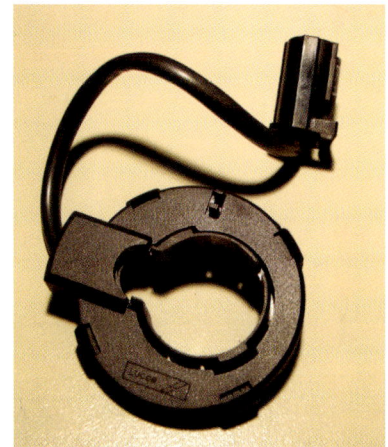

Fig. 5.29 2000 model year cars and later benefit from a passive coil around the steering lock to avoid having to press the fob unlock button if the immobilizer has auto-rearmed.

Fig. 5.30 The passive coil can be retrofitted to earlier cars and is shown being fitted to a 1998 MGF.

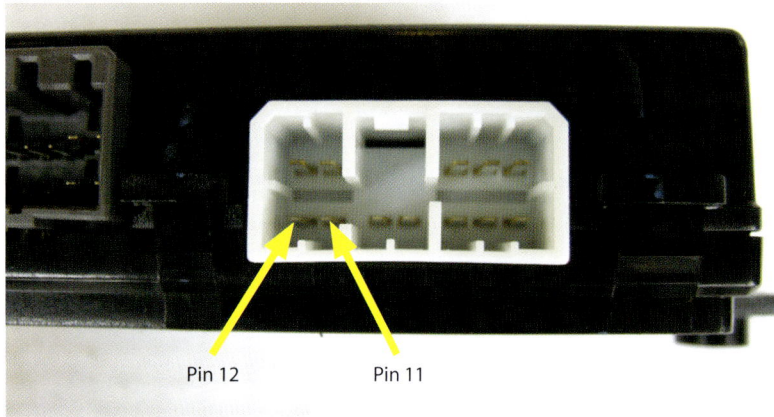

Pin 12   Pin 11

Fig. 5.31   Pins 11 and 12 of the 5AS are used to connect the coil wires.

will also be coded to that 5AS, and you have a complete 'plug and play' set-up. It is quite common to see breakers advertising ECU and fob 'sets' as 'plug and play', but you have to be wary of buying a 'saloon' car set-up instead of an MGF or TF one, and most come with only a single fob.

2000 model year on cars have a passive coil around the steering lock that energizes when the ignition is switched on and this automatically triggers the fob to transmit its disarming signal. Earlier cars do not have this and if the ignition is not switched on within approximately thirty seconds of the car being unlocked, the immobilizer automatically rearms. When the ignition is switched on you get a repeating 'beep' from the alarm system. This demands a

further press of the fob unlock button and is an inconvenience.

Retrofitting the coil to earlier cars is quite simple as you only need the coil with attached wire and plug (up to 2005 model year MG and Rover cars, except 75/ZT), either from a scrapped car or new (part number YWD100082, costing £16 in 2011). You also ideally need a matching plug to meet that from the coil and a couple of specific wire pin connections that will fit the 5AS ECU white plug, so if raiding a scrapped car you may find it simpler to cut off one of the wiring plugs with a few inches of wire.

Clip it onto the exposed end of the steering lock together, if possible, with a matching female plug with about 60cm (24in) of wire. This plug is a common format plug, but if you do not have a female part then you can replace it with any complete two-part plug you have to hand or buy. Then you need two wires to run to the white 5AS ECU plug and the original slate/red wire goes to pin 11 and purple/pink to pin 12.

The coil wires are normally slate on pin 1 of the coil plug and purple on pin 2. Slate connects to the original car's slate/red (S/R) and purple connects to purple/pink (P/K). As you look straight at the white 5AS plug, the lower left two pins are numbered 12 (left) and 11 (right).

Sometimes alarms seem to be triggered for no apparent reason, but there will always be one. The vehicle battery starting to fail is one possible cause, but cars from the 1998 model year and later have an alarm trigger store in the 5AS memory, so it is worth checking

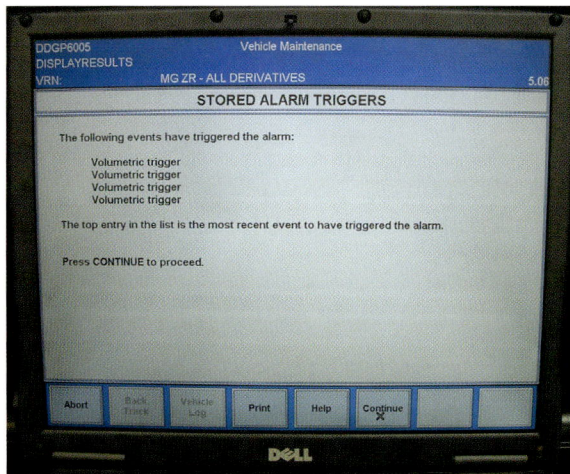

Fig. 5.32   With T4 and other diagnostics you can easily see what has previously triggered the alarm. This test was on a ZR, but it is the same on a MGF or TF.

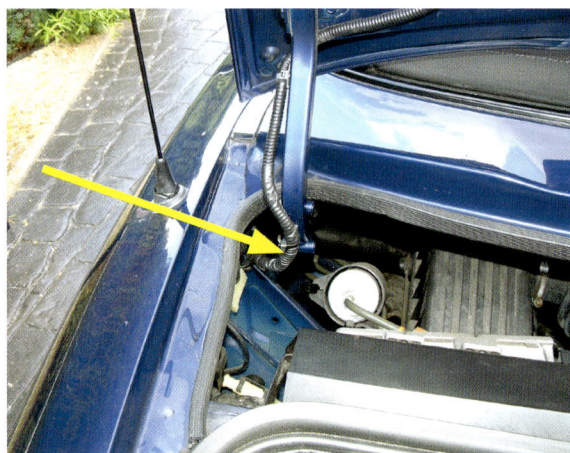

Fig. 5.33   Broken wiring within the loom, where it passes from the car to the left boot hinge, is a common cause of MGF and TF false alarms.

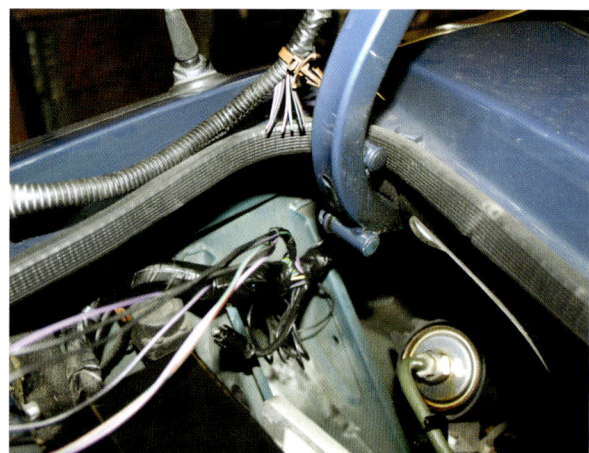

Fig. 5.34   Broken wiring on another car revealed when the loom was taken to pieces.

this via dealer diagnostics as it often saves more than the cost of plugging in diagnostics. A not uncommon cause of alarm triggers can be damaged wiring in the boot around the left hinge.

The 5AS has a very useful self-test procedure. Although this is included in the workshop manual, I feel it should not be missed and so it is reproduced here, together with a similar self-test for the Multi Function Unit (MFU) found in cars using the 5AS.

Pektron SCU

SCU was introduced into TF production on 17 June 2003 and was primarily added to increase the security level to Thatcham Category 1. In security terms this upgrade addressed a number of significant shortcomings in the Lucas 5AS system. In addition to security control, which once again includes central locking, the SCU also took on 'body control' functions from the MFU and window lift control, adding front fog lamp control, wipers and washer control, horn, lazy locking, indicator and hazard light control. There is provision for additional function control within this unit, such as low coolant warning, seat belt warning, speed locking and remote boot opening.

The SCU is much more robust than the 5AS in security terms, which unfortunately is best illustrated by considerably increased owner inconvenience when something goes wrong. Reliability is not this unit's forte and the rate of SCU failures can be too high, often in cold weather, most commonly with the onboard double relays. Common scenarios are that windows won't lower or if lowered won't raise, horns don't work or are on continuously, and the foglight circuit fails. Combining the functions of three separate control units into one was a logical step forward, only undone by the poorer reliability of the single unit. The knock-on effect is that owners need professional help to deal with the increased levels of security, which then drives up repair costs.

SCU has a self-test mode that is entered just as for the instructions for the Lucas 5AS system which is very useful for testing peripheral functions. In the event of repeated false alarms, remember that the SCU memory, like

the 5AS, records the last four alarm activations for diagnostic reading.

The problems that affect the SCU are focused first on the failures of relays mounted on the circuit board. The SCU has five of these rather unusual 'double' relays, effectively two separate relay functions in one box, fitted to the circuit board. The function of these relays can be programmed differently

---

LUCAS 5AS CONTROL UNIT SELF-TEST PROCEDURE

1. Ensure doors, bonnet and boot lid are closed.
2. Sit in the driver's seat and close the door.

Note: The next three actions must be carried out within two seconds.

3. Depress the driver's door sill button.
4. Switch the ignition on, off and on again.
5. Raise the driver's door sill button.

If the test mode has been entered correctly, the horns will give a short beep and the engine immobilization buzzer will sound.

Opening either door, the bonnet or the boot lid, or operating the driver's door sill button, will cause the alarm LED to illuminate for approximately one second.

If the LED does not illuminate, there is a system fault.

The volumetric sensor can also be tested while in test mode. To test the volumetric sensor, press the unlock button on the remote handset several times. The alarm LED will illuminate for approximately one second each time movement is detected in the vehicle.

The test mode is cancelled by switching the ignition OFF.

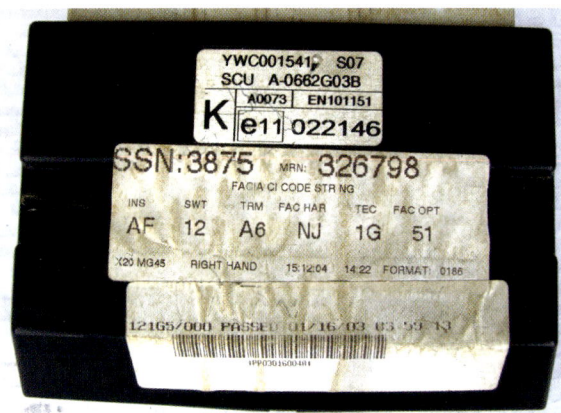

Fig. 5.35 Pektron-made SCU.

PRE-SCU MULTI-FUNCTION UNIT (MFU) SELF-TEST

The MFU (or multi-function unit) deals with many electrical control functions in all cars made before the introduction of the SCU. There is a self-check similar to that used for the 5AS system check, however it requires the car to have a heated rear window (HRW) switch fitted:

1. Press and hold the HRW switch and turn the ignition on – within one second release the HRW switch. The MFU will confirm it is in test mode by giving a brief rapid chime of the 'lights left on' buzzer.
2. A second press of the HRW switch will test the circuits, starting with the HRW switch. Every operation of the appropriate circuit will be confirmed by two chimes from the MFU. The MFU circuit tests are for the HRW switch, intermittent wipe, side lights, head lights, door open switches, rear fog switch and front fog switch.
3. A third press of the HRW switch will force on some of the circuits. Following a chime of the 'lights left on' buzzer, the HRW, rear fog, wipers and interior lamp will operate in turn for one second.

Fig. 5.36   SCU circuit board, showing the five boxes containing the relays. The white relay is a recent replacement.

Fig. 5.37   The failed original relay, cut open to show the double coils and contacts inside.

depending on the car, so it is not possible here to state clearly what each one does. All these relays have the same rating. It would be understandable if the ones that fail more often tended to be those carrying the higher loads, but that is not always the case, which raises doubts about the quality or rating of these components.

By 2011, there were a reasonable number of professionals able to deal with relay failures on SCUs and it is hoped that the range and number of specialists will continue to grow. The original SCU manufacturer, Pektron, has focused on supplying vehicle manufacturers and their spares companies

(MG and XPart), and to date there has been no allowance for a spares, repair or replacement service. The unusual configuration of these relays has meant that they are not off-the-shelf items, but specialists have found sources and new ones have been available on eBay, as we have come to expect in recent years.

Since the replacement relays have become more available, inevitably some have asked whether these new versions would cure the relay problems The jury is out on this one. Replacing a relay is quite straightforward for anyone who works with electronic modules, as it really just involves melting the solder on the pins, sucking it away

and lifting off the old relay, and replacing and soldering in the new relay.

Other specialists have started to offer deeper diagnostics and repairs of the SCU. I expect this to grow as it is generally expected that many SCUs will fail, and the high costs of dealer route rectification makes developing and providing a repair service viable. Remember that the normal dealer solution to a problematic SCU is to renew it and the two fobs. This all needs specific dealer diagnostics-only programming, which in 2011 cost in the order of £700 (SCU £366.95, fobs £77.43 each, both plus VAT plus fitting and programming.) The big advantage of being able to repair

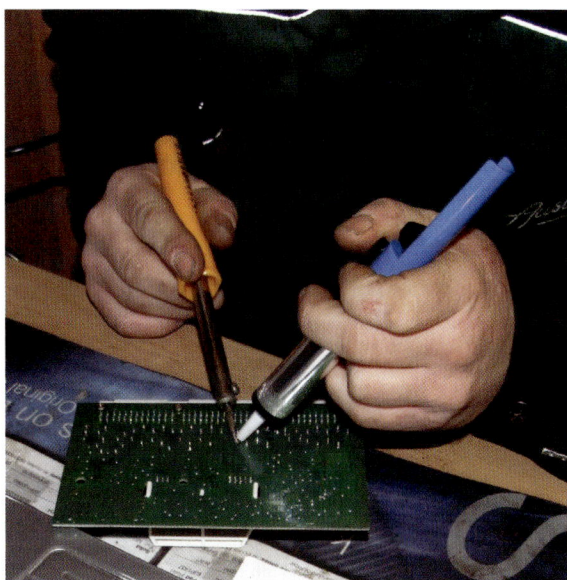

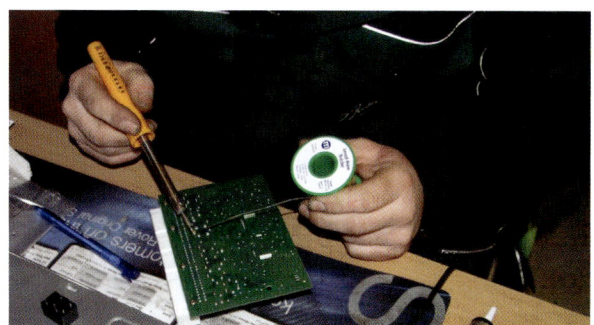

Fig. 5.39   Fitting a new relay and soldering its pins in place.

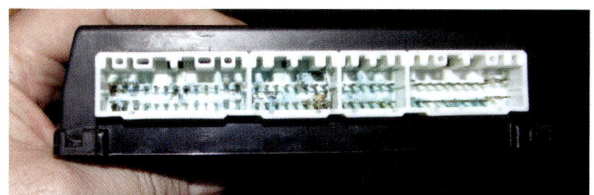

Fig. 5.38   Replacing a relay is a matter of melting the solder holding each pin of the relay to the board and sucking the solder away to release the relay.

Fig. 5.40   Fortunately the position in which the SCU is mounted in the TF doesn't lend itself to water ingress. ZR models, on the other hand, can suffer from water damage that usually destroys the SCU, as here.

the original SCU is that the internal programming is not usually affected, so everything should operate on a 'plug and play' basis. If it is water damaged that makes for a ZR problem and fortunately not one for the TF.

Some dealers seem to have problems programming new SCUs. A huge number of SCUs have been returned to XPart as faulty, since once a programming error has been made the SCU is unrecoverable using dealer diagnostics. One very skilled electronics specialist has shown me how he has made a special rig onto which the SCU circuit board is fitted. This allows him to access the full depth of the SCU, read the original programming errors by dealer fitters, and then 'unlock' the SCU to allow correct coding and programming. With a USB connection to a PC with his software, he demonstrated how he could also extract all the programmed data from one SCU and clone this onto another previously programmed SCU. This equipment has become available from Avon Diagnostics in South Warwickshire (http://avon-diagnostics.co.uk), although only for use by bona fide motor traders (there are no sales to the public), so it would seem that the potential for practical cost-effective solutions for SCU problems is expanding rapidly.

SCU cars still have an EKA, but what this offers is more restrictive. Instead of the 5AS's immobilizer remaining dis-abled for an indeterminate period once the correct EKA is entered, the SCU has a more complex arrangement. This starts with access into the car being given immediately the correct EKA code has been entered: the immobilizer, however, remains active for a further five minutes. Only at the end of that five-minute waiting period can the engine be started, and indeed that must be done before the expiry of a further ten minutes otherwise the immobilizer re-arms. That ten-minute window remains active after the engine is running, so when you next stop the engine and switch off the ignition you have a further ten-minute window to restart, otherwise you have to re-enter the EKA code, wait five minutes and so on.

Fob battery life is about the same at approximately three years, although there is no need to go through the resynchronizing process once a new battery is fitted. The fobs also operate

Fig. 5.41 *Avon Diagnostics SCU 'Unlock Equipment' allows erroneous programming that 'locks' the SCU to be 'unlocked' via direct to circuit board spring pins. When connected to a PC, this allows complete internal reading/programming access. This equipment is only available to registered trade customers.*

on the same frequencies as the previous 5AS system fobs. Where they drastically differ is that you can't use any previously programmed (i.e. second-hand) fobs, unless you have the twenty-two character alphanumeric bar code that was on a sticky label on the blister pack containing the car's original pair of fobs. MG Rover did ask dealers to remove the sticky label from the blister pack and stick it on the service introduction page of the handbook, but it seems this message didn't get through for most cars.

There is also the issue of internal fob programming that doesn't allow them to be recoded to another SCU after the buttons have been pressed a specific (but unknown) number of times. The scenario described was that only a spare fob that has been very rarely used could be recoded to a replacement SCU. This is in addition to needing the twenty-two character bar code mentioned above.

Finally, on the subject of SCU fobs, there is a strange but true piece of information that could become costly: owners of any BMW (including the Mini) or Rover 75/MG ZT and who also

own an SCU-equipped TF must never operate the fobs of these cars in close proximity to an MG Rover SCU fob as irreparable damage will be caused to the MG fob. In addition, if a corrupted fob is then used it can also corrupt the SCU programming, making it necessary to renew both the SCU and the fobs.

Another German connection is with the internal operation and coding of the SCU and you may hear references to ZCS, GM and SA code letters, which are derived from German terms that are shown below.

In very simple terms this information gives the SCU the car's identity data: 'what am I, who am I and what have I got?' The data is seen in diagnostics as a series of alphanumeric characters describing in code the detailed aspects of the car and its equipment. The TF, however, does not operate in such an ordered fashion as the illustration here of the codes that determine how the SCU operates in a late ZR. The TF predelivery inspection has to go through a series of individual question and answers: is air conditioning fitted, yes/no; is ABS fitted, yes/no; are front fog lamps fitted, yes/no, and so on.

ZCS	Zentrale Codierungs System (Central Coding System)
GM	Grund Merkmal (Basic Feature)
SA	Sonderausst Attung (Special Equipment)

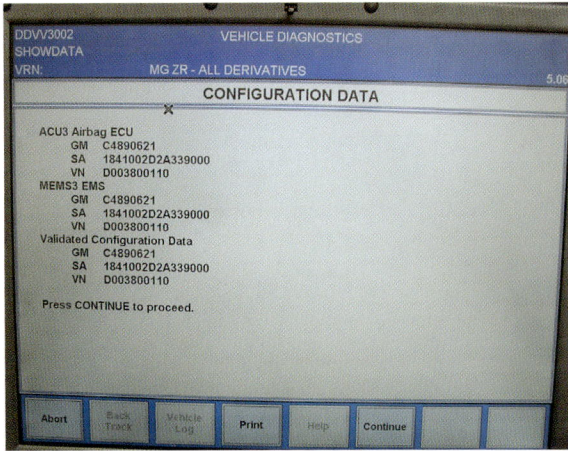

```
DDVV3002                VEHICLE DIAGNOSTICS
SHOWDATA
VRN:              MG ZR - ALL DERIVATIVES              5.06
                CONFIGURATION DATA
                        x
  ACU3 Airbag ECU
     GM   C4890621
     SA   1841002D2A339000
     VN   D003800110
  MEMS3 EMS
     GM   C4890621
     SA   1841002D2A339000
     VN   D003800110
  Validated Configuration Data
     GM   C4890621
     SA   1841002D2A339000
     VN   D003800110

  Press CONTINUE to proceed.



  Abort    Back     Vehicle    Print    Help    Continue
           Track     Log
```

Fig. 5.42   SCU operates with a series of ZCS code letters to instruct it as to 'who it is, what it is and what it should work'. This T4 page shows how the car is programmed.

The mention of fog lamps is deliberately chosen as this is something that is retrofitted to many cars. Even though they are fitted correctly, the lamps fail to operate because the SCU 'simply doesn't know' front fog lamps are fitted and it has to be 'told' of the change. This is done via the dealer diagnostics, going into the Pre-delivery Inspection section and now answering 'yes' to the question about fitting front fog lamps.

The feasibility of buying complete ECU sets, as are available for 5AS systems, still applies. Once again a complete ECU set, engine ECU, SCU and at least one fob, all previously coded together, fitted and working on a car being broken for spares, should work. As the Air Bag control unit also contains vehicle identity data, however, it may be necessary to fit that ECU in order to avoid possible conflicts with the identity data recorded, including the VIN.

Obviously the donor car should be of the same model, otherwise the engine ECU will have the wrong mapping. If this car ever went on dealer diagnostics in the future it would still give identification problems because the embedded vehicle VIN is different.

Overcoming such conflicts needs an operator who is very familiar with T4 diagnostics in order to find their way out of any cul-de-sacs they might encounter, or go to someone with the Avon equipment, such as MG Owners Club Worksop. These issues will probably deter many from thinking about this route, but I mention it more for the unfortunate owner who buys a car whose previous owner has already followed this route and to highlight where the root of some problems may lie.

SCU Modifications

Many are unaware of the option to personalize the TF via the dealer's T4 or GDS diagnostics. The most popular optional extra is speed locking (better than the Rover 75/MG ZT implementation as it unlocks when the ignition is turned off). Other options include setting the mis-lock sounder on or off, a one-shot down driver's window function configured by pressing and briefly holding to activate, setting the interior lights on or off when unlocking the car, and auto relocking on or off. If your local dealer or specialist with the dealer diagnostic equipment can't help you, consult a specialist such as Austin Garages (www.austingarages.co.uk), who have found ways of making wider use of the SCU's capabilities.

Remotely operated central door locking was not fitted to TF 1.6 UK market models until 2005MY, although it seems to have been fitted to export models. The TF 1.6 can be retro-equipped by fitting the specific remote factory latch assemblies applicable for the models with remote locking, since all the wiring is present on all cars built. After fitting they will probably operate as normal – before the alarm goes off! It is a simple procedure with dealer diagnostics to reconfigure the SCU to the status that has remote locking. Retrofitting the interior movement sensor will also require diagnostics to reconfigure the system so that is aware the microwave transmitter is now present.

WIPERS AND WASHERS

Generally speaking this is an area where problems are clear-cut and simple to overcome. The most common failure is wear leading to disconnection of one of the lower arms, which of course always happens when it is raining and you need the wipers working!

The first sign will be that one or both of the wipers suddenly stops, depending on which joint fails, and there is a good possibility that the working arm gets intimate with the static one. The arms that transmit rotary motor movement into wiper action use metal ball joints on the motor output arm, and the two wheelbox arms and the interconnecting rods have plastic moulded sockets that are 'popped' onto the ball joints. Over time wear and moisture will overcome the original lubricated felt pad and some corrosion will develop,

Fig. 5.43   Wiper linkage failure is not uncommon and either or both wipers may stop.

Fig. 5.44   The usual cause is that one of the three ball and socket joints pops. The bright orange rust is the clear cause for this joint's wear.

Fig. 5.45   The joint at the opposite end could also fail.

Fig. 5.46   The middle joint, right behind the wiper motor, could be the cause.

Fig. 5.47   The MG repair kit comprises a pair of new arms.

Fig. 5.49   In time rust will reduce the ball size and the cup will not remain engaged. Rather than replace the whole wiper mechanism, this aftermarket repair kit uses substantial metal 'Rose' and ball joints.

Fig. 5.48   Most wear is usually confined to the plastic cup rather than the metal ball, so this usually provides a simple and effective cure.

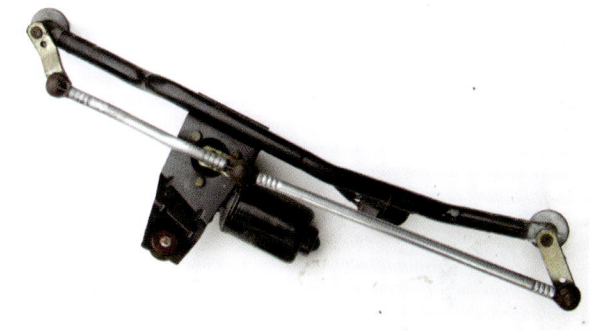

Fig. 5.50   The Brown and Gammons wiper arm conversion after fitting.

which acts as a grinding paste and very rapidly wears the plastic socket until the weakest joint 'pops'.

In most cases when this first occurs the degradation seen on the ball joints is very small. The MG factory solution is to replace both lower arms, which is successful in most cases. Where this route has already been tried and another failure follows, then a more robust, longer-term solution needs to be applied. The MG factory solution is to replace the whole wiper assembly, which in 2011 cost £125 for right-hand drive cars and nearly £170 for left-hand drive cars.

Fortunately the ever resourceful MG specialists have provided a similar solution to the initial repair route that uses a very robust redesigned linkage replacing the original arms. The original ball joints are also removed from the motor and wheel box arms. The new arms have a different design of ball joint that has more in common with a steering track rod end, so will simply not separate like the originals.

Fig. 5.51 A misleading drawing in the workshop manual shows the wiper linkage parked position incorrectly, and with the arm as seen here. This makes removal difficult without potentially damaging the screen panel and paint.

Fig. 5.52 Damage can be avoided by moving the mechanism to this position (see text), as now there is much more free movement.

LEFT: Fig. 5.53 Many MGFs and TFs suffer when the owner accidentally breaks the ends of the plastic screen trim when removing it.

Fig. 5.54 There is a moulded-in clip that hooks under the windscreen glass to ensure there is a tight seal. The trim has to be carefully bent and slid along before the clip can be disengaged.

A more recent development is the arrival of some simple but robust looking spring steel clips, one of which engages below the ball while the other clips over the upper socket, so preventing the socket separating from the ball (Fig. 5.55).

Faults and Repairs

Whichever repair route is chosen, the wiper motor and linkage assembly has to be removed from the car. This removal is covered by the workshop manual, but I need to draw your attention to the removal process for the plastic trim cover seen under the wipers in front of the screen, as when not done carefully the ends of the trim can be broken.

You should be aware that there is an error in the workshop manual where a drawing of the linkage shows the arms pointing the opposite way to how they park. In the normal park position the right-hand wheel box stubby arm will be pointing at the right inner wing and chassis leg. In this position you will not be able to remove the assembly without distorting the screen panel. (For left hand drive cars, this is a mirror image problem.) If the linkage has dropped off the right or centre balls the arm will be free and you can move it out of the way, but it will still be a problem when reassembling the repaired assembly and will need repositioning to facilitate easy reassembly.

First, remove the wiper arms, then reconnect any popped linkage joints so you can see the linkage position in park and judge the position of the arm. Operate the wipers and switch the ignition off when the arm is seen to be in the position in Fig. 5.52, so it stops there and doesn't let the motor 'park' the wipers. When it comes to reassembly, once the wiper arm assembly has been refitted, and before the wipers are refitted, switch on the ignition and the wipers, and then switch off the wipers and let the motor park, before switching off the ignition and continuing reassembly.

Next you have to remove the black plastic screen trim. There are six screws under rounded trim covers immediately below the windscreen glass. These covers need to be picked out with a sharp pointed implement at the six o'clock position. Cup your hand over the cover being removed, otherwise you can expect at least one to fly off to a distant hidden location. At the front edge of this trim are six plastic rivets, which hold the front edge to the edge of the windscreen panel and are usually hidden by the seal folding over them. If you have a trim clip tool, then ease the clips out from this. Otherwise place a flat-bladed screwdriver between the plastic trim and metal panel and ease the two apart to lift the clips.

The plastic grille is now theoretically free to lift out. This is when most people break the ends. There is a moulded tongue at each thin end of the grille that clips under the edge of the glass. You have to take great care to fiddle the trim to disengage this. Originally these were fitted before the bonnet and it is the hinges that restrict the simple removal of the trim by sliding it forward, although with care removal without damage is possible even with the bonnet fitted.

Disconnect the motor electrical plug and loosen the two 32mm nuts holding the wiper wheel boxes to the screen panel. Remove the single 13mm bolt below the motor, followed by full removal of the two 32mm nuts. Push the wheel boxes downwards to disengage from the screen panel and the wiper assembly can now be manoeuvred out.

MG Rover Repair Kit

On the bench, turn the assembly over and pop the cups off their balls, noting the position of the felt washer and arms where they are connected to the centre ball joint and the rubber cup seals. When repairing with the MG Rover repair kit (*see* Fig. 5.47) the balls are cleaned up, but don't be tempted to use any abrasive around them as this will reduce their dimensions. Cleaning with a solvent and rag is all that should be needed.

Lightly grease the balls and reassemble using the new rubber cup seals and felt washer, before clipping the new arms' ball sockets onto the ball joints. Note that more felt washers are supplied in the repair kit than are needed.

Refitting is a reversal of the removal process. Before refitting the wiper arms and blades, however, switch on the ignition and then flick the wiper switch on and off so that the motor returns to the park position. Then you can refit the wiper arms and blades and expect the

wipers to wipe the screen and not the bonnet. Final adjustment of the arm positions is best done after wetting the screen, as this provides lubrication and the arms will travel further.

MG Specialist Repair Kit

The design of this kit replaces the original ball joints of the standard set-up with a threaded pin and nut ball joint, much like a steering track rod end configuration. Having a robust mechanical fitting virtually eliminates any prospect of the wiper linkage collapsing unexpectedly.

The fitting instructions that come with the kits explain the process of modifying the three arms to remove the ball joints and allow the new ball joint threaded pins to fit through. This is not a complex operation, but requires the wiper assembly be removed from the car. Once this and the other instructions are followed, refitting is as per the original linkage.

First Aid Repairs

Quick Clip Solution

A novel approach to providing a first aid approach is another of those internet finds and involves a specially formed spring clip that is able to hold the detached arm onto the ball temporarily while you are seeking a long-term solution. It is very simple in its approach and clearly is applicable to many different wiper systems that have a common ball and socket configuration. Its value is, of course, in being available when the wiper linkage fails, so it has to be bought before a problem occurs. One source at the time of writing is the website www.askthemechanic.co.uk.

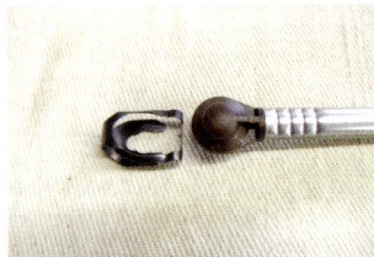

Fig. 5.55 A novel aftermarket first aid spring steel clip can be fitted onto the wiper arm to hold it in place if it 'pops'.

Screw Fixing Solution

There will be occasions when the linkage fails and you have no means of getting a repair kit or a first aid clip, let

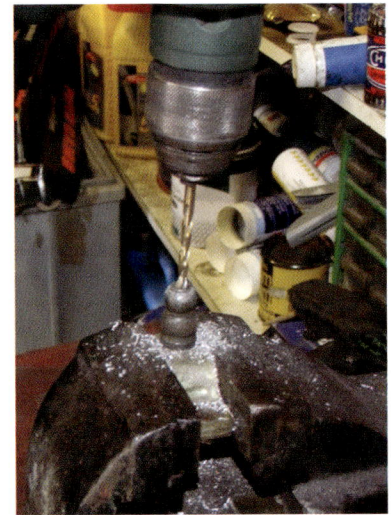

Fig. 5.56 Another first aid approach can be to drill the cup and steel ball.

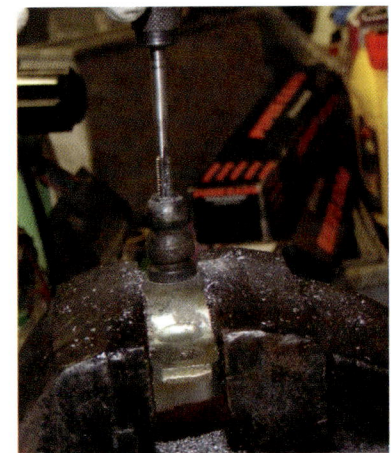

Fig. 5.57 Tap a thread into the ball.

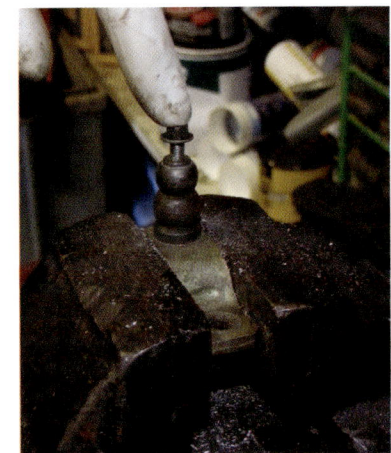

Fig. 5.58 Use a small bolt with a thread lock to hold it in place. This should not be fully tightened, allowing some movement of the cup on the ball, but not enough for it to 'pop'.

alone a new or second-hand mechanism, yet still have to make use of the car. Having faced this problem, I adopted what I regard as a 'sticking plaster' repair that is still going strong nearly four years on at the time of writing.

The process involved refitting the arm to the ball joint and centralizing the arm on the ball. I then drilled through the top of the cup and into the ball with a 3.5mm drill, removed the arm and ran a 4mm tap down the hole in the ball. I then drilled out the hole in the cup to 5mm and found a 4mm bolt and a small washer.

Some thread lock was added to the new thread in the ball and the arm refitted to the ball. The washer was fitted over the bolt, which was screwed into the ball just enough to allow free movement of the arm on the ball but not allow it to lift off. A couple of hours were given for the thread lock to set before refitting the assembly.

I did find that the depth of the bolt head created a contact with the car body, so I ground part of the head away and also added a spacer washer to the lower motor-to-body mounting to provide more clearance. Once completed this provided normal wiper operation again, although I anticipated having to do either of the previous long-term repairs at a more convenient time in the not too distant future. It is nearly four years since that repair, however, and it is still going strong, so it does seem to be a little more than a first aid option.

Wiper Motor Water Ingress

This is the second most common failing and in most cases the cause could easily be prevented. The often derided plastic shield that sits behind the spare wheel and over the rear bulkhead is not just for trim purposes, but it extends under the open section of the screen panel on the driver's side, so covering the wiper motor and thus providing an effective barrier to stop rainwater from otherwise easily reaching the wiper motor. Usually the point of entry will be between the motor body and the end plate.

It appears that earlier cars were more prone to water contamination, but there was no change of wiper part number until late 1999 production, and as water ingress was not

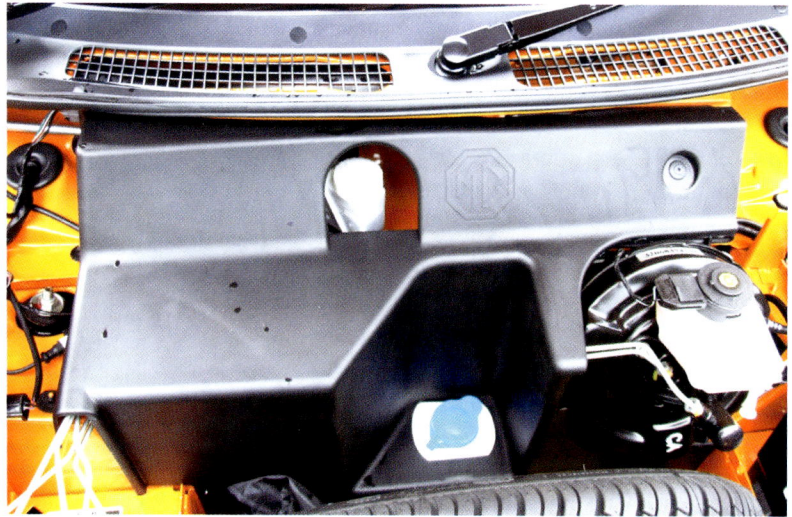

Fig. 5.59 One of the main causes of wiper motor failure through water ingress is the black plastic cover that sits at the rear of the under bonnet area. If this is missing or damaged, water can drip onto the motor.

affecting cars to the same degree throughout the period from 1995 to 1999, waterproofing was clearly improved during production. The clear indicator of water ingress is a noticeable reduction of motor speed and with it slower wiper operation, caused by the motor now not producing as much torque.

Some owners have stripped the motors and cleaned the internals, even identifying and sourcing replacement bearings before rebuilding the motor. This certainly can give the motor an extended lease of life, but for how long is an open question. I have had very mixed results in the past when repairing motors, so I regard this as more of a first aid approach to give you time to source a replacement motor.

One discussion point relating to the MGF wiper motor is the reference to the motor 'drain' being in the wrong place, and that there is an advantage in drilling a hole in the motor body at the lowest point relative to when the motor is fitted in the car. I actually do not agree that the inbuilt 'drain' is a water drain at all: in my view it is nothing more than a breather port. The configuration of the rubber tube is to discourage any water from entering the motor body through that tube. The motor should be fully sealed and not allow water ingress. Draining water out after it has got in offers a small advantage, but that is addressing the symptom and not the cause.

Windscreen Washers

These have individual problems. The commonest is dirt building up in the reservoir, usually as the result of washer additive residues and bacterial action. This is why it often smells like a sewage farm when you remove the lid to top up. When you get to this stage there will be heavy black staining inside and this is not removed with just a light clean.

You can of course use a washing up brush as you can get one inside the bottle quite easily, but I suggest that it is not returned to the kitchen afterwards. It is certainly much easier to remove the reservoir, taking off the large plastic cover to do so, and clean it off the car.

For a number of years I have used a simpler but effective cleaning method. Take the motor out and find a suitable size of bolt to push into the motor-to-reservoir sealing grommet to seal the tank. Add a big handful of horticultural grit, some washing up liquid and add hot water to about an eighth full. Close the lid, shake well and let the small sharp stones do all the hard work in cleaning muck out of the nooks and crannies. Note that with even this small amount of water the tank will become pressurized with foaming soap and the air bleed hole in the cap will be venting vigorously. Relieve the pressure and continue to shake until the inside of the tank is very obviously now clean. Wash the tank out and ensure all grit is removed.

After this there will still be some debris inside, so it is well worth reverse blowing the washer jets, hoses and pump with a low-pressure air line (or mains water pressure when no air line is available).

Winter Driving

Winter with an MGF or TF means encountering a source of aggravation that experienced owners will really appreciate: frozen washer jets. Most other car owners may experience the issue first thing on a frosty morning or only when the temperature drops suddenly, but the occurence of MGF and TF frozen jets is far more frequent simply because the engine is at the back and there is no engine heat to keep the system from freezing.

Even if you fit washer jet heaters the problem is not much better since, if it is cold enough to freeze the jet, you also get a slug of ice further back down the hoses that the heater jet does nothing to remove. This can be much worse when there is any continuous period of freezing weather as the reservoir freezes solid and takes several days of above zero temperatures to thaw.

The only effective solution is not any heating device but concentrated winter screen wash. Even then wind chill across the bonnet and washer jets can still overcome the heater elements, so make sure that your concentration is high and check the freezing point for the winter screen wash: some makes are only just below freezing, while others are many degrees lower. A simple check that the washer jet heater elements are still working is easy to confirm on frosty mornings when small melted rings will surround the jets.

Combined Washer and Wipe on Pre-2004 Model Year Cars

This simple modification provides automatic wiper operation when the washers are operated, an oddity that affected all MGFs and early TFs until the SCU arrived. This facility is common to Rover and MG small saloons using the same hardware, so it has always been a mystery why this was not configured to the MGF and TF.

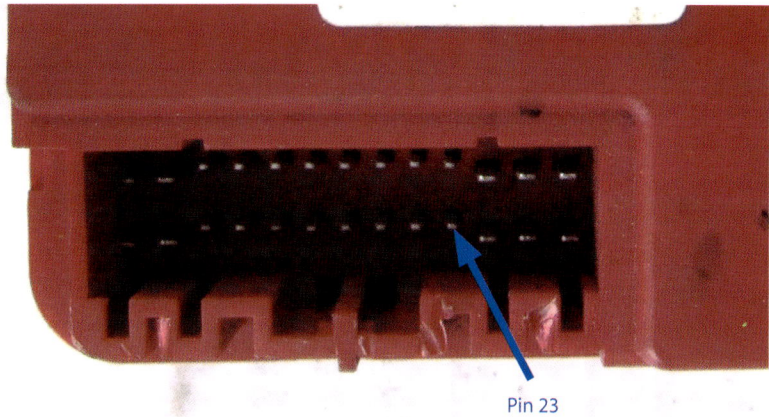

Pin 23

Fig. 5.60   A combined wash and wipe cycle, triggered by just operating the washer switch, was introduced with the SCU in the TF. Most MG and Rover saloons already had this feature.

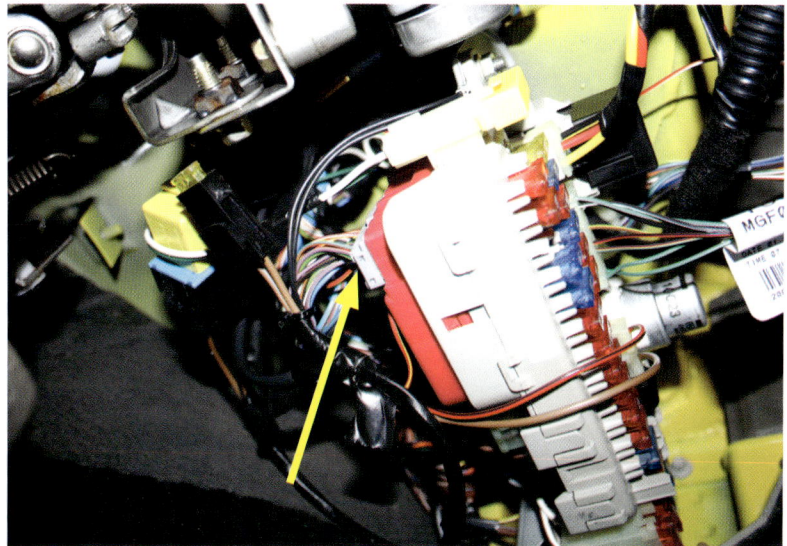

Fig. 5.61   A wire was connected from the washer pump feed to the vacant pin 23 in the MFU via its main connector plug. (Austin Garages)

The modification involves connecting a new wire from the light green/black wire from the washer switch wiring (coming from the column stalk switch) to the washer pump, across to pin 23 of the MGF/TF multi-function unit (MFU), which sits behind the passenger compartment fuse box (*see* Fig. 5.2 above). You need a suitable electrical pin to fit in the MFU electrical plug as pin 23 is vacant, but once connected the function is now active with no programming, just plug and play.

DOOR WINDOW LIFT

Motor Failures

Door window lift motors fail reasonably frequently and ironically it seems that it is TF that suffers most, even though these will be newer units. Nevertheless both MGF and TF can be regarded as the same and dealt with in an identical manner.

There are usually two problems. The first is slowing and lazy operation, mainly on the lift cycle, which eventually sees the motor unable to complete its full movement unless assisted by hand. The other type is a sudden failure accompanied by graunching and clicking noises when the motor is operated. Both demand a new combined motor/regulator assembly. One possible exception is a sudden failure with no prior warning: this could be caused by a fuse, but on SCU cars it could be a relay problem.

Replacement window lift assemblies are for the most part universal now and there may be a couple of differences to the original parts fitted. The first is that the fitted position of the motor may be

ABOVE: *Fig. 5.62   This original window regulator motor has its motor pointing to the right.*

RIGHT: *Fig. 5.63   The replacement shown here has the motor pointing to the left.*

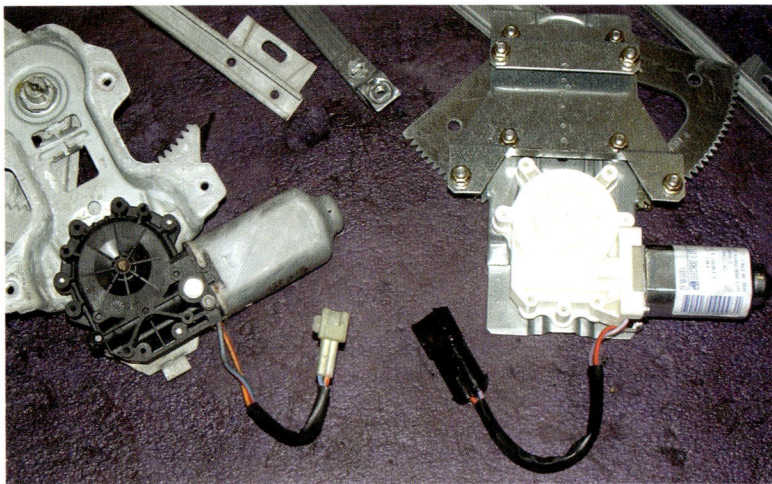

Fig. 5.64   Other replacements have the motor pointing in the same direction as the original. Both orientations will fit, but there are differences in the plugs' wiring and this does matter.

Fig. 5.65   It is easy to damage the tweeter speakers or their wiring on cars from the 2000 model year on.

180 degrees to that of the original. This will present no problems to fitting the replacement and it will work perfectly well. The second issue is that the electrical plug and most motors now come with a replacement plug and terminals in the box. If the fitted plug is different to that on the car's wiring loom, cut off the car's plug and fit the new one.

Removal of the old and refitting the new is a straightforward operation that is well covered in the workshop manual, but it is quite possible to reduce the work involved. Remove the six fixings holding the door trim on, and on 2000 on model year cars take care not to rip out the tweeter speaker wiring when you lift the door trim away. The plastic sheet vapour barrier has to be carefully peeled, but expect it to rip and need some repair with adhesive tape when refitting.

Behind the plastic sheet are two access holes. Lower the window to a position where you can see the bolts inside. These bolts secure the glass to the regulator and will need to be removed once the window has been wedged to stop it dropping when the regulator is removed.

The electrical plug is disconnected and then the six 10mm headed bolts holding the regulator to the door are removed. The wiring is fed through the door and the regulator with its integral motor is removed from the door's rear access hole. The replacement assembly is fitted in a reverse process and bolted in place, followed by either plugging the new motor wiring into the door harness, or changing the plug to suit.

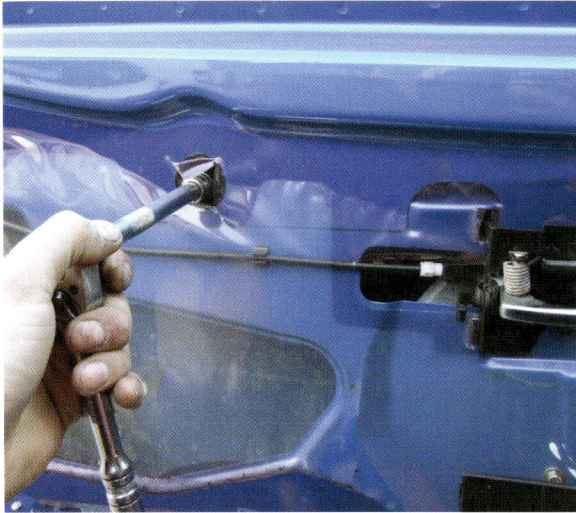

Fig. 5.66   Window glass is fixed in a lower frame, which in turn is attached to the regulator by two bolts, one accessed through this hole when the window is lowered slightly.

Fig. 5.67   The bolts only need to be loosened as the regulator has slotted holes that allow it to be moved sideways and then it lifts off.

Fig. 5.68   The window is wedged with a cushioned wedge or, more effectively, two wedges to stop the glass dropping.

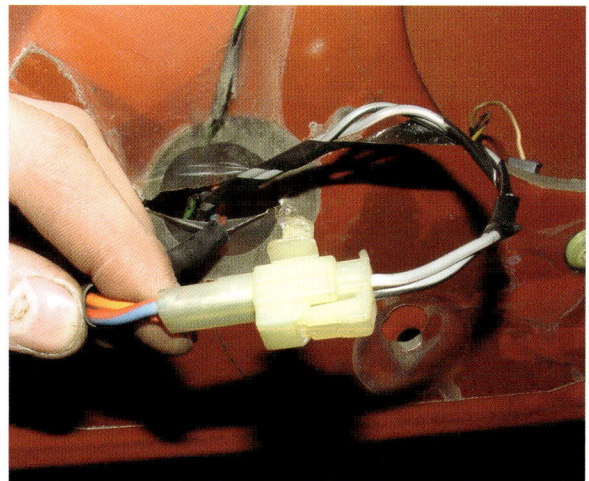

Fig. 5.69   The two-wire electrical plug for the regulator is now disconnected. On cars before 2000 the plug is to the side of the door speaker.

Fig. 5.70   On cars from 2000 the plug is above the speaker. It is also a different fitting.

Fig. 5.71   The regulator can now be removed by taking out the four bolts circled in red and only loosening the two in yellow. The regulator is twisted slightly to allow the two loosened bolts to be pulled through the wider holes.

Fig. 5.72   The regulator is removed through the rear door opening.

Fig. 5.73   The electrical plugs will probably be different.

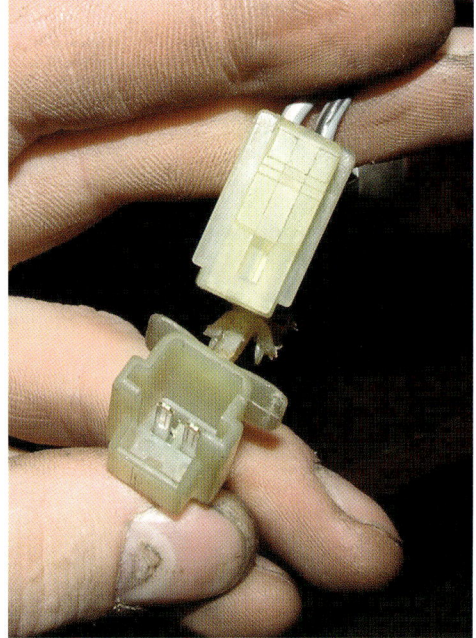

Fig. 5.74   Most new regulators come with a plug on the new regulator wiring and the matching other plug, with terminals and terminal seals, to be fitted to the car's wiring.

Fig. 5.75   If no new plug parts are provided and the plugs differ, cut the old wiring and connect this to the new regulator, as long as the connections are sound and well insulated.

Fig. 5.76   The car's wiring has here had new seals and terminals fitted ready to be inserted into the new plug. If you are unsure of the correct positions for the terminals to go into the plug, wrap some insulation tape around each terminal and carefully insert it into the regulator plug and test the window's operation.

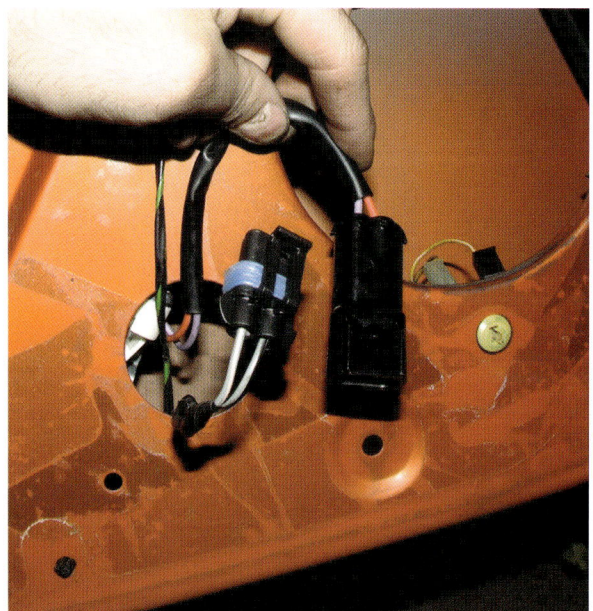

Fig. 5.77   Here the new connections have all been tested and are ready to be connected.

Wiring colour codes are also probably different on the new motor. Matching them up to the car's wiring is sometimes a little confusing. The colour codes are supposed to be common in the car's wiring – slate/pink (S/K) and slate/black (S/B) in the driver's door and slate/white (S/W) and slate/blue (S/U) in the passenger door – although confusingly I have seen original cars with the opposite wiring. This isn't a problem when the wiring of the plug on the new motor is the same as on the car. It should be plug and play, but I advise checking the operation before putting all the trim back.

When the wiring plug on the car's wiring has to be changed, simple crimp-type terminal ends need to be fitted to the wiring. I suggest that you fit these to both wires, but before inserting them into the new moulded plug end, fit each into the motor wiring

plug and ensure they are not touching. Then turn on the ignition and test that the window operation is correct. If it is, switch off and fit the connectors into the new moulded plug to match the positions you have just tested them in. If the function is reversed, just swap the wires over in the new connector.

SUPPLEMENTARY RESTRAINT SYSTEM (SRS)

Before looking at any part of this system there are significant safety issues to consider as the inadvertent uncontrolled activation of an airbag when you are close by will cause injury that can be serious or even fatal. The greatest respect needs to be adopted whenever working with or near the airbag or other parts of the SRS system.

The first consideration is to *always disconnect the vehicle battery and leave*

the car for at least 15 minutes to allow all residual current in the SRS to dissipate. When working with any airbag, do not drop or strike it as an airbag can still be activated even without electrical energy to create the normal trigger.

The SRS on both MGF and TF follow very similar paths. All have a driver's airbag contained within the steering wheel; some cars also have a passenger airbag contained within the dashboard. All cars are equipped with a seat belt pretensioner for both seat belts built into the seat frame. The whole system is controlled by an SRS ECU that sits in front of the gear change mechanism behind the centre console.

There is a failure warning lamp on the centre vertical stack of warning lamps. This illuminates for around six seconds when the ignition is first switched on as a system check, but should then extinguish. If it doesn't, it

Fig. 5.78   All cars have a driver's airbag marked with 'SRS Airbag'.

Fig. 5.79   Some cars are also fitted with a passenger airbag, similarly identified with 'SRS Airbag'.

Fig. 5.80   Both seat belts have a pretensioner mounted on the seat frame.

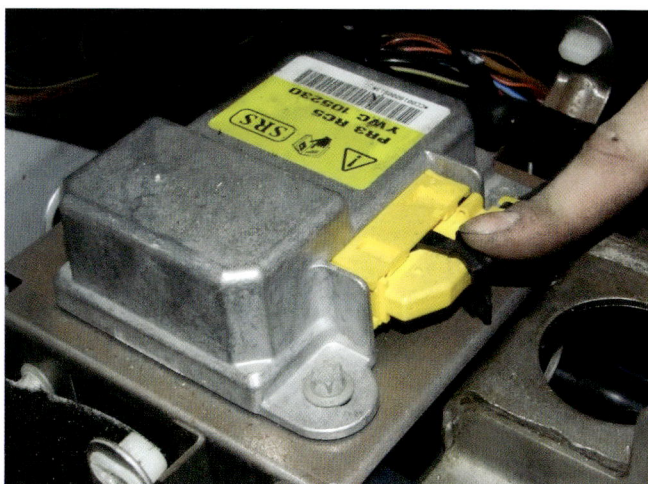
Fig. 5.81   The SRS system is controlled by an ECU mounted in front of the gear change and behind the centre console.

indicates a fault in the system. The system's controlling ECU has a memory that can be accessed with the appropriate diagnostic equipment to identify the trigger and then clear it. If the fault condition has been rectified then the warning lamp will go out after the next 'ignition on' check, but if not then a fault remains.

Under Seat Wiring Problems

Many faults will be found either under a seat or under the steering wheel. All of these are related to movement of wires within the system. The most common by far are the pretensioner connections under the seat. The wiring to these is a simple two-wire feed. To facilitate easy removal of the seat there is a simple plug and socket under the seat and most faults are usually found in a bad connection here. Careful cleaning of the terminals usually helps, but sometimes there is also some free movement in the plug.

A common dealer fix for this was to cut off the plug and socket and then solder the wires together. While this certainly provides the best electrical connection, it creates the problem that the wires need to be cut whenever the seat has to be removed. Before this route is taken, I suggest trying a small cable tie, which is fed between the wires on both sides of the connector and then pulled tight to hold the

connector tightly together. If the seat has to be removed in the future, cut the cable tie and fit a new one when the seat is replaced.

Rotary Coupler Problems

The other common problem area is often within the rotary coupler, a device that maintains electrical continuity between the steering wheel and the steering column. In very simple terms this is a loose coil of wire contained within a round plastic box fitted to the steering column, with its lid fixed to the steering wheel. Inside the box is a loose coil of wire, connected at one end to the car's wiring loom and at the other to a connection for the electrical items on the steering wheel, which are the airbag and the horn for manual transmission cars, and additional connections for the gear controls for the Steptronic/Stepspeed models.

The system operates by having enough free play within the coil of wire to allow full lock to lock movement of the steering wheel with no stretching of the wire in the rotary coupler. While this is a simple and effective means of keeping electrical continuity, the fact that there is movement causes fatigue failures over time in some couplers and it is then that circuit continuity is lost, as shown by the SRS light coming on or the horn or gear change buttons failing to work.

This may be a simple device but repair is far more difficult than might appear, and it is usually necessary to replace the coupler. As the failure rate is relatively low, going for a second-hand unit is much cheaper and a relatively low risk option. If you choose to buy new, however, be prepared for a bill of nearly £150 at 2011 prices.

LIGHTING

MGF Headlamps

Degradation

This is a problem specific only to the MGF and affects the reflectors within the headlamp. The bright reflective qualities are lost and the reflector turns milky. The lamp loses headlamp beam strength and control, and then fails the MOT test. A very simple analogy is to look at your reflection in a bathroom mirror when it is crystal clear, but when the bathroom is filled with steam your reflection is degraded or lost.

The 'steam' in the case of the MGF headlamp reflector is caused by heat from the headlamp bulbs, so the degradation is dictated by use rather than age, although six to eight years' normal use seems to be the average time needed before the dipped beam reflector suffers sufficiently to fail the MOT.

You can tell how bad the problem is by looking directly into the dipped beam area of any MGF headlamp and seeing how milky it looks. Another reference is to look at the main beam reflector and immediately above the side lamp. You can expect to see the dull trail of a 'smoke curl' rising from above the lamp position. This is the heat track from a 5watt bulb and gives some impression of the damage a 55watt bulb can cause in the more confined dipped beam reflector area.

Quite why these reflectors should be so relatively short lived has generated a number of theories, but comment from a company manufacturing similar products has pointed to a stabilizing process being omitted from the original manufacturing operation, probably on cost grounds.

The logical course is to renew the headlamps, which should have degraded at an equal rate. This is a costly exer-

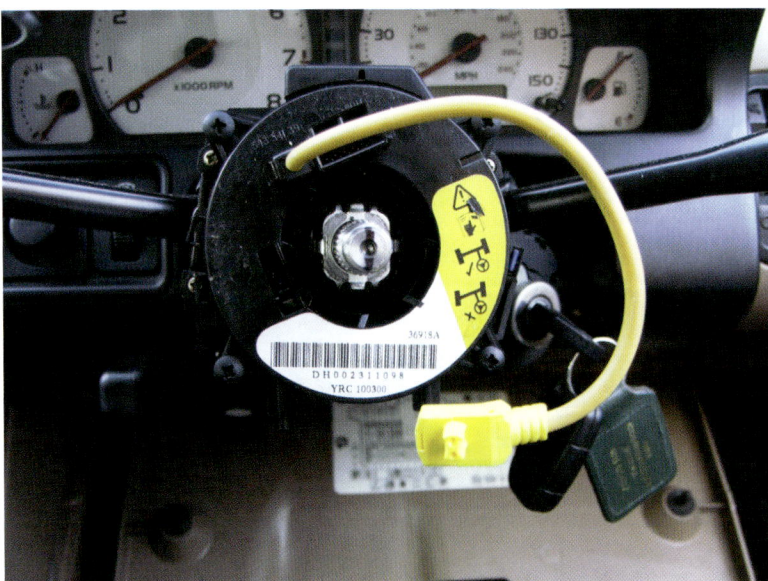

Fig. 5.82   *The electrical connection between the rotating steering wheel and static steering column is maintained by the Rotary Coupler, which sits at the top and around the steering column, directly under the steering wheel.*

Fig. 5.83   The old headlamp (right) shows clear signs of having a 'milky' reflector, which is what causes the problems.

Fig. 5.84   The circled heat damage on the reflector comes from just a low wattage side lamp. Headlamp bulbs with ten times the wattage will cause greater reflector damage as seen on the larger reflector.

cise, however, as in recent years new headlamps have become significantly more expensive. At the time of writing a pair of new headlamps was listed at well over £460, although some MG specialists are able to knock £100 off that figure. If buying second-hand, do check for degradation first.

Aside from replacement there is also the option of reflector refurbishment, so you have to strip your own headlamps, or buy some second-hand and strip them down. This is not without some risk as plastic clips can break and leave you having to find another headlamp to replace them, since only the headlamp glass and bulbs are available as separate parts. For this reason the safer approach is to buy a pair of used lamps to strip and refurbish the reflectors.

Headlamp removal means removing the bumper (*see* Chapter 2). Before doing that it is always useful to park the car on level ground facing, and about fifteen feet away from, a wall, fence or garage door. Switch on the dipped headlamps and mark the beam pattern on the wall, fence or door with chalk. If the car is to be moved then mark the front and rear tyre positions on the ground so the car can be accurately repositioned at the same spot after the work is done. Assuming that the current headlamp aim is correct, when the replacement lamps are fitted the aim can be aligned to the marks and the headlamp aim should be close to optimum.

The headlamp is secured to the car by four fixings. The one on the outside

edge of the lamp is really quite fragile and easily corrodes. Apply too much force to the screw head and the rusted spire nut on the plastic mounting of the headlamp will break the plastic. If it doesn't immediately loosen, drill or grind the screw head off and save the headlamp moulding from damage. Screws and spire nuts are simpler to renew!

Stripping the headlamp is really quite simple, but the operation may be obstructed by over-tightened ball joints holding the inner reflector bowl against the mounting and adjuster balls that are fixed to the main headlamp casing. Taking the headlamp into a warm room and allowing it to heat up for a few hours is a sure way of easing the problem and a hair dryer can help to speed this up.

Fig. 5.85   Once the spring clips are removed, the glass can be eased carefully away from the headlamp body. As it is glass, it will probably be stuck to the headlamp body via the rubber weather seal.

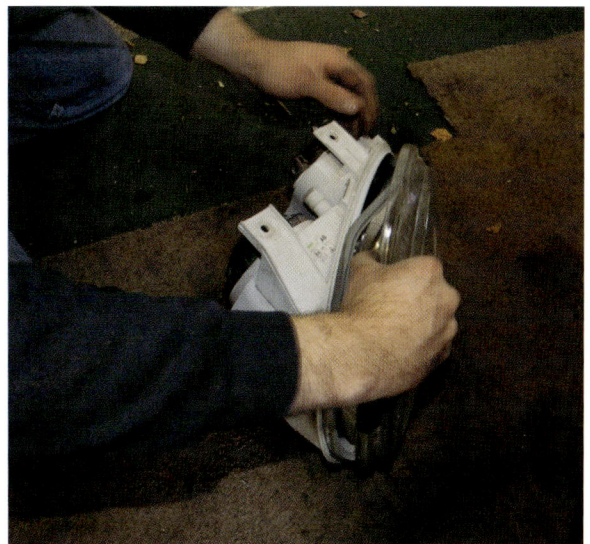

Fig. 5.86   Be very careful that you do not damage the weather seal when easing off the glass. It is not available separately as a spare part, only with a new headlamp glass.

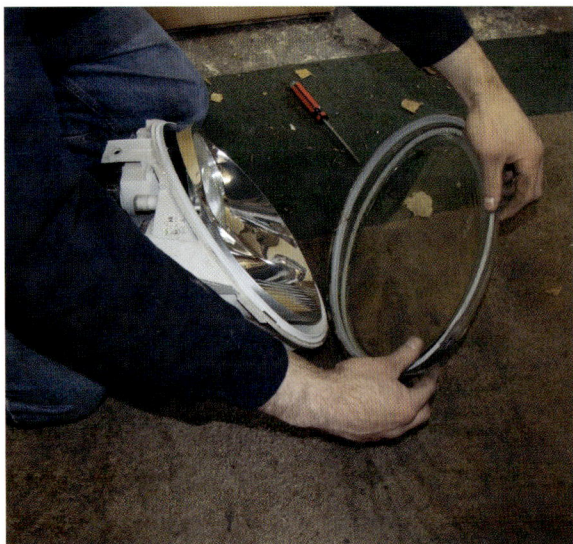

Fig. 5.87   The glass has now been removed from the body and is ready for the seal to be eased off, before washing away the common green algae growth and general dirt.

Fig. 5.88   The bulb covers are twisted off.

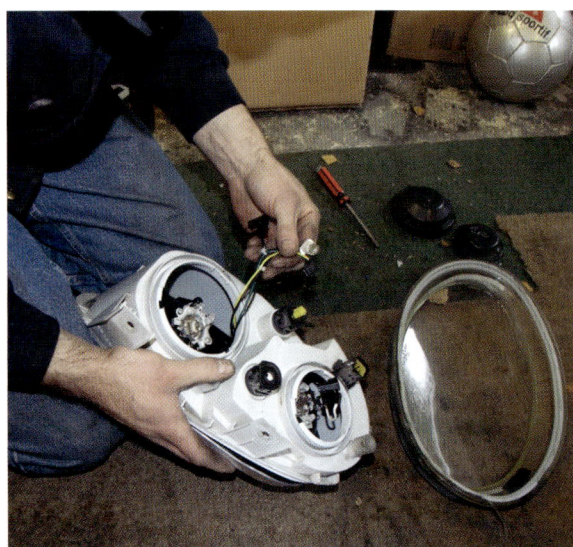

Fig. 5.89   The bulb wiring is disconnected.

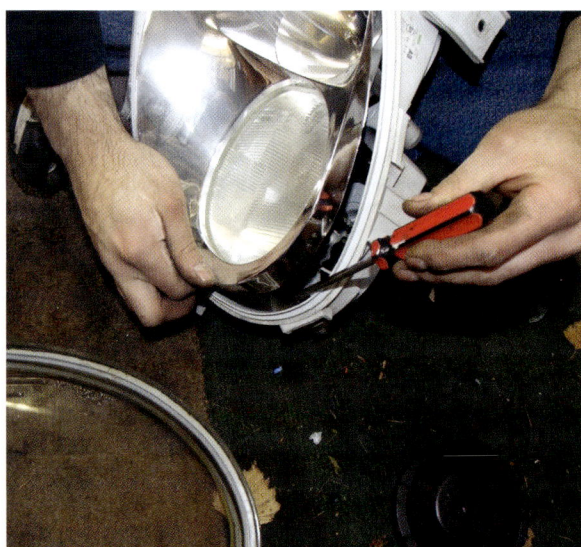

Fig. 5.90   The three inner ball joints holding the reflector into the headlamp body can now be disconnected with great care.

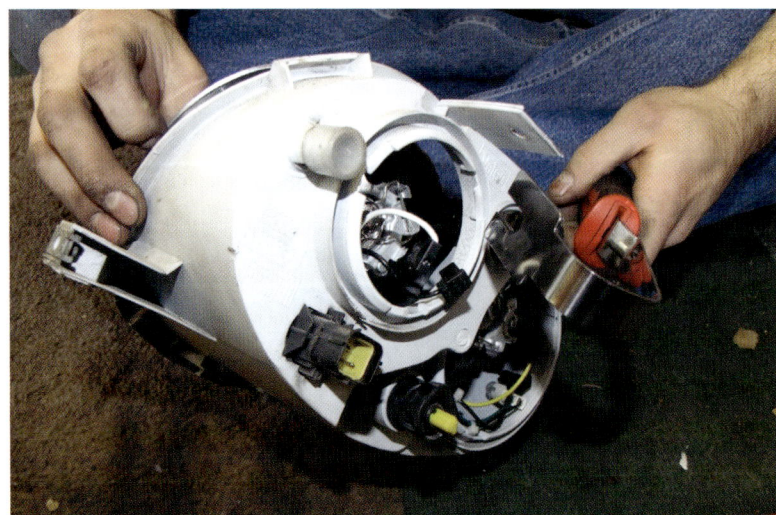

Fig. 5.91   A trim clip removal tool is used to separate the joints.

Also be sure to remove all the separate small clips and fixings from the reflector section: leaving them in is a recipe for losing them. They also become hardened by the heating process used for the re-silvering. Otherwise the accompanying illustrations should guide you through the process.

Dual Metallising in Tyseley, Birmingham, is the only company I know of that is both capable and willing to take on the job of re-silvering the MGF reflector (http://www.dual-metallising.co.uk/reflectors.html). At the time of writing they charged about £75 for a pair of MGF reflectors.

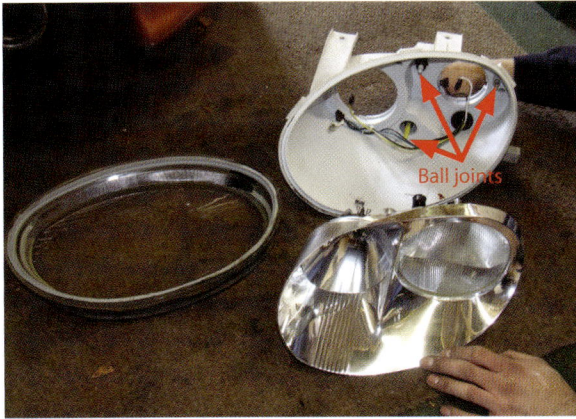

Fig. 5.92   The three ball joints are arrowed.

Fig. 5.93   Remove the four fixing screws and separate the two halves of the reflector assembly. Be aware that the inner dipped beam glass lens is held in place by the two halves. It is not available as a separate part, so take care.

Fig. 5.94   Remember to remove the plastic pegs that act as receivers for the three ball joints. The silvering process involves some heat and if left in place they will harden and become brittle. They are also not available separately.

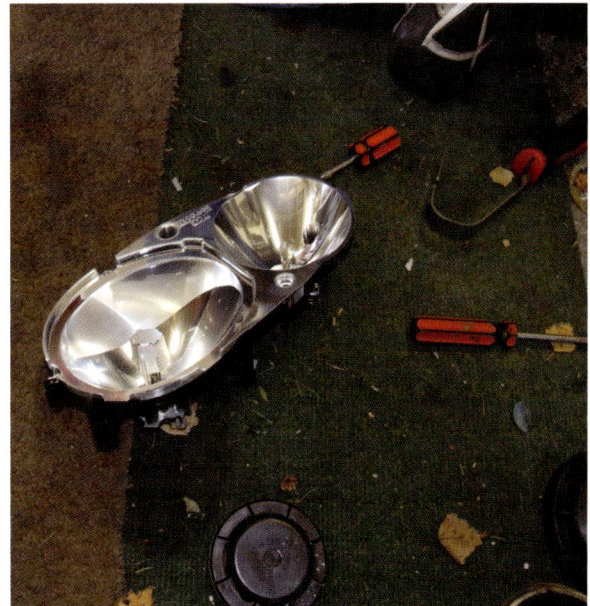

Fig. 5.95   The bulb holders are the last components to be removed before the reflector is ready for resilvering.

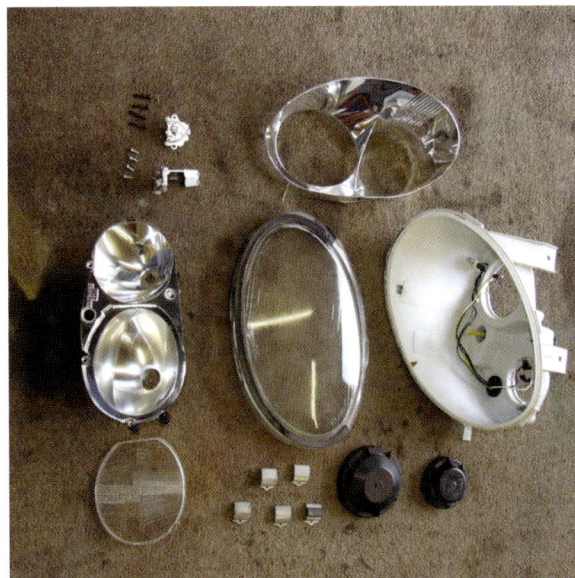

Fig. 5.96   MGF headlamp in kit form. While the reflector is away there is an ideal opportunity to create a Trophy headlamp look or change the silver finish of the outer half to a customized colour.

Fig. 5.97   The same reflector after treatment.

Fig. 5.98   The dipped beam inner glass lens, after cleaning, is placed in position and the two halves of the reflector assembly are secured together.

Fig. 5.99   The three plastic clips are pushed back into the tubular posts and the reflector assembly is carefully pressed back onto the ball joints. Gently warm the clips in order to ease engagement of the ball joints, which benefit from a spray of light lubricant.

Fig. 5.100   The finished job shows obvious improvement.

Alternative MGF Headlamp Options

If you are changing or refurbishing headlamps you have an option to change the style to the Trophy 160 type. The difference is that the silvered area of the lamps that is not part of the two dished reflectors is finished in black and this creates a twinned headlamp look. Other owners have taken this a stage further and painted this section in body colour, but this is very personal. If you just want to change to Trophy headlamps then they are identical aside from the black finish around the reflectors.

Many owners fit uprated bulbs. This is often as a reaction to failing reflector performance, but whatever output bulb is used the headlamp's performance will remain poor until the reflector is dealt with. Bulb heat has already been identified as the main cause of degradation and using higher wattage bulbs just makes things worse. In addition to accelerating the failure of original reflectors, they stress the wiring and I have seen melted plug connectors. The simple advice is don't go there.

Higher performance bulbs of the same wattage as the standard bulbs and carrying required approval marks are widely available, but once again their performance will be directly related to reflector condition.

HID (Xenon) Conversions

In the UK there is a growing interest in using aftermarket HID (High Intensity Discharge) lamp conversions, the ones that flicker for a second when you switch them on and then, starting from a dim level, rapidly brighten. These have the significant advantage of generating more light with less heat and power consumption, but the burners or burner mountings that replace the bulbs are in too many cases made with inconsistent tolerances and so headlamp beam control can be an issue. Set properly, though, they can offer marked improvement in dipped beam operation, but again only with good reflectors.

There has been a long-running discussion about the legal status of these conversions in the UK, and I expect a similar situation exists in other countries, especially in the EU. Specific UK legislation, derived from EU regulations, seems quite clear and the requirements for obligatory lamps, including headlamps, are specified in the various Schedules of the Road Vehicle Lighting Regulations 1989 as amended. Regulation 14 simply states that any obligatory lamp required by the Schedules (found at the back of the legislation), if fitted to a vehicle first used after 1 April 1986, must use a filament lamp that conforms to the regulations and carries an appropriate approval mark. That is the law, so HIDs and LEDs do not conform.

Exceptions to this are granted where vehicle manufacturers develop vehicles that gain type approval with new types of lighting, or a lighting manufacturer develops and gains individual approval for a complete new lamp assembly, not individual components (ECE Regulation 98 dictates requirements from the headlamp assembly, and ECE Regulation 48 relates to how it is fitted to a car). Converting existing lamps from bulb to HID doesn't conform to either UK or EU legislation.

The Road Traffic Act 1988 as amended also contains provisions that make it an offence to supply, fit or use parts that are not legal, yet I have not seen any official desire to pursue either individuals or their suppliers. Indeed there appears to be a distinct stepping back from viewing the opportunity that was presented to include a more proactive course with the UK's 2012 MOT changes. Quite what the future will bring only time will tell, and the rulings described above may be completely reversed.

MG TF Headlamps

TF headlamps are of the projector design that uses the small-diameter, strong lens arrangement similar to HID headlamps, but using normal filament type halogen bulbs. Control of the light generated is better with these headlamps and they have not suffered from the degradation seen with MGF reflectors. Conversion of an MGF to take TF headlamps is not a simple operation, but is possible and this is covered in Chapter 2.

When it comes to fitting uprated bulbs, the practical restrictions outlined above for the MGF similarly apply to using higher wattage bulbs. On the aftermarket HID front, the style of projector lamp is very similar to original equipment HID headlamp systems and would probably not attract as much attention since it mimics an original fit, as long as the beam pattern is well controlled.

One other specific TF light issue relates to the sidelamps and their rather pathetic light output, even though the MGF and TF use the same five-watt bulb. The difference is due to the MGF side lamp projecting through the main

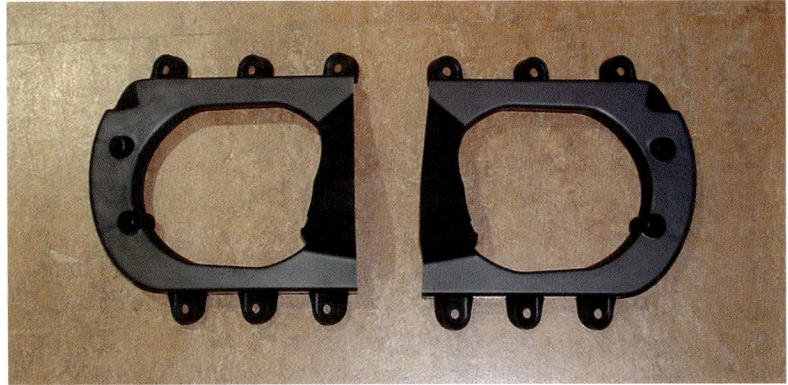

Fig. 5.101   MG TF fog lamps are fitted to brackets glued to the back of the front bumper, wheras MGF fog lamps attach to the body. The brackets needed were not a standard fit.

beam reflector, so the light output is using the whole reflector. The TF, on the other hand, has no reflector as the bulb sits in a tube, and the light output is only what is projected forwards through a small lens at the front of the tube. This makes them only effective as parking lamps, but if lights are needed then dipped headlamps should always be used when driving.

Fitting Front Fog Lamps

Adding front fog lamps has always been a popular addition. The Rover kit for the MGF, which has long since been out of stock, involved mounting the fog lamps on the body panel behind and below the line of the indicator, then cutting holes in the front bumper for the lamp to shine through. Last, there were plastic trim rings to fit around the cut hole, usually after they were painted in body colour. A separate wiring loom was part of the kit, along with the appropriate switch (pre- or post-2000 model year) and instructions.

The TF had a similar kit, but it also is no longer available This had to take into account that the lamps were now fitted to brackets glued to the rear of the front bumper. Many owners have been confused if they were lucky enough to find a kit or decided to do their own fit using a pair of lamps and switch, which are commonly available parts. Many later cars simply didn't have the fixing brackets, although these can be found under part numbers DPL000180 and DPL000190, for the right and left bracket respectively. The original two-part adhesive, found under part number DYM000020, is no longer available, so a suitable adhesive

is needed to glue a plastic bracket to a plastic bumper.

TF owners of cars with a VIN RD620549 and later (mid-2003) have a further difficulty relating to the arrival of the SCU. If you wire fog lamps up exactly according to the instructions for these cars they will not work, even though you have wired things correctly. The reason is that the SCU has to be reset by dealer diagnostics to 'tell' the SCU it has front fog lamps and, when receiving a feed from the new switch, to activate the relay and power the lamps, as long as the side lamps are also on.

LED Bulb Conversions

There are a couple of LED upgrades that do not have legal complications. One is the down light elements of the interior mirror, which on MG Motor TFs uses LEDs in place of filament bulbs. The effect is quite obvious and does give earlier cars a white light boost. The MG (SAIC) part number for this LED interior mirror is 300000264. To fit it you have to carefully pick the wiring connections out of the new plug and put them into your old mirror's plastic plug connector. Naturally they do not have the same colour codes and so this needs a little trial and error. Converting the two festoon bulbs in the footwells to aftermarket LED replacement festoons will complete the whitening of the interior when you open the doors.

The poor TF side lamps highlight an area where an upgrade is beneficial. Before looking at replacing original filament bulbs with LED replacements, however, you should remember that in all known circumstances their use

Fig. 5.102   The use of an LED unit in place of the standard bulb for TF side lamps is quite clear.

Fig. 5.103   An appropriate LED used in place of an MGF front side lamp.

LED replacements and with it a visibility bonus that alone makes the change worthy of consideration. Looking at the standard bulb, the glowing filament projects light at almost all angles, while LED replacements have a reduced number of facets from which light is emitted. This needs to be considered when looking to replace a standard universal bulb. The MGF front side lamp, for example, needs a multi-faceted display, but the TF with its single forward projection of light only needs an LED with that single facet.

This is one area where I have tested a single-facet LED replacement in a TF front side lamp and the difference is considerable. On the other hand, multi-faceted replacements have a use with the MGF and again the improvement in light output is quite noticeable.

There are some issues that may arise in fitting, depending on the construction style and physical size of the LED unit. The style issues come from the fact that most LED units have the correct bayonet base fitting for where the bulb sat, but the LED board section often comes out at 90 degrees from the bayonet section and this can conflict with some light sockets. The other issue is that some LED units are longer and there is sometimes not enough space to accommodate them inside the lamp unit. Therefore you need to confirm the dimensions of replacement LED units and check there is clearance for the different-shaped LED units before buying.

MGF and TF High Level Brake Lamps

High level brake lamps (HLBL), also known as Centre High Mounted Stop Lamps (CHMSL), are fitted to all MG TFs and to most MGFs, but not to all early MPi models. Retrofitting is certainly possible and in most cases relatively simple: the wiring plug is present and sticks out of the wiring loom, which is hidden behind the boot interior light. If this is the case then the light strip (made by Hella under the original part number 8KA 146 751 007) can easily be fitted into the plastic moulding that fits the recess in the central top edge of the boot lid. It is worth noting that this unit uses small individual capless bulbs that can be replaced.

This recess was originally designed to be the air vent from the engine bay.

on MGFs or TFs is not legal. This comes back to the previously mentioned issues with the Lighting Regulations dictating that bulbs must be filament bulbs. There are also minimum wattage standards and LEDs are very low consumption items. This is genuinely a case that LEDs and other light sources were simply never envisaged by those who drew up the original legislation, and since then there have been no amendments to allow LEDs except by the 'type approval' route.

Changing low wattage bulbs (normally up to 21 watts) is not uncommon, but owners change at their own risk, in view of the legal aspects. As the light output doesn't have any dazzling issues, it can be done where the enforc-

ing authorities tacitly look the other way. Comprehensive testing on older classic MG lights with LED replacements for bulbs, which are pretty much common with those on MGF and TF, has led to the surprising conclusion that the light output of the 21-watt brake and indicator bulbs is not bettered by a number of common LED replacements. The speed of illumination from cold of the LED is noticeably faster than a bulb, and the latter's power consumption is very much higher, but the primary function of the lamp, to display the appropriate coloured light, doesn't justify a change.

With the common 5-watt side lamp bulbs the situation is reversed. There is a clear light output advantage with

Fig. 5.104 The MGF high level brake lamp (HLBL) is relatively simple to retrofit, although threading wire through the boot, if needed, can be fiddly. Two screws fit the unit and the backing to the boot.

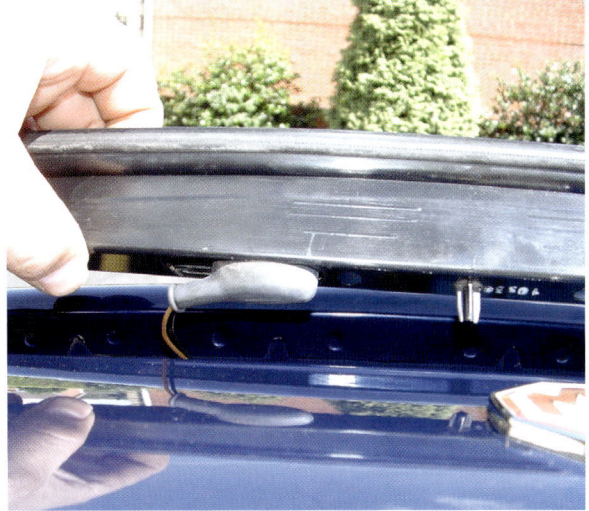

Fig. 5.105 The position of the plug connection is offset, so the actual lamp is upside down and read ALLEH instead of HELLA.

Fig. 5.106 The plug fits only one way.

Fig. 5.107 From the HLBL the wiring passes through the boot bulkhead.

That is why the underside of the boot lid has a much bigger box section than is needed for maintaining rigidity in the boot. Testing showed, however, that insufficient airflow was achieved and so the boot gained the familiar vents in the front of its top skin and the rear vent was filled with a plastic moulding that carries the HLBL.

The MGF HLBL is actually mounted upside down and reads 'ALLEH' instead of Hella! This is because the two-pin electrical connection in the rear of the lamp is not located centrally. For the MGF the connection needs to be towards the passenger side and the plug is towards the driver's side when mounted the correct way up.

Mention of the rear connector raises a second issue for those cars not originally equipped. There is a short Hella connection (Hella part number 8KA 146 751 007) with an important weather boot connection to prevent

Fig. 5.108 The wiring is taken to another connection behind the boot lamp. From there it is part of the main loom, or you have to create your own.

moisture entering the lamp unit. The connector and wiring that this clips into is what may or may not be fitted to the car, depending on its age. If it is not then two wires have to be fitted between this position and run through the boot, down the left-side boot hinge and around behind the interior carpet on the left side of the

boot to terminate near the rear light, where one wire will be spliced into the green/purple, while the other wire connects to earth.

The only difficulty is fitting wiring through the boot voids. Here it is of considerable help to have some welding rod or similar that can be poked through from the various holes in the

Fig. 5.109   The TF has an LED type HLBL, held by two interference plastic clips at each end.

Something that often generates a need for a new lamp is when the original is not removed very, very carefully. The problem is that the red lamp cover extends beyond the base moulding where the simple interference clip is located, beyond the reach of a normal screwdriver or even a trim clip tool. This means that leverage will be against the red cover plastic, which will break as the clips are usually a very tight fit.

Before attempting to remove the HLBL, try warming the surrounding metal and the end of the lamp with a hair dryer to soften the plastic and reduce the effort needed to pop it out. Age also adds to the problems and makes the plastic stiffer and more brittle.

Other Lighting Options

When the 2000 model year MGF was launched in July 1999 it had new clear front and side indicators with amber-tinted bulbs. These became much in demand by owners of earlier cars. Swapping both front and side units is a simple one-for-one change along with the amber bulb. Earlier units can also be fitted to a later car the same way, if desired.

boot panels and then tape the new wiring to the end of the rod and draw it back through. You have to do a section at a time. I also suggest wrapping some tape around the end of any rod so that, when inserted, it doesn't scratch the paint within the closed sections of boot, since that could promote rusting.

The boot lid of the TF was reshaped to incorporate a raised spoiler section at the rear edge and a new shaped LED high level brake light incorporated smoothly and seamlessly. There is no

possibility of fitting the TF LED HLBL into the MGF boot lid, although the boot lid of the TF can be fitted straight onto an MGF.

The LEDs in the TF HLBL are much more effective than the bulbs in the MGF HLBL, although a downside is that the LEDs are not designed to be replaced if one should fail. I expect that those with some knowledge of electronics, however, may be able to overcome this and avoid the rather heavy price of more than £90 for a new unit.

The difference between the rear lights for the MGF and TF is that the MGFs has a darker reverse and indicator section. Otherwise the lamps are the same and can be swapped between MGF and TF, but only in matched pairs as a car with one of each would fail its MOT.

There are also alternative approved rear lamp assemblies to replace the whole rear lamp in what is commonly referred to as the 'Lexus' style. Several different styles have been available over the years and this is an easy way for owners to express individuality without any legal worries. If there is any issue with these lamps it is that the wiring to the individual bulb holders is a little untidy and vulnerable to damage, which is where the next item offers a solution.

Rear Lamp Interior Boot Protection

The standard lamps' rear face inside the boot has always been untidy and it is not unknown for one of the two locating clips of the bulb holder to be broken

Fig. 5.110   The clip here is visible because the red plastic of the lamp is easier to break than the clips that are supposed to be coming out. Make sure you can get a lever under the black plastic base, not the red lens. Warming with a hair dryer should also help.

when placing items in the boot. There has always been a need for a simple cover to protect the lamps and present a finished look. Surprisingly this was not addressed until the 2009 model year TF when MG Motor introduced a simple grey plastic moulding that fits over the existing mounting studs for the rear lamp. These have been made available through XPart, under part number ZUA000640, for about £25 for a pair.

Fitting these is quite simple, but of course is not listed in any manual. The new cover uses the three stud fixings of the original rear lamp-to-body fixings, although when I first fitted them I found that it was much better to obtain six new M5 flange nuts rather than try to use the original lamp-to-body fixing nuts. You can use the original nuts, but usually you then have to have a helper or use your body to lean against the lamp to stop it falling out while you push on the fixing studs when fitting the new cover. Adding new M5 nuts completely eliminates any fiddling and allows a simple and quick fitting. This is also of value when a bulb fails, as you do not want to be messing with holding the light unit in the car while removing and refitting the bulb holder board just for a simple bulb change.

Fig. 5.111   The MGF and TF rear lamps are prone to damage from loads carried.

Fig. 5.112   These neat plastic covers for the rear lamps have proved extremely popular.

Fig. 6.1 MGF styling saw black mesh grilles behind the lower and upper grilles at the front and for each side air intake.

Fig. 6.2 Over time the black painted grille will rust. Optional interwoven stainless steel mesh kits have been a popular replacement, although this entails having to remove the front bumper.

6

personalization and modification

When it comes to modification and personalization, so much is possible with virtually any car. The strong enthusiast following for the MGF and TF drives a thriving trade to supply that demand. There is not enough space to cover everything, and what is covered may not be in any depth, but I hope this chapter will provide some insight, together with appropriate contact details for those interested in following up the suggestions.

Car insurance is a contract between a car owner and an insurance company. The company assesses the risk and charges a premium based on the specification of the car, as it was originally made, and then on any non-standard features that the owner declares to the insurance company. Changing any part to one that is not an original manufacturer's standard part for that specific model essentially changes the insurance risk and should be notified to the insurance company.

Enhanced performance will significantly affect the risk and thus the premium. It might even affect whether the insurance company will still accept the modified vehicle as many insurance companies specifically exclude modified cars. While an owner might not believe that cosmetic and some other changes would affect the risks, some most certainly will. Anything that makes the car more desirable increases the potential of theft of or from the car.

The bottom line is that if you are planning to change anything on your car, the nature of the contract you have with your insurance company is that you are obliged to notify them; otherwise they may choose to cancel your insurance or not cover certain aspects, such as damage or theft. It is sensible to discuss the changes with them to clarify their position prior to any work being done or spending on parts. Get a reference so that, if you carry out the agreed modifications, you can then notify the company that the agreed changes have been carried out and pay any premium increase to retain full cover.

Prior discussion is advised as many of those you speak with in the insurance industry have little understanding of a car other than how to drive it and where the fuel goes. Discussing a proposed change allows enough time for the proposal to reach someone within the company who understands the effect your proposed changes will have on the car and, it is to be hoped, reach a sensible conclusion. If the company doesn't take on modified cars, you have the option of not carrying out the changes or looking for an alternative insurer.

It is also important to note that rarely do modifications enhance the value of a car. It is more likely that they will reduce the value, because a modified car is not going to attract such a wide range of potential buyers and it may be less easy to insure.

COSMETIC ENHANCEMENTS

This section covers potential changes from full body kit to furry dice, although I hope not to see the latter. This area very much depends on personal taste, but it is fair to say that if many owners didn't wish to give their cars a personal touch, they wouldn't have bought an MGF or TF. Rover and MG Rover certainly recognized this and offered a wide range of options for the first buyer and accessories for all.

Factory options and accessories were all relatively low key, often using bright finish parts to replace plain ones, leaving the more radical changes directly in the hands of individual owners. Even so the range of options and accessories was always popular. Among the most popular was a 'Chrome Pack' for early cars, which evolved into the 'Bright Kit' for later cars and offered an attractive interwoven stainless steel grille material to replace the somewhat plain, black-painted grille material fitted in the standard car's front bumper air intakes and the two side air intakes, and in the rear bumper mesh for the TF. The later 'Bright Kit' also included bright finish (chrome effect plastic) door handles, plus a stainless steel ashtray (from the Jaguar XJS), a matching bright finish cigar lighter and, of all things, a bright finish handbrake button.

Pre-2000 cars often had adhesive-backed imitation wood or silver finish

Fig. 6.3   The stainless steel mesh kits provide a marked visual improvement.

Fig. 6.4   When the TF arrived in 2002 a 'Bright kit' was a popular option, although the front upper grille slats would not benefit from a bright grille.

Fig. 6.5   The bright grille for the rear of the TF kit was something that had no equivalent on the MGF.

Fig. 6.6   Pre-2000 model year cars could have the centre console and dash air vents trimmed out with adhesive-backed imitation wood. The darker finish wood seemed more realistic and was also more resilient to sunlight, but after many years most can now be expected to have faded.

centre console and air vent cover trims; these were not as tacky as they sound, at least not until they were approaching ten years of age. You can still find companies specializing in selling these for a wide variety of cars, including the MGF and TF, but in my opinion the factory options for the 2000 model year and all later cars are preferable.

Updating Early Models With Later Parts

Mention of the 2000 model year cars brings forward the fact that many owners of earlier MGFs wanted to update to the later look. This is certainly possible, although the demand has significantly dropped off now we

are more than ten years after the end of MGF production.

Any time you take your car to pieces, and before it goes back together again, I strongly suggest that you have a camera to hand and a quantity of small and medium sized plastic bags and/or ice cream and margarine tubs. Photograph the parts as they are coming off and then place them in labelled bags or tubs to ensure that, when you actually come to fit the replacement parts, you know what came from where.

Some later parts, such as centre console switches, require more than just removing them from the donor car and fitting them to your own. The window winder switches, for example, can stay as they fit the later console

and that eliminates a wiring mismatch. The early and late console HRW and rear fog lamp switches have the same pattern of plug, but each has a specific keyway moulding to ensure it fits only the correct switch. The keyway is a simple plastic moulded protrusion in the switch moulding and a corresponding groove in the wiring plug that only allows a matching switch and plug to engage.

The oddity is that the keyway for the fog and HRW switches is swapped around between these early and late cars, so you can fit the late HRW switch to the rear fog lamp plug and vice versa. Obviously the switch face will be wrong, but there are a couple of ways around this. The switches can

LEFT: Fig. 6.7   From the 2000 model year the main trim moulding could be supplied with a wooden finish that matched with similar door trims when this option was specified.

ABOVE: Fig. 6.8   The ash grey interior plastic fittings and dark seats common to most pre-2000 cars can sometimes be seen as a little depressing. The lighter interior colourways and trim available as options from 2000 could significantly brighten the interior, as in this 2001 model with Walnut interior and walnut/cream leather seats.

Fig. 6.9   From the 2000 model year on the door trim gained by default a silver centre trim rail that looked odd with some interior colours.

Fig. 6.10   The optional wood finish rails worked much better.

ABOVE: *Fig. 6.11   The trim rails are relatively simple to swap once the door card is removed and the centre section is taken away by releasing the seven screw fixings and four bent tabs.*

RIGHT: *Fig. 6.12   The centre section can now be removed from the door card and separated into the two separate parts.*

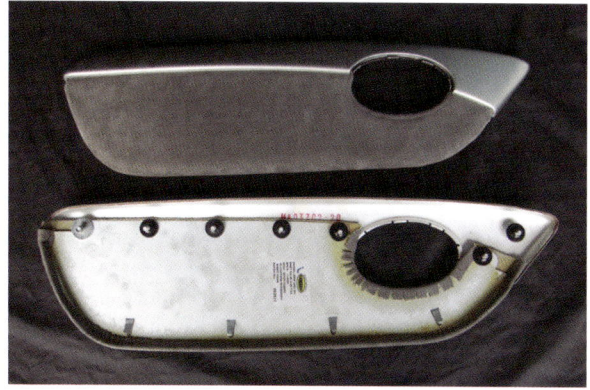

LEFT: *Fig. 6.13   In order to update the pre-2000 centre console, the switches and wiring have to be changed. This wiring on this 1998 MGF is more complicated than usual as it is fitted with air conditioning.*

RIGHT: *Fig. 6.14   The conversion involves changing the wiring plug pins in the mismatching switches in (all) the switch plugs seen here.*

Fig. 6.15   Once the wires have been changed and connected to the post-2000 switches, everything should work normally.

have their fronts carefully unclipped and swapped over, or the later switch plastic keyways can be cut off with a sharp blade, or the wiring plugs can have their electrical pins removed from one plug and fitted in the other. The last of these options is the best in my view as the removal of the electrical pins is very quick with the right tool or a small opened-up split pin.

The later door card design is also a common change as it is a little more glamorous due to the flowing shape of the trim rail and the use of leather or other contrasting trim in the door centre, rather than the earlier cars' pad of either leather or basic trim material. The later card also benefits from a bright finish, oval-shaped interior door handle, in place of the early plain squared one, and the additional tweeter speakers common to all cars from the 2000 model year onwards, except the MGF 1.6 and TF 115.

Fig. 6.16   The standard ash grey pre-2000 interior door trim, shown here, is often changed to the later options.

BELOW: Fig. 6.17   Two later ash grey options.

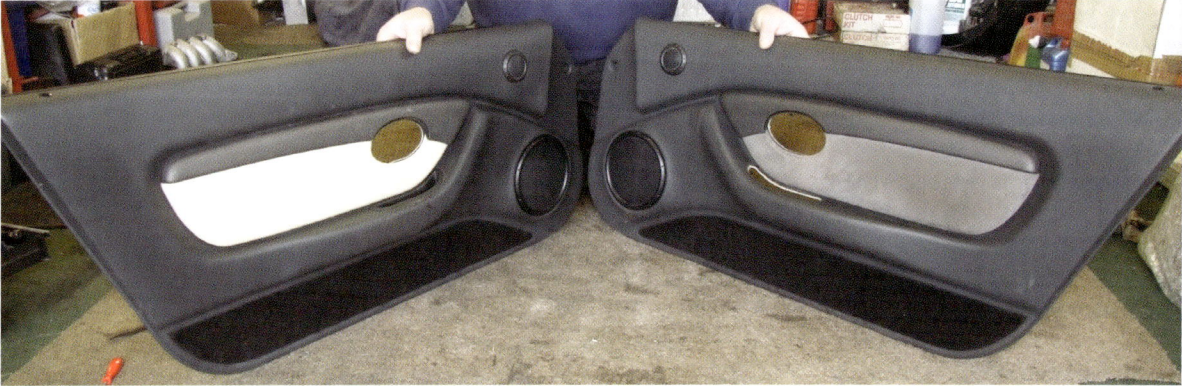

Some owners have taken the MG ZT interior door handle and surround and fitted this to the later door cards for an even plusher look. The ZT fittings have a curved handle, rather than the angular original, and the surround has a bright finish. A degree of modification is necessary for these to fit, so the end result can have a variable finish depending on the skill and effort of the converter.

Attention will now move to the seats. It has to be said that the original cloth seat material on the standard MGF was a little dull. This was only slightly improved on the VVC with the standard addition of black leather bolsters (outer edges). Overall this and the ash grey coloured plastics for the hard trim made for a rather dull interior that many may want to update.

Changing the seats for a pair from a later car is quite simple as long as you strictly observe the specific operating procedures that must be adopted when working with any part of the SRS (airbag) system, which in this case includes the seat belt pretensioners attached to the seats.

Later cars have subtly different shaped seats in a wider range of materials, many with what are called Alcantara central sections. Alcantara is a high-quality, man-made suede-like material with good wear and longevity. Less well looked-after Alcantara often suffers from 'bobbling', which can be dealt with using a 'bobble buster', just as one would with clothes. Other cleaning and maintenance tips may be found at the manufacturer's website (http://www.alcantara.com).

Changing seats gives access to the carpet. As well as finding all sorts of rubbish, and the inevitable selection of coins, there is the opportunity to

Fig. 6.18   The original 2000 on pattern interior door handle and surround.

Fig. 6.19   One possibility is to fit the MG ZT interior handle and surround

Fig. 6.20   Driver's seats trimmed in Alcantara often suffer from 'bobbling' caused by wear.

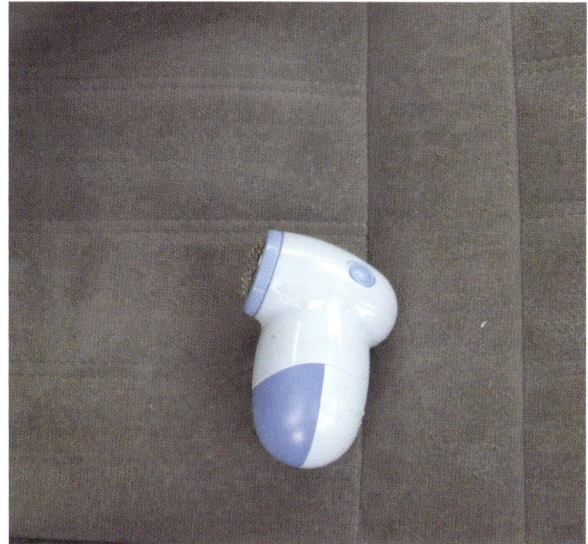

Fig. 6.21   Looks can be significantly improved by using a clothing 'bobble buster' to shave the bobbles.

remove the carpet and the underlying insulation to dry them out if wet and deal with any rainwater leaks. This is also the right time to change the carpet and there is a definite advantage in using a later TF carpet on earlier cars, as the quality is better and the fit of the carpet around the sill-to-door area is tighter. The later carpet also comes as a single piece, whilst earlier TF and all MGF carpets come as separate carpets for drivers and passenger sides.

Fitting the later carpet correctly means that the centre console has to be removed as well as the seats, but that is really very little additional work (*see* Figs 3.20–3.37). One specific issue that applies when fitting this later carpet to an earlier pre-SCU equipped cars (pre-VIN RD620549) is that the carpet foam in the driver footwell has to be cut out, since the later SCU cars did not have the window lift controller mounted down there as its function was taken over by the SCU. The foam removed from the original carpet is used as a template with a can of spray paint to mark out the area that needs to be cut out, which is done with a sharp craft knife.

The ash grey facia colour is practical but can also be depressing. A selection of different colour facias were later offered as options, and the lighter ones can really lift the interior. Where the lighter colour options were fitted it is not just the facia that is affected, but also the centre console, including the Tee bar between and behind the seats, and both door cards. This makes

Fig. 6.22   Individual owner personalization can reach spectacular levels, as on this 1998 MGF with full leather retrimmed interior.

Fig. 6.23   These original MG Sport and Racing XPower branded Sparco competition seats, originally fitted to a rally ZR, needed a custom subframe to allow fitting into the MGF.

Fig. 6.25 The MG Motor TF new main instruments introduce a new format and dark face for the main instruments.

Fig. 6.26 At night the new dark face now matched the dark face of the smaller centre console instruments, something that was not present on earlier MGF and TFs.

Fig. 6.27 Centre console instruments of the MG Motor TF in daylight.

Fig. 6.28 The introduction of a black background on the MG Motor TF's main and centre console instruments gave them the same look at night.

a change of facia essentially a complete interior swap from a scrapped car.

Aside from the range of standard interior trim options, there are always the bespoke specialist supplied options, from a new carpet to a full interior retrim. The upside of a bespoke interior is that personalization can be taken however far you want to go and you are guaranteed an individual end result.

Last, in this area are options relating to steering wheel, instruments and heater controls. Many early cars came with a soft touch plastic steering wheel that is actually better than it sounds, but it falls short of the feel of a leather trimmed wheel. Fortunately there are many leather wheel options and, even if the wheel has been handled for many years and thousands of miles, it is an item that is easily professionally retrimmed.

Instruments are a little more difficult to deal with. While they can all be changed for later ones with the bright finish faces, instead of the cream of the pre-2000 models, there are some differences in function and wiring, not least of which is the change from a mechanical speedo cable drive to electronic sensed operation, and different connections in some cases. With the right degree of commitment almost anything is possible, but this is an area where perhaps changing the face to one of the custom aftermarket options is the simplest route, if the look is something that has to be changed.

Instrument illumination has always been an issue for MGF and TF, as the main instrument panel is forward lit and the smaller centre console clock and oil temperature gauge are back lit. The result is that at night the main instruments retain a light coloured background, while the smaller instruments gain a black background. This mismatch was not changed until the MG Motor TF arrived with a new main instrument pack, which has a black background like the smaller gauges, so wherever the interior illumination comes from it has the same look, matching the small gauges.

Heater controls have seen several changes to the face and control knobs. All factory knobs were plastic and there are different lengths to the main shaft, shorter on cars up to the 2000 model

Fig. 6.29   Using alloy heater knobs is an easy way to add some glamour to the centre console.

Fig. 6.30   The MGF Trophy 160 introduced an additional plastic moulded front bib spoiler that marginally improved aerodynamic performance. The contrasting colour of the Trophy bib shows up well as it is trial fitted.

Fig. 6.31   The Trophy bib once painted and fitted.

Fig. 6.32   Aftermarket fibreglass Trophy spoilers may look similar, but they are thicker and more rigid and do not fit so neatly, as the join to the front bumper shows here.

year and longer for the later cars and TF. The actual heater controls are the same, but the early cars had the heater panel slightly sunken, and the 2000 model year cars saw the panel spaced outwards, giving a smoother look. Obviously for this reason you can't use early pattern knobs on a later heater facia, but then not many would want to. However, this would affect someone with aftermarket alloy or Rover 200 BRM alloy knobs.

Mention of the BRM raises the perfect example of how Rover chose to add 'bling' to the Rover 200 range with leather and alloy trim. A number of these alloy bits can be adapted for use on the MGF and TF. Beyond this there is an enormous range of alloy additions and other trim options available from MG specialists and other suppliers.

Fig. 6.33   The Trophy spoiler was never officially compatible with front fog lamps because the lamp position overran the upper edge of the spoiler. This has not stopped enterprising owners getting around the problem with neat solutions.

Exterior Changes and Front Spoilers

As the exterior is a significantly more hostile environment than the interior, any changes outside have to be done in a very robust manner to survive. Most owners generally only commit to smaller changes, while a few go for major changes that involve complete panel replacement and other additions that come with complete body kits. One of the main attractions of moving into an MGF or a TF is the simple fact that it is already a very individual car, but it has to be said that significantly changing the style of a car by adding a body kit generally reduces the car's value. This may not be a consideration for some, but it is a point many overlook as beauty is in the eye of the beholder: you may be in a crowd of just one, so resale may be impossible.

Smaller changes can be easily reversed, if need be, but a few have wider appreciation, such as front splitters, which are functional as well as cosmetic. MGFs and TFs are light at the front and suffer some front lift during

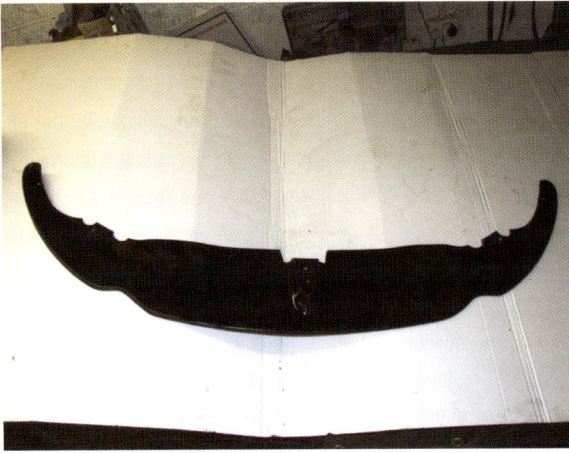

LEFT: *Fig. 6.34 A splitter that attaches to the underside of the MGF bumper, originally supplied by KH and copied by others, has been a popular way to improve stability aerodynamically. Fortunately it is not expensive, as it is highly vulnerable to damage if you get too close to the kerb.*

ABOVE: *Fig. 6.35 When painted to the body colour the splitter loses much of its 'bolt-on' look.*

Fig. 6.36 *MG Sports and Racing sold an extension bib to the front lower lip of the TF bumper to improve aerodynamics. This is also still copied and available.*

Fig. 6.37 *Inventive owners have found that the Seat Leon front splitter can be easily made to fit the front of the TF, although its benefits are questionable.*

driving that leads to a reduction in stability, especially in windy conditions. MG Rover recognized this when introducing the MGF Trophy 160 SE model, which comes with an integrated additional moulding attached to the lower part of the front bumper panel and incorporating a moulded lip to help reduce lift. This Trophy splitter, as it is known, offers a small aerodynamic advantage, but its profile does not project far from the bumper to ensure that it isn't accidentally damaged by contact with low kerbs.

This limitation doesn't apply to what is known as the Krafthaus or KH front splitter, now widely copied, which has a three-point fixing to the underside of the front bumper panel. This has a much stronger aerodynamic effect, but is seriously vulnerable to careless parking and many owners will be on their second or third splitter, especially on lowered cars. Their persistence illustrates how effective this splitter is in reducing front end lift, as these owners want to regain the advantages as soon as possible.

The TF benefits from some front end changes to reduce this issue, although they are only partly effective. MG Sport and Racing developed an additional extension splitter that fits over the lower short lip of the standard front bumper panel. This has been copied by a number of MG specialists and body kit manufacturers. It doesn't give the same step advantage as the KH splitter on the MGF, but a little more than the Trophy splitter. Overall the KH splitter still offers the best aerodynamic advantage, even on the TF but it is not as simple to fit.

MG owners are often quite inventive and find ways to adapt parts from other cars to make changes. A popular modification has been the fitting of the Seat Leon front lower splitter to the TF. The splitter has attracted interest because it is cheap (about £30) and flexible. It

Fig. 6.38 *An interesting feature of the MG TF XPower 500, announced in 2002, was the inclusion of a huge bonnet vent for airflow from the radiator, as well as for reducing front lift.*

can easily be made to fit the underside of the TF front bumper panel and many believe it improves the appearance of the front. I have not, however, been able to quantify any aerodynamic effect after fitting one, beyond the visual aspects.

Vented Bonnets

Many high-end sports cars, coming all the way down to the Lotus Elise and its siblings, have distinctive frontal designs that incorporate a vented bonnet for more effective cooling and aerodynamics. MG showed they were conscious of this with the 2002 announcement of the TF XPower 500 race concept, with a huge bonnet vent for redirected airflow to improve radiator efficiency and lower frontal lift.

Wind tunnel testing by the MIRA (Motor Industry Research Association) found the MGF and TF radiator sees most of the heat exchange done in the lower quarter or so of the radiator, and that on both the MGF and TF air can be seen coming out of the upper grill vents, rather than travelling in through the vents as logic would suggest.

This is why the MIRA/MG Rover TF HPD200 development car did not have these upper vents. It also featured a vented bonnet where airflow through the radiator was allowed to track upwards and out through bonnet vents, mounted towards the front of the bonnet rather than the central area where the XPower 500 vent is located. In addition this car featured several other aerodynamic appendages created directly from the wind tunnel testing, which achieved a 10 per cent reduction in overall drag (down to 0.32Cd) and, more importantly, reduced front and rear lift to zero.

MG Rover was seriously looking into this aspect towards the end. Since cars were increasingly being specified with the IMS systems in place of a spare wheel, this cleared the way for permanent modifications to the front of the car incorporating a vented bonnet that significantly helps cooling and reduces front lift, something that is not very good with the standard MGF or TF. The car shown here, photographed during a 2004 MG Rover test session in the Australian desert, features side vent 'ears' and wheel arch lip appendages

Fig. 6.39   In late 2003 the MG TF HPD200 Hybrid electric/petrol concept, jointly developed by MIRA and MG Rover, was announced. The most effective of its significant aerodynamic advances was the reconfigured radiator airflow through the bonnet, which greatly improved radiator efficiency. Note the forward positioning of the vents, based on the MIRA wind tunnel testing.

Fig. 6.40   This 2004 view, taken during tests in the Australian desert, shows that MG Rover were actively testing bonnet venting for the TF. Note that the vents have moved towards the windscreen, as on the XPower 500, and there are subtle side vent 'ears' and wheel arch 'eyebrows'.

that are all derived from the work at MIRA.

The most significant change is the vented bonnet, where airflow passing through the radiator is actively drawn upwards and through the bonnet rather than being forced under the car. Not only did this improve the radiator efficiency to a point where a significantly smaller radiator was used on the HPD200, but the lower airflow under the car reduced front end lift from more than 0.2 to zero. Lift under most cars is between zero and 0.1, so that is a notable improvement.

Incorporating such changes to an MGF or TF involves not just the process of creating bonnet vents, but also modifying the inner structure behind the radiator. Fortunately this is not as big a job as it first appears and is something of which I have direct experience.

One of the general principles that apply here is that there are both low and high air pressure areas at different points over a bonnet. There is usually a low pressure area just behind the leading edge of the bonnet: cars such as the RS and Cosworth Fords have vents in this general area through which hot

LEFT: Fig. 6.41 Matt Parker's 1998 MGF has a variation on the bonnet vent theme with the vents in the same general area as the TF HPD200.

BELOW LEFT: Fig. 6.42 The bonnet vent arrangement has been shown to significantly improve stability, especially in crosswinds. The flow of hot air from the radiator makes the vent ramps very hot after a few miles, showing significant hot airflow exiting from the radiator.

BELOW RIGHT: Fig. 6.43 Even though the bonnet vents and the modified panels behind the radiator may seem small, they provide a significant bonus.

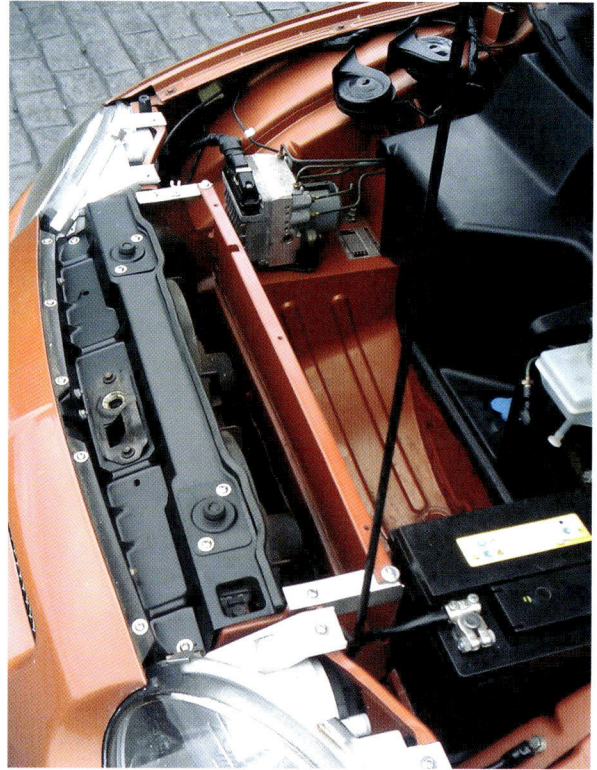

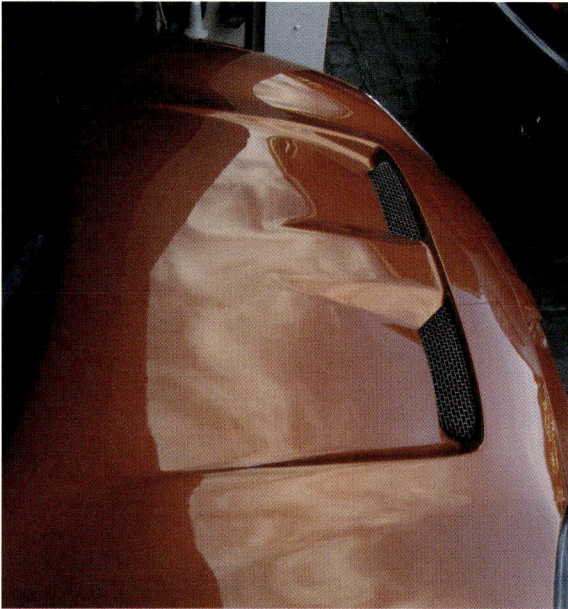

Fig. 6.44 Those wishing to take the vented bonnet to another level can use this VHS track car as a guide.

engine bay air may be drawn. As you get closer to the windscreen, which is creating a block stopping the airflow, then the air pressure increases, and this is why heater vents are located here to take advantage of the pressurized air.

This is not an exact science as the different shapes of cars create variables, but there is a low pressure point, measured approximately one to 1½ times the screen height towards the front of the car from the base of the screen, where you need to see air actively drawn out of the vents before any positive air pressure from air being forced through the radiator is considered.

Keeping panel modifications to a minimum, yet retaining a good chance of achieving positive aerodynamic changes, is actually quite simple, but part of the spare wheel well is lost. The positioning of the battery and the ABS unit (if fitted) restricts how wide simple modifications can be made to the

Fig. 6.45   The critically important bonnet substructure gets in the way of venting the bonnet.

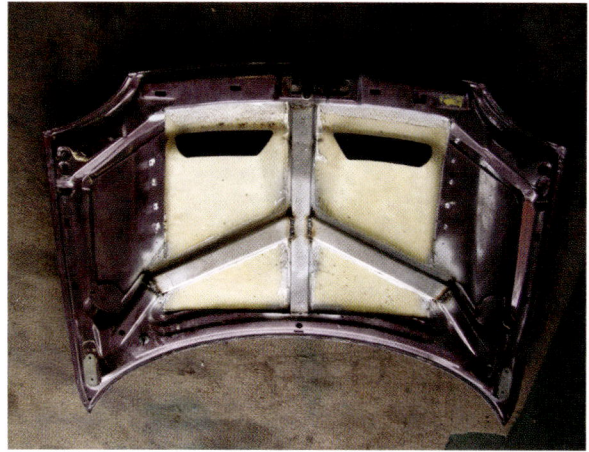

Fig. 6.46   The bonnet substructure has to be cut away to allow venting, but then the structure needs to be replaced. This test bonnet shows how replacement structure has been welded back in.

existing panels. There is scope to go much further if desired, but the VHS competition TF demonstrates that there would be no practical advantage.

Modifications started with removing the bonnet locking platform, which leaves a healthy gap for considerable airflow. Unfortunately this carries the bonnet latch, which keeps the bonnet closed, and the upper radiator mountings, so it can't be dispensed with altogether. There is considerable scope for trimming down the rear section just behind the fold line, leaving a 'letter box' gap of about 50mm for air to pass through, but this is still too small.

The battery gets in the way of increasing the size of the 'letter box' to any extent, but measuring back to the battery increases the opening by 70mm, resulting in a very reasonable 120mm. The spot welds where the spare wheel well panel joins its front side panels were drilled out, down to the level of the battery and ABS mounting trays. This allowed the spare wheel panel to be neatly bent back into a vertical position and then a couple of temporary bracing bars were made to hold it firmly in position (*see* Fig. 6.43).

The position of the 'letter box' was transposed onto the bonnet using masking tape as a marker and the venting cuts straight through the standard bonnet's reinforcement structure. At this point an MGF bonnet found on eBay, which had been roughly fitted with an 'Evo' style fibreglass aftermarket vented bonnet panel, provided a simple and low-cost means of evaluating the modification. If this confirmed the modification were viable,

Fig. 6.47   Clive Johnson commissioned professionals to manufacture a new fibreglass bonnet incorporating venting; it is also available in carbon fibre. (Clive Johnson)

another bonnet would then be made up in steel, as fixing fibreglass to steel invariably sees cracking occur later at the join. As the results were much better than expected, a steel bonnet was made up to a similar design.

A new frame had to be made up and welded in for the test bonnet, as the existing frame is the wrong shape to work with this sort of venting. In the condition as bought the bonnet had lost its supporting frame and was as limp as a piece of fresh bread, but simple new bracing returned it to a useable state. The bonnet was further finished and painted to give a completely presentable look, knowing that cracking around would probably occur. Hairline cracks did eventually show, but this was only intended as a temporary panel.

The first test drive showed an immediate improvement in stability above 50mph. This was even more noticeable on a windy day. If any confirmation of the improved cooling were needed, the lower ramp sections behind each vent were too hot to touch immediately after stopping, while the leading edge above the vent area was stone cold. This was one of those changes where no special tools were needed to prove the changes work, as they were so significant.

Quite whether further benefits can be achieved by increasing the vent size or moving the vents in the bon-

Fig. 6.48   The fibreglass bonnet has an impressive substructure. (Clive Johnson)

Fig. 6.49   Two MG types of MGF boot spoiler have been seen. The Trophy 160 shown here has two main and two small fixing feet.

Fig. 6.50   The visually similar accessory boot spoiler has just two fixings to the boot under each end of the spoiler.

Fig. 6.51   This Trophy spoiler fixing bolts through the boot into a reinforcement bracket inside. The two small outer feet each have adhesive pads to provide location and to stop paint scuffing.

net, or indeed creating a new undertray so that all air passing through the radiator has to exit via the bonnet, is an open question. The latter arrangement is currently being tried with a removable steel panel on one car. Figs 6.47 and 6.48 show an alternative complete replacement bonnet commissioned by Clive Johnson, a stalwart of the enthusiasts' website MG-Rover.org. It is fair to say that this is a subject with plenty of mileage remaining.

Rear Spoilers

At the rear the TF has a subtly reshaped boot lid compared to the MGF, incorporating a kicked-up central section that was part of a package to assist the extraction of hot air from the engine bay vents behind the hood, and also to reduce rear lift slightly. The main advantage in my view, however, is the standard LED high-level brake light, which is so much more responsive than the bulb unit on the MGF.

Boot-mounted spoilers first appeared on the MGF wedgwood blue SE model, followed by the Trophy 160 SE and Freestyle models. Surprisingly each model's spoiler was slightly different. Even though the Trophy release

information indicated that the rear spoiler contributed to an aerodynamic improvement along with the front splitter, it is safer to see the changes at the front as effective improvements, but the rear spoiler as simply a cosmetic item. The TF didn't feature any additional rear spoiler and MGF spoilers do not fit with the ideal mounting angle because of the slope on the reshaped boot lid.

In practical terms the added weight of the rear spoiler often causes the boot to close prematurely, which can be painful if your head gets in the way! The other aspect is that the left side

end of the spoiler will usually make contact with the aerial when the boot is fully opened and over time that will mark the paint.

Body Kits

Stephen Palmer was an MG dealer in the first period of MGF production (unfortunately no longer in business) who recognized that there was a clear demand for more than the standard MGFs. The SP Cheetah model they developed incorporated a full body kit and other modifications including a supercharger conversion for the

Fig. 6.52   Body kits come in various shapes and forms. One of the most widely accepted has been the Stephen Palmer (SP) Cheetah, which featured a supercharged engine.

Fig. 6.62   *The larger four-pot caliper had a much bigger clamping surface.*

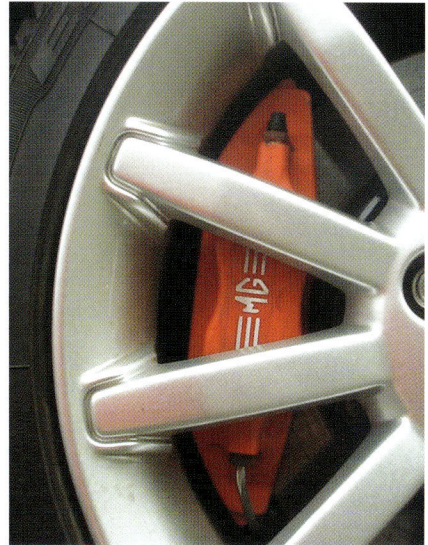

Fig. 6.63   *This car's performance demands high-profile, high-performance braking.*

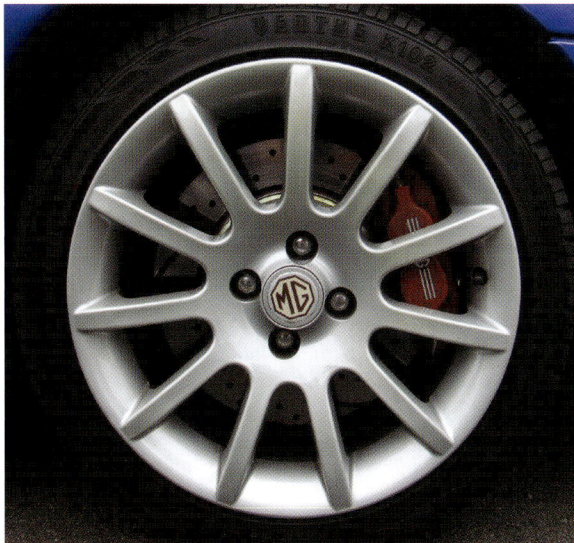

Fig. 6.64   *MG standard wheels designed to accommodate the AP Racing 304mm discs and calipers start with the Trophy 160 11-spoke wheels.*

Fig. 6.65   *The MG TF 160 11-spoke wheels are visually similar.*

Fig. 6.66   *Optional 11-spoke Ultra Lightweight wheels.*

contact area and clamping load on the front surprisingly doesn't upset the front-to-rear brake balance as long as the correct tyres are used and the suspension is in good order. It does certainly push the balance closer to the edge of acceptable limits and over time, and with degradation within the car, some balance issues will eventually develop.

Conversion of any MGF or TF to take the AP Racing brakes is a straight replacement. One big fly in this process is that you really need the specific 16in wheel designs that provide clearance for the AP Racing calipers, and in most cases this adds considerably to the conversion costs. It is not impossible to fit behind other 16in standard wheels as I have seen, but clearances are tight even with a spacer, which adds stress to wheel bearings, so I do not recommend them, only the wheels originally designed to accommodate the AP Racing brakes and shown in the accompanying photographs.

In 2005 there was a planned change of TF 160 brakes to move from the four-piston caliper to a two-piston caliper. The last TF brochure produced by MG Rover shows this in both a full-page image and the specifications pages, where it

Fig. 6.67   The MG Motor period 16in V spoke wheels should not be confused with the MG Rover period 15in V spoke.

Fig. 6.68   The TF 85th Anniversary wheel comes in two rim widths, 6.5in for the front and 7.5in for the rear.

Fig. 6.69   The company went into administration just before an MG Rover planned change to the MG TF brakes to a common 304mm disc with a two-pot AP Racing brake calliper. This would have been a huge boost for mainstream models, but a slightly backward step for the 160 and other cars that would have taken up the Sportpack 2 option.

Fig. 6.70   Cars are seldom driven in a manner that uses brake performance to anywhere near its full extent, so most drivers would not have noticed if MG Rover has discontinued the four-pot caliper and introduced the two-pot.

states 'Uprated MG/AP Racing derived 304mm front discs and red two piston calipers'. Some of these calipers were found fitted to cars subsequently sold by the Administrators and so it is useful for those facing the difficulty of replacing pads, which are substantially smaller than the four-pot caliper pads, to know that AP Racing pads under the CP7700-11 part number are an original option; in addition, Mintex MDB 1890 pads, which were common to front use on the early Lotus Elise and Exige, are essentially the same pad. The restriction regarding the need for specific 16in wheels to clear the bulkier caliper applies to the two-piston calipers as much as it does to the four-piston calipers.

When using bigger brakes with larger discs there is a greater mass to absorb heat and a greater surface area for heat to be dissipated, so as long as there is adequate airflow around the discs there is less need for different pad materials with higher temperature ceilings. This means that it is actually easier to glaze these discs than the smaller ones, especially if you change to a more 'sporting' pad.

Fitting stainless steel braided hoses to these AP Racing calipers can show up an important safety issue when the original caliper banjo bolt is carried over, as it may not fully clamp the banjo even though the bolt is tight. The issue is a combination that the new banjo thickness is approximately 1.75mm thinner than the original brake hose banjo, while the depth of the threaded section in the caliper to receive the banjo bolt is an average of 3.5mm

shallower than the original caliper. The part number for the banjo bolt has changed twice during the MGF and TF production period. Although I have not been able to confirm this, I suspect these have different bolt lengths.

Before fitting, screw the banjo bolt fully into the AP Racing caliper and measure the clearance between the underside of the bolt head and the caliper body. Then check that the combined thickness of the banjo and the two copper washers is ideally 2mm or more, so that even with compression of the copper washers a safe fluid seal will always be maintained. When a problem is found the simplest solution is to shorten the banjo bolts by the shortfall to include that 2mm additional leeway. I do not recommend doubling up on the original copper washers.

Fig. 6.71   Replacing original hoses with one of the stainless steel braided hose conversions is not a problem with original slider calipers.

Fig. 6.72   With the AP Racing calipers, however, the banjo bolt can bottom out in the caliper thread before fully clamping the banjo. Check that the depth the banjo bolt screws into the caliper is clearly greater than the banjo and the two copper washers.

Rear Brakes

The rear brakes of MGF and TF have 240mm diameter solid discs and the caliper is sourced from the Rover 800. Because of the extra rear weight they do more work than the average FWD car. They are, however, no less prone to rusting or seizing up than other cars' brakes, but not immune.

Uprating the rear pads in the same way as the front has slightly more benefit with the MGF and TF because the rear brakes are working harder. When retaining standard 240mm discs front and rear, however, do keep a balance between the material types, which normally means that if first-stage uprated materials are used up front, then the rears should normally stay standard. Go up to a second-level specification at the front and you may then have to uprate the rears to be one notch below the fronts to keep a balance. Where the car has been modified and carries a 280mm front disc conversion and 240mm rear standard discs, you have a little more leeway to have a more aggressive rear pad material if needed, although in fairness it should not be an issue with this combination.

When the significantly bigger 304mm front discs and more effective calipers are used with the now puny 240mm rear discs, there is much more scope for the rear brake size to be increased and the standard calipers spaced out. This will return a degree of balance commensurate with the original car's 240mm front and rear. For comparison the race cars had a 310mm front and 295mm rear configuration.

The 266mm rear disc conversion by Vehicle Handling Solutions is a good example that follows the proven principles of spaced original calipers, as used in the 280mm front conversion that I found so successful. Using a mainstream car's brake disc and converting it means there should always be a good supply of replacement discs and the machining needed to convert to the MGF and TF hub is minimal.

It should be noted that the standard MG disc centres do not sit on the centre spigot bore of the hub and rely on the two locating screws and the wheel stud holes for accurate location on the hub. The clamping forces then used to hold the wheel on are enough to make a long-term secure fitting. If a modified disc has the original stud holes elongated to allow for the MGF's

Fig. 6.73   The MGF Cup and subsequent race cars converted to the TF look used 310mm front discs with much bigger four-pot AP Racing calipers up front.

Fig. 6.74   The 295mm rear discs with two-pot AP Racing calipers are not dissimilar to what was to appear as the 2006 model year TF front brakes, and were also used on the rear of the ZT 260 and the front of the Lotus Elise.

small PCD, then additional central locating rings will be needed to ensure accurate location of the disc to hub, but if the new MGF PCD holes are drilled cleanly a few degrees around from the original holes, along with new screw location holes, then there is no need for a locating ring.

266mm rear discs are a very good balance to the 304mm front brakes. While the car hasn't exhibited any imbalance with the 304mm and 240mm brake combination, 304mm and 266mm is a better balance and will mean not only better braking but less likelihood that the imbalance of the original set-up will manifest itself under harsh braking. I have mentioned VHS's conversion as there is more than a degree of motor manufacturers' quality about their depth of development and their knowledge of MG and Rover cars is second to none, but I am also aware that other companies' conversions continue to appear in what is a growing market.

Suspension

This is one area where the MGF and TF differ so considerably they have to be dealt with separately.

MGF Suspension Changes

Suspension performance doesn't just come from springs, dampers and similar parts we associate with suspension. The actual frame that the suspension bolts onto has a very substantial input

too. The stiffer and more rigid the body of the car, then the more effective suspension operation will be. That is why most will find the TF, the body of which is approximately 20 per cent stiffer than the MGF, a more responsive car at speed.

By the standards of the day the MGF was commendably stiff for a roadster and in manufacturer speak was measured at 7,100Nm per degree. That was better than the competition back in the mid-1990s, but as time passed so the stiffness of cars increased. The MG TF improvements I mentioned in Chapter 2 is where that 20 per cent improvement came from, reaching about 8,500 Nm/degree. To put this in perspective, however, the Rover 75/MG ZT is notably stiffer than many other cars and the level of 24,000Nm/degree that it achieves is immediately apparent when compared to an MGF or MG TF.

This does not mean that the MGF and TF are lost causes as numbers do not always reflect the driving experience. Much of the 20 per cent improvement between the MGF and TF comes from three sets of bracing bars that can be retrofitted to the MGF. First, a cross tube arrangement is fitted from corner to corner of the front subframe, with a central crossover bolt point up to a new bracket on the base of the spare wheel well (*see* Figs 2.121–2.123). Second, a smaller cross tube brace, behind the centre console, fits between the substantial tubular cross brace and the gear change tunnel: this replaces a

rather feeble pressed steel plate. Third, a pair of tubular bars run from the centre of the engine bay/boot bulkhead, forwards and outwards to an anchor point at the side of the engine bay cover.

Sourcing these from a TF is perfectly feasible, but unless you are able to remove them yourself you will not have the opportunity to carefully remove the mounting brackets, which are welded to various parts of the body and are not standard spare parts. The simplest solution to this is to buy the complete kit of bars and fixings from Vehicle Handling Solutions.

There are three fixing points that ideally need to be welded to the body and front subframe. While you can perhaps avoid the latter, and I can show a way of bolting the rear bar's anchor bracket, the brackets behind the centre console bracket on the main cross tube are difficult to fit and welding can't be avoided. Then there is the need for reinforcement plates to be fitted to the lower gear change tunnel, all of which are covered in the VHS kit.

The front subframe involves fitting the crossbar to two existing subframe mounting bolt positions. This then provides positioning to identify where the two front holes for the front bolt mountings should be drilled. The cross brace can then be fitted and ideally the anchor welded to the lower rear corner of the spare wheel.

The rear bracing bars have a single common mounting bracket on the

LEFT: Fig. 6.75   The flat, slightly A-shaped plate in this MGF is to be replaced by the TF's more substantial, tubular steel A-shaped plate to add structural rigidity.

BELOW: Fig. 6.76   The TF 'A' brace needs these dedicated fixing points.

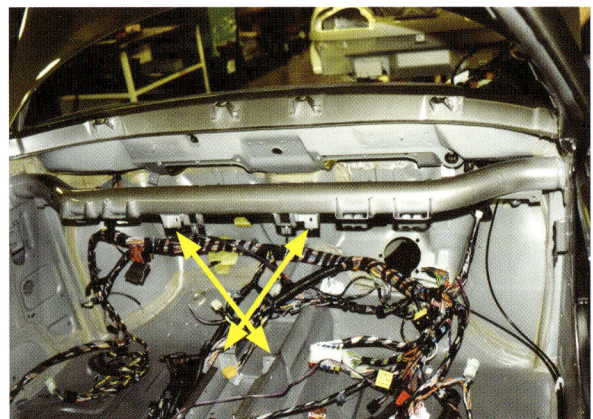

Fig. 6.77   The front subframe cross brace (indicated) fixing to the bottom of the spare wheel well.

the same dampers were used on mainstream and Trophy models. The standard set-up is biased towards a compliant ride and the Trophy was most definitely focused towards a firm track day type of use. If they can be found, fitting Trophy displacers on a standard MGF will not only make the ride quite considerably firmer, it will also sit at the 20mm lower ride height of the Trophy, as the piston rod length in the Trophy displacer is shorter.

Many owners have lowered the ride heights ever since the MGF arrived. In standard form the relatively high ride

engine bay to boot bulkhead. Ideally this is welded, but a reasonable alternative is to bolt it up. Since the bulkhead is actually double-skinned, however, bolting through without a distance tube between the two panels would crush them and would not be secure. The way around this is to mark where the bracket needs to fit on the engine bay side and then transpose where the bolt holes need to go to the boot side.

Drill through for the two fixing bolts and then increase the hole size on the boot side to 20mm. That gives more than enough access room to pass a bolt and socket through to allow two bolts with nuts to securely hold the bracket against the engine bay side of the bulkhead. Paint the exposed metal edges to deter rust and then insert a couple of 20mm rubber bungs to fill the holes and give a neat look.

Hydragas

The MGF uses the Hydragas suspension system. When in good condition and set up properly this can provide a class-leading ride and handling compromise. The problem is that all cars are now more than ten years old and new Hydragas displacers are no longer available, other than when old stocks are discovered. Modification of this suspension system remains viable, however, so long as you are able to maintain a matched set of displacers as the core of your suspension.

The MGF in standard form used different specification displacers at the front and rear because of the different weights being carried at each end of the car. This was also seen in different spec dampers used between front and rear, although it needs to be noted that

Fig. 6.80   Hydragas displacer pistons have different shapes to suit the different applications.

Fig. 6.81   The piston of the standard MGF displacer (left) has a very different appearancxe to the Trophy displacer (right), even before internal differences are considered.

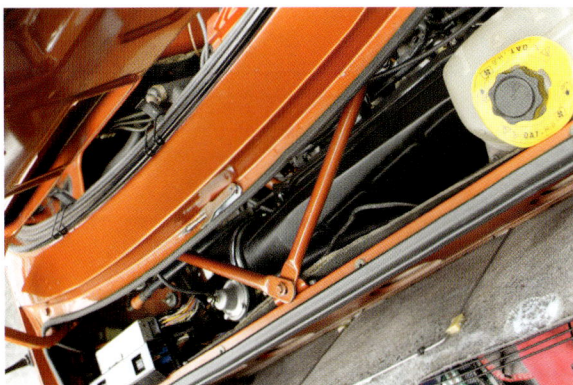

Fig. 6.78   The engine bay brace bar's rear bulkhead mounting bracket is welded to the bulkhead, but a reasonable alternative is to drill two holes in the bracket and bulkhead to bolt it together and dab some paint on the exposed metal.

Fig. 6.79   Since the bulkhead is double skinned, you need to drill a hole 20mm bigger on the boot side, which allows access for a socket to tighten the bolts. When all is bolted up, the holes are filled by a couple of 20mm rubber bungs and the boot carpet is replaced.

LEFT: *Fig. 6.82 An MGF must not be lowered by fluid release. This is best done using lowering knuckles that sit between the upper suspension arm and the displacer piston.*
RIGHT: *Fig. 6.83 The main pin of the knuckle (right) is replaced by the shorter (left), and this provides lowering without reducing the suspension pressure.*

height of 368/363mm (front/rear), as measured between the wheel centres and the wheel arch lip directly above, has led to remarks about the 'Freelander ride height' (an obvious reference to the Land-Rover model's ground clearance).

Lowering must only be done the professional way by shortening the distance between the displacer and the suspension top arm, not the nasty and damaging method of reducing the system's pressure by letting out some of the Hydrolastic fluid.

Fitting the shorter Trophy piston rod is a viable way to lower a standard MGF, but a much more convenient way of achieving a ride height about 30mm lower is to fit what are known as 'lowering knuckles' (officially called roller foot joints or knuckle joints). As can be clearly seen in the photographs here, the lowered versions have a shorter replacement main pin, which means you do not have to carefully calculate

the distance that would have to be cut from the piston rod. For reference, though, the MGF suspension leverage ratio is approximately 4.3 to 1, so for every 1mm reduction in the overall length between top arm and displacer you see approximately 4.3mm reduction in ride height.

My personal view has always been that the standard MGF ride height is around 10mm too high in standard form, so the 358/353mm standard heights for the mainstream TF reflects my ideal all-round level for cars in general use. The lowered height of 348/343mm for the MGF Trophy and all TFs with the lowered Sportpack 1 suspension is today a practical target, provided you bear in mind the practicalities of negotiating 'official assault courses' (speed humps). The lowering knuckles will take you a little below this, so you have to take a little more care when driving over the humps.

The Cup race cars were set at 310/305mm, which I consider far too low for practical road use, but surprisingly many road cars are not far from that either by design or lack of care and maintenance. This ride height is far too close to the suspension's bump stops and way too low to get over humps without under-body contact.

Dampers and Bushes

Using uprated dampers will sharpen the handling, but because the upper damper mounting is in the body of the car, which is not particularly strong, you do have to take care not to have a damper with very stiff settings on the bump (compression) stroke. In severe cases some body cracking has been seen around the mountings. The MGF Cup race series cars use higher rated dampers (with different harder spec displacers) and they also have three strengthening gusset plates welded

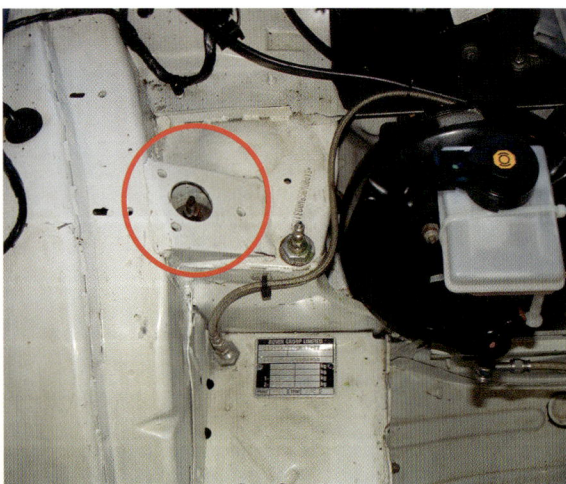

Fig. 6.84 Very stiffly set dampers on MGFs have been known to crack the upper body damper mountings. This is why Cup Race cars had welded-in plates to strengthen the front mountings (indicated).

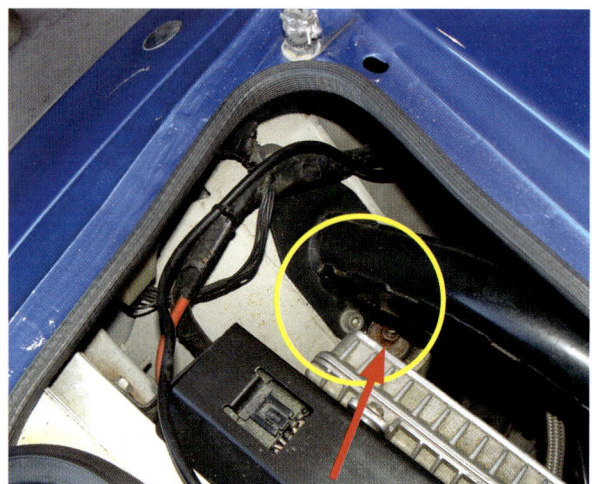

Fig. 6.85 The damper (indicated) and the whole surrounding area (circled) of the rear mountings is strengthened, not just for the damper, but also for a cross brace tube.

around the rear damper mountings to strengthen this area. Additional strengthening pieces are added at the front. What many fail to realize is that the very stiff Trophy specification comes from the displacers, as the dampers are the same as all other MGFs.

Despite this warning about body strength, the degree of damping change that can be accommodated is still more than enough to make the ride very firm. Generally owners tend to make their cars too hard riding, which is fine if you drive on millpond-smooth road surfaces, but not on more common road surfaces where the hard ride reduces tyre effectiveness.

Suspension bushes are often overlooked until the MOT man points out that there is too much play. When the car has done more than 50,000 miles, replacing all the bushes at the same time can bring immediate benefits. It takes some effort, but the improvement will be evident as soon as you take a drive.

This may take a couple of weekends to complete. The fronts especially can be time consuming, since you have to lower the rear of the front subframe from the car to remove the rear lower pivot bolts. In turn that means disconnecting the steering rack from the steering column interconnection shaft. Here it is worth mentioning that the access work to do the bushes takes you more than halfway to removing the rack. If you have thought about fitting a TF rack (2.8 turns lock to lock against the MGF 3.1), plan ahead and do both jobs together.

Replacing the bushes in the lower arms when they are removed is actually quite simple with an extractor: a home-made one can be made out of a nut, bolt, washers and a suitably sized socket and used while the arm is securely held in a bench vice.

Choose a socket big enough to fit on the end of the arm and with enough space for the bush to slide inside. A bolt long enough to pass through the bush and socket is needed and a thick flat steel washer (or two thinner) that is just smaller than the bush diameter, plus another slightly smaller one and a nut, make up the parts of the removal tool.

The bigger washer(s) are slipped onto the bolt and then the bolt is passed through the bush. The socket is held against the other end of the bush and the bolt passed through. The smaller washer and nut are then fitted onto the protruding bolt thread and tightened. Progressively this sees the bush pulled out of the arm and into the socket. The same approach, with a

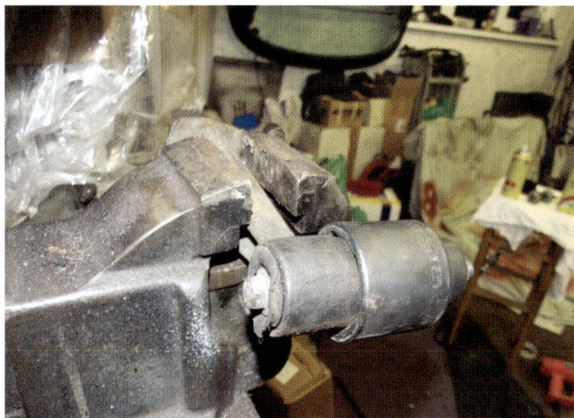

TOP LEFT: *Fig. 6.86 Lower arm bushes and rear arms can be replaced using a home-made extractor, assembled from a big socket, nut, bolt, large washers and a vice.*
TOP RIGHT: *Fig. 6.87 The home-made extractor once assembled.*
MIDDLE LEFT: *Fig. 6.88 It is a simple matter to tighten the nut.*
BELOW LEFT: *Fig. 6.89 Tightening the nut drags the bush into the socket.*
BELOW RIGHT: *Fig. 6.90 A clean and easy extraction.*

Fig. 6.91   Replacing bushes is also simple, starting here with a fully cleaned and painted arm.

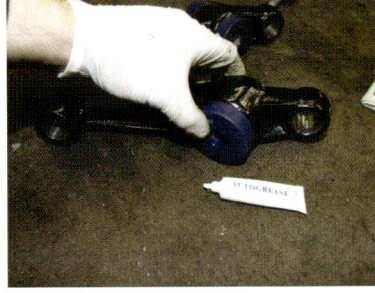

Fig. 6.92   New poly bushes are slid into place with a light coating of grease.

Fig. 6.93   The stainless steel centre tube is greased and slid just into the bush.

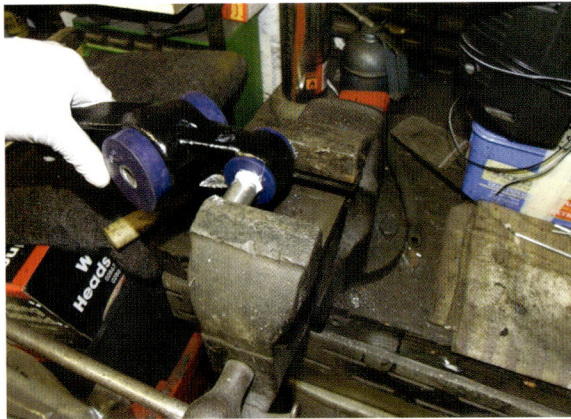

Fig. 6.94   Using a vice makes light work of pushing the tube home.

Fig. 6.95   Repeat for the remaining bushes.

little rubber lube, can be used to fit the new bushes once the arm is cleaned up.

The rear bushes are more numerous, but removing the arms is less complex than at the front. The process of removing the larger track control arm bushes is usually surprisingly the easiest and needs only gentle levering. The end bushes, however, need to be forced out and this is where that home-made tool comes into play again.

There is a choice of either the standard bushes or the widely available poly bushes, as seen being used in the accompanying photographs. In fact the Poly bushes are simpler to fit than the originals as they come in split format with a separate centre metal tube, which is simply slid into place once the two poly halves are put in place.

Before fitting new bushes, though, do take some time to use a small rotary wire brush on an electric drill to comprehensively clean any rust and bits of old bush off the arm. When fitting, don't forget to use the sachet of special grease that accompanies the new bushes. After I replaced my own MGF's bushes at around 90,000 miles with normal first stage above standard poly bushes, I was pleasantly surprised by the noticeable improvement in handling and general precision, and also more unexpectedly by the noticeable reduction in noise and harshness.

I also replaced the anti-roll bar link arms, with their integral bushes, with some alternative supplier's test ones. It was interesting to note that the state of the rubbers in the originals was much better than expected and only the outer edges had degraded. Although I

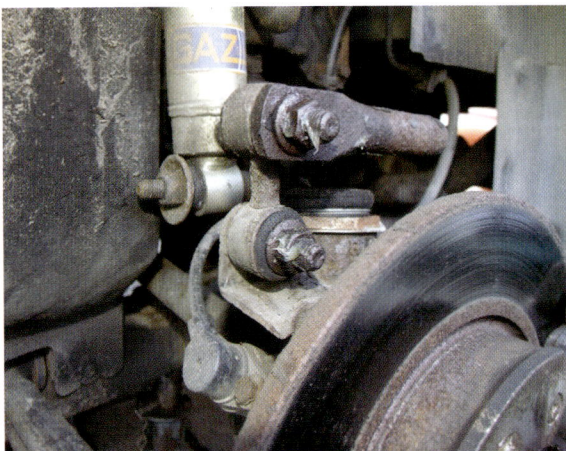

Fig. 6.96   These original anti-roll bar link arms were still serviceable.

Fig. 6.97   Anti-roll bar link arms with uprated bushes.

have seen much worse, these too need to be considered for replacement. I have also seen broken link arms, so any damage or deep corrosion is a warning to change them sooner rather than later. Uprated items for both the metal arm and poly type bushing are available from MGF specialists.

Anti-Roll Bars, TF Subframes and Suspension, Subframe Mountings

Anti-roll bar changes have not been pursued on the MGF, probably because they are found to be more than adequate as supplied. The front bars are the same configuration for both the MGF and TF. Thicker bars are found on some TFs, but there has been little interest in fitting these. For those who wish to try, however, the front experience of both the MGF Cup race cars and the 85th Anniversary TF, both using much thicker front anti-roll bars, should be considered in using uprated links and anchor points on the front lower arms. Slightly thicker bars, up to 2mm bigger in diameter, should see original links cope adequately, but thicker bars demand following the route of the 85th Anniversary TF.

Subframe bushes also have a bearing on the handling of the car, mainly because the attachment brackets holding the subframe to the car's body have two different specifications of rubber inserts on the MGF, although not the Trophy models, which introduced solid mountings with no rubber and shorter bolts to suit.

The MGF's rubber mountings were carried over from the Metro. The originals were painted black, while those fitted from VIN WD26658 were a lurid green, but they are effectively the same. There is, however, an advantage in changing these to the later Trophy 160 and TF type, usually painted light blue, which eliminated the rubber bushings and so gave the subframe a solid mounting to the body. Changing to this solid type, with shorter bolts, will give a much firmer footing for the suspension to work from and so will work better, but a little more noise and vibration will be transmitted (*see* Figs 2.114 and 2.115).

Mention of subframe mountings neatly brings us to the option of using the TF suspension if the maintenance of the Hydragas suspension becomes too acute. Such a change is viable, but requires replacing the complete front and rear subframes along with the attached TF suspension. Aside from being a very big job, in terms of what has to be removed, swapped and refitted, it is also costly in labour terms if the job is done professionally. The parts themselves are cost-effective only if using complete second-hand assemblies, ideally from a single donor car that has not been damaged.

Suplex MGF Coil Spring Conversion

I mentioned that there are no new Hydragas displacers aside from 'new old' stocks, but it also appears that the tooling has been lost. Obviously second-hand displacers will be around to support MGFs for some time to come. Some will argue that there is no problem because you can still see cars on the road belonging to the BMC and BL ranges using Hydragas and its predecessor, Hydrolastic, many years after they went out of production. However, the numbers of these survivors compared to the number made is very small. My view is that the MGF will follow the model set by the MGB and Midget and see many thousands rather than hundreds of cars surviving, which will be a much bigger proportion of the total made. This will clearly present a much stronger demand for parts and be a problem much earlier.

Suplex is a specialist company deeply involved in suspension systems, manufacturing springs and other specialists' suspension parts for a wide

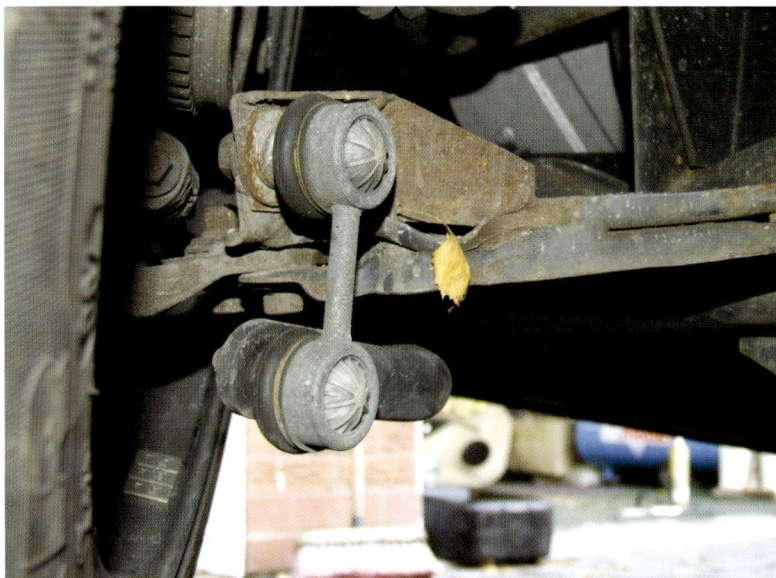

ABOVE LEFT: Fig. 6.98   The TF 85th Anniversary car has a significantly uprated front anti-roll bar that demands improved versions of both the lower arm mounting and the link arm. The birch leaf comes at no extra cost!

ABOVE RIGHT: Fig. 6.99   Since new displacers are no longer made, and second-hand examples vary in condition, a simple long-term solution to keeping MGFs on the road is provided by the Suplex steel spring conversion. This is an elegantly simple design with a canister containing a very finely tuned steel coil spring and matched external damper.

range of clients from major manufacturers down. XPart (the official factory source for MG and Rover parts) is one of Suplex's customers, and they commissioned Suplex to design a solution to the MGF's problem.

What they came up with was a brilliantly simple and elegant solution, replacing the Hydragas displacer with a similar canister unit that sat in the place of the displacer and interacted with the suspension top arm in a similar way. Inside the canister was a finely tuned steel coil spring that connected to the suspension top arm via an adjustable piston.

Unfortunately, for legal reasons, XPart could not fully develop this brilliant idea and for a time it appeared that the project would stay at the prototype stage. It was at this point that I was able to encourage enough momentum through the MG Owners Club to create the favourable business case for the project to be committed to production. This partly involved gaining a measure of potential interest through promoting the product in *Enjoying MG*, the MGOC monthly magazine. I am proud to have assisted seeing this product to the market place as it is hugely significant for the long-term survival of the MGF.

The conversion has to negotiate several technical issues, one of which is the Hydragas displacer has both a spring and partial damper function built into its internal operation, while the Suplex kits canisters contain only a coil spring. The original external damper used with Hydragas has almost no damping action on the compression side, so was now completely unsuited to taking on the whole damping function. Under normal circumstances this would be a simple problem to overcome with a new damper setting, but as I have already mentioned, the possibility for body damage with damper settings that are too harsh creates additional considerations when configuring a new damper.

The end result sees more damping control moved to the compres-

Fig. 6.100   Detailed instructions for fitting the Suplex kit are supplied. First depressurize and remove the original displacers.

Fig. 6.101   Slide the new Suplex spring canister onto the roller foot joint pin (knuckle joint).

BOTTOM LEFT:
Fig. 6.102   Seat the canister into the subframe.

BOTTOM RIGHT:
Fig. 6.103   Refit the cover plate to secure the canister and then wind down the adjuster until resistance stops hand winding.

Fig. 6.104   Mark one of the adjuster faces to provide a reference point.

Fig. 6.105   Continue winding the adjuster with a 21mm spanner the number of turns advised in the instructions to set a preload.

Fig. 6.106   Fit the new dampers supplied with the kit, specifically making sure that the larger dished washer sits on the outside, as shown, to act as a barrier to the damper becoming loose if the bush wears. (Note washer diameters in excess of 32mm diameter have been found to be a source of contact noise, some standard washers are bigger than this.)

Fig. 6.107   Lower the car and settle the suspension by bouncing it a few times. Check and note the ride heights on all corners. Lift the car and adjust each unit on the basis that each full turn of the adjuster equates to approximately 5mm. Road test, recheck and adjust as needed. Any initial settlement may demand further adjustment later.

sion stroke, but still most damping is concentrated on the rebound to reduce body stress and provide a comfortable ride quality. This doesn't mean that the Trophy type characteristics are not going to be available as dampers with stiffer settings are under development at the time of writing, without the need for the Cup race type damper top strengthening modifications.

Fitting a Suplex conversion is very simple and a flavour of the conversion is covered in the accompanying photographs. Safety provisions mean that the original Hydragas suspension should be depressurized using the proper Hydrolastic pump as the internal fluid pressure within the suspension system is nominally 400psi, which is more than enough to cause injury to eyes if the valve is pressed and a stream of fluid hits you in the face.

The experience of using one of these systems on my MGF for some 15,000 miles has been extremely positive and I intend to use this set-up permanently. This length of use has provided some insight into where a few helpful tips may be of use.

The original suspension came with a 3.6mm thick spacer washer at the rear and a 2.3mm spacer for the front. In the original instructions it was stated that these should be

Fig. 6.108   Each MGF was originally fitted with spacers, 3.6mm thick at the front and 2.3mm thick at the rear. Normally this should be removed, but if the ride height is too low with all adjustment taken up, then refit the spacer.

removed, but if the ride height remains too low after the adjuster has reached full travel, then refit the removed spacer. If this were to occur then it would be quite unusual as the adjusters should have more than enough range, unless lowered knuckles have been used. If a lowered knuckle has been used then achieving the recommended ride height should ideally be achieved by replacing the lowered knuckles with standard items.

If you have lost the spacers or there were none, they are no longer available new and you would have to make them up. If a spacer were to be required then I would only suggest that a single original of 2.3mm or 3.6mm be used, otherwise there is a likelihood of more movement between the adjuster and the knuckle pin, which has a tapered shaft. This can then generate suspension noise, especially at the front, which is undesirable. The height increase that these original spacers would deliver using the suspensions 4.3 to 1 ratio would see a ride height increase of 9.8mm and 15.4mm, respectively.

Steering Upgrades

The standard MGF steering is really very good and even with the EPAS it doesn't lose too much feedback. Some, however, will always feel too isolated and want more feedback. For those owners on track days I would suggest removing the main 40 amp EPAS fuse from under the bonnet when they feel the need to have additional feedback. This way the fuse can be replaced for all normal driving and, importantly, will allow the system to work as made and therefore pass the annual MOT, which at present does not allow non-operation of the EPAS.

The commonest MGF steering upgrade is be to replace the original MGF steering rack with one from a TF, so the turns from lock to lock come down from 3.1 to 2.8. This makes the steering slightly more responsive, but having done this change, as well as owning an MGF and TF side by side, I find the difference quite small and question the benefit of this as a stand-alone change. I see it as worthwhile only when the original rack needs to be changed.

Identifying the TF rack can be a problem as externally it is identical to the

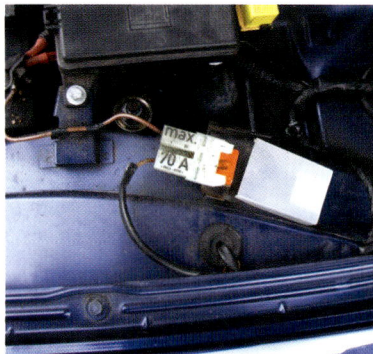

Fig. 6.109   The 40 amp fuse (in a 70 amp holder) Electric Power Assisted Steering (EPAS) main fuse for the MGF and early TF is located here.

Fig. 6.110   Later TFs have a 40amp fusible link in the under-bonnet fuse box.

Fig. 6.111   MGF and TF steering racks are usually identified by a coloured band. This rack on a TF 160 looks red/orange, but is officially red. MGF racks have yellow.

MGF and almost identical to the Rover Metro, especially if the rack has no track rod ends fitted. On paper the MGF rack has a yellow identifying band and the TF up to about 2004 had a red/orange band. The Metro, on the other hand, didn't have any identifying band and confusion set in when post-2004 TF racks didn't have one either; the same applies to new replacement racks. The Metro racks come with a 3.3 turns lock to lock for the GTi, while ordinary models are geared with 3.5 turns, so the door for unscrupulous eBay sellers is wide open!

Alternative Wheels and Tyres

Changing wheels and tyres will have more impact on steering feel and response, although many will want to fit larger diameter wheels and lower profile tyres from an aesthetic perspective. Clearly the most popular route is to go from 15in to 16in using MG wheels, which means moving from 185/55 × 15 tyres to 215/40 × 16 tyres up front, or if using the Trophy size then it will be 195/45 × 16. Aside from the critical aspects of correct tyre choice if handling balance is not to be upset (*see* Chapter 4), there are additional considerations as to the choice of front tyre.

To the casual observer it may seem somewhat odd that the MGF, with the mainstream 15in wheels, has different sized tyres front and rear, but the introduction of the 16in wheel suddenly brought in the same wider, lower-profile tyre size all round. It gets more confusing when you then see the MGF Trophy 160 SE model running with a narrower higher profile front tyre, so falling back in line with the MGF on 15in wheels. Finally, the TF compounds the use of narrower and higher profile front tyres as the mainstream models with 15in wheels follow the MGFs with 15in wheels, but now the cars with 16in wheels follow the MGF Trophy tyre route. Why did it keep changing and are there any differences when driving?

In short there are differences, not all of them good, as I found when experimenting with different wheels and tyres on my MGF some years ago. The car came with standard 15in eight-spoke alloys with the normal 185/55 × 15 tyres front and 205/50 × 15 tyres rear. It performed perfectly normally as an MGF on 15in tyres should, although my preference is for 16in rims fitted with recommended 215/40 × 16 tyres all round, so I took the opportunity to change to these using the originally recommended Goodyear Eagle F1 GSD2 tyres.

Later I obtained a spare set of TF rims fitted with the recommended 195/45 × 16 and 215/40 × 16 Goodyear tyres. As an experiment, as well as getting some use from the spare tyres before they became too old, I fitted them to the MGF and ran them for a few weeks. While the general handling stability and operation was fine, the feel at the front was different and overly sensitive, more so on damp, but not wet surfaces.

To verify that it was not an individual tyre issue, I swapped the wheels and tyres over from my TF 160 and found the same feeling, which wasn't present on the TF. Then, to confirm my findings, I went back to the 215/40 × 16 tyres on the front of the MGF and the feelings of security returned. I also tried different tyre pressures, but that improved things only slightly.

That leads me on to consider whether MGFs subjected to more comprehensive suspension changes that significantly stiffen up the car, such as the Trophy 160 models, would benefit from the narrower front tyres. The answer is vague, at least until the solid subframe mounts are also fitted, when the car will be close to the Trophy and it is possible that the 195/45 × 16 front tyre size will then come into its own.

The MGF 16in Wheel Bump Stop Question

Not everyone who may have heard about this probably knows what it is all about. It involves a modification to the front suspension displacer retaining plate that secures the displacer to the subframe, and which also carries the suspension bump stops.

When the MGF Abingdon variant arrived for the 1998 model year, one of its most interesting features was the use of new 7 × 16in alloy wheels instead of the 6 × 15in wheels previously used on all MGFs. A little-known change, associated with the larger wheels, was made to the displacer retaining plate in the form of a small additional welded plate on the lower edge, and fitted

Fig. 6.112 MGF front bump stops on the displacer retaining plate were modified when 16in wheels were used with small welded additions on the bottom edge; the standard parts (top) are plain.

only to the front of the car. These additional patches are there to reinforce the plate and slightly reduce the maximum height by which the suspension's upper arm can rise.

When this plate was introduced, cars with 16in rims were using a 215/40 R16 tyre up front that was quite significantly wider than the original 185/55 R15 tyres on all other cars. This increased the risk of tyre contact onto the wheel arch liner, a well-documented issue affecting many earlier cars. A technical bulletin issued by Rover described how to reshape the plastic liner to eliminate this problem by very carefully using a hot air gun to soften the plastic enough to mould it closer to the body (though not to melt holes in it, as too many found to their cost).

It is interesting to note that these reinforced plates were a standard fit on all cars specified with 16in wheels, although the Trophy 160 SE models introduced a narrower 195/45 × 16 tyre size that had greater clearance, offset by the fact that the suspension sat 20mm lower.

Owners who choose to replace their original 15in wheels and tyres with MG 16in wheels and tyres are faced with an awkward choice as to whether they should fit, or actually need to fit, these uprated plates? The short answer appears to be no. Many owners, myself included, have operated MGFs with

16in wheels and 215/40 tyres, without changing the plates, for ten years or more without any issues. Even in the competition environment, and specifically the MGF Cup build notes, there is no mention of changing the Hydragas retaining plates, even though the Hydragas units for this race series were changed to a different specification.

Non-MG Wheels

Aftermarket wheels occupy a huge market, but owing to the odd 95.25mm PCD of the MGF and TF there is little choice off the shelf. Many wheel manufacturers cater for this by drilling to suit the MG PCD at extra cost, while some MG specialists offer PCD conversions that allow the more common 100mm PCD wheel options to be fitted.

Style is very much an individual's choice and if the wheel dimensions stay the same as standard there will be no fitting or running issues. If the wheels are wider or offsets different, however, there is potential for tyre to body, or wheel to brake caliper contact. This also applies when cars are lowered: the wheel arch lips of MGF Cup race cars, for example, needed to be rolled flat, but then they were riding very low.

Some owners have gone to 17in diameter wheels, for which there was never any production option. The main

Fig. 6.113   *The TF GT concept used 17in diameter wheels only for aesthetic reasons, since body modifications would have been required if they were adopted for a production version of this or any other TF. (MG Rover)*

reason for this, for example the use of 17in wheels on concept cars such as the TF GT coupé, relates again to front wheel arch clearance, or the lack of it, before any lowering complicates this clearance.

Clearance between the front wheel arch liner and the standard 215/40 × 16in tyres on the MGF can be zero and this requires some careful reshaping of the liner with a hot air gun. There is clearly little scope for a bigger 17in diameter wheel that leaves less space for the tyre. The rear can also see problems with the wheel arch lip making contact with some 16in tyres, and low ride heights and the MGF Cup cars saw the rolling back of wheel arch lips as part of general body preparation.

Suggestions for 17in diameter tyres might be to use 185/40 × 17 front tyres, as these are approximately 0.4 per cent smaller in diameter than a 195/45 × 16 standard tyre, or the 195/40 × 17, which

are about 1 per cent bigger: both have a narrower tread section. Keeping the 215 profile, while maintaining the same overall diameter of a 16in tyre when going to 17in, means a 215/35 × 17 tyre, which ends up just less than 1 per cent bigger in diameter. This size would appear to be the choice to use, but occupying all the space in a wheel arch will inevitably mean that some cars will have body contact and others will not, owing to production variations.

Dynamically there are genuine question marks as to the suitability of using 17in wheels and tyres. This is essentially due to the body restrictions creating a narrow tyre choice and also demanding ultra-low profile tyres that create too much sensitivity. Overcoming these body restrictions would be a major issue with very limited benefits and so has to be seen as impractical. Certainly if 17in was a good move we would see a huge number of cars run-

ning them, but as we don't I take this as a strong indication to steer clear.

MG TF Upgrades – VHS Bilstein Comfort Handling Kit

The story of how the TF suspension arrived in the very firm state it did in 2002 is covered in Chapter 4. As it was deliberately a firm sports suspension, there is little demand for any further stiffening of the suspension, just perhaps lowering. This was catered for by the Sportpack 1 option, which reduced the ride height by 10mm to 348/343mm front/rear against 358/353mm for mainstream. While 348/343mm is the ideal lowered ride height for the reasons I mentioned above, a further drop of around 10mm is offered with aftermarket replacement springs, such as those by XPower and others, where available.

Fig. 6.114   *The TF suspension is very harsh on models made between 2002 and early 2005. The Bilstein damper conversion is specifically designed to smooth that ride without hurting the handling.*

Fig. 6.115   *As supplied, the lower spring platform of the Bilstein conversion has three positions to give three different ride heights: standard 358/353mm, Sportpack 1 348/343mm and an intermediate 353/234mm. Resetting involves just moving a circlip.*

Fig. 6.116   *In order to access the upper damper securing nut, one horn and the under-bonnet fuse box should be removed. Remember to disconnect the battery first.*

Fig. 6.117   At the rear, the engine ECU and the cooling system expansion tank are also removed for access.

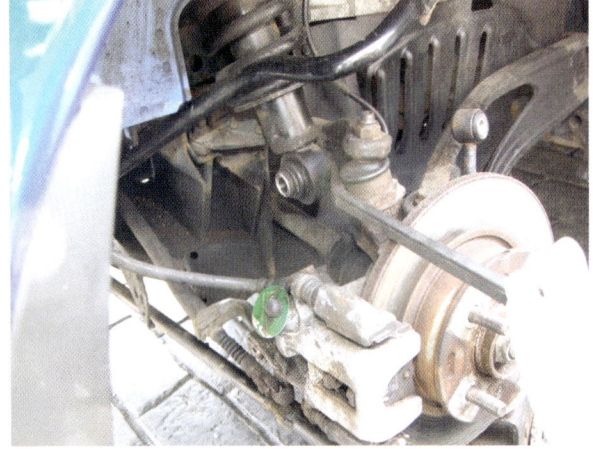

Fig. 6.118   It can often be difficult to dislodge the lower fixing of the self-contained spring/damper units as there is a small degree of an interference fit. Leverage will overcome that difficulty. Use a smear of copper grease when fitting the Bilstein dampers.

Fig. 6.119   Here the rear spring damper unit has been removed from the car, with the Bilstein replacement alongside.

Fig. 6.120   Replacement simply involves undoing the main retaining nut to release spring tension. This will be achieved before the nut is anywhere near the end of its thread, so no spring compressors are needed at the rear.

Fig. 6.121   Spring compressors, though, are most definitely needed at the front.

Fig. 6.122   All the parts are laid out before reassembly onto the new damper.

Fig. 6.123   Reassembly on the rear damper.

Fig. 6.124   Refitting to the car is a reversal of the removal. While the front is exposed, remember that the TF still has grease nipples on the upper arm pivot, so now is a good time to give them some grease.

That there was virtually no demand for any stiffening is clear, but there was always a demand for providing a more flexible ride quality, which was not answered in a production TF until the arrival of the 2005 model year cars. A significant number of components were changed in these late model cars, so using this specification was never an economically viable option.

The first purpose-designed softer suspension conversion was introduced by Vehicle Handling Solutions and the route to its development is also described in Chapter 4. Here I want to cover the fitting of one of these kits to a TF and show how simple the job actually is: the original firm specification springs are retained, yet the damper changes make a big difference to the ride quality (*see* Figs 6.114 to 6.124).

The route followed is the same as that for replacing the standard dampers, as covered in the workshop manual, although I found that spring compressors were only needed for the front dampers. In my experience the rear dampers' spring retaining plate locknut could be wound out sufficiently that the spring was fully free before the nut reached the end of its thread. This may not be the case on all cars, however, so it is safer to ensure that if the spring has not fully released before the nut has reached the end of the thread, you should then fit the compressors.

One of the extra features of the VHS suspension conversion is that the lower spring platform, which dictates ride height, has three adjustable positions: the standard mainstream TF ride height of 358/353mm, the Sportpack 1 lowered ride height of 348/343mm, and also a halfway house at 353/348mm. The dampers come with the platform set at the higher 358/353mm position, the top of the three circlip grooves, and setting to a lower height is simply achieved by moving the platform up out of the way while locating the circlip into the desired lower position. All units should be set at the same ride height.

MG TF 85th Anniversary Suspension

It is significant that the VHS Comfort kit became a core element of the MG Motor 85th Anniversary cars' suspension upgrade, which achieved what I consider to be the ultimate TF

suspension specification for road use. The Bilstein dampers were very slightly modified for use in this production format with the softer 2005 model year on springs, standard on all MG Motor TFs, and, to offset the softer overall setup, the front anti-roll bar was made a whopping 4mm thicker, from 21mm to 25mm, and the rear by 2mm from 18mm to 20mm.

With the big increase in diameter at the front comes a huge increase in the forces that are being transmitted. The original MGF/TF links and attachment points on the lower arms are quite simply too weedy for the job and so new ball joint links and seriously uprated anchor brackets on the lower arm accompany the new anti-roll bars. I mention these additional changes in case anyone comes across an 85th front bar and wants to fit it to their TF (or MGF), since uprated parts are needed to stop the forces ripping out the fixing point or breaking the link (*see* Fig. 6.98).

The use of the Bilstein dampers with the softer springs from 2005 on cars also shows a further route to achieve an even more comfortable ride from a 2002 to 2005 TF. The result should be a match for the brilliant ride quality of the 85th Anniversary cars, but the handling will suffer slightly as there will be more body roll. This is exactly why the 85th cars had the significant increase in anti-roll bar thickness, to counter the increased roll and retain the same degree of handling.

There are other softer riding suspension conversions that change both springs and dampers and owners report a very useful improvement in the ride quality of their cars. Having no direct experience of these, or any other information to provide any accurate comparison with the Bilstein conversion, all I can say is that these offer a price advantage.

Suspension Bushes

The considerations surrounding TF suspension bushes can be seen as exactly the same as for the MGF at the front and so the same use of poly bushes is recommended. At the rear the TF has a much better-located suspension and generally less compliant materials to degrade. This means there is less scope

for the poly bush treatment to deliver the really big gains that are found on the MGF.

The availability of replacement poly bushes for trailing arm front and lower rear bushes, however, along with the long lower rear link arm inner bushes, is a bonus as otherwise it means you need to buy a new arm if considering standard parts. In cost terms many owners feel that, at just over £200, the poly bush set for the TF rear is expensive for the relatively few parts supplied, although to put this in perspective, replacing the affected parts with standard units, not including the cast trailing arm, would cost just short of £400. Additionally the poly bush kit gives you the bonus of the lower rear trailing arm bushes: if these bushes are worn, factory replacements would need two new trailing arms at a cost of £345. (All of these prices are at 2011 rates without VAT.) Note that the 85th Anniversary cars' trailing arms have an uprated bush that is not available separately.

SIMPLE ENGINE UPGRADES

Powertrain in this context means the engine and transmission. This is where most interest will lie, but as I mentioned earlier, 'Safety Fast' means making sure the car can cope with any increases in performance at least as well as the standard car copes with its performance, but ideally better.

I will split engine modifications into two, the relatively simple bolt-on changes and then the more comprehensive changes. It will not be an all-encompassing resumé of all that can be done, but cover most of the common routes to engine improvement intended for a road environment. One other major consideration I always apply to engine modifications is that reliability should not be adversely affected: if it is then the loss should be very small indeed.

How far an owner wants to move away from a fully road-competent specification is an individual's choice, but bear in mind the K series engine is a favourite for Caterham and Lotus cars. Very importantly, what may be acceptable in a Caterham or Lotus will possibly not be suitable for an MGF or TF, for the simple reason that the MGs are steel bodied and heavy in comparison.

Fig. 6.131 The alloy inlet is much heavier than the plastic. There are two extra mounting bolts to the head and a steady bar between the lower engine block and the underside of the manifold. This may be seen when the cylinder head is removed.

the plastic one. This is fitted to a cast-in attachment in the underside of the number one inlet tract of the lower half of the inlet, which then is attached to a lower block threaded boss via a steel bracing bar. This triangulates the fitting of the inlet and is designed to prevent the weight of the inlet and any harsh road shocks causing the manifold to break off at the mounting lugs where the manifold is bolted to the cylinder head.

Another little-known difference is the fuel return pipe that runs under the inlet on both plastic and alloy manifolds. The route and fixings are different and so the return pipe is different as well. More obviously different are the fixings used to secure it to the head: these changed from predominantly nuts and studs to flange bolts, something that can be inconvenient, which you find out only during the job.

Other detail differences depend on the age of the car and the replacement inlet. Serious issues can occur in respect of engine sensors. MEMS 1.9 and 2J (up to and including 2000) have separate MAP and inlet air temperature sensors compared with the MEMS 3 from 2001. The air temperature sensor for the earlier systems is the green one that sits in the number four inlet tract. If using a MEMS 3 alloy inlet, you will usually not see a sensor position as by then both MAP and air temp sensing functions were in a combined sensor on the inlet. You can use an earlier manifold on a later engine by drilling out the MAP sensor hole to take the later sensor, but it is difficult to seal the earlier, smaller sensor when going the opposite way (*see* Figs 4.203–4.208).

When it comes to fitting it is really a matter of removing the old and fitting the new with the additional parts I mentioned above, but other differences can then arise. An air leak between the new inlet manifold and cylinder head's manifold face, for example, can be due to slight differences in dimensions between those of the alloy inlet port and flange and those for the cylinder head.

The VVC head has an inlet port approximately 3mm bigger than the non-VVC engine and the inlet manifold bore matches the VVC head port. Therefore when fitting any of the alloy inlets you have a larger port on the manifold meeting a smaller port on the head. The problem comes from the fact that the VVC alloy inlet manifold gasket matches the bigger ports and so there is less surface contact between the manifold and head, meaning less gasket seal. In some cases this can be thin enough to leak air: perhaps not immediately, but one that develops over time.

TF 135 essentially faces this problem as it uses the VVC alloy inlet on a standard MPi head casting. The leakage issues that appeared on some MPi engines converted to take the alloy inlet do not seem to have affected the TF 135. As far as I am aware the dimensions have not changed, so making it less prone to leaks, and it may be an issue with some non-original inlet gaskets.

There is another possible solution to any problem with the standard VVC inlet gasket. The gasket used on the earlier MEMS 1.6 equipped Rover 214/414 and Metro GTi original MPi engines between 1992 and 1994 used a different alloy inlet manifold. The main difference between the two gaskets is that the port holes on the earlier gasket are clearly smaller than the VVC gasket. Since the head ports are the smaller size, the early gasket can give a better seal between inlet and head without the gasket interfering with airflow.

Fig. 6.133 When the same gasket is fitted on an MPi head (what the TF 135 sees), the smaller port shows clearly. There is potential for air leaks with less accurate or incorrect gaskets.

Fig. 6.134 The earlier alloy inlet used on the first K series MPi engines has smaller ports. The sooty residues on the overlapping sections clearly show that the fit is not perfect.

Fig. 6.132 Inlet gaskets can cause problems when fitting an alloy inlet to an MPi head, due to port size differences. A VVC inlet gasket here shows a reasonable match to the VVC inlet.

It should be noted that the blue injectors used on the TF 135 are the VVC injectors, which flow about 9.5 per cent more fuel than the MEMS 3 MPI black injectors, and are different again to the earlier MEMS 1.9 and 2J system injectors. The bottom line here is to use the injector specification applicable to the car if you are to get fully correct running, as fuel rails and injectors are all interchangeable (*see* Figs 4.215–4.218).

Other detail differences include a potential excess or shortage of vacuum take off points on the plenum. An early TF plenum, for example, has an extra take off, which is ideal if fitting to a pre-2001 MEMS 1.9 car as the MAP sensor is in the ECU and you need the extra take off for the vac line. If you do not have the extra vac take off, however, get a windscreen washer Tee piece and break into the vac take off that goes to the fuel pressure regulator. Last, you need to use a different spacer and the alternative hole on the dipstick/oil filler assembly anchor to the inlet.

Exhaust System Upgrades

This is probably the most popular area for modification, although also one of the less productive in terms of power gains for the MGF and TF, as I shall explain later. There is a huge range of alternative stainless steel exhaust systems offering quite a range of sounds, from those that are only slightly louder than the rather restrained standard sounding systems, to frankly unsociable sound levels, such as the SP system I had on my first MGF and which I dissected after removal. The standard systems offer an impressive longevity – more than ten years is not uncommon – so many cars may still be found with them.

When it comes to looking at the potential life of stainless systems, the way many are constructed without the need for internal wadding means the life of a replacement stainless system for an MGF or TF could literally be for the life of the car. Much of the long life comes from the fact that the engine is towards the rear of the car, leaving quite short pipe runs to the tailpipe. The systems run hotter and there is less internal condensation and less acidic water vapour. As a result the systems run dryer for longer.

The exhaust system is made up of three major sections: the manifold and downpipe; the catalyst; and the silencer and tailpipes. The latter two are mounted across the car under the boot area to make the most of the little space available. The commonest part needing replacement is the silencer and integral tailpipes. On paper this is a relatively simple change as the various sections of the exhaust are bolted together with flange joints. The reality, though, is that most cars will be a few years old and the flange nuts and studs

Fig. 6.137   The lumps on this exhaust flange are typical of the way exhaust system nuts and studs corrode in a relatively short time.

Fig. 6.138   Corrosion can be significantly reduced by using 'cat saver' (tube) nuts, which are less susceptible to corrosion and also seal the vulnerable stud inside the tube nut.

will have corroded much faster than the rest of the system.

For many years special stainless steel tube nuts have been available from many MGF specialists under the title of 'Cat Saver Nuts'. Every MGF or TF owner should buy a set of six and replace the standard original nuts while they are in a good enough condition to save. This is irrespective of whether they intend to replace their exhaust or not: the bonus this gives of not having to struggle cutting off and replacing severely corroded nuts and studs when there is a need to remove the exhaust or catalyst in the future is priceless.

After the sound aspects, most will be interested in whether they will see any power gains from changing the rear silencer and tail pipes. Experiments over the years, including two full days spent testing different exhaust systems with a group of enthusiastic owners, have brought me to some quite clear

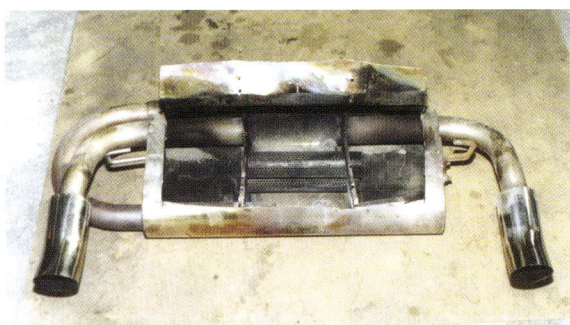

Fig. 6.135   A late 1990s SP DTM style stainless steel exhaust system for the MGF. This largely empty chamber shows why the noise levels were too anti-social early in the morning.

Fig. 6.136   Noise levels are inevitably high especially so with smaller silencer volumes with similar stainless systems.

Fig. 6.139 The MGF Cup race car exhaust used just the right-hand tailpipe and the left was cosmetic, held in place by being welded to the main exhaust pipe. The main pipe remained sealed.

conclusions. The first is that when comparing components in similar condition, such as a new standard system against a new aftermarket one, there will be relatively little difference in power outputs when the cars' engines are producing less than approximately 180bhp.

The maximum gain I have seen is 6bhp and the average gain for most is about 4bhp, which is too small to make any discernible difference to the way the car operates. You may feel the car is sharper and the increased noise level often creates a perception of the car going faster, but unless the old silencer was becoming congested or collapsing internally, those feelings of improvement are usually misleading.

Tailpipe designs on the original cars are oval for MGF and round for TF. Replacement systems, though, come in many different bores, shapes and sizes, paired and quads. In power terms these variations make little difference, only really affecting the sound that the systems produce: the MGF Cup race cars, for example, had only a single working tailpipe on the right side, while the left side tailpipe was purely cosmetic.

One change I had to do with my first MGF followed a series of engine modifications that involved comprehensive head mods. The result was an engine that was so smooth that you could balance the proverbial coin on its edge on the idling engine. One aspect of this with the standard exhaust was that you couldn't hear the engine in noisy traffic. Rattling trucks and buses actually made it more difficult to judge rpms for things like hill starts. As a result I fitted a Janspeed exhaust, which made sufficient noise to overcome the traffic problem but was not so noisy that it was unsociable when starting for work at 5 a.m.

Catalysts

Moving forward from the silencer we reach the catalytic convertor (cat) mounted across the car in front of the silencer. In most countries this is a wholly necessary component if a car is to meet minimum legislative standards, both in terms of meeting specific tailpipe emissions and actually having a cat present. In the UK, for example, from 1 January 2012 the annual MOT test requires that, if a car was manufactured with a cat, this should be present irrespective of whether it is able to meet the emission requirements.

MGFs up to the 2001 model year use a common pattern of cat with a mounting flange at either end. MGFs from 2001 on and all MG TFs have a different configuration in which the flange on the outlet side is moved halfway towards the silencer, meaning that it now has an extended exit pipe with a 90 degree bend. This extended exit pipe allows for the fitting of a second (after cat) lambda (oxygen) sensor, which monitors the efficiency of the cat and engine management to ensure that the composition of the exhaust gas is within required limits. It follows that the differences in cat fitting arrangement also means there are two different configurations for the silencer to match the different flange positions.

Just as with the exhaust silencers, I spent a day at a rolling road getting dirty and checking the efficiency of my welding gloves swapping a range of different cats – standard, sports and aftermarket generic, along with cat replacement pipes – on two test cars, an MGF 1.8i and a VVC. These tests and others since have demonstrated that, if in good working order, the standard cat is clearly not restrictive where the engines are producing under approximately 180bhp.

The test results make disappointing reading for anyone wanting to claim big bhp gains from cat removal. On one car there was actually a small power drop of up to 5bhp, which is not enough to make any real impact on the car's performance, but it is the same level of gain that comes from the best replacement silencer, so at a stroke that particular car would see any gain from a silencer change wiped out by a cat bypass pipe. The cat bypass pipe, of course, would result in emissions outside the UK MOT levels and the missing cat would attract an immediate fail anyway.

Fig. 6.140 The catalyst here is a 2001 and later configuration with a second lambda sensor fitted.

Fig. 6.141 Here it is possible to see the cat's orientation to the silencer. The wire leading off is from the second lambda sensor.

Fig. 6.142   The core of passages inside the cat are coated in the catalytic material. In standard cats the passages are small to ensure a very large surface area for exhaust gas contact.

Fig. 6.143   'Sports cats' tend to have more open passages to offer less restriction to exhaust gas flow.

My reference to standard cats being non-restrictive on engines below 180bhp comes from additional testing where the engines have produced between 180 and 225bhp and demonstrated the benefits of using a sports cat. I think it is a simple reflection that the standard cat's exhaust gas flow limit is reached at about 180bhp, and the more open structure of a sports cat is able to flow more gas, while maintaining the legal requirements.

Downpipes

Next along the exhaust trail is the downpipe that runs between the manifold flange and cat entry flange. It is found with a four-stud fixing to the manifold for cars up to 2001 and a six-stud fixing on cars from 2001.

The standard MG downpipe is actually about as good as it can be, while some aftermarket replacements are of a frankly dreadful quality and impinge on the basic running of the engine. This is more so on the 2001-on applications that carry the upstream lambda sensor, owing to terrible quality control during manufacture.

The threaded boss that the lambda screws into has to be welded over a predrilled hole in the pipe. While mistakes can be made and the boss welded offset to the hole, it is inexcusable for such an obvious and basic error to pass a quality inspection – but they do, and often. The problems are then compounded by fitters who, when finding the sensor doesn't screw in properly, simply resort to brute force and in doing so crush the sensor end. I have

no issue with aftermarket pipes as long as they are accurately manufactured.

Exhaust Manifolds

Moving up to the manifold, both early and late styles are of a tubular steel design with, interestingly, internal welding of the various joints. On the early four-stud pre-2001 type, specifically, it is quite common to see lumpy welding that often noticeably restricts the available port space. While this is untidy, it was not until I saw that the MGF Cup race cars use the same manifold, but with the welds on the outer edges, meaning the inner port areas are completely clean and free of obstruction, that I decided to experiment.

I took a spare manifold and welded the joins on the outside, and then spent a considerable time grinding out the internal weld to mimic the race car manifolds. I then fitted one to a Rover 200 BRM, on the assumption that the more powerful engine would produce more exhaust volume and so any restriction in the exhaust would show up more.

Nothing of consequence came from these labours, which was a little disappointing, but the poor results became more understandable after testing a car to which I fitted a Janspeed exhaust manifold. There was however one clear difference during the maximum power runs and that was the colour difference in the manifold. With the standard manifold the manifold pipes were glowing bright red/orange from the heat within them. With the modified manifold the pipes barely reached a deep red, so

Fig. 6.144   On MGF Cup race cars the pipe joins on the outside of the manifold flanges are welded as in this DIY example.

Fig. 6.145   When the inner welds are ground out, the passage is opened up quite noticeably. The expected gains, however, were not seen, although a reduction from a bright red exhaust under full load on the rolling road to a deep cherry red indicated that less heat was being retained.

Fig. 6.146   Replacing the standard exhaust manifold and downpipe on this 2000 VVC with a Janspeed replacement resulted in only half of the 10 per cent gains seen on FWD K series cars.

170bhp, so the Janspeed manifold had achieved just 5bhp.

The reason the MGF manifold delivered less than half of what is normally seen on FWD cars with the same engine and the same supplier's manifold was clearly down to the fact that there is insufficient space to fit a decent secondary pipe length. Experience of many FWD K series cars has reinforced this conclusion, based on the power and torque benefits that come from designs with long secondary pipe lengths, and nothing has since contradicted these findings.

Heat Insulation

clearly there was less restriction as the heat was escaping more efficiently. With heat on the exhaust side being an issue influencing head gasket failure, this greater heat movement would have long-term reliability benefits.

I have mentioned fitting a Janspeed manifold on another car, replacing the whole manifold and downpipe with a very smooth and beautifully made piece of equipment with four longer smooth primary pipes that are joined into two shorter pipes before the Y piece connects them to a single pipe at the flexible joint, from where there is a short run to the cat.

With the primary pipes effectively eliminating the join where the standard manifold and downpipe connect, there was no effective restriction. It was also known that on FWD cars with the K series engines, an average torque improvement of 10 per cent is usually seen with the Janspeed manifold, so expectations were high.

Fitting the manifold to a 2000 MGF VVC was relatively simple, although the bulk of the Janspeed pipes demanded that the lower rear engine mounting be detached to allow the engine to be swung on the remaining mountings, in order that the manifold could be slipped past the oil filter and alternator. This job was made much easier with the availability of a two-post vehicle lift at Emerald, where the back-to-back rolling road testing was being done. Earlier that day back-to-back changes had shown a gain of 18bhp from fitting an ITG Maxogen filter with a 52mm throttle body against the 147hp delivered by the engine previously. This latter figure was itself slightly higher than standard because the collapse of the original exhaust had made it necessary to install a stainless steel exhaust. There were high hopes of exceeding 170bhp with the Janspeed manifold, but the maximum power stalled at slightly under

Although perhaps not many would give consideration to temperature insulation treatments for a non-turbo engine, in the confined engine bay of the MGF and TF there are certainly benefits to be gained by exploring ways of reducing heat expended into the engine bay, such as those offered by Zircotec (*see below*).

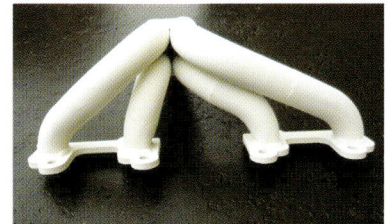

Fig. 6.149   Zircotec plasma treatment of the exhaust manifold significantly reduces the heat radiated from the exhaust, which is a huge bonus in the confined MGF and TF engine bay. It also helps reduce engine heat stress. This manifold is from another MG that suffers from a hot engine bay, the RV8.

ABOVE: Fig. 6.147   The lower rear engine mounting had to be disconnected to allow the engine to be swung on the other mountings.

RIGHT: Fig. 6.148   The manifold could then be eased past the oil filter and alternator.

One benefit is related to intake air temperatures, where 1 per cent power and torque is gained for every air temperature drop of 5°C. The efficiency of the Zircotec coatings can realistically deliver noticeable reductions in engine bay temperature that would be of significant benefit to those with open cone type 'performance' air filters and deserve serious consideration. Another aspect would be that it reduces the effect of radiated heat on the outside of the engine next to the exhaust, which aids long-term reliability, especially with head gaskets.

Engine Remapping

This modification straddles the simple and not so simple engine modifications. The easiest systems to remap are the MEMS 3 (2001 on), as they are true plug and play systems with the right interconnection and software. The earlier MEMS 1.9 and MEMS 2J are far from simple in that circuit board component changes are required, and really need the assistance of suitably skilled and equipped electronics specialists such as Superchips, who developed enhanced mapping for both MEMS 2J and MEMS 3 VVC-engined race cars in the MGOC Race series. These engines would deliver around 165bhp from their 'standard' engines, with a little more potential in reserve.

Just remapping a standard engine is not going to make a huge difference. At best you may hope to achieve a sharper feeling engine, which for the MGF usually sees 5–6bhp more for 1.6 engined cars and 6–7bhp for the 1.8. I have always seen the need for a 10 per cent power or torque gain for the car to be detectably quicker when driving, rather than just feeling sharper, and the sort of gains offered by remapping will generally not reach beyond the sharper feel mode. This still makes it worthwhile, as a sharp and responsive car is much more pleasurable to drive. The reason for the limited gains is simply that, unless the engine is able to flow more air, there will not be enough oxygen to make any more power by adding fuel.

Probably it is the MEMS 3 VVC cars that can see the best gains from skilled remapping. The person responsible for writing the original maps for MG Rover is also perhaps the best you can have

Fig. 6.150   Mark Stacey of Z and F Tuning adding around 12bhp to a TF 160 via a laptop.

to rewrite them: Mark Stacey at Z and F Tuning (www.zandftuning.co.uk) used to write MEMS 3 software for MG Rover, but then had a break from MGs and Rovers and wrote software for 500bhp plus Jaguars. Recently he dusted off his MG and Rover records and started Z and F Tuning. Many owners have appreciated that he is in the best position to rewrite their MEMS 3 cars' software, and their positive response to the results has seen a rapid rise in the company's status.

Mark has two standard rewritten maps for the MEMS 3 VVC engine MGF and TF, one that works within the original rpm limits and delivers around 8bhp more, and a second stage that raises the rpm limit to 7,450rpm (still within the safe ceiling of the standard engine), allowing about 12bhp more. My TF 160 has been running with this spec for a considerable time. The difference in the way the car drives is quite noticeable, yet there hasn't been any obvious change in the excellent fuel consumption.

The benefits of individual remapping by someone who knows the intimate details of the system, and its multiple maps within each ECU, are much greater than a simple off the shelf remap. This is even more so when the engine has had some other airflow-enhancing modifications. The greater benefits that come when the airflow potential of the engine is increased are because maximum power is made from mixing the right amount of fuel with the

available oxygen. Any modification that increases the airflow into the engine means more available oxygen, and will result in bigger gains.

Individual remapping to take advantage of other modifications' ability to flow more air and gain more power and a sharper engine response is not the only avenue for remapping. It can be used to provide better fuel efficiency, especially on the catalyst-equipped cars. I have used Mark's knowledge of the MEMS 3 mapping to hone the mapping of my daily use MGF to extract better efficiency, which stretches the mpg but also allows for a little more power.

The project involved having the expert head tuner Peter Burgess (www.peter-burgess.com) clean up an MPi head so that the ports were smoothed out, the valves featured a three-angle cut, the chambers were tidied up and the head face had a light skim (for more details of the head modifications *see* later).

At this level of tuning an engine there isn't that much difference in the remapping aimed at achieving more power or more economy as you're after greater efficiency. As well as removing additional fuelling to keep the cat lit, some changes were made to advance the ignition and removing the damping element of mapping to sharpen up the throttle. A couple of other tweaks were added to improve economy. Even with this done, though, the biggest gains still come from a different driving style.

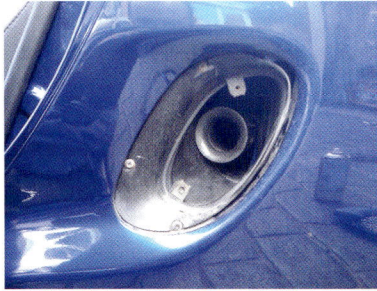

Fig. 6.151   An effective move is to route one of the 160Ps spec air filter cold air pickups to the left side vent to draw air at the outside ambient temperatures. The outer grille cover has been removed to show the pickup.

The engine was already fitted with a 52mm throttle on the plastic inlet and an ITG Maxogen filter, but the latter was swapped with the dual cold air type standard filter from my TF 160, which has one of the cold air pickup pipes in the original position on the rear of the subframe, but the other was fed to the left side air vent for cooler air.

The original changes were made in 2008, well before the remapping, and some interesting fuel economy results had already been logged. There was an issue during the testing period after the fitting of the modified cylinder head. A hesitation that developed, immediately accompanied by a clear drop in fuel efficiency, was traced to a faulty cat causing the second lambda to send spurious information back to the ECU. This was far more difficult to trace than these few words suggest. Nevertheless a new replacement MG Rover cat was obtained on eBay and, once it was fitted, the improvement was immediate.

After remapping in 2010, the test period started towards the end of a hard winter, so many daily drives involved having to warm the car up and clear frozen screens before setting off. This affected the overall returns and was not representative of how the 2008 returns were achieved. Therefore I have compared the results from the same period during the winter and spring of 2009, which had similar cold snaps.

The 2010 comparison shows an improvement of about 4 per cent in overall consumption. The best single tank return was important as it broke the 50mpg barrier, helped by a warm spring day that cut down the engine warm-up. Even then breaking the 50mpg barrier was less than 2 per cent better than had been achieved before. Satisfyingly, 50mpg was reached again during that summer and the overall average is still more than 43mpg, although it hasn't broken that barrier since.

The following results are far from scientifically accurate, but can be used to show a trend as the distances during the test period was sufficient to dampen out short term influences, and weather variations.

2008 returns were completed over a period of nearly 8,000 miles and covered the spring to autumn of that year…

	Average MPG	Improvement over standard	Best MPG on one tank
Standard 2001 MGF 1.8i Official combined consumption	37.1mpg	N/A	N/A
1.8i with ITG and 52mm TB	43.12mpg	16.2%	46.38mpg
As above but with Mod head	42.15mpg	13.6%	46.72mpg
As above but with new catalyst	45.67mpg	23.1%	49.41mpg

See the text to detail how a defective catalyst impacted the consumption and driveability.

In 2010, the testing period was from the end of the winter ice age into spring so many daily drives involved having to warm the car up and clear frozen screens before setting off and so this affected overall returns. This was not representative of the same period during 2008 so direct comparison would be misleading.

Therefore, I have compiled the results from the returns from the period during winter/spring period of 2009, which had some cold snaps too. The car was used for very much the same commuting from Staffordshire to Cambridge over the same route and travelling times as all previous tests.

	Average MPG	Best MPG on one tank
2009 over 1,416 miles	41.72mpg	44.50mpg
2010 remapped over 1,568 miles	43.48mpg	50.38mpg (a very warm April day)

This comparison shows a 4% or so improvement in overall consumption and there is the best single tank return that physiologically was important as it broke the 50mpg barrier, even though it was less than 2% better than the previous best of 2008 and was helped considerably by an exceptionally mild spring day. Taking that one return out of the calculation the next best return on one tank was 47.1mpg. Of note the 50mpg barrier was broken once more outside of the test period in the summer, again with favourably warm weather conditions that shortened the engines warm-up period.

Fig. 6.152   MGF economy modifications – results.

Aftermarket ECUs

A replacement aftermarket ECU gives a degree of flexibility beyond the range offered by normal remapping of an original manufacturer's ECU, since most companies supplying remaps for original ECUs offer only a limited degree of alteration, tweaking the edges, if you like. When you enter into significant engine changes then the original mapping will usually have considerable shortcomings: at the time of writing, owners with highly modified pre-2001 MGFs with the MEMS 1.9 and 2J systems are better off looking at a replacement aftermarket ECU.

One company's products have dominated the MG and Rover market. The M3D, K3 and K6 ECUs made by Emerald (www.emeraldm3d.com) have been so popular largely because they are plug compatible (meaning they plug straight in) to the MEMS 1.6, 1.9 and 2J wiring harnesses – 2J, though, requires some wires moved from the second [red] plug to the main [black] plug, as Emerald has just a single plug connection – and the software is simple to understand and to program.

Even so mapping is not a simple DIY operation. Unless a map for an identical new engine specification has been previously developed, it is unlikely that the base map as supplied in the Emerald (or any other aftermarket ECU) will run the engine properly. Even with such a map it is usual to expect individual fine tuning of the map, although as technology has developed, and the costs of this technology have come down, some of this fine tuning can be done automatically by the ECU through using what is known as a wide band lambda sensor. (Think of the original sensor as a horse wearing blinkers. The wide band sensor takes away those blinkers, so it can see and react to so much more.)

Nevertheless a mapping session on the Emerald rolling road, with Dave Walker making the process look easy, should always be factored into the cost of buying one of their ECUs to get things as close to ideal as possible. It will also highlight any shortcomings or faults you have built in with your modifications, which is quite common.

MEMS 3 cars do not have the same plugs, so the Emerald units are not plug compatible and will require either an interconnection harness made up or the wiring harness **completely** reconfigured to a new single plug. I have followed both routes and this is not a job for the faint-hearted. Additional wiring changes are needed with the now superseded Emerald M3DK and K3 ECUs. The idle air control valve (IACV) has to be switched to the earlier MEMS 1.9 or 2J five-wire unit, which has an external power feed on that fifth wire in place of the four-wire MEMS 3 type.

The current (2012) K6 ECU has much enhanced capabilities over the already impressive K3, including no need to modify the IACV, an internal barometric sensor to enable automatic correction for altitude and weather changes, knock sensing, drive by wire throttle control and enhanced external communication interfaces. This really takes the control options for a K series through the roof.

Not all is lost with MEMS 3. The benefit of Mark Stacey's work for Z and F Tuning is that not all the parameters need to be changed, so the considerable effort Rover and MG Rover put into creating smooth, sweet-running engines with the original mapping can be retained, and there is no need for any fiddly wiring changes.

Fig. 6.153   The Emerald range of plug compatible ECUs has become a favourite for fitting to K series engines. This is the current (2012) K6 unit.

LEFT: *Fig. 6.154   Replacing the car's original ECU with an Emerald will see a base map from a similar spec K series engine loaded that will get you started. There is no substitute, however, for having the engine individually mapped by Dave Walker of Emerald and the mapping costs will be recovered many times over in power and economy gains.*

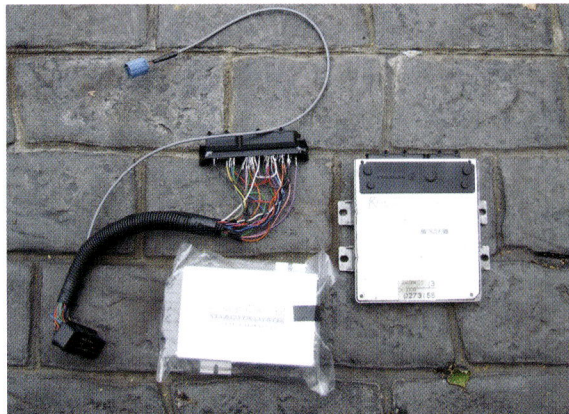

LEFT: *Fig. 6.155   MEMS 3 to Emerald requires an interconnection harness or conversion of the engine loom. The small flying lead is a direct to crank sensor connection for the Emerald.*

ABOVE: *Fig. 6.156   Earlier Emerald ECUs (not K6) require the earlier MEMS 1.9 or 2J systems' idle control valve (left), which has a five-wire connection instead of four. The fifth connection is an external power supply for the valve.*

Emerald ECU on a VVC

I mentioned earlier that I have not seen any shortfall in fuel mixtures with the standard ECU settings when rolling road testing cars with relatively simple modifications. While remapping on naturally aspirated engines will not deliver much when compared to turbo engines, where the ECU also controls boost pressures, I did wonder whether the 220–295 degree inlet cam timing range of the VVC would show any benefits. This option was available because Emerald produced an aftermarket ECU with sufficient processing power and the software to run the VVC.

The car chosen for the test was a 2000 model VVC I had taken to Emerald to measure the improvements associated with a replacement 52mm throttle, ITG Maxogen air filter, Janspeed exhaust manifold and a stainless steel silencer. As the process of changing items had been smooth, there was time to fit an Emerald ECU via a simple plug-in interconnection harness available for Emerald's diagnostic work. With the above modifications the engine was now delivering 170bhp (up from 147bhp) and this would be a good opportunity to highlight any weakness in the fuel supply. Once mapped the peak power went up by just 2bhp, and the excellent exhaust gas mixture readings corroborated the findings seen with the standard set-up.

The next test was to see if alteration of the cam duration at other rpms would show benefits. Reducing the duration in the mid-range picked up torque, so from below 3,000rpm all the way to approximately 5,750rpm there was a solid extra 6lb/ft (4.5 per cent). The advantage tailed off from there, levelling out at about 6,500rpm. In terms of extra power, between 3 and 5bhp was gained from below 3,000rpm all the way to 6,000rpm, after which it tailed off. These were useful gains, but overall they were too small to justify the cost of an Emerald for a road car of this specification, though perhaps that might change with more modifications.

MORE COMPLEX ENGINE MODIFICATIONS

This area covers those changes that demand the engine be partially or fully dismantled.

Probably the simplest change falling into this category will be camshaft changes. Many have responded to attractive sales talk by following this route, but it is not always the bed of roses that general information and discussions may lead you to believe. The profile of a camshaft dictates the character of an engine more than any other single mechanical component: small changes in the cam profile can see quite big changes in that character. The other point is that changes in cam profile often impact significantly on the operation of engine management, so a small increase in overlap often turns a sweet, smooth, likeable character into one with the worst New Year hangover.

I have previously described a negative experience with a mild cam profile change and standard MEMS 1.9, but I haven't mentioned the diagnosis that it was the cams. The first clue to the solution came with the reading from diagnostics of inlet air pressure readings at idle of 60 to 62kPa, which in simple terms was nearly double the figure that should be seen, and there was no air leak. Those higher readings usually equate to an engine being driven, not at idle. This was why the engine cleared its throat and ran off towards the horizon once beyond 3,000rpm.

That the problems were due to the cam profile was proven most conclusively by simply fitting a pair of standard cams. The engine started instantaneously on just the key with no throttle tickling, and immediately settled to a beautifully smooth idle. Driving was equally smooth and normal service had returned. The conclusion to be drawn from this is that, in the absence of any confirmation to the contrary, it must be assumed that cam changes, however mild, will upset engine management operation and remapping will be needed.

To reinforce the conclusion that small cam changes have a disproportionate impact on the engine, the second stage improvements I made on my first 1999 MGF 1.8i involved serious head modifications, a Janspeed exhaust silencer, alloy inlet manifold and an ITG Maxogen. The end result was a 30 per cent increase in power to well over 130bhp at the wheels (approximately 155bhp at the engine). Considering that a pair of cams could achieve about half that at best, it may come as a surprise that my gains were achieved with the original untouched cams and MEMS 1.9 mapping.

In fact I deliberately kept the standard cams so that the standard mapping would not be upset and provide both smooth running and enhanced performance. This proved to be true, but I could feel that full throttle higher rpm power was not quite as sharp as it could be, pointing to fuelling restrictions. I could have increased the fuel pressure, but I didn't want to compromise the creamy smoothness of the engine's operation at other rpms, and the still very good fuel economy. Today I would have used an Emerald, but in 2000 this was not an option.

TF 135 and VVC Exhaust Camshafts on MPi Engines

TF 135 gains its extra power from a pair of cams with greater lift at 9.5mm, and longer duration of 252 degrees for both inlet and exhaust, together with the use of the TF 160 induction system and remapping. The 252 degree duration is the same as on the venerable MGB cam, so it is far from extreme. This compares to the standard 1.4, 1.6 and 1.8 MPi cams' duration of 244 degrees for both inlet and exhaust and their lift of 8.8mm, with slightly different phasing for full lift. I must also mention the 16-valve 1.1 engine's cam, which has a 224 degree duration and only 7mm lift, as some people seem to think these engines have a hotter cam than the 1.6/1.8 cam.

When 135 cams are fitted to a normal 1.8MPi engine these small differences show up in the way the engine runs with a loping idle and less smooth, low rpm steady speed operation and with no performance gain. To obtain the best running and performance benefits, these cams need remapping if the original inlet and injectors are retained, but ideally the 135 ECU (or its map) should be used together with the whole 135 or 160 inlet and different (blue) injectors. There is really no point in failing to complete the job and gain the full benefits.

There is a common misconception that the VVC exhaust cam is the same as

Fig. 6.157   The cast-in number on non-VVC camshafts is not the same as the listed part number but is related, so it provides a sound method of identification. This standard 2001 MPi cam has LGC106970 cast into it: deducting 20 from that number gives the spare part number, LGC106950, useful for identifying TF 135 cams.

Fig. 6.158   The number cast into the VVC exhaust cam, LGC10234, however, has no obvious relationship to the LGC107430 part number.

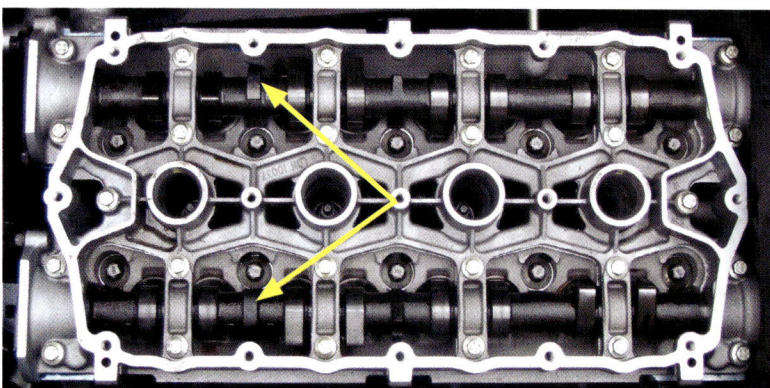

Fig. 6.159   2001 (MEMS 3) engines operate with sequential fuel injection and so need a cam sensor. The sensor picks up cam position timing from a half-moon additional lobe on the exhaust side. As inlet and exhaust cams are the same, there is a half-moon lobe on both cams on this engine.

the 135 cam. The VVC exhaust cam has the same 252-degree duration but lift, at 9.2mm, is less and the point at which peak lift is seen is phased slightly different to the 135 cams. Any reference to the TF 115 using these cams is also incorrect, since its cams are the same as on normal 120Ps 1.8 engines.

Identifying 135 cams is difficult and many cams have been sold as 135 when they are not. If buying new, under the original part number LCG000280, there should be no worry about what you get. Buying second-hand, though, is a completely different ball game as the numbering cast into the cam is *not* the same number that the finished cam is given as a part number. In the case of 135 cams, the cast-in number is LGC000300. For reference purposes, the mainstream cams have LGC000970 cast in, although their part number is LGC106950 part number. It should be noted that these cams can be found with and without the MEMS 3 cam position sensor half-moon lobes.

The VVC exhaust cam can also be identified in the same way, although there is a more immediate visual identification relating to the fact that all 135 cams are operating MEMS 3, which uses a cam position sensor and needs the half-moon additional lobe

Fig. 6.160   The VVC exhaust cam can't be used on MEMS 3 engines because it doesn't have the cam sensor half-moon lobe, which would sit as indicated here.

270 degree duration cam might offer a reasonable compromise between the demands of the track and the comfort expected during the daily commute. Eliminate the need to commute or increase the engine capacity and that 270 degree duration cam becomes much easier to live with. Indeed, even a 285 degree duration can be made to work well with accurate timing (*see below*). Ultimately, though, it is the prerogative of the owner to decide if he/she is prepared to live with the engine characteristics, in the same way that an owner chooses to live with a noisy or quiet exhaust.

With longer duration and greater overlap cams (the time both inlet and exhaust valves are open together) questions arise over the accuracy of the standard keyway fitting of the cam wheels and whether this can be improved. For a standard engine the answer is usually no, but the further you move away from the standard tune of an engine, the greater scope there is to fine tune the power delivery and the section of the rev range where greater power can be developed.

Once again I see this as aimed specifically at those looking beyond just road use, as the result of following this route to its conclusion will mean using adjustable Vernier cam wheels in place of the fixed original cam wheels, which demands very accurate setting up and rolling road testing. Adjustment is

located between the lobes of number 3 and 4 cylinder on the exhaust side. VVC exhaust cams do not have this lobe. Many see fitting two VVC exhaust cams as a performance upgrade on non-135 MPi engines. This is only correct on MEMS 1.9 pre-2001 MP1 engines because there is no cam sensing facility for MEMS 3. The knowledge that the VVC exhaust cam's cast-in number is LGC10234 (note that there are only five numbers, rather than six) should help owners avoid being duped into buying the wrong cams.

Aftermarket Camshafts

There are many companies serving the extensive market for tuning options on the K series engines and cam choice is wide. Knowing that even a very mild cam specification change can seriously upset the standard MEMS 1.9 engine management system, it is certain that anything beyond a duration of approximately 260 degrees will lose more than it gives.

My general advice for road-going engines is that cam changes should be remapped after any work on the induction, exhaust or cylinder heads. Look carefully at how you are actually going to use the car and select a cam that is suitable for moving the relatively heavy steel-bodied MG, not a cam profile that sounds better in club room discussions. You will then be able to impress fellow enthusiasts with the way the car goes.

All too often I have seen owner sensibility blown away by the allure of advertising that promotes 'up to' an extra 15 or 25bhp. Advertising standards dictate that this will have been seen on at least one engine, but that is no guarantee that you will see even half of that, and the impact it might have on the lower rpm ranges remains unspoken.

In reality the TF 135's 252 degree cam will generally cater for most 1.8-litre road engines extremely well. It is only if you are looking at some weekend track work that moving to approximately

Fig. 6.161   The engine becomes more sensitive when fitting longer duration and higher lift cams, so using Vernier adjustable cam wheels can fine tune an engine's power delivery to better suit its use. The rusting belt tensioner shown here was renewed at this time.

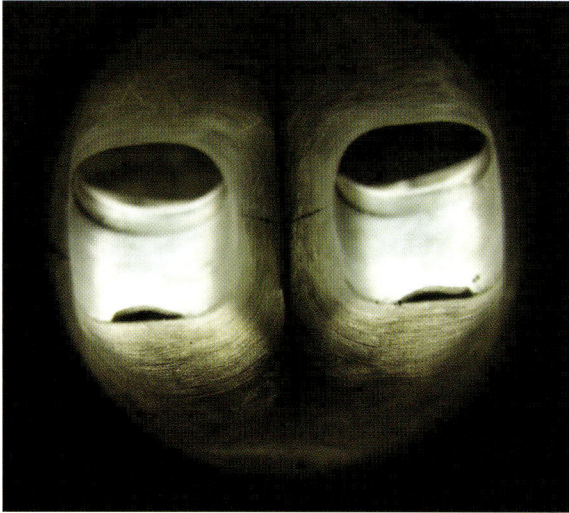

Fig. 6.162 Light cleaning of the ports helps improve efficiency, but still leaves significant scope for more comprehensive and effective modifications.

easy, correct adjustment is not, so this is when the assistance of experienced professionals is required. Those wishing to look further into the subject will find specific information on cam manufacturers' websites, especially, in respect of K series engines, at www. dvapower.com.

The need for remapping or using aftermarket ECUs to get the best from an engine with wider duration/lift cams opens up other options in the bolt-on arena. Some will be content just to bolt on a cam and remap with an Emerald ECU, and in these conditions it is possible to exceed the power of a TF 135. By adding multiple throttle bodies (*see later*) TF 160 power levels can be achieved, but probably at a cost that will exceed the value of most cars if all parts are new. By comparison, a well-modified cylinder head will come in cheaper and deliver more low-down power, and at least as much peak power.

Cylinder Head Modifications

Many fail to appreciate how much scope there is for even simple cylinder head modifications to generate quite significant power gains over the whole rpm range. The twin cam 16-valve configuration is certainly far more effective than overhead valve pushrod designs, but they still suffer from the shortcomings of volume production, which allow careful head modifications to deliver significant power gains. Many head tuners provide this service but my experience only extends to two, Peter Burgess (www. peter-burgess.com) and the renowned K series specialist Dave Andrews (www. dvapower.com)

MPi heads are common to 1.1 to 1.8 engine capacities, meaning that the valve sizes are large for a 1.1 engine but relatively small when fitted to a 1.8 engine. Not all MPi heads are the same, however, and here I will not be

looking at the early 1.4 'low port' head but only the later 1.4 and all other post-1995 MPi 'high port' heads. As the change was introduced more than fifteen years ago, there will probably be few of the pre-1995 heads still in use, but I should mention that the inlet port diameter was smaller on the 'low port' heads, 31mm against the 'high port' 34mm.

The main post-1995 engine difference relates to the two different cam belt tensioners used: the auto tensioner fitted from late 1998 on MPi engines, and the manual one that was common to all previous MPi engines and all VVC engines. The cam belts used are different in length and width, 23mm wide with the manual tensioner and 26mm wide for the auto tensioner on MPi engines. On the VVC there is a different 26mm main front belt with manual tensioner, but no tensioner is used on the short rear belt.

On the MPi engines the mounting bolt positions for the two types of tensioner are different and early manual tensioner heads do not have the 'meat' in the casting to be drilled and tapped to take the auto tensioner bolt positions. Later auto tensioner heads have the meat for both, but as the auto tensioner is kinder to the belt and is less likely to suffer from bearing failure, why would you want to go back to the manual tensioner on any MPi engine? If fitting an early manual tensioner head to a later engine, however, then use a manual tensioner and its specific 23mm wide belt, which will fit all the original pulleys as they are common to both manual and auto tensioner MPi engines.

Fig. 6.163 The manual cambelt tensioner is found on all VVC engines and MPi engines up to late 1998.

Fig. 6.164 An auto tensioner was fitted on MPi engines from late 1998.

MPi Head Retaining Standard Valves

As I have travelled along the modified route many times, starting with my original MGF in the late 1990s, it may be more helpful to describe what I found and achieved rather than provide a summary of what suppliers offer.

My first modified specification was a carefully cleaned up standard head that did not require deep grinding to change port shapes, retaining the standard valve sizes, seats with three angles, 30, 45 and 60 degree cuts and so on. This is the most cost-effective first step and Peter Burgess did the work, which he describes as an Econo-tune spec.

With the engine remaining standard apart from an ITG Maxogen induction system (48mm throttle), the car delivered 22 per cent more power (peaking at 137bhp) than standard. This increase was quite linear across the engine's rev range. Most of the improvement came from the head modifications, with the Maxogen taking away what on pre-2001 cars is a quite restrictive induction and air filter arrangement. The head and filter modifications really do complement each other with the power and torque gains being quite linear.

MPI Head with VVC Inlet Valves

My next stage was another MPi head with more comprehensive modifications, but looking to retain at least the same standard level of driveability from idle speed upwards, and importantly not upsetting the engine management. This meant retaining the original camshafts and not going too wild in the head mods.

Peter decided to experiment with the head and add VVC inlet valves, which are 31.5mm diameter against the standard 27.5mm, but retaining the standard 24mm exhaust valves. Initially I thought this was an odd route, but it is not as odd as first appeared. Naturally aspirated engine exhaust valves generally average about 80 per cent of the diameter of the inlet. In standard MPi form the exhaust valve runs at approximately 87 per cent of the inlet valve size, while the relationship between VVC inlet and MPi exhaust is actually 76 per cent, so it's

Fig. 6.165   This sports exhaust was fitted to make driving a modified MGF easier. The engine was so smooth and quiet, overassisted by the standard exhaust, that smooth rpm and clutch engagement was more difficult in stop-start traffic. Adding a little exhaust rasp made a difference.

closer to that 80 per cent general rule than at first appears.

Installing VVC inlets requires larger valve seat inserts to be fitted into the head and then a fair degree of careful work to open the ports and achieve a shape to exploit the fitting of the larger valve and seat. One aspect was to concentrate on modifications that promoted good flow within the 8.8mm lift of the standard MPi cams, which were being retained. It would be pointless to create flow improvements occurring at 9mm or greater valve lift as the cam would never open the valve that far.

Another aspect of this conversion was that I intended to use the VVC alloy inlet. I had noted that some others following this route had experienced air leaks owing to the different overlaps between manifold and head reducing gasket contact between the two (see above). In addition there was the obvious mismatch of the bigger inlet manifold diameter compared to the head inlet port diameter interrupting the airflow, so a solution was sought (*see* Figs 6.132–6.134).

Examining the VVC head confirmed that its inlet port is 3mm higher than the port on the MPi head. This made the solution for this head quite extreme and involved welding material into the top protruding area of the inlet ports. This extra material then allowed the head ports to be fully opened up and

matched to the manifold ports, and provides a wider gasket footprint.

Once the head and manifold were refitted the engine ran very smoothly from the restart. A power run, still with the ITG Maxogen, recorded 31 per cent more than this car had done in standard form on the same rollers, with a recorded 152bhp. With the standard cams and standard mapping it was so incredibly smooth and pulled well in high gears from just above idle. This was still using the standard cat and exhaust. An issue developed in that the engine was too quiet and, without being able to hear or feel the engine, clutch and rpm synchronization were more difficult in traffic. This gave me the excuse, if one were needed, to fit a sports rear silencer.

This head was later moved over to a Rover 218iS in 2002. Some nine years after it was fitted, and well over 120,000 miles later, the head was still working very well although the head gasket has been changed twice.

Using a VVC Head on an MPi Engine

The next logical step to employing just VVC inlet valves was to use a complete VVC head minus the VVC, and benefit from the port and valves being already fitted. That, however, then raises issues with replacing the VVC mechanism with a solid standard pattern cam. Rover certainly saw the potential for their motor sport aspirations and developed a head with the lower parts using a VVC pattern as far as porting and valves were concerned; the upper part was MPi with the facility to use two standard type cams.

These 'Motorsport' heads, as they were called, were always rare and expensive but there have been others. PTP, for example, produced their own version under the 'Vulcan' name, which they claimed included modifications in the casting that equates to a 'stage 2' Motorsport head, so eliminating the need for much bench grinding work.

In truth, the only practical way most will get to achieve a 'Motorsport' head will be to convert a VVC head. The conversion of these heads has been made simpler by the availability of solid cam conversion kits, offered by a number

of specialists and costing from about £700 upwards (2011 prices).

Most VVC heads often come from damaged engines where either the head has been replaced following a gasket failure, or the cambelt or cam wheel securing bolt has failed, leading to valves-to-piston contact. You have to be very careful when buying second-hand K series heads that have been subject to such problems, especially following overheating incidents, as the alloy of the head can anneal (soften) and this usually shows with clear indentations where the head gasket fire ring around each bore will have indented the alloy. If a head has been recently skimmed, you cannot tell if there have been problems unless a hardness test is carried out on the head (*see* Fig. 4.38).

On the other hand, bent valves usually do not cause terminal damage to the head unless the heads break off. However, they will usually crack the bottom of the valve guides. Sometimes pieces of the guide will have visibly broken, while others will still be in place, so replace all guides and valves (*see* Fig. 4.52).

Converting a VVC head to solid cam operation involves replacing the VVC cam components with a new and specifically designed solid cam to replicate the MPi arrangement, but with bigger journals than an MPi cam. There is also a need to add specially made end plates that replace the now removed VVC mechanisms and provide the mounting for an oil seal. Additionally a cover plate must be added to the defunct and removed hydraulic control

Fig. 6.166 VVC solid cam conversions start with a special cam with bigger dimensions to fill the void left by the fatter VVC cams, as can be seen here with the new inlet cam closer.

Fig. 6.167 Hydraulic followers (lifters) come in two forms, VVC and MPi. The MPi lifters are slightly longer (left), but the easiest way to tell them apart is that on MPi lifters the oil drilling is a small drilled hole, while on VVC lifters the hole has a machined entry, as shown here.

Fig. 6.168 The inside of the MPi lifters (left) has less unused space.

Fig. 6.169 Once the lifters are fitted, the cams are fitted in the same way as MPi cams, leaving voids where the VVC mechanisms and the cross shaft once sat.

unit and, only for MEMS 1.9 series cars, a mounting for a distributor cap and rotor arm.

Going to this much trouble and expense means that selecting a cam profile that is the same as a standard engine is usually going to be right at the bottom of everyone's wish list, although I would be interested in trying it out sometime, perhaps in a turbo application. In the featured application the decision was made to go with Piper 270 cam profiles for both the inlet and exhaust, intending to deliver a good balanced power delivery that initially used the MPi cam wheels, later moving onto Verniers.

Fig. 6.170   At each end of the inlet cam there is a blanking plate fitted with a VVC mechanism gasket.

Fig. 6.171   The trial fit of an MPi cam wheel reveals the inside of the wheel jammed against four points on the blanking plate.

Fig. 6.172   The problem was quickly solved by a local machine shop removing 0.5mm from the inside face of the wheel.

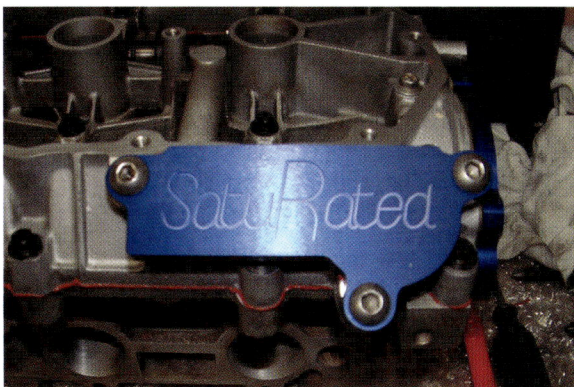

Fig. 6.173   This banking plate, which is part of a Mike Satur kit, fits where the HCU formerly sat.

Fig. 6.174   The front and rear plates are fitted.

Fig. 6.175   The cam oil seals are now fitted. The original seals are coloured because they are made for different cam rotation, black to be fitted front for clockwise rotation and orange for the rear and anticlockwise. It is possible to get unidirectional seals, but it is vital to check the rotation and that they fit correctly.

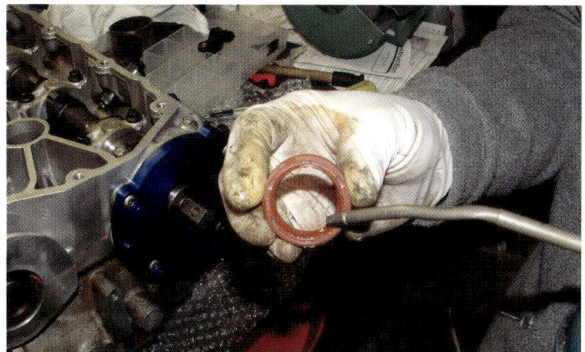

Fig. 6.176   Oil the inner seal lips so the seals do not scorch when the engine first turns before fitting.

Fig. 6.177   This 30mm socket provides the ideal drift to ease the seals into position.

Fig. 6.178   This is the rear of the head. A second plate is fitted over the main plate, via two screws in slots, so that a distributor cap can be fitted, if applicable, when using MEMS 1.9 or Emerald with a single coil ignition.

Fig. 6.179   The VVC cam sensor (indicated) is retained simply as an expensive plug for the hole. It is not connected and has no other function.

The donor VVC cylinder head was one from an engine that suffered a broken cambelt and bent valves. These were replaced along with a full set of valve guides demanding the seats be recut, which in this case was with three angles, 30, 45 and 60 degrees. Later K series engines have these three angle cuts, whereas early engines didn't, and this is one reason why some standard late engine specs are a little stronger than other apparently identical earlier standard specs.

The engine receiving this cylinder head was a standard 1.8 MPi, aside from a 52mm throttle body on an alloy inlet with an ITG Maxogen air filter, and a full Janspeed manifold and system. Initially the engine was run up with the original MEMS 1.9 engine control. While it started first time and idled acceptably, if a little lumpily, as expected it drove very badly. Obviously the new engine spec was way outside the scope of the standard mapping, even beyond the possibility of driving the car anywhere to have it remapped.

MEMS 1.9 may not a user-friendly system as far as owner mapping changes are concerned, but that doesn't mean it can't control a sporting engine as the MGF Cup race cars with 185bhp spec engines with multiple throttle bodies are controlled by MEMS 1.9 systems. As I did not have factory facilities to remap the MEMS 1.9 system, though, it meant moving to an Emerald M3D ECU.

Emerald supplied a new M3D unit with a base map created for a similar spec engine and this allowed the engine to run considerably better than on the original ECU. A few home tweaks via the laptop helped make the car driveable to reach Emerald's Norfolk base. The trip was not easy and used excessive fuel, but within a few hours Dave Walker mapped the new ECU resulting in a very satisfying 170bhp (previously 134bhp) with a solid linear spread of power. Most interesting, though, is the fact that the power of this engine is quite literally identical to the modified VVC mentioned earlier: two completely different routes to reach the same destination!

A comparison between the different resources needed to make these two engines deliver almost identical power makes for interesting reading:

Clearly the longer MPi list adds considerable extra cost in both materials and labour, so in power terms starting with a VVC make more sense. However, things are never that simple and so having alternative routes makes life more interesting.

Converting MPi to VVC

Saying that perhaps it would be better to start with a VVC if you wish to reach 170bhp will only be of value to those who have yet to buy their car. Since most readers will arrive here after making their purchase, it follows that the next question is how difficult is it to convert MPi to VVC. In reality, it is not that difficult. The cost will vary considerably depending whether you need to source parts new or – the cheaper alternative – you have a donor car to hand.

It is important to consider the condition of your car's engine as converting to VVC will be raising the power between 18.5 and 33 per cent, depending on whether you start from 120 or 135Ps and what VVC spec you move to (145Ps or 160Ps). An engine in sound condition will cope with these changes, but if this is the first step towards a series of changes that will take the engine beyond approximately 170bhp, or the engine will be frequently using above 5,500rpm (track days), then the weaker MPi pistons will have a shorter life and changing the whole engine for a VVC one is suggested. The pistons used in VVC engines are also the same in turbo engines and can be identified by having 160 etched into the piston tops.

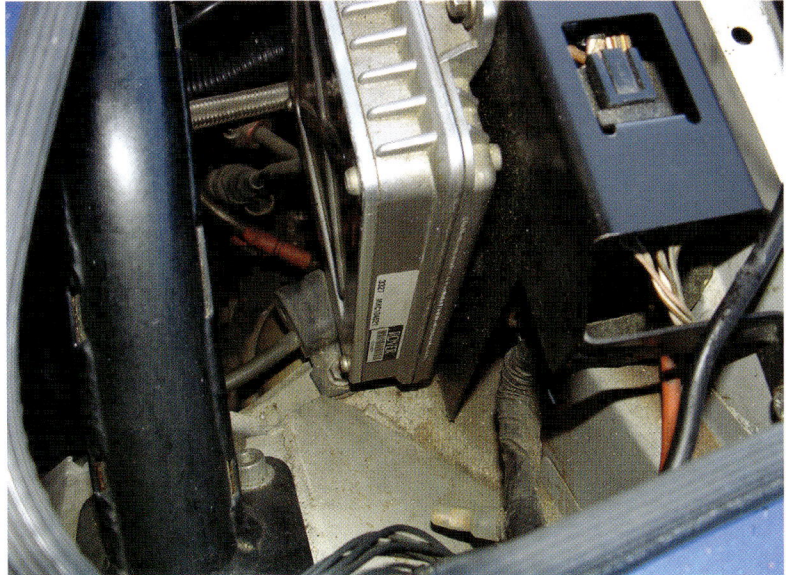

Fig. 6.180   An MGF Cup race car, with about 185–190bhp on multiple throttle bodies, still uses an MG remapped MEMS 1.9 ECU.

Swapping the complete engine is still the obvious first option even for cars that are not going to be subjected to hard use, but that involves dropping the whole subframe from the car. That is a viable route with the right facilities, but many would prefer to be able to do it without the need for such major work and it can be done.

The list of parts will in some areas be very specific to the age of your car and what engine management and security system it has, as ideally you want to match your car's model year with VVC parts from a car of the same era. The list of parts needed is variable depending on detail differences of the cars and your preferences.

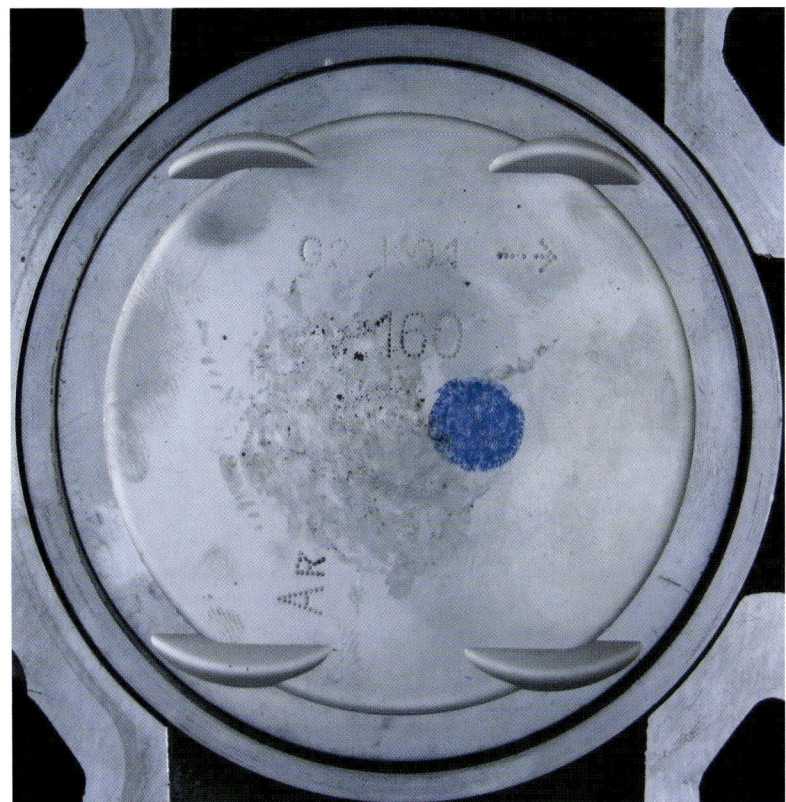

Fig. 6.181   VVC engines use a stronger piston that is identified by having '160' etched into the piston top. This piston is also used in the 160Ps turbo engines, which are not an option in the MGF or TF .

MPi to VVC Parts List

As a guide, a pre-2001 model year MGF running MEMS 1.9 will need:

◆ A complete VVC head, ideally from a pre-2001 VVC. This can include Rover 200 Vi and BRM models
◆ An engine wiring loom from a pre-2001 MGF VVC
◆ VVC MEMS 2J ECU from a VVC MGF (but not from the Rover models, as engine bay and radiator cooling fan controls are different)
◆ An alloy inlet manifold and its supporting bar from a pre-2001 VVC, ideally with MAP sensor still fitted
◆ VVC pattern fuel return, although the MPi one can be crudely adapted
◆ VVC timing belts (2) and new manual adjuster
◆ VVC upper front and rear timing belt covers (inner and outer)
◆ VVC dual coil pack, mounting spacer and bolts
◆ VVC HT lead set.

There are a number of differences for a 2001 on MGF and TF running MEMS 3:

◆ A complete VVC head from a 2001 or later MGF VVC or TF 160. This can

Fig. 6.182 160Ps VVC engines all came with an oil/coolant heat exchanger. This is unlike an oil cooler in that it can see heat transferred from hotter coolant into cooler oil as well as hotter oil passing heat into the coolant.

include Rover 25 GTi and MG ZR 160
◆ An engine loom from a 2001 on MGF VVC or TF 160
◆ VVC MEMS 3 ECU from a VVC MGF or TF 160 (again not from a FWD car as the engine bay and radiator cooling fan control mapping is different)
◆ Alloy inlet and support bar and fuel return pipe from any post-2001 VVC engine or a TF 135

◆ VVC or TF 135 (blue) injectors if not with inlet
◆ VVC timing belts (2) and new manual adjuster
◆ VVC upper front and rear timing belt covers (inner and outer).

An optional fit is the 160Ps VVC engine's standard oil/coolant heat exchanger mounted on the block under the inlet manifold. This can warm the oil during engine warm-up from the hotter

Fig. 6.183 One bright morning between Christmas and New Year this was a 2001 MGF 1.8i.

Fig. 6.184 By late afternoon on the same day the car was now an MGF 1.8 VVC.

coolant, and of course cool it when the oil is hotter than the coolant. If this option is chosen then you need a set of parts that includes the heat exchanger, its mounting bracket, two oil hoses, an oil filter housing where the hoses connect, a 160 coolant rail and hoses to match and assorted fixings. The first problem will be that the heat exchanger is not available new as an MG part. Examine a second-hand heat exchanger carefully to ensure that it is clear internally.

The actual conversion involves removing the original head, which then allows access for easier engine wiring loom replacement and other smaller jobs. The new head can then be fitted and the other parts added as a straight-forward rebuild.

The engine will not be able to run until the VVC ECU is security coded to the car's security system, which in most cases will require a visit from someone with the appropriate MEMS system diagnostic software. Some companies can do security matching if they have the engine and alarm ECUs, although when it comes to the 2004 model year on cars with the SCU, the additional security deliberately designed in will make this job more difficult. It may perhaps be necessary to have the car taken on a trailer to a dealer or special-ist with the appropriate software to work on the SCU.

I have carried out this conversion on several different cars and it is quite an effective way to raise the perform-ance nearly to VVC levels. I say 'nearly' as the MPi models come with gearing that is 10 per cent higher than the VVC cars' and so this creams off some of the sharpness to accelerate. On the oppo-site side, however, this longer gearing can slightly improve on the known good efficiency of the VVC to achieve fuel economy that is as good or better than an MPi, while also giving a notice-able performance boost. A number of suggestions I have with respect to gearing will be covered later.

Modifying VVC Heads

While the VVC head in standard form provides a very significant airflow increase over a standard MPi head, and indeed usually over many modi-fied MPi heads, there is still scope to

Fig. 6.185 The black and blue electrical plugs to the VVC actuators are not aligned to each other as they need to be separated. In practical terms the plugs fit so that they clear the hoses. If the plugs are in line with each other, the engine may not reach beyond 6,500rpm.

improve the VVC head's flow capacity using the same principles that have improved the MPi heads, although the hand of an expert is still required to see worthwhile gains.

My first experience with modi-fied VVC heads was in 1999 with Mat Smith's Rover 200 BRM, which was being used as a guinea pig to try out a Janspeed modified head for PTP. It was a case of Mat having a VVC car and PTP supplying the head for me to fit, so the car could then be run up on the rolling road and the results fed back – and if they were good enough perhaps this might be added to the products offered by PTP.

The head was not extensively modi-fied, but was more a first-stage clean-ing of the ports and valves to remove the negatives of standard casting and production processes, which for most applications is as far as you would want to go. More comprehensive modifica-tions are certainly available and will help to raise peak power ultimately to very attractive levels, but in most cases lower rpm torque would be compro-mised, which brings me back to my comments about the engine power having to move a heavy steel-bodied car.

After fitting the new head the engine initially ran well enough but simply stopped at just under 6,500rpm. I needed assistance to find the cause,

which turned out to be the VVC sole-noids. Many others have fallen into the same trap: it was not the common mis-take that the electrical plugs were fit-ted incorrectly, but the solenoids have to be aligned to each other at different angles, whereas I had aligned them together.

The modified head on the BRM, along with an ITG Maxogen induction, 52mm throttle, an exhaust manifold with external welded pipes (not inter-nally as standard), and an adjustable fuel regulator with a slightly higher fuel pressure achieved a solid 180bhp on the Emerald rolling road, then refused to get much above 170bhp on subse-quent runs.

It turned out that VVC mapping in the standard ECU has a safety feature by which, if the oil temperature is seen to go above a predetermined level, this triggers a reduction in the available maximum valve timing to reduce power. When the 160Ps spec VVC engines arrived, they came with oil-to-coolant heat exchangers that would help keep oil temperatures under control.

On the road this overly hot oil issue was only apparent on a long fast run to Le Mans, but in normal driving, where wide open throttles were only occa-sional events, the acceleration was markedly improved, especially in the standard torque hole around 4,000 to 4,500rpm. With that filled in and the benefit of the close ratio gearbox that the BRM has as standard, acceleration was quite stunning.

Subsequent VVC heads given a similar treatment show that the gains for such work is between 10 and 15bhp, depending on the overall engine spec. Since this is largely cleaning up the shortcomings of the original head, it is an enhancement that doesn't lose any lower rpm power, but actually enhances it.

Multiple Throttle Bodies

I have not included this with the variations of standard throttle bodies because it is a big step away from these. In some respects the subject lies outside the scope of this book, but as it is something that doesn't detract from the driveability of the car, it qualifies for inclusion. Over the years I have

seen various conversions aimed at the owner who has already travelled some distance down the tuning road and has reached the point where the original single throttle is becoming restrictive, usually when approaching the 100bhp per litre mark. I consider a move to these throttle bodies to be a sensible, if expensive, option.

Moving to multiple throttle bodies will cost in the order of £1,300 (2011) for a new throttle body kit, to which must be added the cost of buying an Emerald (or your ECU choice) and mapping it, which will add around £1,000 to the total. I must make the point that while these can be fitted to a standard 1.8 engine, and work well once mapped, doing this as a first stage is definitely a wallet-burning means of keeping up with a TF 135.

However, adding multiple throttle bodies to an engine spec that is already

in the 170 to 180bhp range is something that becomes more effective. At these power levels it is clear that more power starts to cost big money whichever direction you travel. Adding them to the 170bhp MPi engine that had the VVC head and solid cam conversion certainly raised the power after further remapping of the Emerald to a quite respectable 185bhp, with marked improvements in the mid-range too. This is the same power that the MGF Cup race cars delivered and, looking at the similar degree of modification, that should not be a surprise.

Having reached this power level I find that further increases in peak power will start to erode the low to mid-range torque of the engine, which is vital in moving the steel-bodied MGs, so this is where I see a practical ceiling for modifications for the naturally aspirated 1.8-litre K series.

LEFT: Fig. 6.186   Multiple throttle bodies are worth around 10–15bhp over a single throttle, depending on the engine specification.
BELOW LEFT: Fig. 6.187   Multiple throttle bodies from a quality source will include all take-offs for attaching the idle control valve and vacuum take-offs.
BELOW RIGHT: Fig. 6.188   When fitting multiple throttle bodies, it is necessary to replace the specific MGF and TF dipstick and oil top-up tank with a saloon car dipstick and tube. This also means topping up the oil becomes a chore.

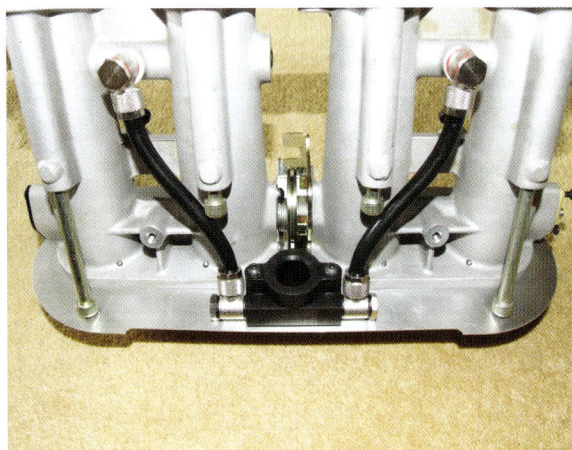

Larger Engine Capacities

Experience has long shown that nothing beats capacity for delivering torque and power. This is still true, although bigger capacities can be mimicked extremely well with modern forced induction (*see later*). Since the K series engine was originally designed with a maximum capacity of 1.4 litres, the scope is limited. The 1.6- and 1.8-litre conversions that followed really did take most of the enlargement capability from the engine.

There is also an ideal capacity for any engine design where the dynamics of the reciprocating parts is at an optimum. It is clear that the 1.6 engine is the sweetest running with the original shorter-stroke 1.4 crank and larger 80mm bore. Its power is extremely close to the 1.8, although torque is the 1.8's advantage. As torque is what the weighty steel-bodied MGF and TF need, the larger capacity rules.

While there has never been any enlargement of the production K series beyond 1796cc, there have been factory-sponsored 2.0-litre competition engines and several specialist companies develop both 1.9 and 2.0 capacity engines. The 1.9 is usually based around new liners that increase the bore to 82 or 82.5mm, depending on which company's product you are looking at, and then the 2.0-litre adds a longer throw crank to give 1985cc or 1997cc, depending on engine builder.

I will deal with the 2.0-litre first as it is probably a non-starter due to its huge cost. The original 2.0-litre project was announced in 2003 by MG Rover's MG Sport and Racing Division when they commissioned Engine Developments Ltd (better known as Judd of F1 engine fame) to develop a 2-litre K series engine for competition under the K2000 project name. Their 1997cc engine was designed only for competition and track use, and at an initial cost of £12,900 plus VAT in 2003 was really only for well-funded competition teams. Later PTP Ltd (John Wilcox Race Engines) introduced their own 1985cc development of the K series, which was intended to have wider applications but cost was still prohibitive. A Spanish company, VGK Racing, is presently offering a range of products to make a complete engine that will cost in the

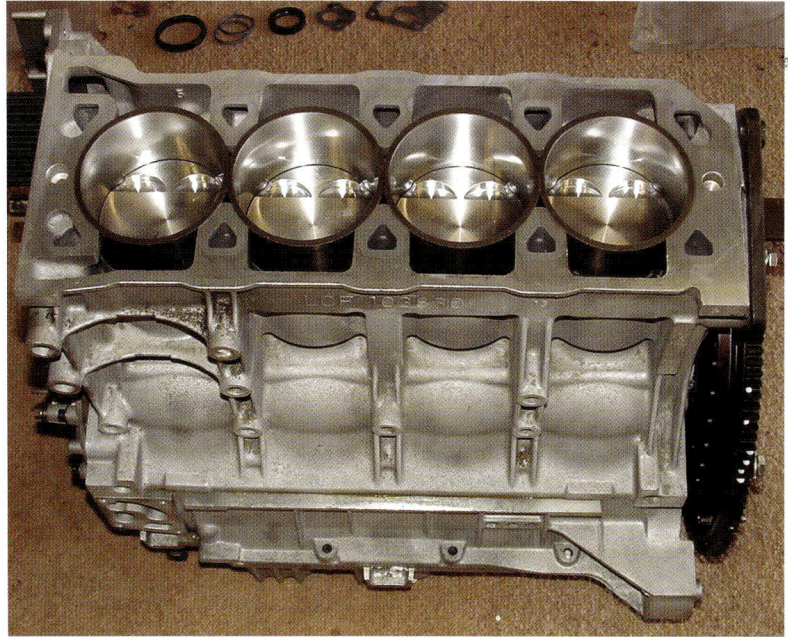

Fig. 6.189   A Scholar 1.9-litre conversion showing the bigger liners and pistons.

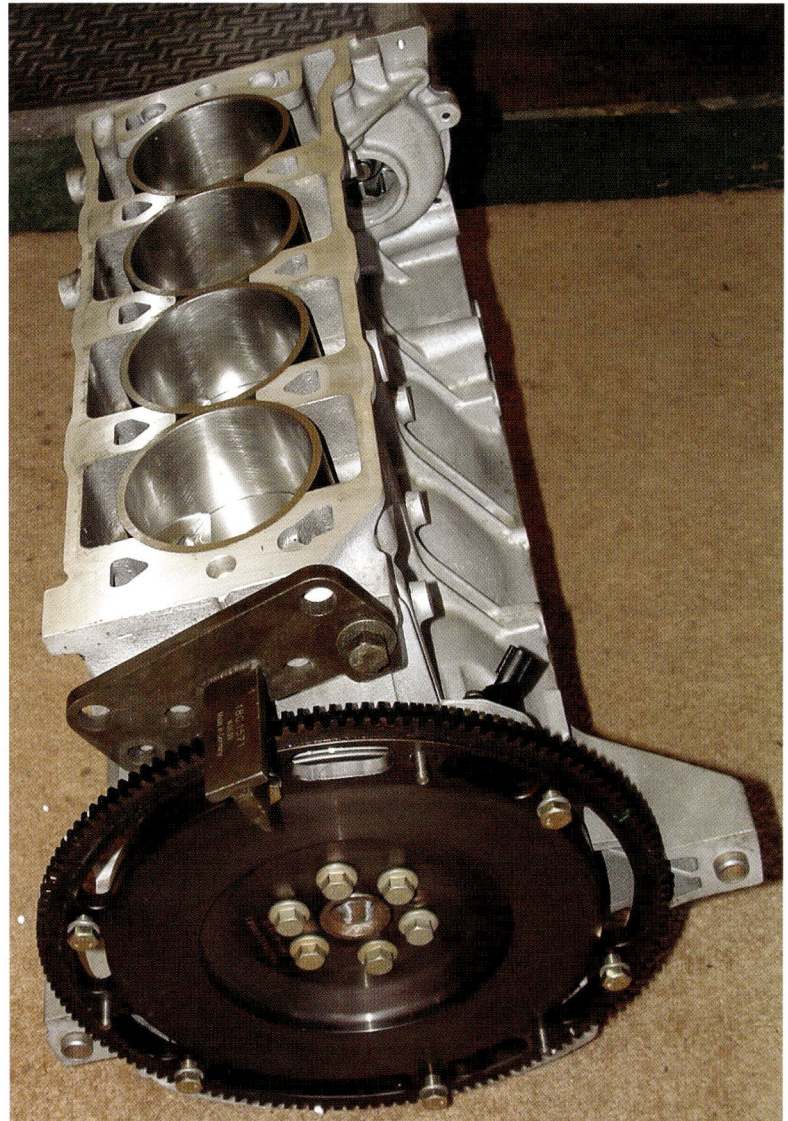

Fig. 6.190   The lightened steel flywheel is locked by the use of a flywheel locking tool to avoid inadvertent crank movement that might displace the liners from the block.

region of £6,500 to £7,500 as a starting point, although for about half that you can get a 2.0 half engine and then build up the rest yourself.

That half-engine approach has driven the more popular 1.9 conversions, where the 82 or 82.5mm piston and liner from the 2.0-litre conversions and your own block machined to accept these is available at between about £1,100 to £1,500 from the likes of Scholar, John Wilcox or VGK. This is a great way to gain torque, but still at a price.

I have experience of the 1.9 route with a Scholar conversion that was the next step of development for the engine to which I fitted multiple throttle bodies. Essentially the engine specification is the same, but with the bigger 1.9-litre capacity. With appropriate mapping adjustments the engine now reached 190bhp at peak, just 5bhp more than in its 1.8-litre form, but the torque gains below that were significant at between 10 and 15 per cent. It is still going fine after more than five years of hard use.

With the cam damping effects that come with increased capacity, changing the 270 cams for 285 degree duration should then enable the engine to get close too or crack the 200bhp barrier, which is about as far as I would want to go for an engine still moving that steel body around.

As getting to 1.9 with just the block costs about as much as a completely reconditioned, off-the-shelf replacement engine, and the overall costs of achieving a K series engine producing 170 to 175 bhp are far less, the question arises whether the results justify the investment. That is an open question that only individual owners can answer.

Forced Induction

The high cost of reaching around 200bhp in naturally aspirated form makes forced induction an obvious alternative, especially as there is a turbo K series engine rated at 160bhp in road-going form. The MGF and TF engine bay temperature issue, however, is a *big* problem that becomes amplified by the nature of a turbo operation, and this demands novel solutions.

An engine-driven supercharger does not have the same exhaust heat issues. Talk of supercharged MGFs was rife during the late 1990s. The first supercharger conversion for the Elise and MGF, marketed by Turbo Technics, was available in two forms, a 190bhp version for the 1.8i and a 215bhp version for VVC engines, probably owing to the piston differences.

Forced induction not only raises peak power, it really increases the engine's torque delivery so acceleration is vastly better. That also adds to engine stress and I can't say that my experiences of supercharged MGFs is good. Over the years I have seen six of these supercharged engines at various venues and three of them have suffered serious mechanical failures before my eyes!

On the other hand, I have more experience with one of these engines removed from an MGF and fitted into a Rover 100. Once Turbo Technics had rebuilt the turbocharger, the engine delivered 239.9bhp and 243.4lb/ft of

Fig. 6.191 A Turbo Technics supercharger conversion removed from an MGF VVC and fitted into a Metro. After the supercharger was fully rebuilt and set up with an Emerald on the Emerald rolling road, the engine delivered 239.9bhp and 243.4lb ft. This application shows the supercharger and component layout.

torque on the Emerald rolling road a very rapid Rover 100! The conversion was still listed by Turbo Technics in 2011 at a hefty price of £5,600 plus VAT, fully fitted, but this would be with their 190 (MPi) and 215 bhp (VVC) specifications.

Those high costs drive the next question as to how easy it is to fit a K series turbo engine into an MGF or TF. The answer is that it is not as easy as it is to fit one in an MG ZS, a route I am very familiar with in the context of the only ZR petrol turbo development car to be built by MG Rover. Certainly that experience has generated a plan to do the same to a TF: at the time of writing, however, although a couple of turbo engines and many ancillaries have been collected, other projects have stood in the way of anything finding its way into the TF 160 bought for the purpose.

Certainly MGF and TF turbo conversions have been done before and the various issues overcome, to a greater or lesser extent, but my approach to all the conversions I have undertaken since the mid-1970s has been to use as many standard off-the-shelf parts as possible to create something that could almost pass as a factory model, since this would become beneficial in sourcing spares in the future.

Fig. 6.192   An MGF engine in its subframe, showing the compact nature of the later standard exhaust manifold.

Fig. 6.193   The trial fit of a standard ZT 1.8 turbo exhaust and turbo in an MGF.

Fig. 6.194   When fitted the mounting position projects out beyond the edge of the subframe, as indicated, which is roughly where the engine bulkhead is located.

Fig. 6.195 MG Rover engineers overcame a similar conflict, when fitting the same engine to a ZR, by fabricating a tubular steel exhaust manifold.

Using the off-the-shelf standard turbo manifold and turbo means that its mounting position projects into the engine-to-fuel tank bulkhead by approximately 50mm. The same issue was met with in the ZR turbo, where a fabricated exhaust manifold moved the turbo closer to the engine. This is a serious possibility for a TF Turbo, but it will not be enough to avoid some bulkhead modifications and that has an impact on the fuel tank behind the bulkhead.

Once fitted, the route for the air pipes can be configured and here there is enough room above the gearbox to be flexible. A charge cooler will be the simplest route, just as with the Turbo Technics supercharger, with a remote radiator and separate coolant pump.

Heat radiated from the turbo and exhaust components was certainly been the main reason Rover/MG Rover didn't pursue a turbo MGF or TF. It is

only recently that effective heat management products have become available at sensible prices. Once again I will turn to Zircotec and I have already had a number of turbo exhaust components treated with a product from their effective 'Performance colour' range.

Engine management is a much bigger issue. As Rover 75 and MG ZT Turbo models are seen running with MEMS 3, it might seem that fitting this to another MEMS 3 car would be simple. Wrong! There are big differences between the two versions of MEMS 3. Then there are the difficulties associated with the partnered BMW EWS3 security system, and that is before we come to the different crank position sensor and reluctor pattern.

Fortunately, the ZR Turbo development car has a version of MEMS that operated with the same platform as most mainstream MEMS 3 cars, but with the operating map from the MG

ZT Turbo, so with the help of Z and F Tuning a suitable MEMS 3 ECU has been set up appropriate for fitting to the TF with none of the BMW security issues and the different reluctor types and pattern problems we faced with the ZS Turbo conversion, and which dictated the use of an Emerald (see Fig. 6.155).

The bonus of the Emerald, though, was that it allowed over 200bhp and more than 200lb ft to be achieved, with a standard turbo engine and only a slight fuel delivery uprating. This has improved as the engine gathered miles, and after 30,000 miles of frequently hard use it has proven to be completely reliable and economic. With the TF Turbo the use of MEMS will mean that the potential for additional power beyond the standard 160bhp level will be less than with the Emerald, but around 182bhp with enhanced turbo torque will still make for faster acceleration than can be achieved in a naturally aspirated TF with the same peak power and gearing.

One of the benefits of using as many standard turbo K series parts as possible to create the TF Turbo is the way costs can be kept down. That is why I am not looking for anything exotic in order to get 250bhp. Indeed there comes a point when chasing big numbers makes fitting other engines and gearboxes a cheaper and sometimes a better option.

Fitting Other Engines

This will not be a route followed by many and will usually end up costing a considerable sum, even if you have the desired donor engine and gearbox sitting in your garage looking for a new home. Buying a previously converted car also has drawbacks unless you know the quality of the build, as it is often the detail that differentiates really good conversions from those that only look good. Some of the more common engine and gearbox conversions use Honda, VAG and Toyota units. Generally, the Lotus Elise/Exige scene provides information on these conversions since their owners tend to spend much more to make their cars quicker and the similarity of layout provides a good basic template for MGF and TF owners to follow.

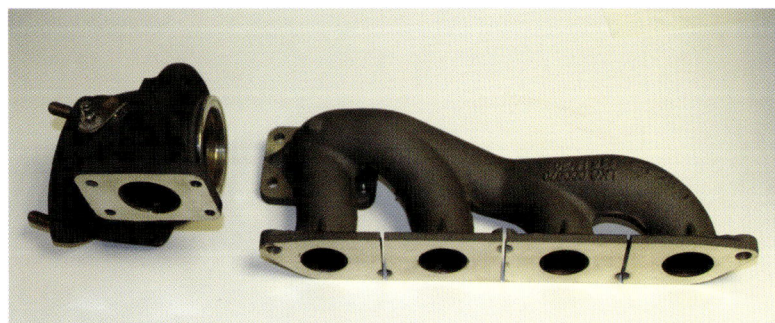

Fig. 6.196 K series turbo exhaust manifold and exhaust housing treated with Zircotec plasma treatment.

Fig. 6.197   *Probably the cheapest 2.0-litre conversion for the MGF and TF would be to use a Rover T16 engine. The alloy inlet and throttle of Paul Gaster's project MGF shows how the T16 differs from the K series.*

At the bottom of the engine conversion pile I must mention a very cheap 2.0-litre conversion that I looked at when first moving from my 240bhp Rover T16 Turbo-engined MG Maestro into a 120bhp MGF. The thought of transplanting the same engine into the MGF was very attractive as there would be no issues relating to a gearbox as the PG1 gearbox is used, with just different clutch housings to suit the different engines. Familiarity with engine management would be no problem as it was running an earlier MEMS 1.6 system. Lastly, they were not expensive and plentiful second-hand.

Things were not quite the same more than ten years later, but the 100,000 plus miles that engine managed delivering 240bhp in essentially standard form, and the relatively low expense involved when compared to a 2.0-litre K series conversion, made it a tempting proposition.

The downside was that initial measuring showed the extra length of the T16 block pushed the engine into conflict with the suspension, or at least I thought it did until meeting Paul Gaster at the 2009 MG Fest event. Paul came along in his MGF project, to which he had fitted a 2-litre T16

Fig. 6.198   *In the late 1990s there were many rumours about supercharged and V6 MGFs and Rover 425 V6 models. This unissued Rover image from September 1997 shows that the 425 was a real product of what was called the 'Skunk Works'. (Rover Group)*

non-turbo engine. The T16 weighs between 65 and 80 per cent more than a K series (depending on which K spec), so this is not ideal, but the 140bhp engine spec as standard and much more torque make it an interesting conversion that can be done for peanuts.

My personal experience of using a T16 turbo in a number of MGs is that 15 per cent more power is released as soon as the original restrictive inlet and exhaust is removed, bringing it up to 230bhp. A little boost increases this by another 10 to 20bhp, taking the power to around 240 to 250bhp, with up to around 275bhp available from the standard turbo, with more boost and fuel.

Paul and his family have a long history of being diesel enthusiasts and their previous MGBs with diesel engines have been very effective and long lived. Paul was hoping to create a diesel MGF using an L series diesel, which is essentially based on the same block as the T series. Utilising one of the modern common rail super sweet diesels with plenty of torque and excellent fuel consumption would indeed make an interesting MGF or TF.

The last engine swap I will mention is the 2.5-litre Rover KV6 engine, which is mated to the same PG1 gearbox in

Fig. 6.199   No Skunk Works MGF V6 has ever been recorded, but Chris Flanagan has built a couple, including this TF.

Fig. 6.200   Chris Flanagan's Skunk Works MGF V6 has suitably subtle external hints.

the MG ZS 180, so the potential for conversion is obvious. Since the V6 is short there are no length issues, but its 90-degree arrangement means that it is quite wide and some engine bay modification is required. There were rumours of a Rover development MGF with the same engine during the late 1990s. I saw a Rover 425 adapted in the same way in 1998, so it seems a good bet that the MGF V6 existed too. These unofficial experiments were termed 'Skunk Works' projects and carried out 'under the BMW radar', hence the genuine secrecy.

Whatever the true story of the Rover development MGF, one owner, Chris Flanagan, has built a very sweet 2.5-litre KV6-engined MGF and also a TF. Once again the main viability for this conversion comes from the fact that the KV6 in the MG ZS 180 uses a version of the PG1 gearbox, which makes for a simpler installation. The engine does not intrude into the suspension area, owing to the relative shortness of the V6, but there is considerable intrusion through the front engine bay bulkhead and into the fuel tank space. On a more positive note, the engine management in the ZS 180 is the same Lucas 5AS or Pektron SCU as on the MGF and TF, so there are no conflicts as exist with Rover 75/MG ZT BMW based electronics.

Chris Flanagan commented that the TF suspension changes reduced available space for the engine conversion. The end results of his work on both cars have been very well received. As the engine is only about 45 per cent heavier than the original K series, it doesn't have a huge impact on the handling.

FLYWHEEL, CLUTCH, GEARBOX AND OTHER POWERTRAIN UPGRADES

Flywheel and Clutch

The MGF and TF use a standard pattern flywheel and clutch, so no fancy, expensive, dual mass flywheels or combined clutch release bearing and slave cylinders here. There are three slightly different versions, however, and, aside from a common clutch release bearing, you do need to ensure that you get the correct parts.

Clutch diameters are the very common 215mm, which is fitted to all

Fig. 6.201   *The reverse side of a lightened steel flywheel for a K series engine showing the reluctor. The ring is machined into the flywheel.*

1.8-litre MGF and TFs, and the smaller 200mm diameter for all 1.6 litre cars (although many don't realize this). There is also a 228mm clutch, which is not used on any MGF or TF applications, but on the old 200bhp Turbo Rovers of the 1990s, Freelander 1.8 and 2.5, and MG ZS180 models.

Those who have uprated their engines significantly, and find issues with clutch grip, may wish to consider using the 228mm clutch rather than an uprated 215mm diameter clutch. This is the largest diameter clutch ever fitted within the clutch housing. Since Freelander 1.8 models also used this 228mm clutch and a PG1 gearbox, a simple upgrade for any MGF or TF is to obtain a Freelander flywheel and then fit the bigger 228mm clutch. Alternatively, take a 215mm original PG1/K series flywheel and then use the 228mm clutch cover as a pattern to redrill and tap the flywheel for the fixing bolts and locating dowels.

The standard basic flywheel for all K series engines using PG1 gearboxes is drilled to suit the appropriate sized clutch for the three different applications. It is also quite heavy and many will feel that there is an advantage in looking at lightened steel flywheels

from a number of sources. These are geared more for competition use where engines will spend much of their time in the upper rpms areas rather than trundling around normal roads.

Their advantages of low weight for rapid engine responses may well make the engine rev faster and sound sportier, but on a road car there is so much weight to accelerate that a few pounds less weight in the flywheel makes no discernible difference in real world road driving. The other aspect is that if too light they can make moving off from standstill more difficult, especially if a competition clutch is also fitted.

Competition clutches tend to have a harsh action rather like a switch, which is not ideal when you are faced with stop-start traffic. Considering the mainstream 215mm clutch was actually standard in the 180bhp/159lb ft torque 1,450kg Rover 800 Vitesse models, the need for uprated clutches in a much lighter MGF or TF often has to be questioned. Nevertheless, if there is a need for an uprated clutch on an MGF or TF, then there are uprated 215mm and 228mm clutches that retain road-friendly characteristics, the latter for up to 270bhp.

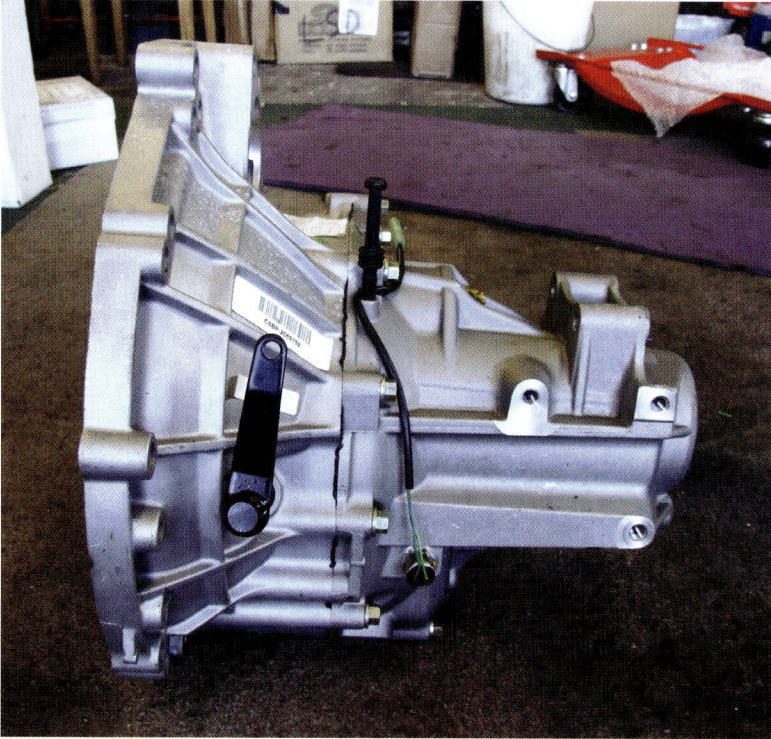

Fig. 6.202   PG1 gearboxes for K series engines all look the same from the outside. Only the ID label or internal examination confirms the details.

Fig. 6.203   All PG1 gearboxes had an external ID label stuck to the clutch housing on the upper face near the clutch arm. The gearbox code C4BP fits 1.6i, 1.8i MGF and TF 115 models and has a 3.9 to 1 final drive ratio.

Fig. 6.204   PG1 gearboxes for the K series all had this pattern of clutch housing.

Gearbox

PG1 gearboxes are all essentially the same, apart from having a different clutch housing to suit whatever engine it was being bolted to. The gearing in the standard MGF and TF applications uses just a single set of intermediate ratios but with either a 3.9:1 or 4.2:1 final drive.

A ratio of 3.9:1 was found in MGF 1.6i, 1.8i and TF 115, while the 4.2:1 was found in the MGF VVC, Trophy 160 SE, TF 135 and TF 160. The 10 per cent overall difference in the final drive variation is to provide sportier acceleration and also to make the most of the engine specifications, which have higher rpm torque and power peaks.

Replacing a gearbox with the higher 3.9:1 gearing with one that has the 4.2:1 gearing will certainly sharpen the way in which the car responds and accelerates. In most cases there will not be a major impact on fuel consumption, only about 1 or 2mpg, but at first drivers will probably tend to use more fuel as the improved sharpness promotes more use of the sharpened acceleration. It is possible to strip and replace the final drive gears, but the reality is that gearboxes are relatively common and so obtaining and fitting a complete gearbox is a simpler and probably cheaper route. Speedo accuracy can suffer, though.

Identifying gearboxes is usually done from the paper bar code label stuck to the top side of the clutch housing, next to the clutch release arm, but after many years it is quite likely that the label may have disintegrated. To confirm that it is a K series application, check the shape of the clutch housing and ideally try to locate the model and year of the car from which the gearbox was removed. Without this you will only be able to confirm the detailed specifications by internal examination.

There is one production gearbox that can be like finding a golden nugget, since when fitted to the VVC or TF 135 engines with a high rpm power peak it will provide a surprising bonus to the acceleration and general driveability of an MGF or TF. This is the gearbox with a label prefix code of B6BST, which was fitted just to the Rover 200 BRM. This gearbox has a close ratio gear set and a second bonus in the

Fig. 6.205   Gearbox codes

Gearbox Code	1st	2nd	3rd	4th	5th	Final Drive	Fitted Too
C6BP	3.167	1.842	1.308	1.033	0.765	3.938	MGF 1.6i, 1.8i and TF 115
C4BP	3.167	1.842	1.308	1.033	0.765	4.200	MGF VVC, MG TF 135 and 160
B6BST	2.923	1.750	1.308	1.033	0.848	3.938	Rover 200 BRM with TorSen LSD

Fig. 6.206   This label is on the sought-after Rover 200 BRM gearbox, which had a close ratio gear set and a Type B Torsen LSD.

Fig. 6.207   When there is no label to confirm that a gearbox supposedly has an LSD, it is possible to establish the truth by looking through the differential where the drive shafts connect. This is a standard differential with the visible dowel running through it.

form of a Torsen LSD (Limited Slip Differential).

This makes the first three gears 'longer', fourth is the same and fifth is shorter. The actual effects are influenced by the use of a 3.9:1 final drive. When compared to the VVC 4.2:1 final drive, the first three ratios are quite noticeably higher and fourth is slightly higher as well. Fifth remains slightly shorter, even with the use of the higher final drive ratio.

One means of physically identifying these gearboxes, aside from the label, is that there is nothing in the way when you look through the driveshaft splines into the gearbox and you can see straight through to the other side. If there is a steel dowel cutting across your view then it is a standard differential. This would raise the obvious question as to whether this is a standard gearbox on which someone has just stuck the label to make more money.

Because of the extensive use of the K series and PG1 gearbox, especially in Lotus applications, a wide range of specialist gearbox applications is available. There are also specialist gearboxes, kits and LSDs from manufacturers such as Quaife (www.quaife.co.uk), including conversions that use the original PG1 case and other applications for competition purposes, including six-speed conversions. Their cost is considerable, however, and they really lie outside the scope of this book.

Fig. 6.208   The internal plate blocking the differential signifies that this is a Type A Torsen LSD, as fitted to the 1993–95 Rover 200 and 400 petrol Turbo models.

Fig. 6.209 The view straight through the differential, with nothing in the way, indicates that this is a Type B Torsen equipped gearbox, probably from a Rover 200 BRM.

LPG

Converting an MGF or TF to run on LPG is not a common conversion, but more frequently found on FWD Rovers and MGs with the same engine. I know, however, of one conversion on a TF 135 owned by Will Thorman, which has covered more than 180,000 miles. Another TF 160 owned by Jon Fischer is a more recent conversion for which Jon transferred all the equipment, except the tank, from his VVC-engined Metro. The main issue for both owners was siting the tank to suit their different daily routines: Will wanted sufficient LPG to complete a long daily commute, while Jon's needs for range were not so stringent. The cars illustrate two options, one requiring no major body modification to place a tank in the boot space and the other needing the spare wheel well cut out and a smaller tank fitted in the vacant space.

The larger 55-litre tank makes more sense in range terms and reduces the frequency of refuelling, but the weight of the tank and contents when full does alter the weight balance of the car. This doesn't make it any less safe, but it is like running around with a full boot all the time, as indeed it is. Having the smaller 40-litre tank up front means rear luggage space is not compromised and the weight of the tank and contents is initially partly

Fig. 6.210 Three LSDs for the K series: (left to right) Torsen Type B, Torsen Type A and Quaife LSD.

compensated by the removed spare wheel well metal. The extra weight up front is like carrying two spare wheels and this actually helps reduce some of the front end lightness that can be experienced, although the downside is the shorter LPG range.

Converting the engine to run LPG is not difficult since there used to be two approved conversions for K series engines and other multi-point systems are readily available. Anyone familiar with running LPG will know that igniting LPG is more difficult than petrol and the ignition and spark has to be first class.

Using silver spark plugs rather than copper, platinum or iridium gives a very positive boost to combustion. Silver has the best conductivity of all the metals used in spark plugs and as such generates a much stronger spark. These plugs are also used in some race engines and may well offer some benefits for higher-tuned road spec engines, but they will not have the longevity of, for example, platinum.

Remapping is also beneficial as LPG has a much higher octane level, so ignition mapping can be altered to take advantage of this. Other mapping changes that benefit a petrol-powered K series also benefit an LPG-powered one. Both cars have benefited from Z and F Tuning remaps and both owners were delighted with the evident gains. Exhaust emissions are also very clean: no cat would be needed to meet the emission requirements in the UK, but it can't be removed from the car without attracting an automatic fail.

Fig. 6.211   Will Thorman has been running his 2003 TF 135 on LPG for more than 180,000 miles to make financial sense of his long daily commute. The 55-litre LPG tank occupies most of the boot space, but has to be this size in order to get to work and back without refilling. (Will Thorman)

Fig. 6.212   The LPG system that Jon Fischer has run for some time in his VVC Metro is now in his 2002 TF 160. As he does not wish to fill the boot with a tank, he has chosen to remove the spare wheel well and insert a new supporting frame for a 40-litre tank, which is adequate for his normal use.

appendix I – specifications

Source: Rover and MG Rover

MGF 1.6

Engine

Configuration/no. of cylinders/valves	In-line/4/16
Main bearings	5
Head/block material	Alloy/alloy
Camshaft drive	Belt
Engine management	MEMS
Displacement	1588cc
Bore/stroke	80 × 79 mm
Compression ratio/fuel grade	10.5 to 1
Max. output	112Ps/84kW/110bhp
Max. output at engine speed	6,250rpm
Max. torque	145Nm
Max. torque engine speed	4,700rpm
Max. intermittent engine rpm	6,800rpm
Cooling system including heater	10.5 litres
Engine oil	4.5 litres
Transmission fluid	2.2 litres (2.0 refill)

Transmission

Gearbox	PG1 5-speed, manual
Ratios	
First	3.167:1
Second	1.842:1
Third	1.308:1
Fourth	1.033:1
Fifth	0.765:1
Reverse	3.000:1
Final drive ratio	3.938:1
Km/h (mph) per 1,000rpm in top	
15in wheels	35.6km/h (22.2mph)

Electrics

Battery/location	63Ah/front
Alternator	85amp

Suspension and steering

Front	Double wishbones, interconnected Hydragas fluid over gas suspension with additional dampers and 20mm anti-roll bar
Rear	Double wishbones, interconnected Hydragas fluid over gas suspension with additional dampers and 18mm anti-roll bar
Steering	Speed-sensitive, electric power-assisted rack-and-pinion
Turns lock to lock	3.1
Steering wheel diameter	355mm
Tyres	185/55 VR15 (front), 205/50 VR15 (rear)
Wheels	6 × 15in
Spare wheel for all models	5.5 × 14in steel rim with 175/65 × R14 officially designated as 'temporary spare wheel'

Brakes

Front	240mm (9.5in) ventilated disc
Rear	240mm (9.5in) solid disc
Optional ABS, type	Bosch 5.3 three channel

Dimensions

Length/width (including door mirrors)	3,910/1,780mm
Height standard/Trophy 160 SE (hood raised)	1,270/1,249mm
Ground clearance standard/lowered	134/114mm
Wheelbase	2,380mm
Front track all wheels	1,400mm
Rear track all wheels	1,410mm
Turning circle	10.5m
Fuel tank capacity	50 litres (11 gallons)
Fuel specification	EN228 95RON Unleaded
Min. weight, unladen (EC Kerb)	1,095kg
Gross vehicle weight	1,320kg
Weight distribution F/R	45/55%
Luggage compartment capacity	210 litres
Max. boot loading with MG boot rack	20kg
Drag coefficient standard suspension	0.36/0.62 Cd/CdA

MGF 1.8I STEPTRONIC TO MAY 2000, STEPSPEED THEREAFTER

Specification as per MGF 1.6, except as below:

Engine

Displacement	1796 cc
Bore/stroke	80 × 89mm
Max. output	120Ps/88kW/118bhp
Max. output at engine speed	5,500rpm
Max. torque	165Nm 122lb/ft
Max. torque at engine speed	3,000rpm
Max. intermittent engine rpm	6,000rpm, gearbox limited

Transmission

'Steptronic' July 1999 to May 2000, 'Stepspeed' thereafter

Type	ZF Constantly Variable Transmission (EmCVT) with 6-speed 'set ratios' in manual mode
Manual mode ratios	
First	2.416:1
Second	1.520:1
Third	1.123:1
Fourth	0.845:1
Fifth	0.681:1
Sixth	0.518:1
Max. gearing in EmCVT mode	0.443:1
Reverse	2.658:1
Overall final drive ratio	5.763:1
Km/h (mph) per 1,000rpm in top	
15in wheels	35.9km/h (22.3mph) manual sixth
	42.1km/h (26.1mph) EmCVT

Dimensions

Min. weight, unladen (EC Kerb)	1,100kg

MGF 1.8I (MANUAL)

Specification as per MGF 1.6, except as below:

Engine

Displacement	1796cc
Bore/stroke	80 × 89mm
Max. output	120Ps/88kW/118bhp
Max. output at engine speed	5,500rpm

Max. torque	165Nm/122lb/ft
Max. torque at engine speed	3,000rpm
Max. intermittent engine rpm	6,800rpm

Dimensions

Min. weight, unladen (EC Kerb)	1,060kg

Gearing

Km/h (mph) per 1,000rpm in top

7 × 16in wheels with 215/40 × 16 tyres (optional)	35.1km/h (21.8mph)

MGF 1.8 VVC

Specification as per MGF 1.6i, except as below:

Engine

Displacement	1796cc
Bore/stroke	80 × 89 mm
Max. output	145Ps/107kW/143bhp
Max. output engine rpm	7,000rpm
Max. torque	174Nm/128lb/ft
Max. torque engine speed	4,500rpm
Max. intermittent engine rpm	7,100rpm

Transmission

Final drive ratio	4.200:1

Brakes

ABS standard, type	Bosch 5.3 three channel

Dimensions

Min. weight, unladen (EC Kerb)	1,070kg

Gearing

Km/h (mph) per 1,000rpm in top

15in wheels (standard up to 2000 Model Year)	33.4km/h (20.8mph)
16in wheels (optional to 1999, standard 2000 Model Year on)	32.9km/h (20.5mph)

MGF TROPHY 160 SE

Engine

Displacement	1796cc
Bore/stroke	80 × 89 mm
Max. output	160Ps/118kW/158bhp
Max. output engine speed	7,000rpm
Max. torque	174Nm
Max. torque engine speed	4,200rpm
Max. intermittent engine rpm	7,100rpm

Transmission

Final drive ratio	4.200:1

Brakes

Front	304mm (12in) ventilated disc
No ABS option	

Gearing

Km/h (mph) per 1,000rpm in top

16in wheels (standard)	32.9km/h (20.5mph)

Dimensions

Min. weight, unladen (EC Kerb)   1,115kg

MG TF 115

Engine

Configuration/no. of cylinders/valves	In-line/4/16
Main bearings	5
Head/block material	Alloy/alloy
Camshaft drive	Belt
Engine management	MEMS 3
Displacement	1588cc
Bore/stroke	80 × 79mm
Compression ratio/fuel grade	10.5 to 1
Max. output	116Ps/85kW/114bhp
Max. output engine speed	6,250rpm
Max. torque	145Nm
Max. torque engine speed	4,700rpm
Max. intermittent engine rpm	6,800rpm
Cooling system including heater	10.5 litres
Engine oil	4.5 litres
Transmission fluid	2.2 litres (2.0 refill)

Transmission

Gearbox	PG1 5-speed, manual
Gear ratios	
First	3.167:1
Second	1.842:1
Third	1.308:1
Fourth	1.033:1
Fifth	0.765:1
Reverse	3.000:1
Final drive ratio	3.938:1
Km/h (mph) per 1,000rpm in top	
15in wheels	35.6km/h (22.2mph)
16in wheels (optional)	35.1km/h (21.8mph)

Electrics

Battery /location	63Ah/front
Alternator	85amp

Suspension and steering

Front	Coil spring over gas-filled damper located by double wishbones. Anti-roll bar diameter 20mm
Rear	Multilink. Coil spring over gas-filled damper. Anti-roll bar diameter 18mm
Optional Sports Pack 1	Trim height reduced by 10mm using uprated dampers with revised valving

These specifications are for the UK market only. Deviations from the model variant described here are possible in various markets.

Steering	Speed-sensitive, electric power-assisted rack-and-pinion
Turns lock to lock	2.8
Overall ratio	17.5 to 1
Steering wheel diameter	355mm

Tyres

15in wheels	185/55 VR15 (front) 205/50 VR15 (rear)
16in wheels	195/45 R16 (front), 215/40 ZR16 (rear)

Spare wheel for all models, except when MG/AP Racing uprated brakes and wheels are used, 5.5 × 14in steel rim with 175/65 × R14 officially designated to be a 'temporary spare wheel'

TF 160 and cars using the 16in wheels use an Instant Mobility System with an option to use a full-size alloy spare fitted with a 194/45 × R16 tyre

specifications

Brakes

Front	240mm (9.5in) ventilated disc
Rear	240mm (9.5in) solid disc
ABS optional until 2004, when it became standard	
ABS type	Bosch 5.3 three channel

Optional uprated 304mm front brakes using MG/AP Racing four-piston callipers, requiring use of TF 160 16in wheels for front brake clearance. (NB not available at all times during production)

Dimensions

Length/width (including door mirrors)	3,943/1,807mm
Height standard/lowered suspension (hood raised)	1,261/1,249mm
Height standard/lowered (hood lowered)	1,219/1,207mm
Height standard/lowered with hardtop	1,264/1,252mm
Ground clearance standard/lowered	124/114mm
Wheelbase	2,375mm
Front track	1,404mm (optional Ultralite wheels 1,408mm)
Rear track	1,410mm (optional Ultralite wheels 1,414mm)
Turning circle	10.56m
Fuel tank capacity	50 litres (11 gallons)
Fuel specification	EN228 95RON Unleaded
Min. weight, unladen (EC Kerb)	1,095kg
Max. permissible axle load, rear	740kg
Luggage compartment capacity	210 litres
Max. boot loading with MG boot rack	20kg
Drag coefficient standard suspension	0.36/0.62 Cd/CdA
Drag coefficient lowered suspension	0.35/0.61 Cd/CdA

MG TF 120

Specification as per TF 115, except as below:

Engine

Displacement	1796cc
Bore/stroke	80 × 89mm
Max. output	120Ps/88kW /118bhp
Max. output at engine speed	5,500rpm
Max. torque	165Nm
Max. torque at engine speed	3,000rpm
Max. intermittent engine rpm	6,000rpm

Transmission

Automatic 'Stepspeed'	
Type	ZF Constantly Variable Transmission (EmCVT) with 6-speed 'set ratios' in manual mode
Manual mode ratios	
First	2.416:1
Second	1.520:1
Third	1.123:1
Fourth	0.845:1
Fifth	0.681:1
Sixth	0.518:1
Max gearing in EmCVT mode	0.443:1
Reverse	2.658:1
Overall final drive ratio	5.763:1
Km/h (mph) per 1,000rpm in top	
15in wheels	35.9km/h (22.3mph) manual sixth
	42.1km/h (26.1mph) EmCVT
16in wheels (optional)	35.3km/h (22.0mph) manual sixth
	41.4km/h (25.7mph) EmCVT

Brakes

Front   240mm (9.5in) ventilated disc (305mm/12in optional)

Dimensions

Min. weight, unladen (EC Kerb)   1,125kg
Max. permissible axle load, rear   790kg

MG TF 135

Specification as per TF 115, except as below:

Engine

Displacement   1796cc
Bore/stroke   80 × 89mm
Max. output   136Ps/100kW/134bhp
Max. output engine speed   6,750rpm
Max. torque   165Nm
Max. torque engine speed   5,500rpm

Transmission

Final drive ratio   4.200:1
Km/h (mph) per 1,000rpm in top
15inch wheels   33.4km/h (20.8mph)
16in wheels (optional)   32.9km/h (20.5mph)

Brakes

Front   240mm (9.5in) ventilated disc (305mm/12in optional)

Dimensions

Min. weight, unladen (EC Kerb)   1,105kg

MG TF 160

Specification as per TF 115, except as below:

Engine

Displacement   1796cc
Bore/stroke   80 × 89mm
Max. output   160Ps/118kW/158bhp
Max. output at engine speed   6,900rpm
Max. torque   174Nm
Max. torque at engine speed   4,200rpm
Max. intermittent engine rpm   7,100rpm

Transmission

Final drive ratio   4.200:1
Km/h (mph) per 1,000rpm in top
16in wheels (standard)   32.9km/h (20.5mph)

Brakes

Front   304mm (12in) ventilated disc

Dimensions

Min. weight, unladen (EC Kerb)   1,115kg
Max. permissible axle load, rear   790kg

MG MOTOR TF 135

Specification as per TF 135, except as below:

Transmission

Final drive ratio	4.200:1

Wheels and tyres

Full-size alloy spare fitted with a 194/45 × R16 tyre to be used as a 'temporary spare wheel'

Brakes

Front	304mm (12in) ventilated disc
Performance	
Km/h (mph) per 1,000 rpm in top	
16in wheels (standard)	32.9km/h (20.5mph)

MG MOTOR TF 85TH ANNIVERSARY

Specification as per MG Motor TF 135, except as below:

Suspension and steering

Anti-roll bar diameter	
Front	25mm
Rear	20mm
Tyres	195/45 R16 (front), 215/40 ZR16 (rear)
Wheels	6.5 × 16in (front), 7.5 × 16in (rear)

'Instant Mobility System' with option to use a full-size alloy spare wheel fitted with a 194/45 × R16 tyre

PERFORMANCE

MGF 1.6i

0–60mph	9.3sec
30–50mph (4th)	8.3sec
50–70mph (4th)	9.0sec
Top speed	186.7km/h (116mph)

MGF 1.8i

0–60mph	8.5sec
30–50mph (4th)	6.8sec
50–70mph (4th)	7.2sec
Top speed	193.1km/h (120mph)

MGF Steptronic/Stepspeed

0–60mph	9.5sec
30–50mph (4th)	N/A
50–70mph (4th)	N/A
Top speed	189.9km/h (118mph)

MGF VVC

0–60mph	8.2sec
30–50mph (4th)	6.7sec
50–70mph (4th)	6.9sec
Top speed	204.4km/h (127mph)

MGF Trophy 160 SE

0–60mph	6.9sec
30–50mph (4th)	6.4sec
50–70mph (4th)	6.6sec
Top speed	220.5km/h (137mph)

TF 115

0–60mph	9.2sec
30–50mph (4th)	8.3sec
50–70mph (4th)	9.0sec
Top speed	189.9km/h (118mph)

TF 120 Stepspeed

0–60mph	9.7sec
30–50mph (4th)	N/A
50–70mph (4th)	N/A
Top speed	189.9km/h (118mph)

TF 135

0–60mph	8.2sec
30–50mph (4th)	6.7sec
50–70mph (4th)	6.9sec
Top speed	204.4km/h (127mph)

TF 160

0–60mph	6.9sec
30–50mph (4th)	6.4sec
50–70mph (4th)	6.6sec
Top speed	220.5km/h (137mph)

MG Motor TF (all models)

0–60mph	8.4sec
30–50mph (4th)	Not stated
50–70mph (4th)	Not stated
Top speed	204.4km/h (127mph)

FUEL ECONOMY AND EMISSIONS

Based upon EU cycle (93/116/EC) mpg/ltr per 100km

This system did not apply for MGFs registered before 1 March 2001, specifically the CO_2 outputs, but the fuel consumption figures are representative.

MGF 1.6i

EU urban	28.2/10.1
EU extra-urban	48.6/5.8
EU combined	34.8/7.4
CO_2	177g/km

MGF 1.8i

EU urban	26.2/10.8
EU extra-urban	49.0/5.8
EU combined	37.1/7.6
CO_2	182g/km

MGF Steptronic/Stepspeed

EU urban	23.4/12.1
EU extra-urban	42.6/6.6
EU combined	32.8/8.6
CO_2	206g/km

MGF VVC

EU urban	25.0/11.3
EU extra-urban	47.6/5.9
EU combined	35.7/7.9
CO_2	189g/km

specifications

MGF Trophy 160 SE

EU urban	25.2/11.2
EU extra-urban	48.8/5.8
EU combined	36.3/7.8
CO_2	190g/km

TF 115

EU urban	29.2/9.7
EU extra-urban	50.4/5.6
EU combined	39.8/7.1
CO_2	169g/km

TF 120

EU urban	24.8/11.4
EU extra-urban	45.3/6.2
EU combined	34.7/7.1
CO_2	194g/km

TF 135 (up to VIN RD617390)

EU urban	25.3/11.2
EU extra-urban	46.9/6.0
EU combined	35.6/7.9
CO_2	189g/km

TF 135 (from VIN RD617391)

EU urban	26.2/10.8
EU extra-urban	47.4/6.0
EU combined	36.6/7.7
CO_2	184g/km

TF 160

EU urban	26.7/10.6
EU extra-urban	49.6/5.7
EU combined	37.6/7.5
CO_2	179g/km

MG Motor TF (whole range)

EU urban	25.4/11.1
EU extra-urban	46.3/6.1
EU combined	35.8/7.9
CO_2	185g/km

appendix II –
service check sheets

Source: Rover and MG Rover

MAINTENANCE CHECK SHEET

MGF
Pre ECD3 only - pre VIN no. RD 522572

Mr/Mrs/Ms

Invoice/Job No

Model

Reg No

VIN

Service type	FS	A	B	A	B	A	B	A	B
Months/,000miles	3	12	24	36	48	60	72	84	96

Odometer reading

Adjust/Lubricate/Replace - Labour cost including in scheduled time except items marked*
Check - After the checking procedure, cleaning, adjusting, repairing or replacing is subject to extra labour and material cost

PRELIMINARY

1 ☐ Before commencing work, check for any outstanding service actions

FIRST SERVICE

FS

2 ☐ 3k Replace engine oil and filter - *First 3000 miles only*
3 ☐ 3k Check suspension height and adjust if necessary - record details
   ☐ LHF   ☐ RHF   ☐ LHR   ☐ RHR

MAIN SERVICE - (VEHICLE INTERIOR)

A   B

4 ☐ Adjust handbrake - *First 12,000 miles only*
5 ☐ Check handbrake operation
6 ☐ Check seatbelt and airbag module covers - *36 months and then every 12 months*
7 ☐ Lubricate strikers, latches (use Rover lock grease) door hinges and door checks
8 ☐ Lubricate hood pivot points (remove hard top if necessary)
9 ☐ Replace alarm handset batteries

MAIN SERVICE - (VEHICLE EXTERIOR)

10 ☐ Annual corrosion/cosmetic inspection - *Using annual corrosion inspection sheet*
11 ☐ Check front brake linings, disc, calipers, hoses and pipes
12 ☐ Check rear brake linings, disc, calipers, hoses and pipes
13 ☐ Grease suspension pivots
14 ☐ Check suspension and steering for signs of leaking or wear
15 ☐ Check suspension height and adjust if necessary - record details
    ☐ LHF   ☐ RHF   ☐ LHR   ☐ RHR
16 ☐ Check wheel bearings, drive shafts and gaiters
17 ☐ Check lamps, horns, and system warning indicators
18 ☐ Check screen wipers and washers
19 ☐ Check front screen number plates and V.I.N. - *36 months and then every 12 months*
20 ☐ Remover front road wheels
21 ☐ Remove rear road wheels
22 ☐ Check road wheels
23 ☐ Check tyre for damage and tread depth including spare (mm)
    ☐ LHF   ☐ RHF   ☐ LHR   ☐ RHR   ☐ Spare
24 ☐ Check tyre pressures and adjust if necessary, including spare (bar)
    ☐ LHF   ☐ RHF   ☐ LHR   ☐ RHR   ☐ Spare

MAIN SERVICE - (ENGINE BAY)

25 ☐ Remove engine service hatch
26 ☐ Remove engine access cover - *Every 60,000 miles*
27 ☐ Replace engine oil and filter

28 ☐ Replace antifreeze* - *Every 2 years AFC, every 4 years XLC (OAT)*
29 ☐ Replace camshaft drive belt - *Every 60,000 miles*
30 ☐ Replace rear camshaft drive belt *VVC - Every 60,000 miles*
31 ☐ Replace manual gearbox oil - *Every 96,000 miles*
32 ☐ Replace automatic gearbox oil
33 ☐ Check automatic gearbox level
34 ☐ Check battery connections and antifreeze
35 ☐ Check brake, clutch & gearbox fluid levels
36 ☐ Check pressure sensing hoses and vacuum pipes
37 ☐ Check cooling system hoses and connections for signs of leakage and condition
38 ☐ Check fuel & clutch pipes and hoses for signs of leakage and condition
39 ☐ Check condition of crankcase vent hoses & valves where fitted
40 ☐ Check air conditioning system, hoses and sight glass
41 ☐ Check auxiliary drive belts tension and condition
42 ☐ Replace air cleaner element
43 ☐ Replace fuel filter - *Every 60,000 miles*
44 ☐ Replace spark plugs - *Every 60,000 miles*
45 ☐ Replace brake fluid - *Every 24 months regardless of mileage* (indicate replacement on service record)*
46 ☐ Check exhaust system and heat shields

10 YEAR REPLACEMENT - AIRBAGS

47 ☐ Replace airbag module(s)*
48 ☐ Replace airbag rotary coupler* - *When driver only airbag fitted*

AFTER EACH MAIN SERVICE

49 ☐ Check oxygen sensor operation - *at 36 months and then very 12 months*
50 ☐ Check CO at tailpipe - *at 36 months and then every 12 months. (Record CO%)*
51 ☐ Carry out road test, check for the correct function of all vehicle systems

The maintenance items listed are those recommended for vehicles operating under normal driving, road and climatic conditions. More frequent attention may be necessary if the vehicle is subject to stop/start operation, extremes of temperature, dusty conditions or frequent towing of trailers.

Service check completed, cosmetic/corrosion inspection check completed and service portfolio book stamped.

Name _____

Signature _____

Date _____

07/01

RCL 0397ENG(4)

Note after these sheets were published cambelt changes were modified to be '60,000 miles or 5 years, whichever comes first' and the airbag change moved to 15 years.

MAINTENANCE CHECK SHEET

MGF

ECD3 only - Vin no. RD522573 on

Mr/Mrs/Ms _____

Invoice/Job No _____

Model _____

Reg No _____

VIN _____

Service type	FS	A	B	A	B	A	B	A	B
Months/,000miles	3	12/15	24/30	36/45	48/60	60/75	72/90	84/105	96/120

Adjust/Lubricate/Replace - Labour cost including in scheduled time cost including in scheduled time except items marked*
Check - After the checking procedure, cleaning, adjusting, repairing or replacing is subject to extra labour and material cost

PRELIMINARY

1. Before commencing work, check for any outstanding service actions

FS FIRST SERVICE

2. 3k ☐ Check suspension height and adjust if necessary - record details
☐ LHF ☐ RHF ☐ RHR ☐ LHR

A B MAIN SERVICE - (VEHICLE INTERIOR)

3. ☐ Adjust handbrake - *First 15,000 miles only*
4. ☐ Check handbrake operation
5. ☐ Check seatbelt and airbag module covers - *36 months and then every 12 months*
6. ☐ Lubricate strikers, latches (use Rover lock grease) door hinges and door checks
7. ☐ Lubricate hood pivot points (remover hard top if necessary)
8. ☐ Replace alarm handset batteries

MAIN SERVICE - (VEHICLE EXTERIOR)

9. ☐ Annual corrosion/cosmetic inspection - *Using annual corrosion inspection sheet*
10. ☐ Check front brake linings, disc, calipers, hoses and pipes
11. ☐ Check rear brake linings, disc, calipers, hoses and pipes
12. ☐ Grease suspension pivots
13. ☐ Check suspension and steering for signs of leaking or wear
14. ☐ Check suspension height and adjust if necessary - record details
☐ LHF ☐ RHF ☐ RHR ☐ LHR
15. ☐ Check wheel bearings, drive shafts and gaiters
16. ☐ Check lamps, horns, and system warning indicators
17. ☐ Check screen wipers and washers
18. ☐ Check front screen number plates and V.I.N. - *36 months and then every 12 months*
19. ☐ Remover front road wheels
20. ☐ Remove rear road wheels
21. ☐ Check road wheels
22. ☐ Check tyre for damage and tread depth including spare (mm)
☐ LHF ☐ RHF ☐ RHR ☐ LHR ☐ Spare
23. ☐ Check tyre pressures and adjust if necessary, including spare (bar)
☐ LHF ☐ RHF ☐ RHR ☐ LHR ☐ Spare

MAIN SERVICE - (ENGINE BAY)

24. ☐ Remove engine service hatch
25. ☐ Remove engine access cover - *Every 60,000 miles*
26. ☐ Replace engine oil and filter
27. ☐ Replace antifreeze* - *every 4 years XLC (OAT)*

28. ☐ Replace camshaft drive belt - *Every 60,000 miles*
29. ☐ Replace rear camshaft drive belt VVC - *Every 60,000 miles*
30. ☐ Replace manual gearbox oil - *Every 105,000 miles*
31. ☐ Replace automatic gearbox oil
32. ☐ Check automatic gearbox level
33. ☐ Check battery connections and antifreeze
34. ☐ Check brake, clutch & gearbox fluid levels
35. ☐ Check pressure sensing hoses and vacuum pipes
36. ☐ Check cooling system hoses and connections for signs of leakage and condition
37. ☐ Check fuel & clutch pipes and hoses for signs of leakage and condition
38. ☐ Check condition of crankcase vent hoses & valves where fitted
39. ☐ Check air conditioning system, hoses and sight glass
40. ☐ Check auxiliary drive belts tension and condition
41. ☐ Replace air cleaner element
42. ☐ Replace fuel filter - *Every 60,000 miles*
43. ☐ Replace spark plugs - *Every 60,000 miles*
44. ☐ Replace brake fluid - *Every 24 months regardless of mileage* (indicate replacement on service record)*
45. ☐ Check exhaust system and heat shields

15 YEAR REPLACEMENT - AIRBAGS

46. ☐ Replace airbag module(s)*
47. ☐ Replace airbag rotary coupler* - *When driver only airbag fitted*

AFTER EACH MAIN SERVICE

48. ☐ Check oxygen sensor operation - *at 36 months and then very 12 months*
49. ☐ Check CO at tailpipe - *at 36 months and then every 12 months. (Record CO%)*
50. ☐ Carry out road test, check for the correct function of all vehicle systems

The maintenance items listed are those recommended for vehicles operating under normal driving, road and climatic conditions. More frequent attention may be necessary if the vehicle is subject to stop/start operation, extremes of temperature, dusty conditions or frequent towing of trailers.

Service check completed, cosmetic/corrosion inspection check completed and service portfolio book stamped.

Name _____ Signature _____ Date _____

07/01

RCL 0408ENG(3)

Note after these sheets were published cambelt changes were modified to be '60,000 miles or 5 years, whichever comes first' and the airbag change moved to 15 years.

MAINTENANCE CHECK SHEET

MG TF

Mr/Mrs/Ms

Reg No

Model

VIN

Invoice/Job No

Odometer reading

Service type

Years / Miles x 1000	A	B	A	C	A	B	A	C
	1 / 15	2 / 30	3 / 45	4 / 60	5 / 75	6 / 90	7 / 105	8 / 120

For full details regarding the operations contained in this maintenance check sheet, please refer to the workshop manual.

A	B	C	
			Preliminary
☐			1 Before commencing work, check for any outstanding service actions

VEHICLE INTERIOR AND EXTERIOR

A	B	C	
☐			2 Fit vehicle protection kit
☐			3 Replace alarm handset batteries
☐			4 Check handbrake operation and adjust if necessary
☐			5 Check lamps, horns and system warning indicators
☐			6 Check screen for damage and operation of wipers and washers - Adjust washers if required
☐			7 Check seatbelt operation, seatbelts and airbag module covers for damage
☐			8 Check air conditioning system operation - If applicable
☐			9 Lubricate locks, strikers, latches, door hinges and door checks
☐			10 Lubricate hood pivot points (remove hard top if necessary)
☐			11 Check battery connections and battery condition indicator colour and charge condition
☐			12 Check and top up brake, clutch and screen washer fluid levels
4/60			13 Remove engine access cover - **Every 60,000 miles or 4 years, whichever is the sooner**

ENGINE BAY

A	B	C	
☐			14 Remove engine service hatch
☐			15 Check brake servo vacuum pipe condition
☐			16 Pressure test cooling system and coolant cap, check hoses and connections for signs of leakage and condition - Use tool No 26R001
☐			17 Check and record anti freeze content ☐ **Concentration % or degrees C** - (Concentration must be corrected if below 50%) - Use tool No 26R003
☐			18 Inspect air conditioning system hoses and sight glass
☐			19 Check auxiliary drive belts, tension and condition
☐			20 Replace air cleaner element
4/60			21 Replace fuel filter - **Every 60,000 miles or every 4 years, whichever is the sooner**
4/60			22 Replace spark plugs - **Every 60,000 miles or every 4 years, whichever is the sooner**
☐			23 Connect T4 carry out Engine Management fault code read and clear codes. Reset Fuelling Adaptions. Check operation of coolant fan/s
☐			24 Check for new tune availability and download new tunes if required - **Charged Separately**

With Vehicle on Lift

No		Item
25	4/60	Replace camshaft drive belt - **Every 60,000 miles or 4 years, whichever is the sooner**
26	4/60	Replace rear camshaft drive belt **VVC** only - **Every 60,000 miles or 4 years, whichever is the sooner**
27	4/60	Replace antifreeze using vacuum fill process - **Every 60,000 miles or 4 years, whichever is the sooner.** - Use tool No 26R002
28	4/60	Check and record anti freeze content □ **Concentration % or degrees C** - (Concentration must be corrected if below 50%) - Use tool No 26R003
29		Replace automatic gearbox oil – **Every 30,000 miles or 2 years, whichever is the sooner**
30	7/105	Replace manual gearbox oil - **Every 105,000 miles or 7 years, whichever is the sooner**
31		Replace engine oil and filter
32		Check wheel bearings, drive shafts and gaiters
33		Mark relative stud and wheel position and remove front and rear road wheels, check wheels for damage
34		Check tyres for damage, uneven wear and tread depth including spare (mm)

LHF □   RHF □   RHR □   LHR □   Spare □

No		Item
35		Visually check front brake pads and rear brake pads, discs, callipers, hoses and pipes for wear or damage
36		Inspect for condition and evidence of leakage from fuel, clutch, transmission and engine systems
37		Inspect exhaust system and heat shields
38		Inspect suspension and steering systems for signs of leaking or wear
39		Replace brake fluid - **Every 30,000 miles or 2 years, whichever is the sooner.** - **CHARGED SEPARATELY**
40		Apply anti seize compound to wheel hub and refit road wheels to original hub and stud position (ensure directional tyres are fitted correctly), apply correct torque to wheel nuts
41		Refit engine service hatch

VEHICLE EXTERIOR (Stage 2)

No		Item
42		Check tyre pressures and adjust if necessary, including spare (bar)

LHF □   RHF □   RHR □   LHR □   Spare □

No		Item
43		Check I.M.S (Instant Mobility System) for pump functionality, kit contents and expiry date of sealant (if applicable)
44		Check I.T.R (Instant Tyre Repair) for previous usage and expiry date of sealant (if applicable)
45	4/60	Refit engine access cover - **Every 60,000 miles or 4 years, whichever is the sooner**

15 YEAR REPLACEMENT - AIRBAGS

No		Item
46	15 Yrs	Replace airbag module(s) Seat belt pre tensioners and rotary coupler - **CHARGED SEPARATELY**

AFTER EACH SERVICE

No		Item
47		Annual corrosion/cosmetic inspection - **Using annual corrosion inspection sheet**
48		Carry out road test, check for the correct function of all vehicle systems

The maintenance items listed are those recommended for vehicles operating under normal driving, road and climatic conditions
More frequent attention may be necessary if the vehicle is subject to stop/start operation, extremes of temperature, dusty conditions or frequent towing of trailers

Service check completed, cosmetic/corrosion inspection check completed and service portfolio book stamped

Name _____   Signature _____   Date _____

Oil Viscosity/Temperature Ranges
02516592642516602882516623362516 63360

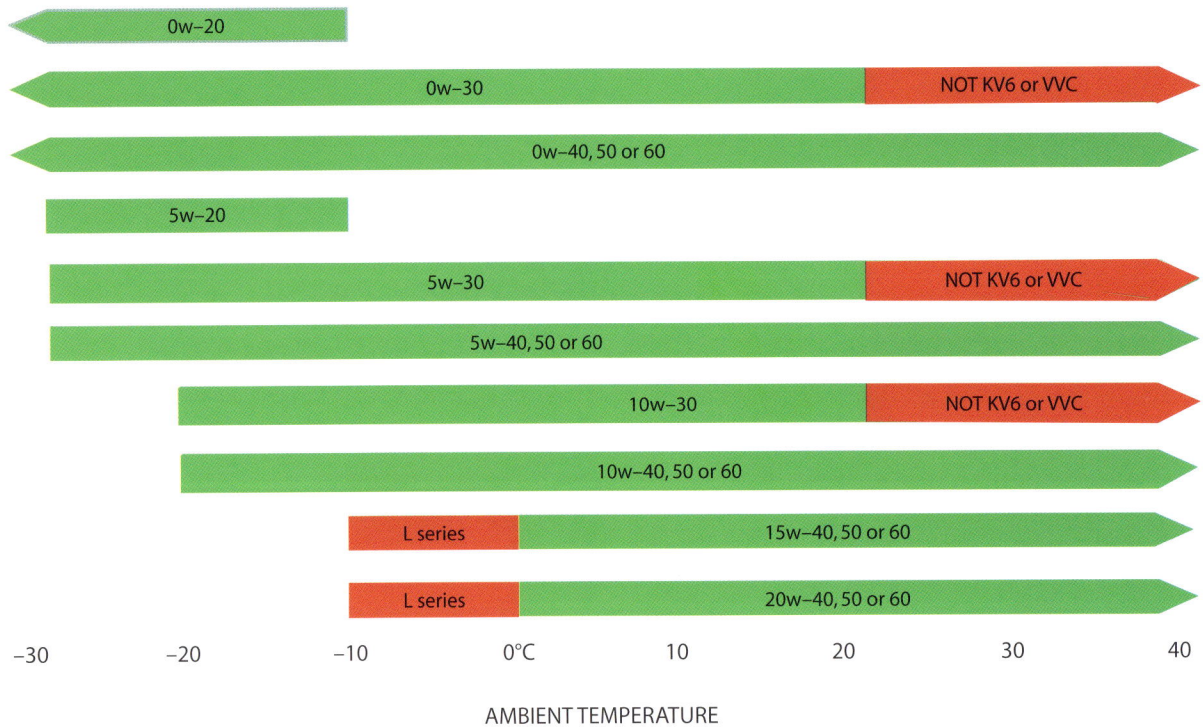

	0w–20	
	0w–30	NOT KV6 or VVC
	0w–40, 50 or 60	
	5w–20	
	5w–30	NOT KV6 or VVC
	5w–40, 50 or 60	
	10w–30	NOT KV6 or VVC
	10w–40, 50 or 60	
L series	15w–40, 50 or 60	
L series	20w–40, 50 or 60	

–30 –20 –10 0°C 10 20 30 40

AMBIENT TEMPERATURE

The above applies to all MG Rover cars that includes MGF and TF with their K series engines.

Alternator
Pulley diameter: 48mm
Regulated voltage: 14.2V (nominal)
Rated output: 85A MGF and TF (different for FWD)

Crankshaft TV Damper
Pulley diameter: Alternator – 120mm

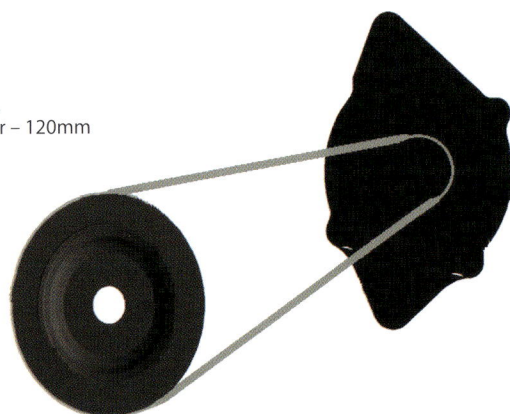

K Series Ancillary units, drive belt layout

Alternator
Pulley diameter: 48mm
Regulated voltage: 14.2V (nominal)
Rated output: 85A MGF and TF (different for FWD)

Drive Ratios
PAS   0.88
Air Con   1.08
Alternator 2.71

Power Steering Pump Not MGF or TF
Pulley diameter: 103mm
Delivery Rate: Application Specific
Relief Valve Blowoff: Application Specific

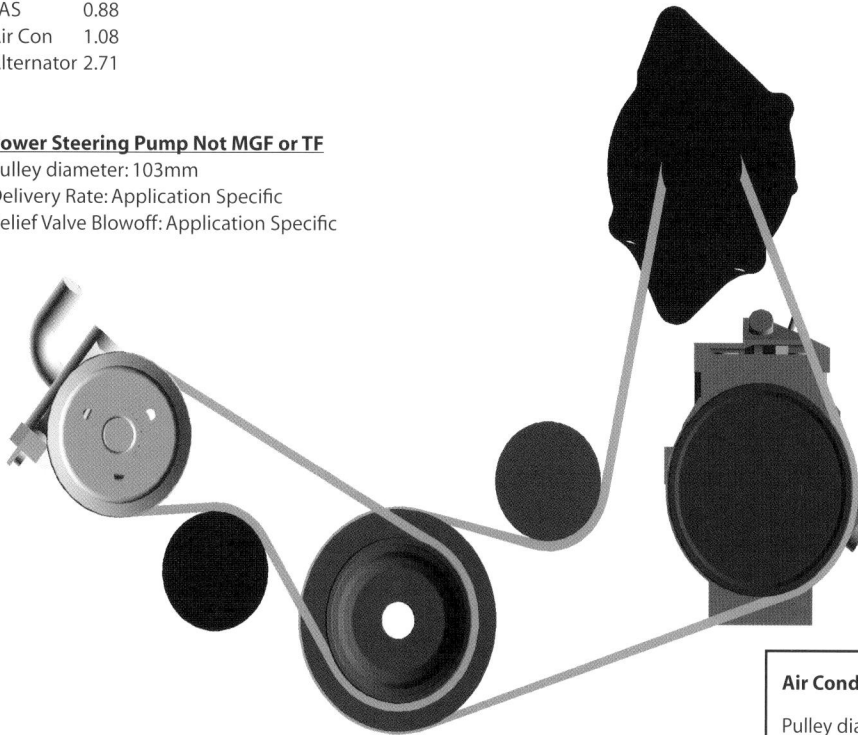

Air Conditioning Compressor

Pulley diameter: 120mm

Displacement: 161.5cm³/rev.

Crankshaft TV Damper
Pulley diameter: AirCon & Alternator – 120mm
                 PAS – 90.4mm

index

RELATED TITLES FROM CROWOOD

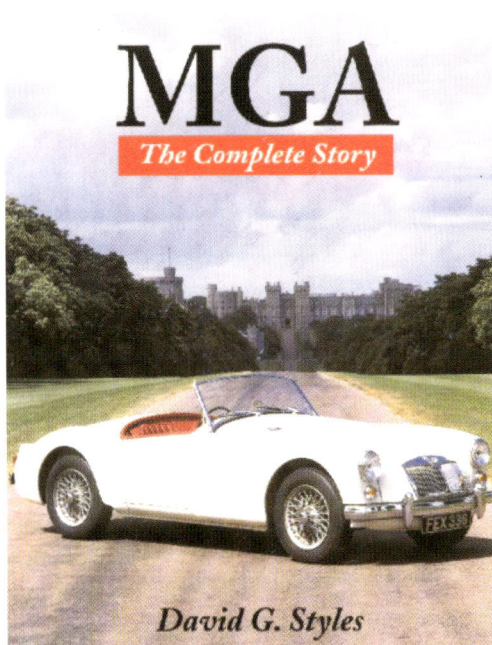

MGA
David G. Styles
ISBN 978 1 86126 466 4
200pp, 150 illustrations

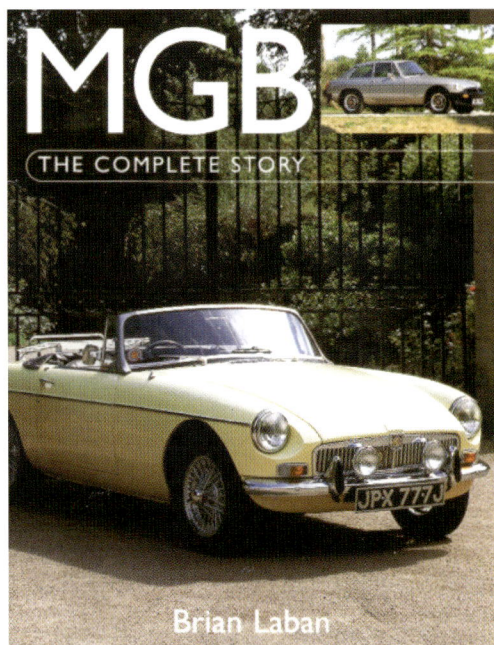

MGB
Brian Laban
ISBN 978 1 86126 752 8
208pp, 180 illustrations

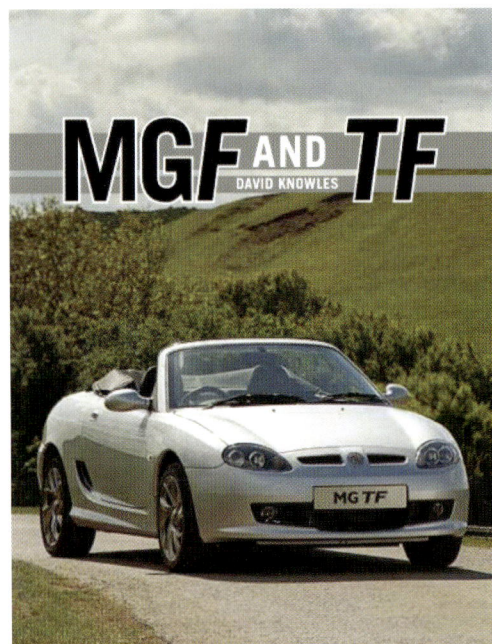

MGF and TF
David Knowles
ISBN 978 1 84797 202 6
208pp, 300 illustrations

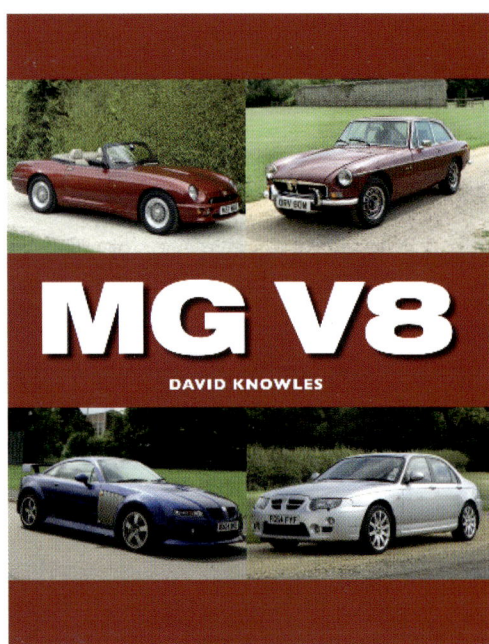

MG V8
David Knowles
ISBN 978 1 84797 451 8
320pp, 400 illustrations

In case of difficulty ordering, contact the Sales Office:

The Crowood Press, Ramsbury, Wiltshire SN8 2HR

Tel: 44 (0) 1672 520320   enquiries@crowood.com